Shadows of Empire

Shadows of Empire

Colonial Discourse and Javanese Tales

Laurie J. Sears

Duke University Press   Durham And London   1996

© 1996 Duke University Press

All rights reserved   Printed in the United States of America on acid-free paper ∞

Designed by Cherie H. Westmoreland   Typeset in Palatino with Optima display

by Keystone Typesetting, Inc.

Library of Congress Cataloging-in-Publication Data appear on the last printed page of this book.

Publication of this book was made possible, in part, with the assistance of the Graduate School

Research Fund of the University of Washington.

Portions of chapter 5 were previously published as "Aesthetic Displacement in Javanese Shadow Theatre: Three Contemporary Performance Styles," *The Drama Review* 33/3 (1989).

Contents

Note on Spelling and Translations

I have not italicized the titles of stories and texts that exist in a variety of tellings. This is to indicate the fluid nature of these oral and written textual traditions. Ramayana, Mahabharata, Bhagavad Gita, or the titles of shadow play stories are thus not italicized. When I refer to the written texts of particular authors, I italicize. When I refer to texts that exist in a variety of inscriptions, I do not.

I have used the spellings for proper names preferred by those who bore them. In the early part of the twentieth century, many Javanese, like Indonesia's first president Soekarno, favored Dutch spellings for their names. There are many inconsistencies in the spellings of Mahabharata and Ramayana characters, texts, and performances; to banish these inconsistencies entirely, I believe, does violence to the nature of these traditions. Because this book argues that Javanese Mahabharata and Ramayana stories are no less "authentic" than Indian ones, and occasionally the Javanese and Indian spellings overlap, it is difficult to maintain a clear separation. An added complication comes with Dutch spellings of these names. Spellings in translated or quoted passages have not been changed. Alternate spellings of names and places from these story-worlds can be found in the glossary at the end of the book.

Unless otherwise indicated, all the translations from Javanese, Indonesian, and Dutch—with all their failings—are my own.

Preface

When I first came to Java in 1982 to begin my study of the shadow theatre tradition, I always found out about the all-night performances *after* they had happened. Javanese friends and colleagues would regale me with tales of the wonderful plays I had missed and would offer vague promises to inform me of future celebrations. After a year or so in Central Java, I came to know about performances weeks and months before they happened; I began to attend so many performances that I regularly went to bed after my eight-year-old daughter had left for school, to awaken when she returned five hours later. In the summer of 1990, during a month's stay in Solo (Surakarta) in the wedding season, puppeteers invited me to attend performances almost every night.

In fact, it has now become a status symbol among Javanese shadow play puppeteers to have as many foreigners as possible at performances. Some of these mostly American, Australian, Dutch, French, or Japanese visitors to Java are studying Javanese performing arts, and their talents may, on occasion, be blended into the performances of daring puppeteers. Javanese shadow puppeteers are pleased that foreigners can play the difficult instruments of the Javanese *gamelan* ensemble and sing the intricate Javanese poetry, and that the most skilled can perform as shadow puppeteers. I see the incorporation of foreigners into Javanese performance arts in historical terms; the Sultans and Sunans of the Central Javanese courts used to keep albinos, dwarfs, Dutchmen, and other exceptional people around them in the old days, as these unusual beings were considered to have special powers. Today, perhaps, strange-looking foreigners are still thought to have special powers, or at least disposable income.

Becoming aware of this made me realize that I tend to see this complex oral tradition through the eyes of the puppeteers. For the most part, I traveled to performances with the puppeteers, partook of the preperformance and postperformance meals along with the musicians and singers, and often witnessed the subtle struggle between patron and performer over what story was to be chosen for a night's entertainment. Occasionally I traveled to performances with a Javanese friend whose family was sponsoring the celebration or with a foreign friend as an uninvited guest. Javanese of a certain status would never consider going to a ritual celebration uninvited; only foreigners and *wong cilik* (little people, village people) can get away with such behavior.[1] But each shadow play performance has both an invited and an uninvited audience. The invited guests usually sit in a special place—in older days they sat inside the patron's house and saw the shadows—while the uninvited guests remained outside—usually they stood in back of the musicians and the puppeteer—free to come and go as they chose.[2]

In the last six months of 1984, I became, through the generosity of a Ford Foundation grant to the government-sponsored fine arts academy in Solo (Sekolah Tinggi Seni Indonesia or STSI), the patron of a half-dozen performances. I helped to plan three meals for about fifty people for each night's performance, ensure an unending supply of Jasmine tea, coffee, and cigarettes, choose the puppeteers, and decide what story would be presented. Some of the puppeteers, unaware of the Ford Foundation's intervention, thought of me as a very rich woman who was able to sponsor six performances in as many months. This experience let me see the tradition from a new perspective, be more aware of audience reactions to the performance, and realize how much behind-the-scenes female labor

1. Except for Dutch-language passages, foreign words and quotations are Javanese unless they are labeled otherwise. Javanese is spoken at home by most Javanese in Central and East Java, but it is slowly being displaced by Indonesian—Bahasa Indonesia—which is the language of schooling, commerce, most media, and government. Many Javanese words have been absorbed into Indonesian. But, as a language with distinctive hierarchical vocabularies that distinguish power relations in each utterance, Javanese is felt by many to be inimical to the *modern* Indonesian rhetoric of equality. Please refer to the glossary at the end of this book for definitions of frequently used Javanese, Indonesian, and Dutch terms.

2. The gendered nature of seating arrangements at shadow play performances has been a topic of concern for Dutch scholars since the nineteenth century. See J. W. Winter, "Beknopte Beschrijving van het Hof Soerakarta in 1824," *Bijdragen tot de Taal-, Land- en Volkenkunde* 54 (1902): 15–176, for one of the earliest discussions of seating arrangements at *wayang* performances. The Dutch structuralist W. H. Rassers, writing in the 1930s, argued that shadow theatre originated in special "men's house" rituals, which women were forbidden to see. A curtain was hung for privacy, and women were only allowed to see the shadows of the men's rituals—and thus the shadow theatre was born. Rassers had little actual data on which to base these speculations, but the wives of invited guests at village performances often do sit behind the men or are segregated from them in various ways. See W. H. Rassers, *Panji, the Culture Hero* (1931; The Hague: M. Nijhoff, 1959).

goes into the preparations for each ritual celebration. From these two different perspectives—of patron and puppeteer—I learned how the puppet masters contour each performance to match their own skills and experiences to the tastes of their audiences.

This study of the Javanese shadow theatre is grounded in research in Holland and Java. It spans the elusive gap between history and ethnography and tries to strike a balance between the two. Dutch sources shed light on how Dutch scholars saw the tradition in the nineteenth and twentieth centuries and how this way of looking at the shadow theatre influenced not only succeeding generations of scholars but also those of Javanese performers. In Dutch and Javanese libraries there are descriptions of the tradition from the nineteenth century that help create pictures of the shadow theatre's past. All researchers must gratefully acknowledge the rigor and care that went into the compilation and preservation of these materials by Dutch scholars and their Javanese colleagues.

Conversations with puppeteers and scholars in Java complemented the written Dutch sources, giving me an understanding of the tradition as it was heard and passed on to new generations by Javanese puppeteers. I discovered how new methods of transmission contrasted with earlier patterns by attending the courses for shadow puppeteers in Surakarta, both the older-style course taught by teachers associated with the Mangkunagaran palace and the courses offered at the Academy. Most important, of course, was the opportunity to attend over one hundred performances, as many as the season and occasion would permit.

But how should one assess the vast array of performances, conversations, and texts that this work draws together? Historiographical methods urge historians to assess the moral viewpoints of authors and analyze their perspectives to contrast the texts of Europeans writing about Java with Javanese writing about Java and to ask if the Javanese author is an observer of the tradition or a performer of the tradition. But the oral sources presented different problems. Over the past twenty years, oral historiography has come a long way in elevating the credibility of oral sources to equal that of written ones.[3] But critics have questioned the purpose of

---

3. J. Vansina, *Oral Tradition* (Chicago: Aldine Publishing Company, 1965), and *Oral Tradition as History* (Madison: University of Wisconsin Press, 1985).

creating historically legitimate oral documents as an end in itself.[4] Reflections on my field experience eventually brought home the realization that the questions raised by oral testimonies—the words of an informant who is speaking or performing—can both enrich and provide a means to interrogate the written texts. Older educated Javanese puppeteers are as likely to have read the Dutch works on the shadow theatre tradition as the foreign researcher, and their testimonies can seem to validate these sources; informants often want to please the researcher by giving the "right" answers, and what seems right is usually what has been documented in written texts. The flows of information tacked back and forth in bewildering ways among patrons, puppeteers, and scholars, producing myriad opinions. Although it would be misleading to equate written texts and oral testimonies, by rubbing each across the other's grain, new ways of looking at the world can emerge. My own interests and politics of location have been the critical lenses through which these texts and testimonies have been brought momentarily into focus.

As a historian, I, in fact, had little preparation for undertaking field research at all. My mentor John Smail had spent time in Bandung in the early 1960s, interviewing people for his study on the Indonesian Revolution, but he, too, never thought about *interviewing*, about the process, as he has recently recounted.[5] I had read all the available anthropological scholarship on Java, but at that time I encountered little discussion about what "participant observation" actually meant. This was just before the explosion of self-reflexive studies in anthropology that would come in the mid-1980s. I did have the advantage of having lived in Solo, the site of the research, for several years in the early 1970s. Thus I had good friends and knew the town, the language, and the environment. In a sense, this was a return that I had been working toward for ten years. I did not feel that I was going to Solo as an observer; rather I felt that I was returning home.

The only information I received about field research came from Jan Vansina, who occupies a chair in history at the University of Wisconsin, although he is a trained linguist. I had the opportunity to study historical methods with Vansina and listen to his informed comments on every

4. R. Rosaldo, "Doing Oral History," *Social Analysis* 4 (1980): 89–99.

5. Laura Smail, "John Smail: Reflections on an Academic Life," in *Autonomous Histories, Particular Truths: Essays in Honor of John R. W. Smail*, ed. Laurie J. Sears (Madison: University of Wisconsin Center for Southeast Asian Studies, 1993).

Preface

possible type of historical source, from dumb traces—monuments and other archaeological remains—to the latest anthropological theory. I discovered over the years that about five minutes of Vansina's time provided food for thought for at least a year. He was the one who turned my attention to the transmission of the *wayang* as oral tradition. He also pointed out that there was very little chance of finding sources for the period before the late eighteenth century.

Vansina could also, though an Africanist, listen to my Javanese tapes of shadow plays and tell me things that no one else in Madison could at that time. He said the work of Parry and Lord on oral tradition would be of no use to me, after listening to my tapes for a few minutes, since the *wayang* tradition is not metrical and thus did not fit Lord's pattern for oral epic. Vansina gave me two warnings: never visit the family of one performer with a member of another known performer's family if you want to learn anything. His second comment had to do with questions: never use questionnaires. Be patient, he said, and wait quietly until the performer starts to talk about what he or she believes is important. The last instruction, although a particularly difficult one to pass on to my colleagues at the Academy in Solo, provided this book with many useful insights.

Javanese *dhalang* (puppeteers) are as wise, talented, and inspiring a group of human beings as exist, but proved to be enigmatic informants. They are storytellers, creators, authors, and entertainers. They often want to please people, especially foreign researchers who come to their village and who, through a wave of their magic wand, can invite puppeteers or musicians to America. Here is where Vansina's advice was so useful: depending on whom I was with, I always received different information. If I went to see an older puppeteer with a younger member of his or her family, I was treated as a member of the family and the puppeteer felt free to talk about anything. If I went with a teacher from the Academy, especially one with a high position, the puppeteers might become quite nervous and reticent. If I went with my daughter, then seven or eight years old, everyone would concentrate on her and I could fade into the background. I also learned that in large families of puppeteers, the more puppeteers present, the more formal and less interesting the discussion. Puppeteers were most open when they were alone or among their immediate family.

Lastly, I learned a lot about the Javanese puppeteers when I took chances like lending money. Some researchers do not believe in lending money; they feel it might compromise the research, or it might lead to embarrassing situations, or they are afraid they will never get it back. I learned that the best way to handle lending money is only to lend what you do not need to get back. I did research in the days before many Javanese discovered that European, American, or Japanese researchers could (should?) be asked to pay for Javanese knowledges. Many of the puppeteers I knew were happy just to have me along, especially at performances. When visiting their homes, I always brought cigarettes, tea, and sugar, the required items when visiting the villages, or European biscuits when visiting in the city. But very few of the puppeteers I knew were wealthy. They lived on the edge. If a child was sick, they needed money for "Western" medicine. Sometimes they had to sell their puppets or their instruments to survive. When times were good, they might be able to buy them back. I learned to give a part of what was asked, a part that I felt good about giving. As I look back, I wish there had been more to give.

This book is about Javanese Ramayana and Mahabharata stories: the former cycle of stories tells of the demon-king Rahwana's abduction of Rama's virtuous wife Sita and the latter tells the stories leading up to the fratricidal war between the Pandhawa and Korawa cousins over the rights to the kingdom of Ngastina. In 1991 I organized a symposium at the University of Washington to examine Ramayana stories in India, Malaysia, and Indonesia from several perspectives: as vehicles of aesthetic transmission, as collections of texts in numerous tellings and translations, and as a vast repertoire of performance traditions.[6] Because the Indonesian and Indian scholars and intellectuals I had invited could not attend, predominantly American and European views of Ramayana traditions were expressed. But I did engage a large group of Indonesian and American performers, singers, and musicians, the full complement required to stage a Javanese shadow theatre performance; they, of course, offered a different kind of commentary. The Javanese puppeteer Ki Widiyanto gave a masterful performance supported by several famous Javanese musicians

6. I use the word "tradition" in this book to refer to particular story cycles or performance practices. The symposium referred to above was funded by the National Endowment for the Humanities and the Rockefeller Foundation as part of an explanatory program connected with the 1990–91 Festival of Indonesia.

Preface

and a group of American musicians who made up the Lewis and Clark College *gamelan* ensemble in the fall of 1991. Unique to this performance was the presence of an accomplished translator. A. L. Becker worked with the Javanese puppeteer to make the shadow play more accessible to a non-Javanese audience. In original ways, he interspersed his English translations of a long-lived, poetic Old Javanese Ramayana text with the songs and chants of the puppeteer.[7]

In the academic stories that unfolded both before and after the shadow theatre play, the scholars of Malay-Indonesian history tended to equate Ramayana tales with puppet and human performance traditions, while the South Asianists often found more connections with written textual traditions.[8] Toward the end of the symposium, Imam Ahmad, a Javanese intellectual studying anthropology at the University of Washington, accused the American scholars present of reducing the shadow theatre tradition—synonymous, as he explained, with Ramayana and Mahabharata stories—to a series of performances and texts. Although Imam Ahmad is Muslim, the Ramayana and Mahabharata stories conveyed in shadow theatre traditions were still more than texts or performances to him; they were the expression of a unique worldview or epistemology whose existence was becoming less and less important in the intellectual life of many Javanese. Ahmad mourned the passing of what he recognized as a hybrid colonial discourse of social and moral values even as he acknowledged his own position in its construction.

To use Javanese shadow theatre as a metaphor to introduce the terminology of *colonial discourse*, the puppetmaster's lamp, which illuminates the darting shadows enclosed within the carefully fabricated frame, conceals much more than it reveals. In the demystifying light of dawn, as the puppets are returned to their box and audiences disperse, intersections of labor, art, ritual, and power are exposed to show the maintenance of an

7. A. L. Becker is Professor Emeritus of Linguistics and Anthropology at the University of Michigan and a longtime student and scholar of Javanese shadow theatre.

8. Stuart Blackburn's research on South Indian shadow theatre described a tradition closely connected to written texts. See his "Epic Transmission and Adaptation: A Folk Ramayama in South India," in *Boundaries of the Text: Epic Performances in South and Southeast Asia*, ed. J. B. Flueckiger and L. J. Sears (Ann Arbor: University of Michigan Center for South and Southeast Asian Studies, 1991). But see also W. Doniger [O'Flaherty], "Fluid and Fixed Texts in India," and J. B. Flueckiger, "Literacy and the Changing Concept of Text: Women's Ramayana *Mandali* in Central India," in the same volume.

intricate system of hierarchy and patronage in which everyone knows his or her place. Colonial discourses are similar to artfully constructed shadow plays—as sites of surveillance and resistance—concealing machineries of power as they reveal stories packaged to please particular audiences, even though both performers and patrons know the value, in monetary and symbolic terms, of the labor and goods required to produce the show. This book is an analysis of colonial discourses as they have penetrated the workings of a repertoire of stories transmitted through a variety of older and more contemporary media. The book moves from a discussion of the cultural politics of empire to retellings by local intellectuals and performers that contested colonial and postcolonial categories by enacting allegories of resistance.

The performance mentioned above, which took place at the University of Washington in the fall of 1991, shows how shadow plays serve as allegories of power and patronage, even when displaced from Java to Seattle. When I called Ki Widiyanto, the Javanese puppeteer who was teaching *gamelan* at Berkeley at the time, and asked him what he would need for his performance, he said only a complete Central Javanese *gamelan* ensemble (which meant at least fifteen musicians as well as a set of instruments), a *pesindhen* (female singer), an accomplished drummer, and an expert *gender* player—the performer who must closely follow the words and songs of the *dhalang* and play almost continuously throughout the performance. Fine, I said, as I looked at our meager budget and wondered how in the world I would be able to assemble all those people in Seattle. I enlisted the support of Ragamala, the nonprofit Indian music organization in Seattle, run ever so proficiently by Professor Ramesh Gangolli, head of the Mathematics Department at the University at that time and connoisseur of Indian music. He was familiar with Javanese shadow theatre and thought we could work together. Without Professor Gangolli's support and knowledge, the Seattle shadow play would never have happened.

I began to ask A. L. Becker, with whom I communicate regularly on e-mail, what story would be performed. I was surprised when Becker told me he had no idea about the story and that he would need at least ten days to work with the *dhalang* before the performance so that the story could take shape. He had, in fact, had several months to practice with Widiyanto before the Michigan performance where I had first seen them work together. He said the collaboration was delicate business, and it was difficult for Widiyanto to get used to the interruptions that Becker's translations demanded. Ten days was reduced to a week and then to a weekend. A conveniently timed invitation for Becker to lecture at Berkeley helped to bring *dhalang* and translator together. Widiyanto had an accomplished *pesindhen* and a *gender* player in San Francisco, who both agreed to practice for several days before the performance and to come to Seattle. In a final stroke of luck, I remembered that Peggy Choy, who was giving an academic paper at the symposium, was also one of the most accomplished *rebab* players in the country. Everything seemed complete.

Becker believed that he and Widiyanto had decided to perform the story of the burning of the evil kingdom of Langka by Rama's dutiful devotee, the white monkey named Hanuman—Hanuman Obong as the story is known in Javanese. Becker had been busy for weeks translating that episode from the Old Javanese text. A few days before Becker was due to arrive at Berkeley to begin rehearsing, Widiyanto told him that he wanted to perform the story *after* the burning. The story after the burning told of noble Wibisana's parting from his wife when he decides to leave home, family, and country and join Rama because he can no longer tolerate the despicable behavior of his older brother Rahwana, who had stolen Rama's beautiful wife Sita. Becker started madly translating the next episode as he departed for Berkeley. Eerily, he arrived in Berkeley right after the Oakland fires of the fall of 1991—right after the burning. Widiyanto had had to flee his house to save himself from the fires. When they met, Widiyanto said with particular Javanese tact and subtlety to the bemused Becker, "You were so right, Pak[9] Becker, to insist that we do the story after the burning."

They practiced a few times with the *pesindhen* and *gender* player amid the chaos of the devastated Bay area and flew to Portland to rehearse with the Lewis and Clark *gamelan* once before the performance. The next day the entire group of twenty performers filled two minibuses, and they made their way to Seattle, arriving only several hours before the performance. A Thai dinner arrived backstage after the setting up of the instruments and a brief rehearsal, and it worked to revive the tired travelers. The performers ate quickly and began to dress for the performance. All the Lewis and Clark performers had purchased or been supplied with batik

---

9. *Pak* is a term of respect for older Javanese and Indonesian men.

cloth and short black jackets, their required performance attire. The audience began to arrive. Several hundred people showed up, quite unaware that the translator, who would make the performance understandable to them, was unique to this performance. As a perfect complement to the performance, a friend and *gamelan* aficionado had called to ask if he could bring a Halloween party of children, also in full costume. As children are a welcome part of any audience for Javanese shadow theatre, I gladly acquiesced.

As the performance began, the children were drawn irresistibly to the stage, and the layout of the concert hall allowed the audience to take turns viewing the performance from both the puppet and the shadow side. The children added a Fellini-esque touch to the performance, their costumes and delighted faces glittering along with the brightly colored puppets. Widiyanto moved effortlessly between the pathos of the parting and the humor of the clown scenes, which he performed in English. Although I did not expect it, into this dialogue he wove the tale of the Seattle performance. At only one point did he falter slightly. He knew that I had invited him to come and that I was in the History Department at the University. So, slightly puzzled, he had the Ramayana characters tell the large audience that the History Department had sponsored his visit, to the great enjoyment of Jere Bacharach, chair of the History Department at that time—and to the chagrin of Ramesh Gangolli and me, who had not made it clear enough that Ragamala was sponsoring the performance. As always, audience and patrons entered the performance domain.

The scene where Wibisana takes leave of his wife seemed particularly moving. Later I found out why. Widiyanto was sad; he, too, was being forced to part from his wife for a while because she had to return to Java. And, in the way that skilled Javanese *dhalang* weave together mythical and existential realms, Widiyanto had chosen a story that became an allegory, allowing him to reflect upon his loss. So he had chosen to perform the story after the burning. The Oakland fires, the *dhalang*'s sadness, children in Halloween costumes, the generosity of the sponsors, the visiting musicians and instruments, all were drawn momentarily together, endowed with a fleeting meaning experienced in different ways in the lives of those listening and speaking, anchoring the event in individual memories to be told and retold and finally fixed as a fitting beginning to my history of Javanese stories.

Acknowledgments

The field research for this book was supported by fellowships from the Social Science Research Council and the American Council of Learned Societies (SSRC-ACLS) and Fulbright Hays. I spent five months in Leiden at the beginning of the research period reading Dutch sources, attending Dr. Stuart Robson's advanced Javanese classes at the State University, and playing in the gamelan group connected to the Tropenmuseum in Amsterdam. I left for Indonesia in May of 1982 and was settled in the city of Solo in Central Java by June of that year.

In early 1983, with the encouragement of Dr. Terry Bigalke, a program officer with the Ford Foundation in Jakarta, I served as the coordinator for the Lakon Carangan Documentation Project sponsored by the Ford Foundation and the Academy of Performing Arts in Solo [Sekolah Tinggi Seni Indonesia (STSI)]. The intent of the project was the documentation of branch stories (*lakon carangan*) of the Solonese shadow theatre (*wayang purwa*) repertoire. Branch stories are those considered to be among the most fleeting in the repertoire, although our research overturned this definition. I was active in the design and research stage of this project. Worried that our efforts might standardize as well as document the tradition, I made sure that the emphasis of the research would be the collection of numerous tellings of particular stories. During the period in which I worked on the Branch Story Documentation Project, about fifty interviews were carried out, eight performances were sponsored, and a conference was organized and held. Of the eight performances, five were different tellings of the same story and three were tellings of another story. When I had to leave Java in the summer of 1984, the data was turned over to Alan Feinstein who had agreed to oversee the editing of these materials. In turn, Dr. Mary Zurbuchen had taken over the Ford Foundation supervision of the project, and she has remained a supportive friend and critical colleague. After two years of painstaking work, the results of this project were published under the direction of Alan Feinstein by the Academy in Solo.[1]

1. See Alan Feinstein et al., eds., *Lakon Carangan*, vols. 1–3 (Surakarta: Akademi Seni Karawitan Indonesia, 1986).

In the summer of 1990, I had the opportunity to return to Indonesia for two months with the support of a summer stipend from the National Endowment for the Humanities and a Graduate School Research Fund grant from the University of Washington. These two months allowed me to assess the validity of my arguments and to see how the tradition had changed over five years. The Graduate School Research Fund of the University of Washington provided much-needed financial support in the later stages of this undertaking, as did the Keller Fund of the University of Washington History Department. Both Jere Bacharach and Richard Johnson, past and present chairs of the University of Washington History Department, were exceedingly kind and supportive in seeing this project through to completion.

I am very grateful to the Indonesian organizations that assisted me during the years of my field research. The Indonesian Institute of Sciences (LIPI) and the Academy in Solo were always responsive to my needs as a foreign researcher.

Most important to this research were the many Javanese puppeteers who shared their knowledge with me. In particular I would like to thank Ki Naryacarito, the late R. Soetrisno, Nyi Kenyacarita, the late Ki Sukasno, Ki Sindhu, Ki Narto Sindhu, Ki Bambang Suwarno, and Ki Widiyanto S. Putro. The late director of the Academy, Bp. "Gendon" Humardhani, was both supportive and demanding. The Academy instructors who were my colleagues on the Lakon Carangan Documentation Project— Bambang Murtiyasa, Suratno, and Kuwato—were enthusiastic, efficient, and patient with my concerns about standardizing the oral tradition. Other Javanese teachers and friends include the late Ki Martopangrawit and the late Bp. Suranto Atmosaputro. Ki W. Hardjanto Pradjapangarsa and Bp. Suwondo—friends and teachers for over twenty years—supported my work in innumerable ways. Putu Wijaya—novelist, playwright, and director—and his wife Dewi became dear friends and important influences on my thinking about Indonesian theatre and performing arts.

There were also many personal friends and colleagues without whose ideas and encouragement this project could not have been completed: in Holland, Stuart Robson was exceedingly kind, as were E. L. Heins, Greet Heins, Saskya Heins, Marleena Heins, and Victoria Clara van Groenen-

Acknowledgments

dael; in Java, Ben Arps and Jumilah, Timothy E. Behrend, Carol Block, Mark Hoffman, Raymond Weisling, Sri Lestari, and Joan Suyenaga.

Certain colleagues and mentors deserve special thanks: John Smail, whose historical vision inspired me and a generation of students; V. Narayanarao, who opened up the world of oral traditions for me; Jan Vansima, who focused my attention on the transmission of oral traditions; and Benedict Anderson, who first suggested I question the Dutch influence on shadow theatre. Exceptional gratitude goes to Dan Lev and Arlene Lev—my harshest critics—who helped enormously in the revisions of the manuscript. Albertine Smit patiently helped me with my Dutch translations. The e-mail missives of A. L. Becker sustained me during the past two years of rewriting. Extraordinary thanks are due to those who read and commented on all or part of the manuscript: Jane Atkinson, A. L. Becker, Robin Bush, Gail Dreyfuss, Richard Eaton, Nancy Florida, Hendrik Maier, Jan Opdyke, Marc Perlman, Amin Sweeney, Jean Tayler, and Philip Yampolsky. I owe an enormous debt of gratitude to Alan Feinstein who painstakingly read every page and every footnote and offered invaluable suggestions for improvement. Without the help of my research assistants Robin Bush and, especially, Jacquie Ettinger, this project would never have seen its way to completion. Ken Wissoker of Duke University Press has remained a supportive and insightful editor. Cherie Westmoreland from Duke designed the cover, April Ryan from the University of Washington designed the map, Stanley Shockey from the University of Washington made excellent prints of my photos from Java, and Nancy Donnelly from Imagery Photography provided excellent new photographs for the book. Lastly, twenty-five years ago, Paul Stange first introduced me to the world of Javanese *wayang* and mysticism. Despite the generosity of these friends and critics, inaccuracies or inconsistencies in this work are the sole responsibility of the author.

I must not forget to acknowledge my daughter Tikka who never failed to distract me in delightful ways from this work. She spent half of first grade in a Dutch-language school in Holland, second and third grade in an Indonesian-medium school in Solo, has made several other trips to Java and Bali, and remains productively confused about her own ethnic and religious identity.

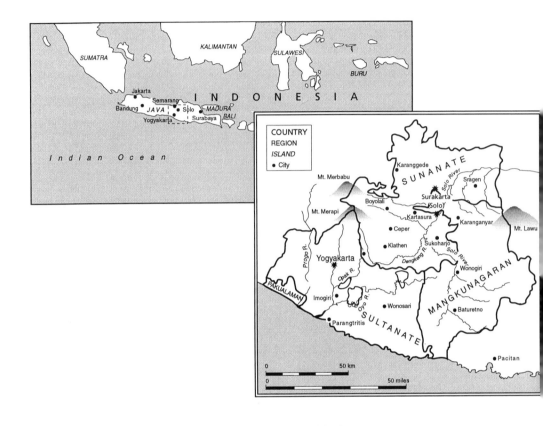

Map of Principalities of Surakarta and Yogyakarta with borders of Sunanate, Sultanate, Mangkunagaran, and Pakualaman.

Introduction   Histories, Mythologies,

and Javanese Tales

In this sense, no text is original, yet no telling is a mere retelling—and the story has no closure, although it may be enclosed in a text. In India and Southeast Asia, no one ever reads the *Ramayana* and *Mahabharata* for the first time. The stories are there, "always already."[1]—A. K. Ramanujan

Thus the traces of the storyteller cling to the story the way the handprints of the potter cling to the clay vessel.[2]—W. Benjamin

Ramayana and Mahabharata tales have often been compared with the Iliad and the Odyssey of ancient Greece. But Ramayana and Mahabharata stories are much more alive in India and Indonesia today than the stories of Homer are in Europe or America. The stories of the former are not only performed in human and puppet theatres to celebrate national and regional holidays, but they are read avidly in novels, romances, and comic books, and the characters appear in creative and commercial guises in radio and television programming. Tales of Rama's battle to regain his wife Sita from the demon king Rahwana (Ramayana) or the great conflict and war between the Pandhawa and Korawa cousins (Mahabharata) were already traveling to Java along the trade routes from the Indian subcontinent by the first centuries c.e. and possibly much earlier.[3] By the tenth and eleventh centuries, the stories were sung in Old

1. A. K. Ramanujan, "Three Hundred Ramayanas: Five Examples of Three Thoughts on Translation," in *Many Ramayanas: The Diversity of a Narrative Tradition in South Asia*, ed. Paula Richman (Berkeley: University of California Press, 1991), p. 46. Following the late A. K. Ramanujan (ibid., p. 24), in this book I use the term *tellings* rather than *versions* or *variants* to indicate that there are no original or primary texts that underpin the stories or the story cycles.

2. W. Benjamin, *Illuminations* (New York: Schocken, 1969), p. 92.

3. This book focuses on Java, one of the major islands that today make up the nation of Indonesia, which proclaimed independence from the Dutch in 1945 and gained it in 1949. Densely populated, Java is home to over half of Indonesia's 190 million people. The Javanese are the dominant ethnic group on the island but there are Sundanese peoples in the western part and Madurese peoples in the eastern part. Chinese minorities in the urban centers of Java wield significant economic power. The dominant religion of Java is Islam, which is observed in various ways. This forms a point of tension

Javanese poetic meters and performed as shadow plays, continually changing as they interacted with various elements of Javanese religion and belief. Just as Ramayana and Mahabharata tales have attracted the attention of non-Javanese scholars and travelers for hundreds of years, they have continued to engage Javanese audiences.

The shadow theatre, above all a storytelling medium, has been one of the major vehicles for the transmission of Ramayana and Mahabharata tales in Java. The stories may be religious, exorcistic, political, or purely entertaining, but puppet masters consistently turn *crita* (story) into *lakon* (formulaic plot) in oral performances. Puppeteers may do this with or without puppets, in the comfort of their sitting rooms or under the *blencong* (oil lamp or electric lightbulb) that illuminates the leather puppets on the white cotton screen and produces the fleeting shadows throughout each nine-hour performance.[4] While there are various dramatic traditions in Java using leather puppets, wooden puppets, and human actors, this book is concerned with the Solonese theatrical tradition known as *wayang kulit* or *wayang purwa* (leather shadows or ancient shadows), based on the association of certain leather shadow puppets with a particular repertoire of stories and a particular musical ensemble.[5] Some of these stories derive

---

between those who interpret Islamic doctrine strictly, those who lean toward more secular worldviews, and those who see themselves as Muslims but still follow local village practices and beliefs. Most Javanese and Sundanese, and many Chinese in Java, have some familiarity with the heroes and heroines of Ramayana and Mahabharata stories.

4. Geertz's description of the skills and talents of the Javanese shadow puppeteer (*dhalang*) is excellent: "He imitates all the voices called for, sings when singing is appropriate, kicks an iron clapper with his foot to keep the rhythm and to symbolize the sounds of war, and, as he has only the bare outline of the story given to him by tradition, makes up most of the details of the plot as he goes along, particularly in the comic scenes, which often contain elements of contemporary social criticism. He does this the whole night long, sitting until dawn with his feet folded inwards in the formal Javanese sitting posture, performing with a dexterity, a fertility of invention, and a physical endurance which are altogether remarkable." C. Geertz, *The Religion of Java* (1960; Chicago: University of Chicago Press, 1975), p. 263. See also W. Keeler, *Javanese Shadow Plays, Javanese Selves* (Princeton: Princeton University Press, 1987), pp. 3–14.

5. This study concentrates on the shadow theatre traditions of Solo (Surakarta) and the surrounding villages, whose artistic traditions were sometimes influenced by one of the court traditions of Solo, i.e. the Kraton Solo or the Mangkunagaran. I do not include the equally important shadow theatre traditions of Yogyakarta, which have their own history, style, and development.

Histories, Mythologies, and Tales

The puppeteer becomes a shadow as he sits in front of the clown puppets (left) and the refined hero.

from Indian oral and written Ramayana and Mahabharata plots, although the Javanese feel and believe the stories to be their own.[6] Most of the stories are Javanese creations, using the Indic heroes and heroines but painting them in Javanese hues.

In this book I avoid the use of the word *epic* when I refer to Javanese Ramayana and Mahabharata stories. This decision signals my reluctance to apply the European genre of "epic" to Javanese—or Indian—textual repertoires.[7] Not only is the epic a European category, but the frequently used term "Indian epics" obscures rather than clarifies what it means to talk about Ramayana or Mahabharata stories in Java. There is no Javanese word for epic, although *epik* is now found in Indonesian dictionaries.

6. See A. Sweeney, "Literacy and Epic in the Malay World," in Flueckiger and Sears, *Boundaries of the Text*, for a lucid and cogent analysis of the imposition of European categories on Malay and Indonesian literary genres, and the essays in A. Appadurai, F. Korom, and M. Mills, eds., *Gender, Genre, and Power in South Asian Expressive Traditions* (Philadelphia: University of Pennsylvania Press, 1991).

7. See Flueckiger and Sears, eds., *Boundaries of the Text*, and S. Blackburn et al., *Oral Epics in India* (Berkeley: University of California Press, 1989), for various discussions about what it means to talk about epics in India, Malaysia, Java, and Bali.

Puppeteers speak of *crita wayang*, or *wayang* stories, to refer to the ocean of stories from which they derive the plots or *lakon* for particular performances.

Often puppeteers connect these stories of Rama and Sita and Pandhawa and Korawa with the idea of *sejarah*, a word of Arabic origin. As with the Arabic *sjihjara*, in Javanese *sejarah* means genealogy; in Indonesian *sejarah* means history. Genealogy is a critical concept when puppeteers speak about their art, for puppeteers must remember the intricate genealogies of hundreds of characters, and the puppeteer's own genealogy is quite important for establishing his or her place in the *wayang* world. In a recent essay, Pramoedya Ananta Toer, the famous Javanese author, defined the Mahabharata as "a monstrous construction consisting of philosophical and ethical stories, religious references and, it goes without saying, social and political proscriptions."[8] As this book argues, Javanese definitions of Mahabharata and Ramayana stories changed over time, and it is most useful to use the terms Ramayana and Mahabharata to mark specific genres within Javanese story-worlds rather than trying to fit the stories into imported categories. Although a tenth-century Old Javanese Ramayana text is one of the oldest and most respected pieces of Javanese literature, *dhalang* (puppeteers) in Java today often refer to Rama stories as *lakon kethek*, or monkey plots, because the tales of Rama have many monkey characters whose movements are considered undignified to perform. In the following chapters, I use "cycles of stories" interchangeably with *wayang* stories or *wayang* tales, terms that only hint at the richness and complexity of these story-worlds. I argue that the abiding appeal of the shadow theatre lies in the ability of the puppeteers consistently to create new stories with the materials at hand, to recombine and re-present old and new elements.[9]

Shadow play performances have been held in connection with religious events and life-cycle rites for centuries. Weddings, births, circumcisions,

8. "Ma'af, Atas Nama Pengalaman," *Kabar Seberang*, no. 23 (1992): 1–9 at p. 1. This essay was brought to my attention by Alex G. Bardsley, a graduate student at Cornell University. I have slightly modified Bardsley's translation.

9. I thank A. L. Becker, Nancy Florida, and Amin Sweeney for discussing these naming problems with me at length. Becker prefers *fable* over *story* or *epic*; Florida rightly cautions that my choice of *story* or *tale* rather than *epic* may not convey the importance of these "epic" stories in Javanese thought-worlds; and Sweeney prefers *tales* in his work on Malay shadow theatre.

vows, and the commemoration of deaths are all suitable occasions for performances. In addition, certain families or villages occasionally hold performances for exorcistic purposes, to cleanse the members of a family or village and protect them from future harm. Patrons almost always pay puppeteers for their services, and delicate bargaining takes place weeks or months before performances.[10] Today performances are also held to celebrate national and religious holidays; in the past, puppeteers were often called to the palaces to associate their voices with court ceremonies.

In addition to ritual purposes, the shadow theatre has been a vehicle of social teachings. Scholars have long noted that proper behavior, manners, and important points of Javanese history and mythology are all emphasized in performances. Yet Javanese aficionados of the *wayang* delight in the puppeteers who can cleverly reproduce unacceptable behavior in humorous ways: the stuttering of Citraksi, the incorrect grammar and coarse language of Dursasana, and the flatulence of Semar seem more important to Javanese audiences than the virtuous behavior or elegant speech of the more refined characters. When they do appear, didactic elements are usually balanced with humor, and the most sought-after puppeteers are celebrated for their caustic or coarse wit.

Although scattered phrases of Old Javanese poetry and prose document the existence of shadow theatre performances as far back as the tenth century, detailed Javanese, Dutch, and English descriptions date only from the late eighteenth and early nineteenth centuries.[11] Various

10. Sometimes the puppeteer is paid a lump sum that includes the cost of hiring musicians and singers. Puppeteers who are in demand often have their own troupe of musicians and singers. Only very wealthy puppeteers can afford to transport their own puppets and selected instruments, and most villages have access to puppets, musicians, and the musical instruments needed for performances.

11. In the middle of the ninth century the word *arringgit* (*ringgit* = *wayang*) is mentioned in a Javanese inscription along with other words connected with dramatic performances and with "servants of the inner apartments" who came from Campa (Champa), Kalinga, Aryya, Singha (Ceylon), Gauda (Bengal), Cola, Malyala (Malabar), Karnataka, Reman (Pegu), and Kmir (Cambodia)—various regions of India and mainland Southeast Asia. See H. B. Sarkar, *Corpus of the Inscriptions of Java, up to 928 A.D.*, vol. 1 (Calcutta: Firma K. L. Mukhopadhyay, 1971), pp. 76–99. Sarkar notes that J.L.A. Brandes, "Pararaton (Ken Arok) Tweede druk bewerkt door N. J. Krom," *Verhandelingen van het Bataviaasch Genootschap van Kunsten en Wetenschappen* 62 (1920): 112–16, considered this inscription to be a fifteenth-century production. Sarkar and L. C. Damais think that it is a copy of a ninth-century original L. C. Damais, "Etudes d'épigraphie indonesienne, III Liste des principales inscriptions datées de l'Indonesie," *Bulletin de l'Ecole*

aesthetic, political, and religious visions were represented in shadow theatre traditions both before and after Javanese encounters with European ideas and customs. The meeting of Javanese and non-Javanese intellectual worlds was often reenacted on the stage of the Javanese shadow theatre, illuminating and interweaving mythical and political discourses. While the Javanese shadow theatre has remained an oral performance tradition, written texts have influenced as well as documented it.

Preoccupation with distinctions between oral and written traditions was a characteristic of nineteenth-century ethnography, in particular as European and American social scientists attempted to interpret the varied oral literatures of peoples in Asia, Africa, and the Americas whom their governments colonized or incorporated into their nation-states. The ethnographers included the oral/written dichotomy in a series of similar dichotomies: they distinguished the savage from the civilized, myth from history, and magic from science. In positing each of these oppositions, nineteenth-century Europeans saw their status as scientific, historical, civilized peoples superior to the uncivilized, magic, and mythical "natives."

Distinctions between the oral and the written fade in light of the complex intersections of mythical and historical discourses that kept Javanese shadow theatre traditions alive. If art is both the reflection and distortion of daily happenings, as I believe it is, then artistic expressions serve to communicate how people feel, think, embrace, or resist the forces that impinge upon their lives. In this sense, shadow play performances reenact power relations in order to negotiate the terms under which those relations are recorded in memory. In the words of Walter Benjamin, "*Memory* creates the chain of tradition which passes a happening on from generation to generation."[12] Tradition, in this case, includes the written, spoken, and performed stories that puppeteers continually combine and rearrange in response to the tastes of audiences and patrons. This focus on power relations moves away from a rehearsing of developmental stages that ultimately privileges European culture toward an analysis of how stories

---

Française d'Extrême Orient 46 (1952): 11. If it is not an original ninth-century document, that means that the shadow theatre would be dated a half-century later. In C.E. 907, another Javanese inscription mentions Ramayana and Mahabharata characters and stories and the word *wayang*; see Sarkar, *Inscriptions of Java*, 2:96.

12. Benjamin, *Illuminations*, p. 98.

Histories, Mythologies, and Tales

captured in texts and performances are ways of recording, transmitting, and interpreting human experience.[13]

Colonial Allegories

Many Javanese shadow play stories ask what in the present, believed to be real, can be explicated by the past. This technique is elaborated in the Javanese use of the term *pasemon*.[14] *Pasemon* comes from the Javanese root *semu*, "to seem like" or "to be colored by."[15] In Javanese performance traditions, *pasemon* can refer to the use of a story as a subtle caricature of reality; thus, the technique of *pasemon* serves to bring the observer/hearer's attention to those domains which often lie outside the boundaries of any particular story. By commenting on the present through the past, the allegorical nature of *pasemon* technique sets up a special relationship between the author and certain people in the audience. The events that *pasemon* stories represent can be as grand as the fall of an empire or as simple as the philandering ways of the patron of a play. In fact, elements of *pasemon* can be found in most of the performances of any good Javanese puppeteer. Today, puppeteers—if they are not already familiar with the

13. See the essays and the introduction to Flueckiger and Sears, eds., *Boundaries of the Text*, for a brief summary of the oral/written dichotomy, and Johannes Fabian, "Keep Listening: Ethnography and Reading," in *The Ethnography of Reading*, ed. J. Boyarin (Berkeley: University of California Press, 1993), for a new look at practices of constructing and reading texts. In his important work on Central Javanese perceptions of self and other, *Javanese Shadow Plays*, Ward Keeler examines power struggles between patrons and performers of shadow play to support his analyses of Central Javanese family, villlage, and societal structures. Of major importance in Keeler's work is his focus on village rather than court shadow theatre traditions.

14. *Pasemon* can refer to the use to which a story—or any part of a story—can be put, that is, as an allusion to something else. As one Javanese scholar explained the word: "*pasemon* is real-life drama, drawn as if it were in a *wayang* for performance. Thus the origin lies in the reality of true human dramas, not just stories adapted for the performance." R. M. Sajid, *Bauwarna Kawruh Wajang* (Surakarta: "Widya Duta," 1971), p. 56. Thus Mahabharata and Ramayana tales inscribed in court poetry can either serve as or be the result of *pasemon*. Following Nancy Florida, *Javanese Literature in Surakarta Manuscripts*, vol. 1 (Ithaca: Cornell Southeast Asia Program Press, 1993), pp. 15 and 24, I use the word *inscription* to refer to the fixing of ideas in Javanese texts because those who produce the ideas may be different from those who inscribe the words in manuscripts.

15. Poerwadarminta, *Baoesastra Djawa* (Batavia: J. B. Wolters, 1937), p. 555.

foibles of their host—are often told information about the family sponsoring the shadow play before or on the way to the performance, and the puppeteer is expected to make humorous or edifying references to the family of the host through the story. In the same way, puppeteers will often mock and make caricatures of their musicians and singers when they perform, keeping them awake and laughing, or miffed and embarrassed, in the wee hours of the night by comparing them to the heroes and heroines of the past. Thus the Ramayana and Mahabharata characters serve as a standard against which to measure the behavior of living people.

The late Javanese scholar Moertono translated *pasemon* as "covered information," and he mentioned the necessity for this type of communication in a colonial society like Java where subtle insinuation was preferred to direct articulation.[16] Thus the Javanese Mahabharata and Ramayana stories that came closest to European notions of truth approached verisimilitude cautiously. If historical observations needed to be clothed in allegory in Javanese colonial society, then ephemeral performances and sung court poetry may have been more fitting vehicles than written chronicles.[17] Court chronicles in Java were intended to express only the most desirable pasts, and they needed to be rewritten constantly as new court rulers required different pasts to effect desired changes in the future. In contrast to written historical genres, most tellings of shadow tales could only be captured in memory; the shadow puppeteers, respected for their ability to remember—stories, genealogies, and characters—could, perhaps, be bolder than others, as Dutch power penetrated deeper into Javanese life after 1830, because they knew that their ephemeral words were difficult to reproduce.[18] But, by the early twentieth century, Dutch

16. S. Moertono, *State and Statecraft in Old Java: A Study of the Later Mataram Period, 16th to 19th Century* (1968; Ithaca: Cornell Modern Indonesia Project, 1981), p. 19.

17. See M. C. Ricklefs, *Jogjakarta under Sultan Mangkubumi 1749–1792* (London: Oxford University Press, 1974), pp. 188–90, for a discussion of Javanese written texts as historical allegories. See also J. J. Ras, "The Historical Development of the Javanese Shadow Theatre," *Review of Indonesian and Malaysian Studies* 10 (1976): 50–76, at p. 65, where Ras discusses "lakon pasemon" as systematic allusion. J. Kats mentions a story that mirrored the abdication of the Sultan of Yogya in 1921 in *Het Javaansche Tooneel I, De Wajang Poerwa*, vol. 1 (Weltevreden: Commissie voor de Volkslectuur, 1923), pp. 110–11.

18. Often scholars have assumed that the clown dialogues were the site of most political commentary. In creating *pasemon*, however, the puppeteer can fill the clown

scholars and Javanese intellectuals were engaged in a subtle struggle to control shadow theatre repertoires and the puppeteers who kept those repertoires alive.

Pramoedya Ananta Toer, mentioned above, poignantly expressed the growing Javanese ambivalence toward and Dutch celebration of the shadow theatre in the final novel of his historical quartet on the first decades of the twentieth century and the rise of Indonesian national consciousness.[19] The main character in the fourth novel is a Menadonese police official, raised in France and married to a French woman. When the story opens in the Indies in 1912, we learn that the Menadonese policeman has become skilled at helping the colonial government understand the constitution of various Indies peoples as subjects of a rising national consciousness. Early in the novel, his Dutch archivist friend asks the Menadonese man if he has ever seen an entire *wayang purwa* play, and he replies no. The would-be Dutch scholar then goes on to explain to this non-Javanese Indies man the meaning of the shadow theatre.

It takes time indeed to study the major lines of thought in the *wayang*. To understand *wayang* is to understand the history of a philosophy of life and the worldview of the Javanese people. To master the study of *wayang* as a subject, Sir, means to master the Javanese people. This is one essential element for becoming an expert on the colonial Indies. If there were a Javanese person who was able to master it as a subject, who was able to free himself from the grip of that *wayang* world, it would still be a long haul to remake himself, Sir. This *wayang* world is a unique structure that is unable to be touched by modern ideas. Whether the Javanese person is Christian or Muslim, or has no religion at all, they are all sucked into it just like Prapanca and Tantular envisioned.[20]

---

scenes with slapstick jokes and still make pointed political statements through his/her characterization and rendering of plot.

19. Pramoedya Ananta Toer, *Rumah Kaca* (Kuala Lumpur: Wira Karya, 1990), p. 78.

20. Prapanca and Tantular were poets who wrote in Old Javanese hundreds of years ago. They were among the first to describe the syncretic nature of Javanist Shaivite and Buddhist thought that Pramoedya's Dutch archivist blames for the failure of the Javanese to resist the Dutch. Ruth McVey succinctly describes the perceived relationship between shadow theatre and Hindu, Buddhist, and Islamic beliefs in Java: "For this amalgam—the Agama Jawa, or the Religion of Java—*wayang* was the supreme expression." Ruth McVey, "The Wayang Controversy in Indonesian Communism," in *Context, Meaning, and Power in Southeast Asia*, ed. M. Hobart and R. Taylor (Ithaca: Cornell Southeast Asia Publications, 1986), p. 22.

There is no element of chance in Pramoedya's ironic decision to have the Dutch scholar lecture the Menadonese policeman about the *wayang*. As a Javanese himself, Pramoedya sees the web of *wayang* stories as an intoxicating veil that mystifies the Javanese, both in their own eyes and in the eyes of others. And he sees, too, the ways in which the *wayang* was constituted in colonial discourses as a significant part of the interlocking apparatuses of Dutch control.[21] In Pramoedya's view, to begin to become objective about the *wayang*, to be able to see the *wayang* as a subject of study, was to free oneself from the power of colonial constructions of Java. To show how Javanese Ramayana and Mahabharata tales became the shadows of empire, this book explores Dutch and postcolonial Indonesian government efforts to use the *wayang* as a means of control. It also examines the several generations of Javanese who, as they constituted themselves and saw themselves constituted as Indonesians, learned to use the *wayang* for their own purposes.

During the 1960s, when many aspects of Javanese—and Indonesian—life were politicized, shadow plays were used to convey Marxist, Islamic, and nationalist messages. Both before and after the fall of the Soekarno government, the fate of Soekarno and his colleagues might be announced through analogies with the characters on the shadow play screen.[22] The technique of *pasemon* allows puppeteers to insert veiled political allusions and commentary into performances. Thus the political critiques embed-

21. Pramoedya told me this in July of 1990 when I visited him in Jakarta, where he was still under tacit house arrest. It is worth noting also that Pramoedya does not identify the *wayang* with religion—all Javanese are subject to its power until they can master it as a subject. The term *colonial discourse*, in this book, shows how Dutch scholars, administrators, and missionaries chose to speak about Java and the Javanese and the ways in which these images that were produced for European consumption circulated among the Javanese. Other recent definitions of colonial discourse, based on the work of theorists like Gayatri Spivak and Homi Bhabha, can be found in Patrick Williams and Laura Chrisman, eds., *Colonial Discourse and Post-Colonial Theory: A Reader* (New York: Harvester Wheatsheaf, 1993), and David Spurr, *The Rhetoric of Empire* (Durham: Duke University Press, 1993). Williams and Chrisman and Spurr all distinguish between colonialism and imperialism in their discussions of colonial discourse. Although the colonial era has ended, the politics of empire have not disappeared.

22. See C. J. Koch's historical novel, *The Year of Living Dangerously* (New York: Penguin, 1983) for one description of the shadow plays held at Soekarno's palace in Bogor. See also Benedict Anderson's "Languages of Indonesian Politics," reprinted in *Language and Power: Exploring Political Cultures in Indonesia* (Ithaca: Cornell University Press, 1990), pp. 123–51.

ded in shadow theatre performances often appear as allegories, unintelligible to those who are not intimately familiar with the tradition.[23] The use of Javanese Mahabharata and Ramayana tales as a metalanguage for politics, village gossip, commentary on court intrigue, and entertaining repartee is stressed in several chapters of this book. Because the stories can be used to comment on the vicissitudes of daily life, and this commentary changes with each telling, it becomes increasingly difficult to fix the "meaning" of any story. Each story has the potential to be renewed in each telling, and each new telling leaves its traces on the story told. The persistent ability of stories both to charge and change past and present marks the constitution and celebration of these stories as allegories. But the power of allegory lies in its very ambiguity: "Thus in allegory an ambivalence occurs between the power to lend meaning to things on the one hand, and the inability to fix this meaning essentially on the other."[24]

Although the shadow theatre of Java served as a transmitter and preserver of Ramayana and Mahabharata stories and as a vehicle for texts and performances to travel through the centuries, this book questions whether it ever was the dominant expression of a Javanese philosophy, religion, or "worldview." Certainly foreign scholars and travelers perceived the shadow theatre as the emblem of exotic, impenetrable, and mystically rich "Java."[25] To argue that *wayang purwa* theatre[26] and its stories were more

23. In his biography of the late President Soekarno, both in its structure and focus, Bernhard Dahm illustrates how Soekarno used these stories as a subversive political discourse. See B. Dahm, *Sukarno and the Struggle for Indonesian Independence*, trans. Mary F. Somers Heidhues (1966; Ithaca: Cornell University Press, 1969).

24. This comment on allegory comes from Lislotte Wiesenthal, *Zur Wissenschaftstheorie Walter Benjamins* (Frankfurt am Main: Athenaum, 1973), p. 58. It was quoted in Susan Buck-Morss, *The Dialectics of Seeing: Walter Benjamin and the Arcades Project* (Cambridge: MIT Press, 1989), p. 426 n. 68.

25. One of the earliest sources to mention shadow theatre in Java is the Malay *Hikayat Raja-Raja Pasai* dated perhaps to the fourteenth century. See A. H. Hill, "Hikayat Raja-Raja Pasai," *Journal of the Malay Branch of the Royal Asiatic Society* 33, no. 2 (1960): 161. Rijklof van Goens mentions shadow theatre in his memoirs of his visits to the court of Mataram in the mid-seventeenth century. See J. J. de Graaf, *De Vijf Gezantschapsreizen van Rijklof van Goens naar het Hof van Mataram 1648–1654* (s' Gravenhage: M. Nijhoff, 1956). Detailed descriptions appear in the works of British scholars and administrators. See T. S. Raffles, *The History of Java* (1817; 2d ed. [2 vols.], London: John Murray, 1830), and J. Crawfurd, *History of the Indian Archipelago*, 3 vols. (Edinburgh: Archibald Constable, 1820).

26. The *wayang purwa* is distinguished from other Javanese shadow theatre traditions by its use of Ramayana and Mahabharata tales for its main repertoire.

than a shifting assemblage of puppets, performers, and plots held together by repeated voicings of Ramayana and Mahabharata stories, I ask what powers and purposes were served by the preservation of the storyrealms these characters inhabited. To discern why the Ramayana and Mahabharata characters were nurtured for several hundred years in the Islamic communities of Central Java, I examine how the stories came to life not only in shadow play performances but also in chronicles, manuscripts, scholarly journals, romances, and novels. These media mixed older ideas with contemporary ones, and Javanese ideas with Dutch, in order to meet the needs of new constituencies. But, if Ramayana and Mahabharata tales have survived in Java because they continued to engage Javanese audiences, the categories of knowledge maintained by these stories have also created tensions among Javanese intellectuals. Like Pramoedya, intellectuals since the first decade of the century have attempted to extricate themselves from their "exotic" and "mystical" past and position themselves within a more Indonesian future.[27] Chapters 3 and 4 of this book address the changing thought-worlds of urban and rural Javanese intelligentsias in the twentieth century to show how these intellectuals used the shadow theatre to construct both ethnic and national identities. Shadow play stories serve as allegories rather than myths or "tradition" because allegory became a necessary strategy for historical survival and social critique in Javanese colonial and postcolonial society.

Shadow Theatre and Orientalism

For the purposes of this book, I have avoided positing a past time of tradition that has been overcome by modernity. As I see it, "tradition" and "modernity" both come into focus at the same time, and scholars can only recognize tradition in the light of modernity. My discussions of Javanese shadow theatre as a point of entry to Dutch colonial discourses suggest

27. As Ben Anderson perceptively notes: "For the fact is that the Javanese language and Javanese culture have for almost a century now been much more of a problem to the Javanese themselves than to anyone else: a problem that cannot be resolved by any obvious or easy means, since it involves and implicates almost all sectors of Javanese society." B.R.O'G. Anderson, "*Sembah-Sumpah*: The Politics of Language and Javanese Culture" [1984], in *Language and Power: Exploring Political Cultures in Indonesia* (Ithaca: Cornell University Press, 1990), p. 235.

that these ways of speaking are a product of Dutch-Javanese encounters that began in the early seventeenth century. In the Napoleonic period, Java and other Dutch colonial possessions were taken away from the Dutch and put, albeit briefly, in British hands. Sir Stamford Raffles, discussed in chapter 1, held power in the Indies in those years and attempted a radical reconstruction of the colony. Raffles promoted the study of Javanese "culture" on orientalist terms that discounted Javanese Islam, and when he departed, the Dutch were left to face the repercussions of his actions.

What is known as the Javanese shadow theatre comes into focus in this moment of the Dutch-Javanese confrontation. The shadow theatre existed before the early nineteenth century, but little is known of its contours, its performance practices, its role or position in Javanese communities. The shadow theatre cannot be separated from the colonial moment and posited as an essential, unchanging part of Java waiting for Europeans to uncover, interpret, document, or eventually reconstruct it. The shadow theatre, as it is known today, developed within an atmosphere where nineteenth-century discourses of science and progress were percolating, both contributing to and drawing from Javanese and Dutch intellectual exchanges. This book contributes to a reenvisioning of European histories that show the influence of Asian, African, and New World knowledges on the constitution of European mentalities.

Edward Said's work *Orientalism* has been immensely influential in challenging scholarly thinking about representations of the Middle East and South Asia by Europeans and Americans, most effectively in the modern period. Said suggested that the Orient was not allowed to represent itself; it was always already represented as the Occident's "other."[28] This representation was not innocent: colonial and postcolonial scholars were implicated in the production of the "Orient" as much as were colonial administrators, travelers, merchants, and artists. The Orient was exoticized and feminized in European literary and scholarly representations and thus was both dominated and relegated to an inferior status. Said's work has

---

28. Said states: "Orientalism is a style of thought based upon an ontological and epistemological distinction made between 'the Orient' and (most of the time) 'the Occident.'" And again: "Orientalism assumed an unchanging Orient, absolutely different (the reasons change from epoch to epoch) from the West." E. Said, *Orientalism* (New York: Vintage, 1979), pp. 2, 98.

provoked a wide range of scholarly debate with critiques from both ends of the political spectrum.[29] Said's identification of orientalist discourses has distinguished, in acknowledged Foucaultian fashion, ways in which the Orient and, more importantly, Islam have been presented to European and American audiences. Said focuses mainly on British, French, and American imperial attitudes, but his arguments can be extended to include Dutch behavior in the Indies and especially Dutch attitudes toward Islam. This book shows a particular example of orientalist discourse in the tensions of empire that influenced both European and Javanese representations of Javanese literary and historical traditions. In this light, one reaction to Said's ideas is pertinent.

A notable feature of Orientalism is that it examines the history of Western textualities about the non-West quite in isolation from how those textualities might have been received, accepted, modified, challenged, overthrown or reproduced by the intelligentsias of the colonized countries: not as an undifferentiated mass but as situated social agents impelled by our own conflicts, contradictions, distinct social and political locations of class, gender, region, religious affiliation, and so on. . . .[30]

Although inadequate as a criticism of Said's work on English literature, this observation cogently captures the intent of my project.[31] I do present Dutch discourses about Java and Javanese traditions, but I am equally interested in showing how the actions of local intelligentsias, "as situated

29. See, for example, the "Review Symposium," in the *Journal of Asian Studies* 39, no. 3 (May 1980): 481–518; James Clifford's "On Orientalism," in *The Predicament of Culture: Twentieth Century Ethnography, Literature, and Art* (Cambridge: Harvard University Press, 1988); and Bernard Lewis, "The Question of Orientalism," *New York Review of Books*, 24 June 1982. One recent and controversial critique appears in the work of Aijaz Ahmad. Ahmad suggests that Said has essentialized both Orient and Occident by following the same master narratives—what Ahmad calls "Auerbachean High Humanism"—that he critiques in the work of others. See Aijaz Ahmad, *In Theory: Classes, Literatures, Nations* (London: Verso, 1992), p. 167. Some scholars have felt the need to defend Said's work against Ahmad's criticisms, as illustrated by the essays in *Public Culture* (December 1993).

30. Aijaz Ahmad, *In Theory*, p. 172.

31. Said clearly states that his purpose is to show how the Orient has been produced in European and American texts. Had Said's *Orientalism* not focused on European discourses, it is doubtful whether it would have received the attention that it did. In effect, his work presents a clear challenge to Asians and Middle Easterners, and those who write about them with empathy, to explore the reception of and resistance to the discursive formations of Orientalism.

social agents," were impelled by their own logics and needs and how these activities intersected, obstructed, or occasionally meshed with Dutch efforts to represent and control Javanese literary and historical productions.

Dutch attitudes toward and representations of Javanese Mahabharata and Ramayana traditions also illuminate the ways in which Dutch scholars promoted these traditions at the expense of Islam. I do not mean to say that the Dutch in any sense "created" Javanese shadow theatre traditions. In fact, the number of Dutch scholars or administrators who could even understand these traditions was quantitatively insignificant even while the influence of those who could was qualitatively profound. Rather, Javanese patrons, authors, and performers of Javanese Mahabharata and Ramayana stories chose to write or perform their texts in ways that would allow them to accrue cultural capital according to the tastes and styles of the time.

In the 1920s and 1930s, for example, this meant that Javanese authors and patrons sought to show that shadow theatre and the stories it conveyed were intrinsically mystical because of the values that were placed on mysticism by groups of Javanese and Dutch intellectuals influenced by Theosophical thought.[32] The key representation of shadow theatre in the 1930s was, in fact, written in Dutch by the noted scholar, military officer, businessman, and ruler Mangkunagara VII, head of the minor court in Solo. The prince, greatly influenced by the ideas of Dutch Theosophists, suggested that every Javanese shadow play was a reenactment of a spiritual search for mystical knowledge.[33] He offered these ideas with mixed intent in a learned lecture to a gathering of Dutch and Indies intellectuals: the prince realized that his audience of Dutch scholars and spiritual seekers placed value on mystical knowledge, and the mystical world was one realm in the era of high colonialism where Javanese could be superior or at least equal to the Dutch. This interpretation suggests that the Javanese prince was impelled by his own conflicts and contradictions, but it also

32. Theosophy was an eclectic religious movement that began in America in the last quarter of the nineteenth century and quickly spread to Europe and the colonies. The movement attempted to combine aspects of the various world religions and to posit a mystical essentialism that they all shared. I discuss Theosophy and its impact on Javanese intellectuals at length in chapter 4.

33. Mangkunagara VII, *On the Wayang Kulit (Purwa) and Its Symbolic and Mystical Elements*, trans. Claire Holt, Data Paper no. 27 (1933; Ithaca: Southeast Asia Program, Cornell University, 1957).

shows that he negotiated knowledges on his own terms to accrue power and prestige in the hybrid[34] Javanese-Dutch intellectual world of the inter-war years.

Mangkunagara VII's interpretation has been accepted by many followers of Javanese mystical groups (*aliran kebathinan*), which have proliferated in Java since the revolutionary period.[35] The text was translated into English in 1957, making it accessible to many Americans who do not read Dutch. Whether from Dutch or English editions, Mankunagara VII's ideas have been portrayed in much of the secondary scholarship on the Javanese shadow theatre as one of several definitive statements about the mystical essence of the tradition, and the essay has been used by scholars to judge and limit the many meanings of the shadow theatre performance tradition.[36] What began as a strategic move at the boundaries of colonizer and colonized has become a critique of the efficacy of individual textual re-enactments, a prescriptive paradigmatic model for both Javanese and non-

34. *Hybrid* is a term I questioned in L. J. Sears, "The Contingency of Autonomous History," in *Autonomous Histories, Particular Truths: Essays in Honor of John R. W. Smail*, ed. L. J. Sears (Madison: University of Wisconsin Center for Southeast Asian Studies, 1993), p. 9. In the present work I have found the term invaluable for describing the colonial interlacing of Javanese and Dutch thought-worlds while recognizing that those thought-worlds are, at all times, being constituted and reconstituted in nonessentialist and complex ways.

35. By revolutionary period, I refer to the years from 1945, when Indonesia proclaimed its independence from the Dutch in the wake of the Japanese defeat, and 1949, when that proclamation became a reality after four years of bloody struggle. For important studies of Javanese mysticism in the revolutionary period, see Paul Stange, "The Logic of Rasa in Java," *Indonesia* 38 (October 1984): 113–34, and "Inner Dimensions of the Indonesian Revolution" in Sears, *Autonomous Histories, Particular Truths*.

36. For example, see James R. Brandon, *On Thrones of Gold* (Cambridge: Harvard University Press, 1970); R. McVey, "The Wayang Controversy in Indonesian Communism," p. 42 n. 3; B.R.O'G. Anderson, "The Idea of Power in Javanese Culture" (1972), in *Language and Power*, p. 55; J. J. Ras, "The Historical Development of the Javanese Shadow Theatre," p. 41. Geertz posits mysticism as the essence of Javanese religion as represented in shadow theatre, using the comments of a Javanese informant, who presumably was a member of a mystical group, in C. Geertz, *The Interpretation of Cultures: Selected Essays* (New York: Basic Books, 1973), pp. 136–37. Keeler, *Javanese Shadow Plays*, p. 244, notes that most Javanese discussion of the meaning of shadow theatre focuses on the Dewaruci story, one of the two plays discussed by Mangkunagara VII. A. L. Becker notes that most Europeans and Americans like the Dewaruci story because it appeals to their linear sense of narrative time in "Text-Building, Epistemology, and Aesthetics in Javanese Shadow Theatre," *The Imagination of Reality*, ed. A. L. Becker and A. A. Yengoyan (Norwood, N.J.: Ablex, 1979), p. 219.

Javanese scholars and *wayang purwa* enthusiasts who see performances that fail to reproduce sufficient mystical depth as a sign of the degeneration of the shadow theatre tradition.[37]

Several chapters of this book present examples of Dutch scholarly representations of Javanese shadow theatre as well as the conflicting Javanese and Indonesian nationalist agendas that both incorporated and resisted Dutch ideas. My intent is to open up spaces for rewritings of colonial and postcolonial Javanese histories in which the boundaries as well as the content of the categories of history and story, myth and allegory, or colonialism and "culture" are questioned rather than taken for granted.[38] These examples of changing constructions of shadow theatre traditions arising out of negotiations among Javanese and Dutch patrons, performers, and scholars are intentionally suggestive; they point to the need for a reconceptualization of art forms and performance traditions that have been nurtured by the tensions of European and Asian colonial relationships.

Mythologies and Histories

This exploration of Javanese Ramayana and Mahabharata traditions begins from the premise that myth, history, and story live on in cultures in complex ways. Definitions of myth identify it with fable, illusion, and universal experience; mythic as an adjective implies characters and tales that appear larger than life. All these meanings converge in Javanese shadow theatre traditions and the stories people tell about them. Certainly the Ramayana and Mahabharata tales that form the major repertoire of the Central Javanese shadow theatre are myth in the sense of fable. The stories tell the exploits of heroes and heroines—the battles fought, the maidens won, the heroes fallen. Because shadow theatre performances are patron-sponsored, puppeteers shape performances to fit the tastes of those who

37. See B.R.O'G. Anderson, *Mythology and the Tolerance of the Javanese* (Ithaca: Cornell Modern Indonesia Project, 1965), and C. Geertz, "'Popular Art' and the Javanese Tradition," *Indonesia* 50 (October 1990): 77–94, as well as Bambang Murtiyasa, "Sebuah Tinjauan tentang Pakem dan Masalah-Masalahnya," *Gatra* 19, no. 1 (1989): 7–11.

38. For an important collection of essays on the interactions between colonialism and culture, see Nicholas Dirks, ed., *Colonialism and Culture* (Ann Arbor: University of Michigan Press, 1992), and Dirks's insightful introduction to the volume.

sponsor them. The stories have a wide range of tellings, and there are no "correct" tellings or tellings that are more "basic" than others;[39] the pleasure of the patron and the audience he or she has attracted decides the success of a night's performance. But these stories of Java serve many purposes as they move between story and myth and between myth and history.

What is the difference between myth and story? Myth signifies the distortion of a story, the stretching or reworking of a story to illustrate more universal themes. Stories are both more naive and more event-centered than myths. As Walter Benjamin put it, the story

. . . is one of the oldest forms of communication. It does not aim at transmitting the pure in-itself of the event (as information does) but anchors the event in the life of the person reporting, in order to pass it on as experience to those listening.[40]

The stories people tell about the past, in simple and stylized renderings, form the content of histories written by scholars. Most of the stories that have organized Javanese culture and society for Dutch and other non-Javanese scholars and travelers mention the shadow theatre and anchor it in the life of the people reporting, and their tales are passed on as experience to those listening.

The Dutch interest in Javanese court and village traditions may be seen as part of a larger European interest in folk cultures that had been inspired by the writings of Herder from the late eighteenth century.[41] In nineteenth-century European intellectual circles, belief in religion had often been

39. See Barbara Herrnstein Smith's thought-provoking essay "Narrative Versions, Narrative Theories," in W.J.T. Mitchell, ed., *On Narrative* (Chicago: University of Chicago Press, 1981). She argues that the dualistic belief in an "original" or "ur" text of a popular tale, which lies beneath all tellings of the tale, is a naively Platonic one; such a "basic" text can only exist in an ideal world. She suggests (p. 217) that the many versions and variants of any tale, in fact, constitute the tale. As I understand her argument, each tale is both constructed from and contingent upon its collection of tellings.

40. This quote is from Benjamin's "Uber einige Motive bei Baudelaire," and is quoted by Susan Buck-Morss in her recreation of Benjamin's Arcades Project, *The Dialectics of Seeing*, p. 336.

41. This discussion draws ideas from M. Jay, *Adorno* (Cambridge: Harvard University Press, 1984), p. 112, and George W. Stocking, Jr., *Victorian Anthropology* (New York: Free Press, 1987), pp. 20–23. Stocking notes that Herder's depiction of the *volksgeist* or folk spirit led to a celebration of the mythopoetic uniqueness of each national culture, which was essentialized in the character of the "folk."

Histories, Mythologies, and Tales

displaced by a glorification of high culture—the humanistic pursuit of the arts—and a reification of "folk" culture. These beliefs were a source of pluralist but also racialist assumptions in which only the temperate climate of Europe could have produced such obvious civilizational heights, and they emerged from a Romanticism that valued the mythopoetic uniqueness of each "culture." The European Romanticist movement of the late eighteenth and early nineteenth centuries combined a belief in culture as both social practices and humanistic artistic pursuits. For the European orientalist scholars in Asia, various performing arts embodied these two meanings of culture.[42] Although some Dutch scholars beginning in the mid-nineteenth century saw evidence of Java's Indic antiquity in the myths of the shadow theatre tradition, most dismissed Javanese notions that equated the shadow theatre tales with Javanese history. Although European scholars wrote about the history of shadow theatre, only in the 1960s did they begin to propose methodologies for evaluating and interpreting the information contained in oral traditions as historical data.[43] If myths are repositories of historical as well as societal data, distinctions between myth and history, and between history and anthropology, have become effaced as scholars have pursued these methods of analysis.[44]

Javanese shadow theatre, in particular the *wayang purwa* of Central

42. For discussions of culture and the Romanticist movement, see A. Sweeney, *A Full Hearing: Orality and Literacy in the Malay World* (Berkeley: University of California Press, 1987), pp. 17–22; W. J. Ong, *Rhetoric, Romance, and Technology* (Ithaca: Cornell University Press, 1971); and J. Barzun, *Classic, Romantic and Modern* (1961; Chicago: University of Chicago Press, 1975). My definitions of culture are drawn from R. Williams, *Keywords: A Vocabulary of Culture and Society* (1976; rev. ed., New York: Oxford University Press, 1983), pp. 87–93. In this work, my general use of the word *culture* refers to social practices rather than artistic pursuits.

43. The Dutch scholar C. C. Berg did suggest rather elaborate methodologies for understanding Javanese chronicles, but few people besides Berg were able to understand these obscure methods. See C. C. Berg, "Javaansche Geschiedschrijving," in F. W. Stapel, *Geschiedenis van Nederlandsch Indie*, pt. 2 (Amsterdam, 1938).

44. Jan Vansina sought to move oral traditions from the realm of myth into the purview of history and to argue that they could be legitimate historical documents, in *Oral Tradition* and *Oral Tradition as History*; cf. A. Lord, *The Singer of Tales* (Cambridge: Harvard University Press, 1960). David Henige has documented the proliferation of oral historical materials by his use of the phrase "oral historiography," in his book by that name (London: Longman, 1982). See also the collections of articles commenting on Vansina's ideas in *Social Analysis* 4 (1980), and J. C. Miller, *The African Past Speaks* (Hamden, Conn.: Archon Books, 1980).

Java, has received a lot of scholarly attention since the early nineteenth century.[45] Often it is presented as the "essence" of Javanist (*kejawen*) culture, a vision of Java in which Islam is often unfairly marginalized. This notion has become a tautology or a circular myth within scholarly debates because it assumes what it professes to explain. The shadow theatre is believed to be a microcosm of Javanist culture. To understand Java it is necessary to understand the shadow theatre, and to understand the shadow theatre is to understand Java. These suppositions are rarely questioned; they blur cause and effect as they weave myths and stories into history. As I trace the changing contours of Javanese Mahabharata and Ramayana stories in dramatic and narrative traditions, I also trace the evolution of scholarly discourses inspired by the efforts of non-Javanese scholars to explain these stories of Java. The mythological tales and studies of those tales continually influence one another, producing new stories and new interpretations of them. But distinctive problems arise when the scholars who describe "exotic" textual traditions are also administrators who wield power in colonial governments. In the politics of empire, scholarly descriptions become part of the machinery of colonial rule. To describe them meant to assign to different Javanese practices and traditions lower or higher places in a European hierarchy of values.[46] As this

45. As noted above, what distinguishes the *wayang purwa* shadow theatre repertoire is its preference for primarily Mahabharata, and occasionally Ramayana, tales, rather than other story cycles. For a detailed discussion of dramatic elements of the tradition, and translations of three shadow play texts, see Brandon, *On Thrones of Gold*. The best ethnographic studies include C. Geertz, *The Religion of Java*; V. M. Clara van Groenendael, *The dalang behind the wayang* (Dordrecht: Foris, 1985); and Keeler, *Javanese Shadow Plays*. For a fine philological study, see Becker, "Text-building." For penetrating studies of political and mythological issues, see Moertono, *State and Statecraft*, and Anderson, *Mythology and Tolerance of the Javanese*. For attention to stories and characters, see R. Hardjowirogo, *Sedjarah Wajang Purwa* (Djakarta: Balai Pustaka, 1968), and Paul Stange, "Mystical Symbolism in Javanese Wayang Mythology," *The South East Asian Review* 1, no. 2 (1977): 109–22. J. J. Ras's "The Historical Development of the Javanese Shadow Theatre" and *De schending van Soebadra: Javaans schimmenspel* (Amsterdam: Meulenhoff, 1976) are important historical and literary studies. McVey's analysis of *wayang* and Communist discourse in "The Wayang Controversy in Indonesian Communism" is exceptional. V. M. Clara van Groenendael's comprehensive bibliography of scholarship on various shadow theatre traditions provides rich information on many available works. See *Wayang Theatre in Indonesia: An Annotated Bibliography* (Dordrecht: Foris, 1987).

46. Aijaz Ahmad, "Jameson's Rhetoric of Otherness and the 'National Allegory,'" *Social Text* 17 (Fall 1987) has commented perceptively on the consequences of colonial descriptions: "It was by assembling a monstrous machinery of descriptions—of our

Histories, Mythologies, and Tales

book argues, myths are both embedded in structures of power and constitutive of various forms of power. Political necessities shape the way the past is understood and portrayed for each generation. Mythology and ideology are intricately connected, and I suggest that historical writing is impelled by a desire to resolve or record tensions or contradictions in this relationship that become visible at particular moments in time.[47]

Rather than being members of a mystified subaltern class, Javanese village performers use the well-known characters and plots of shadow tales to communicate their criticisms of power. The performers have led me to see the Javanese shadow theatre as a site where myth, story, and ideology confront one another, both revealing and blurring the boundaries that separate them.[48] Javanese puppeteers are sharp observers of society and its ills, and shadow tales are among the tools they use to elucidate the workings of power within Javanese society. The stories bring into being textual communities of patrons, performers, and the scholars who study and, in the past, governed them.[49]

---

bodies, our speech-acts, our habits, our conflicts and desires, our politics, our socialities and sexualities—in fields as various as ethnology, fiction, photography, linguistics, political science—that the colonial discourse was able to classify and ideologically master the colonial subject, enabling itself to transform the descriptively verifiable multiplicity and difference into the ideologically felt hierarchy of value" (p. 6).

47. There is an Indian oral tradition about Mahabharata stories that accounts for the many moral paradoxes that have kept South and Southeast Asian audiences arguing about these tales for centuries: Ganesha, the elephant-headed god and son of Shiva, was given the task of writing down the Mahabharata as it was narrated by the sage Vyasa. Sometimes Ganesha would become overwhelmed with the speed of the sage's words or he would want the sage to hurry and finish his tale. At these moments, the knots or moral quandaries would appear to keep sage and scribe arguing over these quandaries, allowing Ganesha to catch up with his writing or Vyasa to think about how he wanted to order his tale. See Wendy Doniger [O'Flaherty], "Fluid and Fixed Texts in India," in Flueckiger and Sears, Boundaries of the Text, pp. 33–34.

48. I use the term subaltern here as it has been defined since 1981 in the writings of a group of scholars of South Asia known as the Subaltern Studies collective. The major theorist of the collective is Ranajit Guha, whose work suggests that most Indian history has been written from a colonialist and elitist point of view, even though that history was enacted by the "subaltern classes" or the "people" (terms Guha uses interchangeably and whose inspiration comes from Antonio Gramsci's Prison Notebooks). See R. Guha and G. Spivak, eds., Selected Subaltern Studies (New York: Oxford University Press, 1988), for a selection of representative articles including Spivak's important feminist and deconstructive critique of the intellectual goals of the collective.

49. Brian Stock has developed the notion of "textual communities" in The Implications

When colonial scholars defined the textual communities of the colonized, they took part in the constitution of those communities. Within Javanese textual communities focused on Ramayana and Mahabharata stories in the nineteenth and twentieth centuries, different groups of intellectuals interacted and different types of knowledge were exchanged.[50] What complicated these Javanese struggles over cultural meanings was an intellectual environment already transformed by colonial relations. Shifting lines of power and patronage among Javanese elites, Dutch scholar-administrators, and village puppeteers entwined intellectual, artistic, and political discourses as dominant and dominated groups engaged in negotiations that left some measure of agency and awareness in the hands of village puppeteers. Through puppeteering schools strategically connected to the Solonese courts, Javanese nationalists and their few Dutch patrons hoped to constitute the puppeteers as thinkers of a modernizing underclass. By suggesting that village performers can be both players and pawns in games of power, my critique places myth, broadly defined, and the activity of mythmaking at the center of political and intellectual alliances in colonial and postcolonial Javanese society.[51]

More than just acknowledging the connections among mythologies,

---

of Literacy: Written Language and Models of Interpretation in the Eleventh and Twelfth Centuries (Princeton: Princeton University Press, 1983) and *Listening for the Text: On the Uses of the Past* (Baltimore: Johns Hopkins, 1990). Stock says, "We can think of a textual community as a group that arises somewhere in the interstices between the imposition of the written word and the articulation of a certain type of social organization. It is an interpretive community, but it is also a social entity." He notes that the idea was developed originally "to interpret the beliefs and activities of small, isolated, heretical and reformist groups in medieval Europe" in *Listening for the Text*, pp. 150–51.

50. For this discussion, I have drawn on the ideas of Antonio Gramsci, *Selections from the Prison Notebooks* (New York: International Publishers, 1971), pp. 3–23; Gramsci discusses the elaboration of rural and urban, as well as traditional and organic, intellectuals in Italian society in the early twentieth century.

51. Notions of agency within the oppressions of colonial structures that I introduce here mesh well with the ideas of accommodation and resistance suggested by Eugene Genovese in his important work on the world of the slaves in the American South: "The slaveholders established their hegemony over the slaves primarily through the development of an elaborate web of paternalistic relationships, but the slaves' place in that hegemonic system reflected deep contradictions, manifested in the dialectic of accommodation and resistance" *Roll, Jordan, Roll: The World the Slaves Made* (New York: Vintage, 1972), p. 658. I do not mean to equate American slavery with high imperialism in simplistic ways, but there are similar patterns in these different systems of subjugation.

ideologies, and scholarly discourses, I suggest that a continual, often unacknowledged, activity of mythmaking takes place as scholars shape stories and position those who tell them within historical or anthropological narratives. Scholarly myths can last for decades, even centuries, if they serve heuristic ideological purposes. For a variety of reasons that this book examines, the majority of Dutch, American, and Indonesian scholarship on Javanese shadow theatre has described the tradition in religious or ritual terms rather than political or historical ones because of the useful belief that the tradition *is* the unchanging mythical essence of Javanese culture.[52] It was in the interests of Dutch scholar-administrators to believe that shadow theatre was synonymous with Javanist religion because that allowed the colonial government to identify and nurture a sector of Javanese society in which Islam could become Java's "other"—where Islam was believed to be a shallow overlay on deeply entrenched older Indic traditions of Hinduism and Buddhism.[53]

Islam continued to be seen by the Dutch as a threatening menace to European colonial rule, and this fear of strict Islam was inherited by the

52. McVey's political study of Javanese Marxist attitudes toward shadow theatre traditions, "The Wayang Controversy," is a brilliant study, but she, too, posits the *wayang purwa* as the essence of Javanese belief. Anderson addresses ways in which Javanese shadow tales reflect political beliefs as well as Javanese notions of power, in *Mythology and the Tolerance of the Javanese* and "The Idea of Power in Javanese Culture." See also the political discussions in P.B.R. Carey, "The Role of *Wayang* in the Dipanagara War," *Prisma* 7 (1977): 15–27, and Takashi Shiraishi, "The Dispute between Tjipto Mangoenkoesoemo and Soetatmo Soeriokoesoemo: *Pandita* vs. *Satria*," *Indonesia* 32 (1981): 93–108. H. Ahmad Muhsin, *Perang Tipu Daya antara Bung Karno dengan Tokoh-Tokoh Komunis* (Jakarta: Golden Terayon Press, 1989), and G. J. Resink, "From the Old Mahabharata—to the New Ramayana—Order," *Bijdragen tot de Taal-, Land- en Volkenkunde* 131, nos. 2/3 (1975): 214–35, give somewhat fanciful or fantastic accounts of *wayang* and politics, J. J. Ras gives a historical chronology based on Javanese mythological and literary texts in his "The Historical Development of the Javanese Shadow Theatre" and his *De schending van Soebadra: Javaans schimmenspel.*

53. In an insightful critique, Richard Robison examines political studies of Indonesia where analyses of culture and power "can be explained essentially in terms of the persistence of Javanese cultural perspectives." See Richard Robison, "Culture, Politics, and Economy in the Political History of the New Order," in *Interpreting Indonesian Politics: Thirteen Contributions to the Debate*, ed. B. Anderson and Audrey Kahin (Ithaca: Southeast Asia Program Press, 1982), p. 131. In a similar vein, I am suggesting that these "Javanese cultural perspectives"—epitomized by the shadow theatre—change over time, and their construction and reconstruction must be investigated rather than taken as foundational beliefs.

postcolonial state. In several chapters of this book, I look at the contradictory relations between Islam and shadow theatre and the ways in which these relations have been represented in history and myth.[54] Without setting up history as a privileged discourse, I show how Javanese shadow theatre traditions changed over time by focusing on their complex negotiations with the social and political forces that surrounded them.[55] Rather than the foundational "essence" of Javanese religion and culture, Central Javanese shadow theatre remained important as allegorical critique and historical commentary in colonial and postcolonial society. If shadow play stories are allegories rather than myths, perhaps history is always already allegory, no more, no less.

Overview

This study of changing boundaries between myth and history in Javanese Mahabharata and Ramayana tales over the past two centuries analyzes what happens when stories move from village performances and palace manuscripts into Dutch texts and nationalist journals and, in the final chapter, into comic books (*cergam*) and novels. The stories told by the scholars, patrons, and performers who manipulate the shadow tales become the threads that are woven into mythical or historical patterns. The anomalies in these patterns present opportunities for exploring ideological battles that have been fought to control the meanings of Javanese cultural symbols. I identify different performers, patrons, and scholars whose ideas inspired reinterpretations as these stories passed through Javanese time: Indic, Islamic, Euroamerican, and Indonesian voices blend

54. This is not to suggest that Dutch reactions to and relations with Javanese Islam remained the same over the centuries of Dutch rule in the archipelago. See Karel Steenbrink's study *Dutch Colonialism and Indonesian Islam: Contacts and Conflicts 1596–1950* (Amsterdam: Editions Rodopi B.V., 1993).

55. Tony Bennett argues that as a discourse, history has been seen as more "real" than literature and more easily knowable independent of textual representations. He continues: "The effect of this dualistic ontology is to privilege history as both literature's source and its ultimate referent." T. Bennett, *Outside Literature* (London: Routledge, 1990), p. 42. The work of historians has often been to create the contexts in which the texts of an age can be understood. But the shaping of text and context are mutually interdependent and mutually creative acts.

and overlap, each new voice challenging and altering the sounds of older ones.

In chapter 1 I discuss the role of Islam in "Hindu-Javanese" culture as it was defined by British scholars during the British interregnum in Java in the early nineteenth century. Contrary to accepted belief, Islamic ideas do penetrate Ramayana and Mahabharata traditions by displacing older meanings within particular stories. I present stories about the birth of the demon-king Rahwana and compare different tellings of the story from its earliest appearance in the Sanskrit Ramayana attributed to Valmiki to its reinterpretations in Javanese court poetry in the eighteenth and nineteenth centuries. These eighteenth- and nineteenth-century renditions of the story served to document a stage in the accommodation of Javanist religious traditions to stricter interpretations of an originally mystical Islam. Islamic authority was becoming established in the texts and performances of the period, and, as part of that process, Islam was being molded to the shape of indigenous Javanese religious belief.[56] Mystical ideas in nineteenth-century Mahabharata and Ramayana tales were usually expressed in Islamic terms, something that would change by the end of the century as Javanese elites began to receive a Dutch-language education.

This exploration of Islamic authority within so-called "Hindu-Javanese" texts suggests that nineteenth- and twentieth-century Dutch colonial discourses, appearing as coercive power and scholarly analysis, minimized the important religious role that Islam had already assumed in Central Javanese villages. By the second half of the nineteenth century, the intertwining of *wayang* and Islam begins to fracture. This arises out of the contact of some Javanese Muslims with the Arabian Wahhabi movement, the colonial suppression of the outward expression of Islam by Bupati (Regents) and others connected to the colonial regime, and systematic

---

56. N. Florida, "Reading the Unread in Traditional Javanese Literature," *Indonesia* 44 (October 1987): 1–15, at pp. 11–13, summarizes a mid-nineteenth-century anonymous poem, *Babad Jaka Tingkir*, in which the poet describes the "rebelliousness" of the sixteenth-century mosque in Demak, on Java's north coast. The mosque refuses to align itself with the central mosque in Mecca. "The solution is a radical one effected by the famous Islamic saint Sunan Kalijaga who miraculously stretches his arms and takes hold of the two mosques, manipulating them into agreement." See also N. Florida, *Writing the Past, Inscribing the Future: History as Prophecy in Colonial Java* (Durham: Duke University Press, 1995), for an elegant translation and exegesis of this text.

Dutch scholarly preferences for "Hindu-Javanese" rather than Islamic knowledges.

Chapter 2 looks at the influence of these Dutch scholarly preferences on Javanese Ramayana and Mahabharata traditions. From a historiographical perspective, it is clear that Dutch philological efforts to preserve Javanese manuscripts and describe performance traditions have influenced the development of these traditions. Dutch scholars were among the first to acquaint the Javanese with European conceptions of textual authority and history. These values included a preference for written texts, a sense that Javanese Mahabharata and Ramayana stories were Indian, thus not originary, and a sense that Javanese *wayang* traditions that served as vehicles for these stories were corrupted, fallen, degenerate, and vulgar. The scholars scoffed at Javanese ideas that saw Ramayana and Mahabharata stories as historical genres—ideas that multiplied in the nineteenth century in response to Dutch scholarly attempts to define the shape and discount the meanings of older Javanese historical writings. These meanings constantly changed as the stories flowed between court and village poetic and performance environments. Efforts to define court styles by refining village traditions were creative Javanese adaptations of influences from Dutch scholars who were interested in preserving and purifying Javanese traditions in the late nineteenth century.

Chapter 3 shows how Dutch-speaking Javanese intellectuals took the initiative and combined features of Javanese traditions with Theosophist ideas and influences in the 1910s and 1920s, producing nationalist agendas to challenge Dutch rule and cultural cleavages that would shape communal identities in the postcolonial period. I explore how patterns in which village traditions were refined in the courts and court styles flowed out into the villages changed as the Solonese courts were faced with challenges from Indies nationalists and colonial administrators in the first decades of the twentieth century. In this period, Javanese who held conflicting nationalist agendas competed for control over the Mahabharata and Ramayana stories and the shadow puppeteers who told them. Among the Dutch-educated Javanese intellectuals, increasingly conservative cultural nationalists used European techniques of organization and communication to constitute "tradition" through the formation of cultural congresses, schools for shadow theatre, music, and dance, and organizations

Histories, Mythologies, and Tales

like the Java Institute.[57] The goals of Javanese cultural nationalists meshed with those of Dutch scholars and administrators as the strengthening of "Hindu-Javanese culture" seemed useful to colonial agendas. By the establishment of court schools that taught the art of shadow puppeteering, the conflicting values of both radical Indies and conservative Javanese nationalists were inculcated among village puppeteers and their village audiences.

But I do not mean to attribute overwhelming power to the Dutch in setting Javanese intellectual agendas. In the early twentieth century, Javanese elites and their Dutch patrons were engaged in critical negotiations over the meanings of Javanese, Eurasian, and newly emerging Indonesian identities. It took a Dutch-language education to convince the new intelligentsias that they could never be Dutch. As regional Javanese identities merged into more inclusive Indonesian ones in the 1920s and 1930s, Javanese "tradition" was redefined and Malay became the language of Indonesian nationalism.[58] This chapter shows what it was possible to say and what was considered worth saying in spaces of unequal power relations at the boundaries between colonizer and colonized.

Despite efforts to redefine village ritual as "high art" and despite the movement of stories into journalistic and scholarly discourses in the 1920s and 1930s, Javanese shadow tales did not successfully serve as narratives of the nation. National narratives produced under colonial conditions needed to encourage an intellectual shift in which feelings of difference become effaced in relation to neighboring ethnic groups and magnified in relation to the colonizer. To force Javanese shadow tales on other ethnic groups in the Indies would have been as unwise as choosing Javanese as the national language. Even among Javanese audiences, other story cycles competed with Ramayana and Mahabharata tales.[59] The attention that the shadow

57. Heather Sutherland, "Pudjangga Baru: Aspects of Indonesian Intellectual Life in the 1930s," *Indonesia* 6 (October 1968): 106–29, at pp. 115–16.

58. See Raymond Williams's indispensable *Keywords*, rev. ed., where he notes: "It is sometimes observed, by those who have looked into particular *traditions*, that it only takes two generations to make anything *traditional*: naturally enough, since that is the sense of *tradition* as active process" (p. 319).

59. The Amir Hamza repertoire has been popular in the northern and western parts of Central Java, perhaps since the fifteenth century. These Islamic tales of a historical uncle of the Prophet can be traced to Indo-Persian stories; they were inscribed in

tales received from Javanese intellectuals and Dutch scholar-administrators shows how colonial might interacted with intellectual glamour. Stimulated and attracted by the accouterments of scientific "modernity," Javanese intellectuals took European ideas and forged fresh interpretations of supposedly ancient Javanese cultural values.

In chapter 4 I discuss the responses of another group of learned Javanese—in this case village storytellers[60]—to the Dutch and elite Javanese interest in village traditions. Ideas circulating among Dutch-educated Javanese intellectuals were communicated to village performers through the schools for shadow puppeteers set up by the Solonese courts in the 1920s. In the world of village Ramayana and Mahabharata stories and performances, responses to the new intellectual and nationalist pressures included the mythical association of their traditions with new written texts, the refining of spirit beliefs into a Theosophical mysticism, and the production of increasing numbers of written *pakem* (plot scenarios). Older Indic influences authorized and reinforced by Dutch scholarship were disseminated among village audiences. Although village puppeteers rejected or reworked the re-Indicized traditions, many chose to incorporate new styles and techniques because these styles provided those who used them with the cultural capital they needed to attract audiences who were both fascinated and oppressed by Dutch power. As the targets of these overlapping attempts by Javanese intellectuals and Dutch scholars to minimize the importance of Islam and to strengthen Javanist traditions in the 1920s and 1930s, puppeteers and their audiences were to suffer unfortunate results in

---

Solonese court poetry in the late eighteenth and early nineteenth centuries along with Ramayana and Mahabharata stories. Nancy Florida (personal communication, 16 January 1994) suggests that Islamic Amir Hamza stories, read and sung in *macapat* poetry, were more popular among court elites than Ramayana and Mahabharata tales in the mid-nineteenth century. The Panji cycle of stories, thought by scholars to be indigenous to Java, is another popular repertoire in Java and Bali. See Th. Pigeaud, *Literature of Java*, vol. 1 (The Hague: M. Nijhoff, 1967), for discussions of these and other story cycles.

60. Robert R. Jay notes the presence of what he terms "the learned professions" in Javanese villages, in *Javanese Villagers: Social Relations in Rural Modjokuto* (Cambridge: MIT Press, 1969), pp. 273–74. For Jay, these professions include *imam* (leaders of congregational Islamic ritual) and *kyai* on the Islamic side and *dhalang* (both shadow puppeteers and dance teachers) and *guru* on the Javanist side. He says that usually villages have either *kyai* or *dhalang* and that *kyai* and *dhalang* tend to outrank the other professions. Although orthodox Muslims may not go to a *dhalang* for curing and advice as they would to a *kyai*, they do respect the *dhalang*, and more secular Javanist villagers feel the same toward powerful *kyai*.

Histories, Mythologies, and Tales

the postcolonial period of the new Indonesian state. The cleavages encouraged by colonial efforts to constitute shadow tales as the essence of Javanese culture lingered after independence.

In the postcolonial period, Soekarno, first President of Indonesia, came to be associated with Mahabharata stories and the Javanese shadow theatre. Soekarno's name and personality not only evoked images of several important Mahabharata characters, but Soekarno himself was known as both a patron and a performer of the tradition. The period from 1950 to 1965 was a disjunctive moment in the trajectory of twentieth century Javanese history. In the period of Dutch rule, the shadow theatre was seen to enhance colonial control because it reinforced hierarchical values. In the 1950s and 1960s, however, shadow theatre and the stories it conveyed were used by Soekarno to combat what he felt were the degenerate influences of American culture and to support his call for continuing the revolutionary struggle.

After the brutal killings in 1965 and 1966 of many people believed to be affiliated with Communist organizations, the New Order (Orde Baru, name for the current government) state returned to colonial techniques of repression and censorship, shoring up its power through military might, myths of Communist and Islamic threats to the state, and vigilant efforts to regulate the circulation of Javanese stories.[61] Puppeteers were among the many who suffered the consequences of the violence of the 1960s. Some were killed, others imprisoned, and many remain under government surveillance or are forbidden to perform. The rest of chapter 5 discusses the patrons of new performance environments that I encountered in the 1980s and the blurring of the categories of patron, performer, and scholar that occurred in those domains. In ritual exorcist perfor-

61. After the night of the 30th of September 1965, on which six generals and one adjutant of the Indonesian Armed Forces were killed by other army men, the army blamed the Communists for the brutal murders of their national heroes and implicated the Communists in a nefarious and unproven plot to overthrow the government. The army, vigilant Islamic bands, and various student groups wreaked vengeance on all those supposedly associated with the Indonesian Communist Party. It is estimated that between 500,000 and one million Indonesians may have been killed in the violence of late 1965 and early 1966, many of them from Central and East Java. For an informed and sober discussion of these brutal events, see H. Crouch, *The Army and Politics in Indonesia*, rev. ed. (Ithaca: Cornell University Press, 1988), and R. Cribb, ed., *The Indonesian Killings 1965–1966* (Clayton, Victoria: Centre of Southeast Asian Studies, Monash University, 1990).

mances, the puppeteer's authority derives from his[62] command of magical and mystical knowledges that stand in opposition to the myths of scientific modernity. The next environment I analyze focuses on *Rebo Legi* performances, which take place once every Javanese *lapan* (thirty-five days) in the home of a famous Solonese puppeteer. The last performance environment includes the *padat* or condensed performances, patronized by the government-sponsored performing arts academy (STSI, Sekolah Tinggi Seni Indonesia) in Solo and developed over the past fifteen years.

Trained in Euroamerican academic traditions, Javanese scholars at the Academy have been writing essays which interpret and analyze shadow theatre in self-conscious ways.[63] These Javanese artists-turned-academics (or, in Humardhani's case, doctor–turned–art critic) are seeking to preserve and upgrade Javanese traditions, just as the Dutch scholars tried to preserve and upgrade the traditions in the early twentieth century. The scholars at the Academy want to make Javanese performing arts relevant to the urban, modernizing sectors of the Javanese population, who no longer have the time or the patience for *gamelan* (gong-chime ensemble) concerts or all-night performances but still feel a need for rituals that such performances celebrate. These scholars seek to reshape the stories to support contemporary values and lifestyes. I analyze the intersection of village and Academy styles, the use of electronic gadgetry, and the popularity of new musical innovations in performances that continue to tell Mahabharata and Ramayana tales.

In the concluding chapter, I continue the focus on new texts and technologies by looking at printed Mahabharata and Ramayana tales available in the bookshops of Java in the 1990s. The stories have moved from Javanese to Indonesian, from poetry and drama to romance and novel, and from stylized, intricately carved puppets to the superhero images of popular comic books. In response to the continual displacement of meaning noted in previous chapters, several points raised at the beginning of this chapter are reassessed. Do shadow theatre performances still

62. Although there are a few women who perform as shadow puppeteers, and some are quite good, I have never seen a woman perform an exorcist (*ruwatan*) play.

63. S. D. Humardhani, *Kumpulan Kertas tentang Kesenian* (Solo: Akademi Seni Karawitan Indonesia, 1983), and Bambang Murtiyasa, "Kegelisahan kehidupan seni yang menggelisahkan" (unpublished manuscript presented at the Diskusi Teater, PKJT Sasanamulya, 10 April 1984).

constitute categories of knowledge through which Javanese audiences perceive the world? Is the shadow theatre still the material face of a unique worldview, or is it but one among the proliferating subject-positions signaled, transformed, and disseminated by the technologies of electronic representation?

In Putu Wijaya's novel *Perang* (War), Mahabharata characters move into contemporary villages. Newspaper reporters (and Wijaya is a reporter himself) go into these villages to interview the shadow play heroes in mythical kingdoms that have sprung up like so many Brigadoons in the Javanese countryside. Out of Wijaya's imagination come puppeteers who perform and charge different fees for different endings. He changes the stories—moving among text, context, and even hypertext—as the powerful god Kresna[64] (Krishna) works at his computer changing the past and future with a few swift keystrokes. Wijaya suggests that Kresna's role in the Mahabharata may be less benign than many have believed, as he uncovers the ideological and mythical constructs that support the tales. Here again, the legacies of the 1960s surface in suppressed and guarded discourses of violence, ethnic strife, and the loss of something that scholars are apt to call Javanese "tradition," for lack of a better word.

Although several Frankfurt School critics[65] worried about the increas-

64. In general, I use accepted Javanese spellings for the names of Mahabharata and Ramayana characters throughout this book. Occasionally I put Sanskrit spellings in parentheses for those readers more familiar with scholarship on India. The use of Javanese spellings, however, makes the point that the late and beloved scholar Ramanujan made in the quote that opened this chapter: there are no versions, tellings, or even spellings of Mahabharata and Ramayana tales that are more correct than others. Every region of India, Java, Bali, Nepal, Thailand, and other places where these tales are told have their own preferred usages.

65. The Frankfurt School thinkers, including T. Adorno, W. Benjamin, M. Horkheimer, and H. Marcuse, were among the first scholars to analyze the intersection of electronic technologies, artistic forms, and capitalist forces of production. Many of them espoused Marxist ideas and reassessed those ideas in the interwar years, as fascism engulfed Germany in the 1930s. Those who could escaped from Nazi Germany and came to America in the late 1930s, and they reconstituted their work in the Institute of Social Research in New York. Although some of their critical theories are now forty or even fifty years old, they remain among the most cogent cultural analyses of this century. Some of the ideas of Benjamin, Adorno, and Horkheimer appear again in the concluding chapter of this book. For an authoritative history of the Frankfurt School and the Institute of Social Research from 1923 to 1950, see Martin Jay, *The Dialectical Imagination: A History of the Frankfurt School and the Institute of Social Research, 1923–1950* (Boston: Little, Brown and Company, 1973).

ing authority of texts as commodities rather than as performances in the age of electronic media, performances were still flourishing in Java in 1990, whether the performance was produced from a memorized playscript, by the long-lived patterns of oral transmission, or through the secondary orality of television programming or radio and cassette recordings. But Mahabharata and Ramayana stories sold as comic books, cassettes, or modern fiction are becoming increasingly prevalent in urban Java. Java- nese children who grow up in Jakarta often learn the stories from comic books rather than from performances. As the Mahabharata and Ramayana characters are drawn in the comic-book style of American superheroes, the visual connection of the characters with shadow puppet forms is also transformed. Recently, episodes of the Ramayana and Mahabharata pro- duced for Indian televison have been shown in Indonesia, emphasizing once again Indian tellings of the stories. A well-known, college-educated Solonese puppeteer who recently visited Seattle asked me to procure for him the dozens of volumes of the P. Lal English translations of a Sanskrit edition of the Mahabharata. Since viewing the Indian episodes televised in Jakarta, he had begun to suspect that the "correct" tellings of the stories might reside in these books.

The ability of Ramayana and Mahabharata stories to provide opposi- tional discourses for Javanese audiences in the late twentieth century maintains these storyrealms in contemporary Javanese life even if one re- grets the passing of nineteenth-century heroic worlds and flinches when forced to watch, for example, a battle between the noble hero Bima and his traditional ally, the all too human clown-servant Petruk. It is poignant for Javanese and Euroamerican scholars, who found comfort and delight in the orientalist interpretation of Javanese traditions as exotic, deep, impene- trable, and mystically potent—who found the Javanese shadow theatre meaningful in the face of a perceived meaninglessness in contemporary European and American life—to realize that Ramayana and Mahabharata tales for many Javanese may in fact come to life in comic books or in soap operas, movies, or Broadway-style plays.

Tracing scholarly discourses on the shadow theatre from colonial to postcolonial periods allows me to present Javanese Ramayana and Maha- bharata tales as appealing and ambivalent reflections of societal change rather than degenerate remnants of "tradition" or derivative reactions to recent American media influences. This is a study of the weavings of

Histories, Mythologies, and Tales

narrative forms in social and political networks. It shows the ways in which the Ramayana and Mahabharata stories can be used to disseminate or displace the voices of different patrons. Continuing negotiations over the meanings of stories and the subjectivities brought into being by them reconstitute the boundaries between history and story, and myth and allegory, for each generation. In colonial days, perhaps Javanese never heard or read Ramayana and Mahabharata stories for the first time. In postcolonial Indonesia, people often do.

1 Hearing Islamic Voices in

"Hindu-Javanese" Tales

Ki Cabolek said: "I first embraced mystical knowledge in Yemen, when I studied / under a teacher, whose name was *Ki* Shaikh Zain, / the doctrine he taught was simialr to that of *Dewa Ruci;* / that was the mystical knowledge passed on [to me] / which was similar to *Bhima Suci.*"[1]—Yasadipura I

If myth is the form in which truth is miraculously revealed in the domain of Eastern spirituality, then it is myth that must be affirmed and the quibbles of a skeptical rationalism declared out of bounds.[2]—Partha Chatterjee

To hear Islamic voices in Javanese Ramayana and Mahabharata tales, this chapter focuses on several discursive moments in the web and flow of *wayang* stories when particular densities of beliefs and symbols coalesce to reveal new textual authorities. The study of power within societal and historical narratives has been enriched over the past decades by Michel Foucault's interest in intellectual genealogies as points of analytical access to the discourses—what it was possible to think—in a certain age. Foucault was concerned with how different discourses came into being and who could appropriate such discourses for his or her own purposes. Foucault's description of the movements of power in society is especially useful.

Power's condition of possibility . . . must not be sought in the primary existence of a central point, in a unique source of sovereignty from which secondary and de-scendent forms would emanate; it is the moving substrate of force relations which, by virtue of their inequality, constantly engender states of power, but the latter are always local and unstable.[3]

1. In S. Soebardi, *The Book of Cabolek* (The Hague: M. Nijhoff, 1975).
2. Partha Chatterjee, *The Nation and Its Fragments: Colonial and Postcolonial Histories* (Princeton: Princeton University Press, 1993), p. 49.
3. M. Foucault, *The History of Sexuality*, vol. 1, *An Introduction* (1978; New York: Vintage, 1990), p. 93. Cf. Anderson, "The Idea of Power in Javanese Culture," pp. 21–23, and Foucault, *History of Sexuality*, pp. 92–96, for discussions of power and how it is conceptualized in both Javanese and European worldviews. Although Foucault's defini-

These continually unfolding local and unstable relations of power constitute narrative traditions like *wayang* tales as sites of contestation and
accommodation in the search to hear new voices of authority in specific
story cycles. Exploring these local sites allows us to see the absorption
and appropriation of imported religious, intellectual, or technological
ideas as creative acts with unpredictable consequences. Rather than proposing that Javanese poets or performers were compelled by powerful
patrons to incorporate new symbols and ideas into their stories, I suggest
that they chose to adopt and adapt new concepts because these concepts
allowed them to accrue cultural capital while introducing intellectual tensions that enhanced their art. In this chapter, I trace the emergence of
Islamic ideas in Javanese Mahabharata and Ramayana stories by examining particular poetic and narrative texts from the late eighteenth and
nineteenth centuries. Later chapters continue the focus on the adoption
and adaptation of new ideas and technologies as the shadow theatre and
its stories became sites of interpretative struggles in colonial and postcolonial Javanese society.

Time, Narrative, Event

The seventeenth century was a turbulent period in Javanese history.[4]
Historical texts—both Javanese and Dutch—tell how early in the century

---

tion of power is a useful one for my purposes, I do not intend to offer a critique of his
ideas. Some scholars have criticized Foucault for presenting a bleak view of the world
with few possibilities for resistance. In contrast, this book argues that the localization of
power endows forms of everyday resistance with meaning. See also M. C. Ricklefs's
recent critique of American-based scholarship on ideas of power and kingship in pre-
colonial Java, in "Unity and Disunity in Javanese Political and Religious Thought of the
Eighteenth Century," in V.J.H. Houben, H.M.J. Maier, and W. van der Molen, eds.,
Looking in Odd Mirrors: The Java Sea, Rijksuniversiteit Vakgroep Talen en Culturen van
Zuidoost-Azie en Oceanie, Semaian 5 (Leiden: Rijksuniversiteit te Leiden, 1992), pp. 61–
62 n. 1. This critique loses much of its sharpness if one reads, for example, Ben Anderson's 1984 work "*Sembah-Sumpah*: The Politics of Language and Javanese Culture,"
p.203.

4. The following discussion of eighteenth- and nineteenth-century Javanese history
is summarized from M. C. Ricklefs, *Jogjakarta under Sultan Mangkubumi 1749–1792* (London: Oxford, 1974), *A History of Modern Indonesia since c. 1300* (1981; rev. ed., Stanford:
Stanford University Press, 1993), and *War, Culture and Economy in Java 1677–1726: Asian
and European Imperialism in the Early Kartasura Period* (Sydney: Asian Studies Association

Sultan Agung (r. 1613–46), a strong and ruthless ruler who had received the Islamic title of Sultan from Mecca, inherited the throne of Mataram. He was able to consolidate the power of the kingdom by crushing the thriving port cities of the north coast. Constant warfare marked the seventeenth and early eighteenth centuries as the descendants of Agung fought to keep volatile regional princes under the Mataram state's control. To complicate matters, a new political actor had appeared on the scene in the seventeenth century: the Dutch East India Company (voc), headquartered on the far western tip of Java, vied for economic dominance and maritime control over the north coast of Java. At this point in Javanese history, the Dutch Company was just another regional power hoping to continue its economic activities despite the wars of succession that were ravaging Java. The voc wanted peace so that trade could flourish; the Company had little intention of ruling Java.

It was Agung's son, Amangkurat I (r. 1646–77), and then his grandson Amangkurat II (r. 1677–1703), who first turned to the voc in 1677 for help in restoring their authority over regional leaders and unruly peasants in Central Java. With Dutch aid, Amangkurat II was barely able to get his kingdom back from the rebellious Madurese prince Trunadjaja; in return for this aid, the ruler had to promise to deliver great quantities of rice to the voc. When the voc realized that the court treasury was bankrupt, they demanded that Amangkurat II temporarily surrender the lucrative seaports of the north coast of Java, the *pasisir*, to the Dutch until his debt could be paid.[5] This loss of the *pasisir* seaports was to become permanent in 1744. More war and rebellion brought more debt and allowed for the continuing Dutch presence in the affairs of Central Java. Finally, on his deathbed in 1749, Susuhunan Pakubuwana II supposedly ceded his entire kingdom of Mataram to the Dutch.

Although the noted historian of this period M. C. Ricklefs finds little support for those who argue that Pakubuwana II may only have intended to give his kingdom to the Dutch temporarily, Javanese ideas of ruler and ruled suggested that he wished the Dutch to watch over the kingdom until

---

of Australia in association with Allen and Unwin, 1993); P.B.R. Carey, *The Cultural Ecology of Early Nineteenth Century Java*, Occasional Paper no. 24 (Singapore: Institute of Southeast Asian Studies, 1974), and "Aspects of Javanese History in the Nineteenth Century," in *The Development of Indonesian Society*, ed. Harry Aveling (New York: St. Martin's Press, 1980); and N. Florida, *Writing the Past*.

5. Ricklefs, *War, Culture and Economy*, p. 47.

it could be safely turned over to his heirs. Power in Java at that time was dependent upon "men and gunpowder," and the Dutch were in no better position to control Java through military means than the other contenders for the throne.[6] In fact, the treaty of 1749 meant little and the voc's position as the eighteenth century drew to a close was exceedingly precarious. The voc was financially weak and its armed forces understaffed and prone to illness. The Dutch Company could not have been more than an overseer of Javanese affairs, and perhaps that is just what the dying Pakubuwana II wanted.

Von Hohendorff, the Dutch Governor of Java's northeast coast (r. 1748–54), proceeded to install the late ruler's son, Pakubuwana III (r. 1749–88), as the new sovereign of Mataram with the understanding that the new ruler was ascending to power as a vassal of the Dutch East India Company and not through his own rights of inheritance. Meanwhile Mangkubumi, Pakubuwana II's younger brother, had rebelled and was finally subdued and paid off by the Dutch with an allotment of land to the southwest in the area to be known as Yogyakarta. Mangkubumi had the backing of princes and court officials who had fled from the court of the dying Susuhunan to join Mangkubumi and proclaim him the new heir to the throne. Since elite consensus was one of the legitimizing forces that supported the rulers of Java, Mangkubumi had as much if not greater claim to the kingdom of Mataram than the Dutch-supported Pakubuwana III. The warfare continued, and finally, in 1755, with neither party able to claim victory on the battlefield, the Dutch oversaw the partition of Java between Susuhunan Pakubuwana III of Surakarta and his uncle Sultan Hamengkubuwana I (Mangkubumi, r. 1749–92) of Yogyakarta. Mas Said, or Mangkunagara I (r. 1757–95) as he came to be known, was a third contender for power in Central Java as a nephew of both the late Pakubuwana II and Mangkubumi; he was destined to become the first ruler of the house of Mangkunagara, the minor court of Surakarta. Two years later he laid down his arms, contented himself with a sizable portion of the kingdom of Surakarta, and submitted to the voc, the Susuhunan of Surakarta, and the Sultan of Yogyakarta.

6. Ricklefs, *Jogjakarta under Sultan Mangkubumi*, pp. 50–51; Soemarsaid Moertono, *State and Statecraft in Old Java*; Ricklefs, *War, Culture and Economy*, p. 37; and Vincent J. H. Houben, *Kraton and Kumpani: Surakarta and Yogyakarta, 1830–1870* (Leiden: KITLV Press, 1994), p. 217.

The voc was certainly pleased with the cessation of warfare in Central Java. They saw division of the kingdom, which their presence made possible, as the only way to keep the Javanese states from draining the Company's economic energy and military capabilities. None of the four recognized contenders for power in Central Java—the Susuhunan, the Sultan, the Mangkunagara, or the voc—could militarily prevail over the others, making warfare an impractical means for attaining political goals. Although the Dutch saw the division of Java as the permanent solution to the Javanese governmental situation, the Javanese rulers saw the division as a temporary solution and assumed that in the future Java would again be reunited under one ruler.[7]

As peace returned to Java in 1757 after centuries of warfare, the Sultan and the Susuhunan were able to devote their energies to acquiring the necessary accoutrements of power: collecting royal heirlooms (*pusaka*), writing court chronicles and poetry, and erecting their royal palaces. When one of the Susuhunan's wives finally gave birth to a legitimate heir in 1768, both Hamengkubuwana I (Mangkubumi) and Mangkunagara I (Mas Said) were forced to accept the possibility that neither of them would inherit the throne of their nephew, the Susuhunan of Solo. Over the next thirty years, the political situation in Central Java was filled with intrigue and suspicion as the voc drew nearer to bankruptcy. In their role as mediators between the Sultan and the Susuhunan, the Dutch oversaw the succession of the Crown Prince in Surakarta in 1788. Although the Dutch could not claim power in Central Java for themselves, they could, by their presence, insure that the Javanese kingdoms could not reunite under one ruler. It is at this tense moment of Javanese-Dutch interaction that one begins to see, albeit through imperial eyes, the ways in which stories of rival kingdoms and foreign ogre kings fitted into the histories and myths of Central Java.

Narratives of War and Empire

In what some Indian and European scholars have considered the master narrative of the innumerable waves in the Mahabharata ocean of stories,

7. See Ricklefs's *Jogjakarta under Sultan Mangkubumi* for extensive discussions of this point.

Hearing Islamic Voices

The five Pandhawa heroes and their mother. From left to right: Nakula, Sadewa, Dewi Kunthi, Yudhistira, Arjuna, and Bima.

two sides of the same family spend many years fighting over the rights to the kingdom of Ngastina.[8] Although the father of the ninety-nine Korawa brothers, and one sister, was the eldest son of the last legitimate ruler, he was born blind and thus the succession passed to his younger brother Pandu. Pandu had five sons through divine intervention and then died, leaving the kingdom back in the hands of his blind older brother, who was supposed to act as regent until Pandu's sons came of age. When the virtuous sons of Pandu reached maturity, they were deprived of their

8. See van Buitenen's multivolume translation of the critical edition of the Sanskrit texts of the Mahabharata, attributed to the sage—and a character in the story—named Vyasa. (J.A.B. van Buitenen, *The Mahabharata*, 3 vols. [Chicago: University of Chicago Press, 1973–78]). There is nothing comparable to this in Java, although the past few decades have seen a proliferation of narrative retellings of the Mahabharata in Indonesian rather than Javanese by Sunardi D. M. and Heroesoekarto. Probably the most widely read retellings of the stories, and those that are believed to incorporate Indian over Javanese or Sundanese retellings, are the multivolume comic books of R. A. Kosasih. Kosasih's influential comic books will be discussed at length in chapter 7. For Sanskrit equivalents of Javanese names for Mahabharata and Ramayana characters, see the glossary.

rights to the kingdom of Ngastina by their Korawa cousins, who believed that the kingdom was rightfully theirs.

After repeated treachery at the hands of their cousins, the Pandhawa are finally given a portion of the kingdom—a tract of land that must be reclaimed from the tropical forest by burning. The Pandhawa clear the land and build their new kingdom of Ngamarta. Although animosity remains between the cousins, for a time they each rule their individual kingdoms in a precarious accommodation marked by intrigue and suspicion.[9]

One of the most popular tales to be situated within this moment of accommodation before the fratricidal Bratayuda War between the Pandhawa and Korawa is the shadow play story known as Kilat Buwana (Lightning of the World).[10] The story tells of the strange priest named Kilat Buwana, who appears at the court of Ngastina. The mysterious priest has a plan to reunite the Pandhawa and Korawa so that the Bratayuda War, which will decide the future fate of the kingdom, will not have to take place. Kilat Buwana convinces the Korawa court of his mystical powers and converts them to his new plan. The Pandhawa appear at the court of Ngastina to collaborate with the Korawa and their new advisor Kilat Buwana. Kresna is then summoned to the court of Ngastina as the Pandhawa tell Kilat Buwana that they cannot agree to anything until their loyal ally and god incarnate Kresna gives his approval. When Kresna arrives, he debates with Kilat Buwana. Kresna demands to know on what basis Kilat Buwana thinks he can put off the Bratayuda; the Bratayuda has been preordained by the gods. After his brilliant defense of the need for the Bratayuda War to be fought, Kresna storms out of the court of Ngastina.

Kilat Buwana is not put off; he demands an offering in order for his new plan to work—the blood of the royal Pandhawa servant Semar and, in some tellings, Kresna. Arjuna, the third and most popular of the five Pandhawa brothers—or occasionally his son Abimanyu—is chosen to kill

9. In his close reading of v o c documents and Javanese chronicles, Ricklefs suggests, in *Jogjakarta under Sultan Mangkubumi*, that Mangkubumi's elaborate water palace may have been modeled on the stories of the eldest Pandhawa King Yudhistira, as both were forced to build their palaces by clearing a patch of jungle near the kingdoms of their rival relatives.

10. I thank Ben Anderson for pointing out to me that a similar story was known as the *lakon* Semar Papa in the early twentieth century. See J. Kats, *Het Javaansche Tooneel I, De Wajang Poerwa*.

Kilat Buwana (left) faces Semar, the clown-servant who is really the high god Ismaya.

the loyal and wise Semar, who is really a powerful god and older brother of the god Siwa. Semar submits but asks to be burned. Arjuna reappears at the court of Ngastina with Semar's ashes. Kilat Buwana receives a challenge from an unknown prince. Kilat Buwana fights with the prince, who turns out to be the recently cremated Semar in his godly (*bagus*) form. Semar chastises Kilat Buwana, who turns out to be his younger brother—and the high god—Siwa. Siwa says that the whole episode was ordained by the gods to test the purity and strength of the Pandhawa. The Pandhawa and Korawa realize that there is no way to reconcile their differences; the necessity for the Bratayuda to be fought in the future is strengthened.

In this story, Kilat Buwana, the disguised god-priest, demands the death of Kresna and Semar as the requirement for canceling the Bratayuda War. In Javanese mythology, the gods have given King Kresna, incarnation of the god Wisnu, the responsibility of insuring that the Bratayuda War takes place. The gods have given Semar, the clown-servant cum powerful god, the duty of maintaining peace and protecting the Javanese kings. Semar and Kresna serve as the special protectors of the Pandhawa, leading them to the moment when they will defeat their ignoble cousins in the Bratayuda War.

By opposing the reunification of Ngastina and Ngamarta and reinforcing the necessity for the Bratayuda to be fought, Kresna's actions in these stories might reflect in an uncanny way the political division of the Kingdoms of Solo and Yogyakarta and the increasing Dutch hegemony. By the late eighteenth century, most Central Javanese rulers and nobles had come to accept as permanent the division of Mataram into the rival courts of Surakarta (Solo) and Yogyakarta (Yogya). The young Solonese ruler Pakubuwana IV in 1790 and, thirty-five years later, Dipanagara, the Yogyanese grandson of Hamengkubuwana II, destined to lead the Javanese against the Dutch in the Java War of 1825–30, were the last two Javanese rulers to have attempted a reunification of the Javanese realm.[11]

In the Kilat Buwana story, whose various tellings and retellings are today still performed all over Central Java, the ways in which the division of Java under Dutch control entered into Javanese myth and history become perceptible. In the Mahabharata tales of Central Java, poets and puppeteers may have believed that the Bratayuda War had to take place, but *lakon* (plays) that enacted the horrible events of the war were approached very cautiously by performers, if they were performed at all.[12] The historical narratives had their reflections in the repertoire of the Central Javanese shadow theatre. Since the division of the historical realm into the rival kingdoms of Surakarta and Yogyakarta seemed increasingly permanent, these shadow tales of rival kingdoms—related through strong blood lines—seemed an apt metaphor for the tensions between Yogya and Solo. Each *wayang lakon* also introduced in almost every performance an ogre kingdom where demonic foreign kings attempted to attack Ngamarta or Ngastina and carry off their beautiful princesses. As the stories mirrored the very tangible tensions between Solo and Yogya—or alternatively be-

11. See Ricklefs's *Jogjakarta under Sultan Mangkubumi*, pp. 285–340, for a detailed discussion of a plot supported by the young Pakubuwana IV (r. 1788–1820) in the late 1780s to reunify the divided realm under his control. It is possible that the story of Kilat Buwana originated as a *pasemon* story of Pakubuwana IV's strong attachment to several Islamic teachers (*santri*), who were perceived as a threat to Dutch interests in Central Java and eventually exiled.

12. See Alan Feinstein et al., eds., *Lakon Caragan*, vols. 1–3 (Surakarta: Akademi Seni Karawitan Indonesia, 1986) for complete transcriptions of four performances of Kilat Buwana, summaries of eight other tellings, and references to several other written texts that tell the story of Kilat Buwana. See also Nancy Florida's *Javanese Literature in Surakarta Manuscripts*, vol. 1, pp. 214–33, for lists of *wayang lakon* from the early nineteenth century. What is surprising about these lists is the number of birth and wedding stories and the lack of any of the Bratayuda stories that would be recognizable by their titles.

Hearing Islamic Voices

tween the Kraton and the Mangkunagaran in Solo itself—and the Dutch, the Bratayuda War of the narrative tradition became the logical conclusion in both mythological and historical futures. New stories that took place in the period when the Pandhawa lived in their kingdom of Ngamarta and the Korawa resided in Ngastina expanded the time period between the division of the mythological kingdom of Ngastina and the bloody, fratricidal war that would eventually reunify the kingdom.[13] In the historical realm—and chapter 3 will show the intricate weavings of *wayang* stories and Javanese histories—the war that was needed to reunite the real Javanese kingdom of Mataram receded into a distant future.[14] This offers one explanation for why it is considered so dangerous to perform the stories of the Bratayuda War in Central Java; if verbal art recorded or mirrored reality, the portrayal of these events might cause them to happen.[15]

But this innocent accounting of Javanese stories as a way to harmonize

13. In Indian Sanskrit Mahabharata traditions, this time period is brief; in van Buitenen's translation of the Sanskrit Critical Edition of the *Mahabharata*, which runs to thousands of pages, the time period between the burning of Khandava forest and the famous dicing (whereby the Pandhava heroes must retire to the forest for twelve years) only fills sixty-two pages (vol. 2, pp. 33–95). It is in this time period that most of the Javanese shadow play stories occur. Brandon comments perceptively on the *carangan* (branch story) plays that spring from this period: "It is not surprising that the true essence of *wajang* lies in the invented *tjarangan* plays. The very special world of *wajang*, centering on the glorious and adventurous period of Amarta, was created in them. And from them the 'classic' form of *wajang* play, with its conventionalized structure and highly systematized techniques of performance, gradually evolved." Brandon, *On Thrones of Gold*, p. 14.

14. Of the 149 Pandhawa cycle plays that Kats lists in *Het Javaansche Tooneel I* as part of the standard repertory in the 1920s, ninety-four are set in the period when the Pandhawa rule their kingdom of Ngamarta. The stories that recount the Bratayuda War were only performed in central Java for ritual purposes until they were revived in the 1970s and 1980s in the government-sponsored fine arts academies. In West Java, where different political tensions existed, Bratayuda stories seem to have been popular tales for village performances. This observation comes from discussions in August of 1994 with Endo Suanda, who is completing a dissertation at the University of Washington on the shadow play traditions of Cirebon and Bandung.

15. McVey, "The Wayang Controversy in Indonesian Communism," p. 49 n. 63, tells of the Bratayuda performance sponsored by LEKRA (Communist arts organization), held in Yogyakarta in January of 1964. The LEKRA sponsors purposely did not burn incense or hold traditional rituals in order to flout the superstitions connected with the performance tradition (*Harian Rakjat Minggu*, 9 February 1964). The tragic violence of the mid-1960s could, of course, be interpreted by Javanese *wayang* followers as ghastly evidence that the LEKRA plan had backfired.

historical and mythical narratives leaves out the important way in which these popular myths gave the Dutch a legitimate role in Java. Although chronicles that relate histories of late seventeenth and eighteenth century Java suggest that Javanese rulers used VOC support to enhance their power, the Dutch benefitted most from the division of the kingdom. The Dutch were also the ones who wished to insure that this division was maintained. By keeping the Javanese divided, through a variety of means, the Dutch strengthened their position as the rulers of Java despite the small number of Dutch soldiers and administrators in Java.[16] The Dutch, in fact, presented themselves as the only ones able to keep the Javanese from falling back into the constant state of warfare that filled the seventeenth and the first half of the eighteenth centuries.[17]

The Java War of 1825–30 was the last stand against oppressive Dutch control, when the rebel prince Dipanagara appealed to all Javanese to unite under the banner of Islam and reclaim the Javanese state. After Dipanagara's failure, the war that the political situation demanded to return the Javanese kingdom to its rightful heirs, of necessity a bloody, fratricidal war, was pushed into a future beyond Dutch rule.[18] This suggests the beginning of a new mythical cycle in late eighteenth-century Java, when the Dutch first appeared in Javanese chronicles and stories in ambivalent and contradictory ways.[19] On the one hand it is easy to see the uncouth and threatening foreign kings (*raja sabrang*) who appeared in each *wayang* play as representing the Dutch usurpers. On the other hand,

16. See C. Fasseur, *The Politics of Colonial Exploitation: Java, the Dutch and the Cultivation System* (Ithaca: Cornell Southeast Asia Publications, 1992), who argues persuasively that even in 1860 there were only ninety Dutch controleurs to keep roughly twenty-five million Javanese under control (p. 240).

17. This argument is presented most forcefully by Ricklefs's *Jogjakarta under Sultan Mangkubumi*.

18. In this sense, the postcolonial killings that accompanied the fall of the Soekarno government in 1965–66 fulfilled the Dutch prophecy for the Javanese without the restraining Dutch presence: seen very simplistically, Javanese united under the banner of Islam and slaughtered those among their brothers who were not willing to accept a unified Islamic state. Chapter 6 explores and documents this argument.

19. Soedarsono, *Living Traditional Theaters in Indonesia* (Yogyakarta: Akademi Seni Tari Indonesia, 1974), pp. 3–4, suggested that in the late eighteenth century the Mahabharata tales became very popular in Central Java because they reflected the political realities of the time. For discussions of the portrayal of the Dutch in Javanese manuscripts, see John Pemberton, *On the Subject of "Java"* (Ithaca: Cornell University Press, 1994); Florida, *Writing the Past*; and Ricklefs, *Jogjakarta under Sultan Mangkubumi*.

Hearing Islamic Voices

the Dutch also presented themselves as the protectors and elder brothers of the Javanese rulers, similar to the relationship between King Kresna and the Pandhawa heroes.[20] Javanese Mahabharata tales, as they were retold in shadow plays and, in the late nineteenth century, emphasized in European scholarship to counter the strength of Javanese Islam, became tales of empire, allegories of the colonial encounter.

Colonial Constructions of Islam

The dates for the arrival of Islam in Java have been pushed back earlier and earlier over the past decades. One of the earliest Islamic graves on Java is now dated back to the eleventh century.[21] Although some Islamic traders came directly to Java from the Middle East after the eleventh century, it is also clear that the arrival of Islam in Java can be seen as a continuation of intellectual influences emanating from India in the preceding centuries and traveling to Java over the expanding trade routes, which were still controlled by Arabs and Asians in this period. Islam was steadily taking hold on the north coast of Java throughout the heyday of Majapahit, the last great inland Hindu-Buddhist empire that flourished in the fourteenth century. The rise of the Islamic trading states on the north coast in the fifteenth and sixteenth centuries marked the integration of inland Java into the *pasisir* (coastal) network running between India and the archipelago, which combined a reliance on trade with adherence to Islam. The dynamic of Javanese politics was to return to the inland regions of Central Java in the late sixteenth and seventeenth centuries with the rise of the kingdom of Mataram and the continuing spread of Islam.

As Indonesian, European, and American scholars translate more of the Javanese literary heritage into Indonesian and European languages, the important role of Islam in Java continues to emerge from the silences of colonial scholarship. The translations and analyses of Simuh, Day, and Florida, among others, illustrate how Islamic the life and literature of the

20. See P.B.R. Carey, *The Cultural Ecology of Early Nineteenth Century Java*, and his fascinating brief study "The Role of *Wayang* in the Dipanagara War," *Prisma* 7 (1977): 15–27. See also Ricklefs, *Jogjakarta under Sultan Mangkubumi*, pp. 28–30.

21. H. M. Ambary, "Epigraphical Data from 17th–19th Century Muslim Graves in East Java," in *Cultural Contact and Textual Interpretation*, ed. C. D. Grijns and S. O. Robson (Dordrecht: Foris Publications, 1986).

Central Javanese courts were as far back as the late eighteenth century.[22] Carey has described the early education of Dipanagara, grandson of Sultan Hamengkubuwana II of Yogyakarta, who was to lead the last major revolt against Dutch rule in Java in 1825. As was typical for a member of the royal family of the Yogyakarta Kraton (palace) born in the late eighteenth century, he was sent to live with his great-grandmother, the Ratu Ageng, at Tegalreja, an estate on the outskirts of the city.

There he was given a disciplined education in Islamic law and Koranic exegesis, and had frequent contacts with the religious teachers and students (*santri*) who lived in the vicinity. The Ratu Ageng also had amicable relations with many of the members of the Islamic hierarchy in Yogyakarta and the legal experts (*ulama*) in the legal establishments.[23]

Even the great nineteenth-century Solonese court poet Ranggawarsita, known for compiling the Javanese Ramayana and Mahabharata stories that form the repertoire of nineteenth- and twentieth-century Javanese theatrical and literary traditions, received his education in a *pesantren* (rural Islamic school), where he, too, studied Islamic texts. In the next

22. Simuh, *Mistik Islam Kejawen* (Jakarta: Penerbit Universitas Indonesia, 1988); J. A. Day, "Meanings of Change in the Poetry of Nineteenth-century Java" (Ph.D. diss., Cornell University, 1981), and "Islam and Literature in South-East Asia: Some Premodern, Mainly Javanese Perspectives," in *Islam in South-East Asia*, ed. M. B. Hooker (Leiden: E. J. Brill, 1983); N. Florida, "Writing the Past, Inscribing the Future: Exile and Prophecy in an Historical Text of Nineteenth-Century Java, Volumes I and II," (Ph.D. diss., Cornell University, 1990), "Crossing Kraton Walls: On Santri Aspects of the Literary Culture of a Premodern Javanese Court" (paper presented at the 1991 Annual Meeting of the Association for Asian Studies, 1991), and *Writing the Past*. New scholarship on this theme has been appearing since Mark Woodward's revisionist study *Islam in Java* (Tucson: University of Arizona Press, 1989), argued dramatically that Islam had been unjustly dismissed in most studies of Javanese history. Although some of Woodward's arguments were insufficiently documented for knowledgeable Javanists, more recent studies have followed his lead in rethinking the history of Javanese Islam. See, for example, M. C. Ricklefs, ed., *Islam in the Indonesian Social Context* (Clayton, Victoria: Monash University Centre of Southeast Asian Studies, 1991), and Anthony Reid, ed., *On the Making of an Islamic Political Discourse in Southeast Asia* (Clayton, Victoria: Monash University Centre of Southeast Asian Studies, 1993). But even in the early 1980s, a number of scholars had been arguing for the importance of Islam in Java. See, in particular, P.B.R. Carey's "Aspects of Javanese History in the Nineteenth Century," and the essays by Anthony Day and Roy F. Ellen, in M. B. Hooker, ed. *Islam in Southeast Asia* (Leiden: E. J. Brill, 1983).

23. P.B.R. Carey, *The Archive of Yogyakarta*, vol. 1 (London: Oxford University Press for the British Academy, 1980), p. 64.

Hearing Islamic Voices

chapter, I discuss the complex interweavings of history and myth in nineteenth-century Java. Here I suggest that for Javanese poets and pup-peteers of the late eighteenth and early nineteenth centuries, Mahabha-rata and Ramayana tales were seen as history, stories of an older age that preserved the memories of the Indic heroes as ancestors of the Javanese.[24] The anonymous encyclopedic collections of eighteenth-century tales in which Ramayana and Mahabharata stories were enfolded and trans-formed—the Serat Pakem Ringgit Purwa or Serat Kandhaning Ringgit Purwa, for example—gave the Indic heroes genealogies which led them back to the Islamic Nabi Adam.[25]

As A. H. Johns explained in several important essays,[26] there was little discontinuity at first between the Indian tales and Islamic stories; thus, although Dipanagara fought the Java War (1825–30) under the banner of Islam, and required that all of his followers be circumcised, it was still possible for the Javanese of that time period to see the war as a reenact-ment of the Bratayuda War,[27] as well as an example of *prang sabil* or a Holy War for Islam against the infidel Dutch. It is after the Java War, as the Dutch begin their intensive reorganization of Javanese economic, agricul-tural, and cultural life, that Islam is discounted in Dutch scholarship as something intrinsic to Java.[28]

24. Chapter 3 will document this view that nineteenth-century Javanese saw the Mahabharata tales as stories of their ancestors, stories of the days when gods walked on the earth and interceded in human affairs.

25. W. L. Olthof, ed., *Poenika Serat Babad Tanah Djawi wiwit saking Nabi Adam doemoegi ing tahoen 1647* ('s Gravenhage: M. Nijhoff, 1941); Moertono, *State and Statecraft in Old Java*; J. Padmapuspita, *Serat Kandhaning Ringgit Purwa*, Jilid 2 (Jakarta: Penerbit Djam-batan dan KITLV, 1985).

26. A. H. Johns, "Sufism as a Category in Indonesian Literature and History," *Journal of Southeast Asian History* 2, no. 2 (1961), "The Role of Structural Anthropology and Myth in Javanese Historiography," *Journal of Asian Studies* 24, no. 1 (1964): 91–99, and "From Buddhism to Islam: An Interpretation of the Javanese Literature of the Transition," *Comparative Studies in Society and History* 9, no. 1 (1966–67): 40–50.

27. Carey, *The Archive of Yogyakarta*, p. 71.

28. Jean Gelman Taylor, a scholar of the VOC period, noted that this construction of Islam as something foreign to Java has pre-nineteenth-century roots (personal com-munication, 7 October 1994). The VOC documents often mention "Morse papen" or Muslim popes. As I discuss in the next chapter, Raffles began to discount Javanese Islam in his *History of Java*, 2 vols., when he devoted four pages to Islam and sixty pages to the then defunct Hinduism and Buddhism in Java. See Karel Steenbrink, *Dutch Colonialism and Indonesian Islam*, for a discussion of the systematic discounting of Islam in Java by Dutch colonial administrators and scholars. W. Ph. Coolhaas, *A Critical Survey of Studies*

Up until the British interregnum (1811–16) in Java, when the British took over Dutch colonial possessions during the Napoleonic wars, many Dutch traders had ignored the cultural life of the Javanese. The VOC, which sank into bankruptcy at the end of the eighteenth century, had been a commercial enterprise concerned to insure the smooth workings of the Dutch trading network in the archipelago. Although the Dutch colonial government that succeeded the Company was preoccupied with intrigue and war until 1830, various missionary and scholarly activities were begun after the Java War and especially after the publication of the encyclopedic British studies of Raffles and Crawfurd, who each devoted hundreds of pages to Javanese history and culture.[29] The Java War had shown the Dutch the dangerous potential of Islam as a rallying force for anticolonial activity; thus the Dutch scholars who came to the Indies after the War to translate the Bible into local languages began to reconstruct the ancient Indic heritage of Java with decidedly anti-Islamic inclinations.[30]

Islam and Javanese Shadow Tales

J. J. Ras, a noted scholar of Javanese literatures and *wayang* traditions, suggested in 1976 that the modern Javanese shadow theatre was created to

on Dutch Colonial History ('s Gravenhage: Martinus Nijhoff, 1960) hardly mentions Islam and discusses Christianity in chapters that survey religion in the Indies.

29. H. Kraemer, "Het Instituut voor de Javaansche Taal te Soerakarta," *Djawa* 12, no. 6 (1932): 262; T. S. Raffles, *The History of Java*; J. Crawfurd, *History of the Indian Archipelago*. Raffles, who was in charge of the Dutch possessions during the British interregnum in Java (1811–15) may have been the first to conceive of a "classical" literature of Java, which he saw as essentially Indic. It was this literary heritage that the coming of Islam supposedly obliterated and that would need to be resurrected by the Dutch in the latter part of the nineteenth century. Day, "Islam and Literature," p. 133 and Florida, "Reading the Unread in Traditional Javanese Literature," pp. 1–15. Donald E. Weatherbee, "Raffles' Sources for Traditional Javanese Historiography and the Mackenzie Collections," *Indonesia* 26 (October 1978): 63–93, has shown that Raffles relied on earlier Dutch studies both to structure and document his own work, a reliance that Raffles mentions only in passing. But the work of Raffles still remained crucial for setting up the categories through which the study of Java could be pursued throughout the nineteenth century. As Jean Gelman Taylor pointed out in her communication of 7 October 1994, some of the Dutch scholars and travelers who did comment on the social and cultural life of Java in the VOC period include Rijcklofs van Goens, François Valentijn, J.C.M. Radermacher, W. van Hogendorp, and even Pieter Erberveldt.

30. Kenji Tsuchiya, "Javanology and the Age of Ranggawarsita: An Introduction to

Hearing Islamic Voices

meet the needs of the rising Islamic commercial elites inhabiting the thriving *pasisir* city-states in the sixteenth century; a decade or so earlier several American scholars had maintained that Islamic influence on the shadow theatre was minimal.[31] Even Ras did not suggest that the *wayang* was Islamic, but he did connect the origins of the Serat Kandhaning Ringgit Purwa (Book of Tales of the Wayang Purwa) texts—which he and Pigeaud see as closely connected to the Javanese shadow theatre traditions—to the Islamic influences that were circulating through the archipelago in the fifteenth and sixteenth centuries.[32] While specifically Islamic elements in the *wayang purwa* can be summarized in a few sentences— such as the connection of Yudhistira's amulet Serat Kalimasada with the Islamic profession of faith (*kalimah sahadat*) or the Persian-style turbans and shoes worn by the Hindu-Javanese gods—I question what the rebirth of the tradition in a particularly Islamic atmosphere means.[33]

Moertono cites genealogy and *wahyu* (from the Arabic *waḥy*), a sign of spiritual/religious merit symbolized as a gift or boon from the gods usually in the form of light, as two of the major ways in which the Javanese rulers of Mataram enhanced their power and glory.[34] Both of these factors pervade the Javanese Mahabharata stories embedded in Serat Kandha texts, where genealogies link the historical Javanese kings to the mythological heroes, and *wahyu* are continually released by the gods to reaffirm the power of the legitimate rulers. *Wahyu* stories remain among the most popular in the ever-changing repertoire of the shadow theatre. Although Moertono sees these principles as quintessentially Javanese, the concept of *wahyu* as a sign of light permeates Islamic thought as does the importance of genealogy.

Nineteenth Century Javanese Culture," in *Reading Southeast Asia* (Ithaca: Cornell Southeast Asia Program, 1990); Kraemer, "Het Instituut voor de Javaansche Taal de Soerakarta."

31. J. R. Ras, "The Historical Development of the Javanese Shadow Theatre"; Geertz, *Religion of Java*; Anderson, *Mythology and the Tolerance of the Javanese*.

32. Th. Pigeaud, *Literature of Java*, vol. 1. See Padmapuspita, *Serat Kandhaning Ringgit Purwa*, pp. viii–ix. The introduction was written by J. J. Ras.

33. I say rebirth here because of the existence of shadow theatre traditions as far back as the tenth century. See L. J. Sears, "Rethinking Indian Influence in Javanese Shadow Theatre Traditions," *Comparative Drama* 18 (Spring 1994). For an interesting discussion of the impact of Islamic writing on oral cultures in Africa, see J. Goody, *The Interface between the Written and the Oral* (Cambridge: Cambridge University Press, 1987), pp. 125–38.

34. Moertono, *State and Statecraft in Old Java*, pp. 61 ff.

In particular, the Islamic stress on genealogy brought a more linear conception of the connections between the past and the future to cyclical Hindu-Javanese ways of perceiving the world. The Arabic word *shihjara* encompasses both genealogy and history, and the word *sajarah* (or *sejarah*) that sprang from this Arabic root means "genealogy" in Javanese and "history" in Malay/Indonesian. The Javanese word *sarasilah* (Ar. *silsilah*), another word for genealogy, interlaces the concepts of genealogy and personal histories, evoking the Islamic sense of transmission reflected in the *hadith*, stories of the life of the Prophet, whose narrative lineage must be traced back to the time of the Prophet to be considered authentic. The shadow play stories, which derived their legitimacy from the recitation of the genealogies of the Mahabharata characters and the credibility of the genealogy of the puppeteer, are permeated with these Islamic notions of genealogy. The *Sajarah-dalem urut saking pangiwa tuwin panengen*, or genealogies of the left and right, are the traditions that connect the Javanese kings to the highest religious authorities.[35] The fact that both of the genealogies situate the Javanese kings firmly within Islamic traditions—the right genealogy begins with Nabi Adam, an origin figure for Semitic traditions, and then connects the Prophet Muhammad (Kanjeng Rasul) to the kings of Mataram while the left genealogy also begins with Nabi Adam but then connects the Mahabharata heroes to the Pakubuwana line of Surakarta—shows how deeply the Javanist traditions have accommodated themselves to Islamic oral and written traditions.[36]

In assessing the impact of Islamic beliefs on Javanese Ramayana and Mahabharata traditions, I will sidestep the ongoing debate about the orthodoxy or heterodoxy of Javanese Islam. Suffice it to say that the spectrum of opinions ranges from those who see Javanist religion as Hindu-Buddhist covered with a thin veneer of Islamic terminology and mysticism[37] to those who argue for placing Javanese Islam within the mainstream of pan-Islamic belief.[38] In general, the debate about Javanese

35. Ibid., p. 63. See Pigeaud, *The Literature of Java*, 1:171 and Florida, *Javanese Literature in Surakarta Manuscripts*, 1:61 and 63.

36. Woodward, *Islam in Java*, pp. 218 ff.

37. Geertz, *Religion of Java*; Anderson, *Mythology and the Tolerance of the Javanese*.

38. M. Hodgson, *The Venture of Islam: Conscience and History in a World Civilization*, 3 vols. (Chicago: University of Chicago Press, 1974); Woodward, *Islam in Java*. A few of the scholars who have contributed to the growing research on Javanese Islam include G.W.J. Drewes, "The Struggle between Javanism and Islam as Illustrated by the Serat Der-

Hearing Islamic Voices

Islam assumes the existence of an essentialist or normative form of Islam, which, research shows, may not even exist in the Middle East. As Geertz has documented in his ongoing work on Java and Morocco, other parts of the Islamic world may be as far from "orthodox" or normative Islam as Java.[39]

Shadow Theatre in Javanese History

Sources that document the existence of the shadow theatre from the waning of the last great Shaivite-Buddhist kingdom of Majapahit in the fifteenth century until the late eighteenth century are scarce. While the tradition existed during these centuries, the transition of the performance tradition to the all-night shadow plays that are known today must have been a complicated one. Evidence does show, however, that the tradition was known in both the courts and the villages. As I have argued else-

---

magandul," *Bijdragen tot de Taal-, Land- en Volkenkunde* 122 (1966): 310–65, *The Admonitions of Seh Bari: A Sixteenth Century Javanese Muslim Text, Attributed to the Saint of Bonang* (The Hague: M. Nijhoff, 1969), and *An Early Javanese Code of Muslim Ethics* (The Hague: M. Nijhoff, 1978); Robert W. Hefner, *Hindu Javanese* (Princeton: Princeton University Press, 1985); A. H. Johns, "Sufism as a Category in Indonesian Literature and History," and "From Buddhism to Islam"; A. Kumar, *The Diary of a Javanese Muslim: Religion, Politics, and the Pesantren, 1883–1886* (Canberra: Australian National University, 1985); M. C. Ricklefs, "Six Centuries of Islamization in Java," in *Conversion to Islam*, ed. Nehemia Levtzion (New York: Holmes & Meier Publishers, Inc., 1979); S. Soebardi, "Santri-religious Elements as Reflected in the Book of Tjentini," *Bijdragen tot de Taal-, Land- en Volkenkunde* 127, no. 3 (1971): 331–49, and *The Book of Cabolek*; and Woodward, *Islam in Java*. In his three-volume study on the expansion of Islam, Hodgson regrets that Geertz's work has led to popular misconceptions about the nature of Javanese Islam. In speaking of Geertz's *Religion of Java*, Hodgson notes: "For one who knows Islam, his [Geertz's] comprehensive data—despite his intention—show how very little has survived from the Hindu past even in inner Java and raise the question why the triumph of Islam was so complete" *The Venture of Islam*, 2:551 n.

39. Geertz, *Islam Observed* (Chicago: University of Chicago Press, 1968). The great Dutch Islamicist C. Snouck Hurgronje, writing at the turn of the century, commented on this in an essay on "Islamic Law and Customs": "Besides the indispensable and inevitable elements, of which without doubt the domestic law is the most important in practice, each nation adopts that portion of Islam which harmonizes most with its character, its customs and its past history, and in doing so seeks involuntarily to preserve under the new regime as much as possible of its ancient lore." C. Snouck Hurgronje, *Oeuvres Choisies de C. Snouck Hurgronje* par G.-H. Bousquet et J. Schacht (Leiden: E. J. Brill, 1957), p. 295.

where, both Sanskritic and non-Sanskritic Ramayana and Mahabharata traditions entered the archipelago from India in the first millennium of this era.[40] Sculptors and poets used both traditions in the creation of their works of art, some of which exist to this day. Court traditions followed both Sanskritic and Indian regional tellings of the Indic stories, and villagers must have been the ones to build the statues and temples whose sculptures recorded the stories sung in the courts and performed in the countryside. Old Javanese poems developed in the courts told stories that are still performed as part of the popular repertoire of the *wayang* theatre.

While the existence of the shadow theatre in Java is documented in inscriptions and manuscripts surviving from the tenth and eleventh centuries,[41] the major extant text, the *Nagarakertagama*, describing the fourteenth-century east Javanese kingdom of Majapahit, is strangely silent about it. The Malay *Hikayat Raja-raja Pasai*, however, states:

The land of Majapahit was supporting a large population. Everywhere one went there were gongs and drums being beaten, people dancing to the strains of all kinds of loud music, entertainments of many kinds like the living theatre, the shadow play, masked-plays, step-dancing and musical dramas. These were the commonest sights and went on day and night in the land of Majapahit.[42]

Pigeaud speculates that the *Nagarakertagama* may have been silent on the subject of *wayang* performances because they were too sacred or too powerful to mention.[43] A sixteenth-century poem, the *Kidung Sunda*, describing

40. L. J. Sears, "Epic Voyages: The Transmission of the *Ramayana* and *Mahabharata* from India to Java," in *Aesthetic Tradition and Cultural Transition in Java and Bali*, ed. S. Morgan and L. J. Sears (Madison: University of Wisconsin Center for Southeast Asian Studies, 1984).

41. For a new look at Indian influences on Javanese shadow theatre traditions, see Sears, "Rethinking Indian Influence in Javanese Shadow Theatre Traditions." See P. J. Zoetmulder with the collaboration of S. O. Robson, *Old Javanese-English Dictionary*, 2 vols. ('s Gravenhage: Martinus Nijhoff, 1982), p. 2228 for references in Old Javanese texts to the word "*wayang*."

42. This is quoted from A. H. Hill, "Hikayat Raja-Raja Pasai," *Journal of the Malay Branch of the Royal Asiatic Society* 33, no. 2 (1960). Supomo adds that while Hill attributes this Hikayat to the late fourteenth century, the last part of the work may have been added at a later date. See S. Supomo, "The Image of Majapahit in Later Javanese and Indonesian Writing," in *Perceptions of the Past in Southeast Asia*, ed. Anthony Reid and David Marr (Singapore: Heinemann Educational Books [Asia] Ltd., 1979), pp. 174–76.

43. Th. Pigeaud, *Java in the Fourteenth Century* (The Hague: M. Nijhoff, 1960–63), 4:482.

Hearing Islamic Voices

the days of Majapahit mentions "splendid *wayang* performances (*pawa-yangan*),"[44] and a passage from the early seventeenth-century *Pararaton* relates:

The queen of Koripan had three children: born (first) a Batara Prabhu (crown prince); his names in youth (?) were Sri Ayamwuruk Raden Tetep; his sacral bynames (?) were, when he danced in the mask-dance (*anapuk*); Dhalang Tri-taradju; when he played a feminine role, Pager-antimun; when he played *wayang* and *bañyol* (*awayang bañyol*), Gagakketawang. . . .[45]

From this passage it is evident that King Hayam Wuruk, the major figure of the *Nagarakertagama* and a historical ruler of Majapahit, could perform *wayang* and *bañyol* (comedy).[46] The information above indicates that *wayang* traditions were known in both the courts and the villages in the days of Majapahit.[47]

Turning from Majapahit to the intervening years before the rise of the Central Javanese Islamic kingdom of Mataram, *dhalang* reappear again in the Babad Tanah Jawi textual traditions that were consolidated between the seventeenth and nineteenth centuries.[48] The author(s) of this text

44. C. Holt, *Art in Indonesia: Continuities and Change* (Ithaca: Cornell University Press, 1967), pp. 288–89.

45. Th. Pigeaud, *Javanese Volksvertoningen* (The Hague: M. Nijhoff, 1938), p. 493, as quoted in Holt, *Art in Indonesia*, p. 289.

46. There seems to be a distinction here between a *dhalang* and the performer of a *wayang* play. We know that the word *awayang* meant to perform *wayang* with puppets or dancers. See B.R.O'G. Anderson, "The Last Picture Show: Wayang Beber," in *Proceedings of the Conference on Modern Indonesian Literature*, ed. J. Taylor (Madison: University of Wisconsin Center for Southeast Asian Studies, 1974), for an interesting discussion of the *wayang beber* (scroll-painting) tradition, its connections with the art of court painting, and his implication that the shadow theatre may have been very different from scroll painting and poetic recitation and that the traditions only came to be associated after the fall of Majapahit.

47. A. Reid, in his recent survey of material culture, social organization, and festivals in fifteenth- through seventeenth-century Southeast Asia, states: "Royal courts were the cultural exemplars, setting patterns, authorizing new trends, attracting outstanding performers from the countryside. In this period when the royal capitals were at the same time the dominant economic and political centres and the crucibles for foreign ideas, it is impossible to distinguish between court and popular culture." *Southeast Asia in the Age of Commerce: The Lands below the Winds* (New Haven: Yale University Press, 1988), p. 202.

48. For a definitive study of the growth of the Babad Tanah Jawi traditions and the scholarly arguments surrounding the texts, see J. J. Ras, "The Babad Tanah Jawi and Its Reliability," in *Cultural Contact and Textual Interpretation*, ed. C. D. Grijns and S. O. Robson (Dordrecht: Foris Publications, 1986).

attempted to link Mataram to the previous dynasties of Majapahit, Demak, and Pajang. Senapati, the first ruler of Mataram, is thus linked to
Jaka Tingkir of Pajang (near the present day site of the city of Surakarta).
Senapati's father, Ki Gede Pamanahan, and Jaka Tingkir were classifica-
tory brothers as pupils of the same guru, Sunan Kalijaga, one of the nine
mythical *wali* (saints) who brought Islam to Java. Following a Javanese
textual tradition from the north coast *Babad Cerbon*, Sunan Kalijaga is
depicted as telling the Sultan of Demak: "The *wayang* show is indeed a
[mirror]-image of the One, one can call it the image of the Law. The *wayang*
stands then for all mankind, [and] the *dhalang* (puppeteer) is to be compared with Allah, the creator of the Universe. . . ."[49]

Senapati's father was also a great-grandson of Ki Ageng Sela, the guru
who had directed Jaka Tingkir to the throne. Ki Ageng loved Jaka Tingkir
because he could perform as a *dhalang*, and among Jaka Tingkir's more
touted claims to fame and legitimacy were a father who was a devotee of
wayang and Jaka's auspicious birth during a *wayang beber* play.[50] Intertwined with Jaka Tingkir's relationship to the *wayang* tradition were his
connections with Islam. Jaka's father and three other friends studied Islam
and prayed together on Fridays at Pengging.[51] Their guru was said to be
none other than Seh Siti Jenar, an Islamic saint who was later put to death
for divulging to the uninitiated the oneness of humanity and god.[52] Jaka's
mother chided him for meditating in mountain caves and sent him off to
study with Islamic devotees (*mukmin*) so that he would not be considered
a *kafir* or unbeliever. There is no indication of discontinuity in the text
between performing as a *dhalang* and professing adherence to Islam.

These scattered fragments from Java's past indicate that during the days
of Majapahit, a shadow theatre tradition was known in the courts and in
the villages. The tradition may have been too powerful for the author of the
Nagarakertagama to write about, although either Hayam Wuruk himself is
glorified by the suggestion that he could perform as a *dhalang*, or he actually

49. This passage is from D. A. Rinkes, "De Heiligen van Java V: Pangeran Pang-
goeng, zijne honden en het wajangspel," *Tijdschrift Bataviaasch Genootschap* 54 (1912):
145. I have taken the citation and translation from Carey, *Cultural Ecology of Early
Nineteenth Century Java*, p. 8.

50. Olthof, *Poenika Serat*, pp. 34–35.

51. Ibid., pp. 23–24.

52. For an intriguing discussion of Seh Siti Jenar, see Florida, *Writing the Past*,
chapter 6.

could. Since the tradition seems to have been sacred and powerful, it is possible that rulers attempted to acquire the knowledge of the *dhalang*, or at least power over the *dhalang* themselves, to enhance their own authority. Connections with a village-based *wayang* tradition legitimize the ruling dynasty of Mataram, the next major kingdom of Java. Senapati is connected to Jaka Tingkir of Pajang, who wielded great power and came to the throne from distinguished origins. Jaka Tingkir is often said to be directly descended from the kings of Majapahit; I have noted that the Babad Tanah Jawi claims Jaka Tingkir was born at a village *wayang beber* performance, his guru was a *dhalang*, his father was a devotee of *wayang*, and he himself was supposedly a famous *dhalang*. These images suggest strong village performance traditions in the eighteenth century—when the *babad* were composed—connected with exorcism, black magic, and spirit possession, the remnants of which still exist in contemporary shadow theatre. It must have been during the seventeenth and eighteenth centuries—and possibly earlier—that older Shaivite/Buddhist ideas of power and knowledge in the shadow theatre traditions began to be expressed in Islamic terms. To trace the growth of Islamic ideas in Javanese mythology, I compare different tellings of a story fragment describing the birth of the demon-king Rahwana. This illuminates the workings of power that bring Islamic imagery into specific and localized sites.

Stories of Rahwana's Birth in History

To explore the penetration of Islamic ideas and imagery into Javanese literature and drama in the late eighteenth and nineteenth centuries, I investigate a particular story which has circulated through Javanese culture for over a thousand years. In the repertoire of shadow theatre, the story is called "The Marriage of Sukesi" or Alap-alapan Sukesi, and the germ of the story, the birth of the demon-king Rahwana, can be traced back to the Sanskrit Ramayana attributed to Valmiki. The story was first rendered into Old Javanese in the tenth century C.E.[53]

53. P. J. Zoetmulder, *Kalangwan: A Survey of Old Javanese Literature* (The Hague: M. Nijhoff, 1974), pp. 95–96. The following discussion of the story of Rahwana's birth is meant to be suggestive rather than definitive. For a detailed discussion of eighteenth- and nineteenth-century Javanese sources for Arjunawijaya texts, transliterations, and

The permutations of the story of Rahwana's birth in the nineteenth century document a late stage in the history of Islamic penetration into the archipelago, when Javanist Sufi mystical traditions were making an accommodation to more orthodox interpretations of Islam. As part of this accommodation, Islam was molded to fit the shape of indigenous Javanese religious beliefs. Certain mystical practices that had flourished freely under the older Indic kingdoms were increasingly frowned upon in the Central Javanese courts, where Islamic titles and rituals were adopted by Javanese rulers—new practices which both shored up the charisma of the courts and antagonized the Dutch. These attitudes are reflected in the written texts of the story of Rahwana's birth produced by Javanese court poets in the late eighteenth and early nineteenth centuries. Although for several centuries Islamic ideas had grown together with *kejawen* traditions, Islamic and Javanist traditions began to fragment into separate domains demarcated across class and urban/rural lines in the latter part of the nineteenth century due to pressures from Dutch administrators on local Javanese elites. The next chapter will explore some of these pressures on Javanese Islam in the second part of the nineteenth century.

The earliest mention of the story of the birth of Rahwana occurs in the *Uttara Kandha* of the Sanskrit Ramayana attributed to Valmiki. While the Valmiki Ramayana is believed to date back to at least 200 B.C.E., the *Uttara Kandha* is a later addition which assumed its present form by the second half of the second century C.E.[54] In the Sanskrit *Uttara Kandha*, a *rakshasa* (demon) named Sumali emerged from the netherworld with his beautiful daughter Kaikesi. Seeking to increase the power of the demons, he wished to marry his daughter to the sage Vishravas, so that she might beget sons equal to Vaishravana (Vishravas's son), also called the Lord of

---

translations of selected texts, and an excellent discussion of *sastrajendra* teachings, see Barbara McDonald, "Kawi and Kawi Miring: Old Javanese Literature in Eighteenth Century Java," 2 vols. (Unpublished Ph.D. Diss., Australian National University, 1985). Other important secondary sources for the Arjunawijaya stories include Bernard Arps, "Sekar Ageng: Over Antieke Javaanse Versvormen" (Unpublished master's thesis, Leiden University, 1986), and *Serat Lokapali* [sic] *Kawi: An eighteenth-century manuscript of the Old Javanese Arjunawijaya by Mpu Tantular, A facsimile edition of manuscript Cod. Or. 2048 in the Library of Leiden University*, introduced by Bernard Arps and Willem van der Molen (Leiden: Manuscripta Indonesica, vol. 3, Indonesian Linguistics Development Project and Legatum Warnerianum in the Library of Leiden University, 1994).

54. S. Supomo, *Arjunawijaya: A Kakawin of Mpu Tantular*, 2 vols. (The Hague: M. Nijhoff, 1977), p. 18.

Hearing Islamic Voices

Wealth. On her father's instructions Kaikesi went to Vishravas, but she inauspiciously interrupted him as he was engaged in the Fire Sacrifice. He replied thus to her brief admission of her name and that she had come at her father's request.

I know well, O Fortunate One, what brings thee here, thou art desirous of having sons by me, thou whose gait is like unto an intoxicated elephant! But, having presented thyself at this hour, hear me, O Fortunate One, thou shalt bring forth offspring of a dark aspect delighting in the companionship of doers of evil deeds. O Lady of Lovely Form, thou shalt beget Rakshasas of cruel exploits.[55]

When Kaikesi bemoaned her fate, Vishravas relented and said that her last son would be virtuous, like him. Thus were the demons Rahwana, Kumbakarna, and Surpanaka, a daughter, born, as well as Wibisana, the promised son of virtue.

The Old Javanese *Uttara Kandha*, which Zoetmulder groups with the prose *parwa* literature recounting the episodes of the Mahabharata, is believed to date back to the late tenth century C. E.[56] In the Old Javanese *Uttara Kandha*,[57] the story of Rahwana's birth remains basically the same. Sumali wishes his daughter to have children equal to Waisrawana (Vaishravana) in order to strengthen the power of the rakshasas. He thus manages to give his daughter to Wisrawa (Vishravas), and she begets Rahwana and his brothers and sister. The identity of the authors of the *Uttara Kandha* and the rest of the Old Javanese *parwa* is not known.

The first Javanese author to be connected to the story of Wisrawa and Kaikesi is Mpu Tantular, who rendered a prose text of the early history of Rahwana into poetry, the *Arjunawijaya Kakawin*. Scholars agree that it is most likely that Tantular used the Old Javanese *Uttara Kandha* as the basis for his story rather than a Sanskrit text, although Tantular may indeed have had a firsthand knowledge of Sanskrit. According to Balinese tradition, Tantular was supposedly a Buddhist in Kadhiri during the reign of Jayabhaya, but it is now accepted that he lived and wrote in the late fourteenth century, during the reign of Hayam Wuruk in the Majapahit kingdom.[58]

---

55. H. P. Shastri, *The Ramayana of Valmiki* (London: Shanti Sadan, 1959), 3:398–99.
56. Zoetmulder, *Kalangwan*, pp. 96–97.
57. Supomo, *Arjunawijaya*, p. 28; Zoetmulder, *Kalangwan*, p. 83.
58. Supomo, *Arjunawijaya*, pp. 1–15.

The telling of the story recounted in the *kakawin* of Tantular agrees with that of the Sanskrit and the Old Javanese *Uttara Kandha* and again mentions that Wisrawa was engaged in devotions when Kaikesi came to him. In the *kakawin*, however, there is no mention of inauspiciousness, and Kaikesi is said to have been granted favors by the great sage as he answered her request for children. The *kakawin* also describes how Sumali's daughter Kaikesi "assumed a form unlike that of a descendant of the great demons; as a goddess in visible form descending into the world. . . ."[59] Supomo recounts that there are more than twenty manuscripts of the Old Javanese *Arjunawijaya Kakawin*, coming from Java, Bali, and Lombok,[60] which were copied and recopied over the next few hundred years.

Concerning the literature of the following centuries, the Serat Kandha (Book of Tales) literature mentioned above includes examples of how older Indic traditions were blended with Islamic stories. When Islam entered the archipelago, it had already been filtered through the fabric of Indian religious philosophy, which emphasized meditative practice in the effort to contact the divine. Traders, who were often connected with sufi *tarekat* (paths or schools of esoteric teachings), brought their interpretations of Islam to the north coast cities of Java, where merchants, who perhaps had not been participants in the elite mystical Shaivite-Buddhist faith of the inland kingdoms, were quick to adopt the new religion, which required no priests or rituals other than the observance of the five pillars of the faith. The mythological carriers of Islam to Java were the nine *wali* or saints, some known for their spiritual and mystical powers and others known for their knowledge of Islamic textual traditions. In the ensuing centuries Islamic stories and Indian legends were intertwined in the Serat Kandha texts as they were in the plays of the shadow puppet theatre. Serat Kandha tellings of the Arjunawijaya story differ from the older texts; these renderings have more in common with storytelling traditions and shadow theatre plays.[61]

Writing in the early years of the nineteenth century, Raffles recounted a story of Rahwana's birth which he took from a Serat Kandha text extant at

59. Ibid., p. 183.

60. Ibid., p. 83.

61. Pigeaud, *Literature of Java*, 1:142; J.L.A. Brandes, "Pararaton (Ken Arok) Tweede druk bewerkt door N. J. Krom," pp. 207–8.

that time. He says that it is to the Serat Kandha ". . . that the modern Javans constantly refer for an explanation of their ancient mythology." He commented on the many passages in this work "otherwise written in a very correct style" which were "unfit for a chaste ear" and his inability to entirely purge this quality from the work. He also mentioned that the word *Pepakem* was another name for the Serat Kandha. The work *pakem* is used in modern Javanese to refer to the most stable stories of the *wayang purwa* repertoire, as well as to written outlines of the stories, and will be discussed in detail in chapter 5. The rendering of the story of Rahwana's birth that Raffles recounts is quite different from the Old Javanese renditions as well as from the later renditions in New Javanese.

Brama then following the example of *Narada*, purifies himself, and at his desire, first there appears before him a boy of strong make, on whom he confers the name of *Brama Tama*: secondly, a boy, also of strong make, whom he names *Brama Sudarga*; and thirdly, a beautiful girl, on whom he confers the name of *Bramani Wati.*

The two boys, when they attained maturity, descended from *Suralaya. Brama Sudarga* united in marriage with a female from the earth: from them, in the third degree, were descended *Raja Sumali* and *Mangliawan.* In the reign of the latter of these a destructive war is stated to have taken place. *Mangliawan* laid waste *Suralaya* and slew *Sri Gati* [Wisnu's son], but afterwards, when he shewed a desire to possess *Sri* [Wisnu's wife], *Wisnu* exerted all his strength, and put him to death. As *Mangliawan* expired *Wisnu* heard a voice saying unto him, "The work is not yet complete; hereafter, when there shall be on the earth a man named *Rahwana*, who will be descended from *Brama Tama*, beware of him: in his time the peace of heaven will again be disturbed, and he will lay it waste." *Brama Tama* espoused a princess of *Champa*, named *S'rati Dewi*, by whom he had a son, named *Brama Raja*, who became *Raja* of *Indrapuri*, and had a son named *Chitra Bahar* or *Angsarwa*, to whom, when he became advanced in age, he delivered over charge of the country, proceeding himself into the forests as a devotee, and assuming the name of *Resi Tama.*

Sumali had a daughter named *Sukesi Dewi*. This prince, alarmed at the accounts of [his brother] *Mangliawan's* death, fled with her to *Chitra Bahar* {his generational uncle and third cousin}, and requested him to protect her as a maiden, giving him authority to sanction her marriage on any proper occasion which might offer. He himself fearing the vengeance of *Sang yang Guru*, fled further into the woods for concealment, but died on the way. *Chitra Bahar*, forgetting the nature of his charge, became enamoured of the girl [who could have been his grandchild]. This happened when he was performing a penance; for he had two sons, named *Misra Warna* and *Bisa Warna*, to the former of whom he had entrusted the charge of his government. The girl resisted on account of his age, but he at last succeeded. During the first amour he received from her nine strokes on the head with a stone. In due time she became pregnant and was delivered of a boy, having nine marks or excrescences on his head, which added to his natural face, making as it were ten fronts to his head: he was thence called *Dasa muka* (ten-faced). In the second attempt she pulled the lobes of both his ears with great strength, and when delivered she produced a child in the form of a *Rasaksa*, and having immense lobes to the ears: this child was named *Amba karna*, or long-eared. In the third she scratched him all over, and the fruit of it was a girl, born with long nails and claws at the end of each finger: she was named *Sarpa kanaka*, or serpent-nailed; the wounds inflicted by these nails are said to have been mortal. But the fourth being unresisted, she was delivered of a most beautiful boy, who, having a countenance and mouth beautiful like those of a girl, was named *Bibisana*.[62]

I have quoted this passage at length as it throws light on the transformations of the story of Rahwana's birth as well as on the ways in which Indian stories became recontextualized in Java. Several themes and variations which will be stressed in the texts of the story produced in the eighteenth- and nineteenth-century courts already have surfaced in the Serat Kandha story. Rather than Sumali emerging from the netherworld as a demon, here Sumali's ancestor descends from Suralaya. Brama Raja turns his kingdom over to his son Chitra Bahar and retreats to the forest where he becomes known as Resi Tama. Sumali, who is fleeing from the wrath of Batara Guru, gives his daughter to Chitra Bahar, who is supposed to marry her off properly. Instead, Chitra Bahar marries the girl himself even though he is much older than she. Chitra Bahar, who has turned his kingdom over to his son, falls in love with Sukesi while he is performing a penance or sacrifice. Then follows the explanations of the physical forms of the children of Chitra Bahar and Sukesi in accordance with the style of their lovemaking.

While it is tempting to see in these folk etymologies indigenous Javanese interpretations, the theme echoes the Indian Mahabharata stories of the births of Pandu, Dhritarashtra, and Vidura where the three sons

62. Raffles, *History of Java*, pp. 417–18, 424–26.

acquire different characteristics according to the degree of repulsion which their various mothers felt for their father, the sage Vyasa (Jav. Abiyasa), during the lovemaking act.[63] The Indian antecedents and Javanese explanations of the names of Rahwana and his brothers and sister show the recontextualizations of the stories that made them more understandable to their audiences and bring to mind the etymologies (*jarwa dhosok*) that all Javanese puppeteers create to explain the names of major characters in the *wayang* stories.[64] The importance of the interpretation lies, not in an approximation of fact, but rather in the ability of the puppeteer to draw together disparate images into a coherent whole. These stories that recount the early history of Rahwana are known as Arjunasasrabahu or Lokapala stories, after King Arjunasasrabahu of Lokapala, who finally defeated the demon Rahwana. The Arjunasasrabahu cycle of stories is considered to be the earliest cycle of the Indian-inspired stories from which many Javanese oral and written traditions draw their repertoire. After the Arjunasasrabahu cycle comes the Ramayana cycle and then the Mahabharata cycle. The Javanese believe that the action of the earlier cycles took place in the distant past, before the action of the later cycles.

A Late Eighteenth-Century Tale of Rahwana's Birth

In the late eighteenth and early nineteenth centuries, a so-called "renaissance" of Javanese literary arts unfolded in the Central Javanese courts, in particular in Surakarta, residence of the famous court poets (*pujangga*), the elder and younger Yasadipura and Ranggawarsita. Ricklefs suggests that this literary renaissance may have fit into a cyclical pattern of Javanese history that saw an outpouring of literary works at the end of each hundred-year epoch in the Javanese calendar.[65] The literary revival may have camouflaged not only the Javanese inability to remedy the political situation of the late eighteenth century, when the Dutch were assuming more

63. Cf. C. V. Narasimhan, *The Mahabharata* (New York: Columbia University Press, 1965), pp. 15–17.

64. Cf. A. L. Becker, "Text-Building, Epistemology, and Aesthetics in Javanese Shadow Theatre," pp. 236–38, and chapter 3 below.

65. Ricklefs, *Jogjakarta under Sultan Mangkubumi*, pp. 187–88. See Florida's introduction to *Writing the Past* for a fresh discussion of the birth of what came to be known as "traditional" Javanese literature.

and more political power, but also the Javanese prophetic tradition that called for a new dynasty to arise at the turn of each hundred-year cycle. I am suggesting that the interest in Mahabharata and Ramayana stories at the end of the eighteenth century was inspired by the ways in which those stories of an ancestral past served as allegories of the colonial present. Tales of the rival kingdoms of Ngastina and Ngamarta reflected the growing rivalry between the courts of Surakarta and Yogyakarta, and stories of wars between powerful foreign kings and virtuous princes served to mirror the expanding power of the Dutch and British over the noble princes of Java.

The next written text of the story of Rahwana's birth, although no longer extant, is attributed to this late-eighteenth-century revival. This was the *macapat* (sung poetry using indigenous Javanese meters) text of the famous Yasadipura I (d. 1803), which is mentioned in the later *macapat* text of his son Yasadipura II.[66] A text that has survived is the *tembang gede* (or *kawi miring*) telling of Yasadipura II, which rendered the Old Javanese *kakawin* into modern Javanese with metrical forms based on the Sanskrit-derived Old Javanese prosody. In 1819, Yasadipura II wrote a *macapat* text of the Arjunasasrabahu, the larger work, also called the *Arjunawijaya* or the *Serat Lokapala*, which contains the story fragment of Rahwana's birth. It is the *macapat* text which Day believes most effectively translated the Old Javanese poetry into modern Javanese poetry, making it comprehensible to the audiences of the nineteenth century.[67] The tellings of the story of Rahwana's birth produced by Yasadipura I and Yasadipura II differ considerably from those recorded in earlier texts.

A Nineteenth-Century Telling of the Story of Rahwana's Birth

This text narrates the actions which take place in three countries: Lokapala, Ngayodya, and Mahispati. What is narrated first takes place in the kingdom of Lokapala. The king is named Wisrawa and he wishes to retire to the forest to undertake

66. Supomo, *Arjunawijaya*, p. 338; Day, "Meanings of Change in the Poetry of Nineteenth-century Java," pp. 54–58.

67. Day, "Meanings of Change in the Poetry of Nineteenth-century Java," pp. 60–77.

Hearing Islamic Voices

ascetic practices. He turns the kingdom over to his son, who is named Dhanapati or Wisrawana.

Then it is said that there is a king of the demons named Sumali, who holds his court in Ngalengka. He has one daughter named Sukesi of exceeding beauty.

King Dhanapati hears of the beauty of Sukesi and asks his father to make the proposal for the hand of Sukesi. Wisrawa agrees to his son's wishes and quickly departs for the kingdom of Ngalengka to meet with King Sumali and make the necessary arrangements. Sumali says that he is willing to accede to Wisrawa's request but before the marriage can take place he would like Wisrawa to give them mystical teachings that will bring well-being to body and soul in this life and the next. Wisrawa agrees and Sumali is then given the teaching he has requested as well as other mystical teachings. Sukesi is sitting in back of her father.

Batara Guru (Siwa) and his wife Betari Durga descend to the earth and head to the kingdom of Ngalengka, to the very place where the teaching is being given. Guru enters the body of Wisrawa and Durga enters the body of Sukesi. At that moment, Wisrawa becomes fatally attracted to Sukesi and he asks Sumali if he might marry the girl himself. Sumali and Sukesi both agree and soon Wisrawa and Sukesi are married.

King Dhanapati is waiting for his father's return when he hears the news that his father has married Sukesi himself. He becomes very angry and orders his soldiers to prepare to go to Ngalengka to fight with Wisrawa. They have not yet departed when the god Endra appears and informs Dhanapati that it is the will of the gods that Sukesi marry Wisrawa. Dhanapati is asked to give up his battle plans and then he is given two celestial nymphs, Nawangsih and Sasmitaningsih. Dhanapati is then satisfied and his anger towards his father disappears.[68]

In Yasadipura II's rendering, Waisrawana or Dhanapati, his more common Javanese name, hears of the beautiful Dewi Sukesi, the daughter of Sumali, the king of the ogres, and Dhanapati asks his father, Wisrawa, to arrange the marriage. Sumali is unwilling to give up his daughter unless the sage Wisrawa initiates him into certain esoteric mystical teachings.

68. C. F. Winter, *De Brata-Joeda, de Rama en de Ardjoena-Sasra*, uitgegeven door T. Roorda (Amsterdam: Johannes Muller, 1845), pp. 152–53. Winter's text gave summaries of the Ramayana, Bratayuda, and Arjunasasrabahu stories in Javanese script.

Wisrawa agrees and Sumali is so pleased with his new knowledge that he asks if Wisrawa will initiate his daughter Sukesi also. When Wisrawa explains the *sastra harjendrayuningrat* (*sastrajendra*)[69] to Sumali and Sukesi, the gods in the heavens feel the heat and turmoil (*gara-gara*) which the unauthorized revelation of this mystical teaching has aroused. Batara Guru (Siwa) and his wife Durga, wishing to punish Wisrawa, descend to earth and incarnate into the bodies of Wisrawa and Sukesi, causing them to fall in love and marry. From this union the three *raksasa* (ogres), Rahwana, Kumbakarna, and Surpanaka, and the noble Wibisana are born. Dhanapati is enraged when he hears of his father's marriage. He plans to take up arms against his father until he is calmed by a visit from the god Indra, who offers him two beautiful celestial nymphs to compensate for the loss of Sukesi.[70]

The new elements in the story center on the conflict between Wisrawa and Dhanapati and the unauthorized expression of the mystical teaching *sastrajendra.* In speaking of Yasadipura II's macapat text of 1819, Poerbatjaraka says:

But here resi Wisrawa has already been made to carry out dishonorable actions. He was asked by his son King Dhanaraja to look for a wife; he proceeds to petition the prospective bride on his son's behalf, and then winds up marrying her himself. These happenings are not found at all in the kakawin rendering of the story. But how or why resi Wisrawa has been made to undertake these dishonorable actions has not yet been investigated.[71]

Several scholars give clues which help to explain this new turn of events in the story of Sukesi and Wisrawa. Since the first telling of the

69. In *Javanese Literature in Surakarta Manuscripts*, 1:317–19, Nancy Florida lists seven *sastrajendra* manuscripts in the library of the Kraton Surakarta in the section "Javanese Mysticism (Kejawen)." Florida describes these texts as "Javano (Islamic) mystical speculations," or "conversations by Hindu deities." All the manuscripts were copied during the reign of Pakubuwana X (r. 1893–1939). Florida also points out that these texts relate to an earlier inscription of a *sastrajendra* text in the Serat Centhini, said to have been composed in the early years of the nineteenth century. See Kamajaya, ed., *Serat Centhini* (*Suluk Tambangraras*) (Yogyakarta: Yayasan Centhini, 1986), 3:12–33.

70. Drewes, "Struggle between Javanism and Islam," p. 356 n. 52; cf. Winter, *De Brata-Joeda*, pp. 152–53.

71. R. Ng. Poerbatjaraka, *Kapustakan Djawi* (Djakarta: Penerbit Djambatan, 1952), p. 138.

story connected with the elder and younger Yasadipura was the macapat text of Yasadipura 1,[72] which is dated during the reign of Pakubuwana III (1749–88), other writings by Yasadipura I might clarify Wisrawa's dishonorable actions. Soebardi argues that in the *Serat Cabolek*, Yasadipura I uses a motif which was common in the literary traditions of the period—the conflict between Javanist mysticism and orthodox, legalistic Islam.[73] Day says that both Yasadipura I and II were critical of "the sorts of heterodox, intuitive, anti-court and anti-Dutch mystical methods of acquiring knowledge and power. . . ."[74] In Day's opinion, Yasadipura I is a rationalist establishment figure worried about village-style magic and *kejawen* mysticism. Soebardi, however, presents Yasadipura I as a self-conscious continualist but also as a preserver of secret knowledge in this passage from the *Serat Suluk*:

The reason that Wisrawa, the *rsi*, incurred the wrath of God, was because he dared to lift the (Divine) veil, and claimed to be God: This happened a long time ago. . . . Those who behaved in similar fashion were (as follows): during the period of the *wali* a man named Shaikh Siti Jenar; during the reign of the second ruler of Demak: Pangeran Panggung; and during the period of Mataram: Shaikh Among Raga.[75]

Soebardi contends that this passage was written by Yasadipura I for the purpose of establishing continuity between the traditions of the three periods mentioned above with the pre-Islamic period that Wisrawa represented. The characters mentioned above, well known in Javanese literary tradition, all shared the same fate of revealing mystical knowledge to the uninitiated, and being put to death or otherwise suffering for their indiscretion. These figures bring to mind the life of the Islamic heretic al-Hallaj, who was put to death in Baghdad in the tenth century for the same reason.[76] Inappropriate revelation of mystical knowledge was a theme that appeared in many Javanese Islamic textual traditions of the eighteenth and nineteenth centuries. Wisrawa, in these particular nineteenth-century

72. Supomo, *Arjunawijaya*, p. 338.

73. Soebardi, "The Book of Cabolek" (Ph.D. diss., Australian National University, 1967), p. 43.

74. Day, "Meanings of Change in the Poetry of Nineteenth-century Java," p. 56 n. 86.

75. Soebardi, "The Book of Cabolek," p. 38.

76. A. H. Johns, "Muslim Mystics and Historical Writing," in *Historians of Southeast Asia*, ed. D.G.E. Hall (London: Oxford, 1961), pp. 46–48.

tellings of the story, suffers the anger and virulent curses of his own son, comes to actual battle with his son in several interpretations, and, through his marriage to Sukesi, causes the destruction of the *raksasa* race. Elements of the Yasadipura nineteenth-century rendering of the story of Rahwana's birth can be seen in the Serat Kandha story recounted by Raffles: an older man inappropriately marries a young maiden intended for someone else; the man falls in love with the younger woman in the course of a penance; Batara Guru takes revenge against the family of Sukesi.[77] What is lacking in the Serat Kandha telling of the story is the mystical teaching, which could have been preserved in an oral rather than a written form.

The events of the story of Rahwana's birth that are higlighted in the nineteenth-century texts of Yasadipura II and Sindusastra indicate a preoccupation with problems of religious orthodoxy. Day comments on the number of renditions of the Arjunasasrabahu story that were commissioned by the Solonese kings in the late eighteenth and early nineteenth centuries, and he isolates Arjunasasrabahu's victory over Rahwana as the theme of the stories that the audiences of that day probably found most central.[78] The inappropriate revelation of mystical knowledge seems to have been an equally pressing subject, as this theme was also stressed in shadow theatre tellings of the story.

Rahwana's Birth in Shadow Theatre Traditions

Tracing the story of Rahwana's birth in shadow theatre traditions presents problems, as the only extant sources in an oral tradition date from the present day. There are, however, testimonies from older puppeteers, who remember the ways in which the story was handled in earlier times, as well as court summaries of the *wayang* stories.[79] The outstanding feature of

77. LOr 6379, as described in Th. Pigeaud, *The Literature of Java*, vol. 2 (The Hague: M. Nijhoff, 1968), p. 356, in the library of the University of Leiden, records another version of the Serat Kandha. In this version, Wisnu and his wife Sri take human shapes in order to resist Rahwana, which suggests the incarnating of Guru and Durga in the bodies of Wisrawa and Sukesi.

78. Day, "Meanings of Change in the Poetry of Nineteenth-century Java," p. 54 n. 80.

79. K.G.P.A.A. Mangkunagara VII, *Serat Padhalangan Ringgit Purwa* (1930–32; Jogjakarta: U. P. Indonesia, 1965). The compilers of the 1965 edition of the *lakon* collected under the auspices of K.G.P.A.A. Mangkunagara VII over a three-year period from 1930

Hearing Islamic Voices

this story in the shadow play tradition, or what is significant to the puppeteers about this story, is the mystical teaching, the *sastrajendra*. Drewes discusses a passage from the Serat Dermagandhul which explains the meaning of the *sastrajendra*, called the *sastra rancang* in this passage.

The attendants give a symbolic interpretation of the different parts of the human body, adding from the *Tajussalatin* that it exists of 208 parts, 32 teeth and 1993 veins. In connection with this they stress the importance of the *ngelmu wirasat* (Arab. *ilmu 'l-firasa*), the knowledge of human character as derived from physical features. In former times this knowledge was kept a secret by the gods, but Resi Wisrawa divulged this secret knowledge to his prospective daughter-in-law, destined for his son Dasamuka [*sic*]. Tempted by Hyang Girinata (Lord Siwa) he became enamoured of her and eventually married her himself. Their children were monsters, by way of punishment for his disclosing this secret of the gods.[80]

This passage contains, perhaps, one of the more clearly Islamic explanations of the mystical teaching *sastrajendra*, which has become a blanket expression in Javanese mysticism for all types of esoteric and exorcist knowledge. The origin of the expression, which is not found in Old Javanese literature, has been explained by Supomo as an example of cacography that arose in the process of rendering the Old Javanese tellings of the Indic stories into modern Javanese.[81] The expression *sang stryahajong* (beautiful woman) in the *kakawin* of Mpu Tantular becomes *sastra harjeng* (auspicious writings) in the modern Javanese poems by Yasadipura's and Sindusastra. How and when this phrase became associated with the sorts of heterodox mystical knowledge with which it was associated in the

---

to 1932, and published by Balai Pustaka, mention in their introduction that the *lakon* "Sastra Djendra Juningrat" (the story of Sukesi and Wisrawa) was among the three *lakon* that they added to Mangkunagara VII's original 177. The telling of the story that they present is credited to Kamadjaja and U. J. Katidja Wp. This telling is very similar to the nineteenth-century version of the story except for a reference to the relationship between the brothers Sumali and Mangliawan that was recorded in the Serat Kandha. Djambumangli is presented as Mangliawan's son, who lost his chance to rule when the kingdom of Ngalangka went to Sumali, Mangliawan's brother. Thus Djambumangli wishes to marry Sukesi so he can get control over the kingdom.

80. Drewes, "The Struggle Between Javanism and Islam," p. 356.

81. S. Supomo, "Sastra Djendra: 'Ngelmu' yang timbul karena kakografi," *Majalah Ilmu-Ilmu Sastra Indonesia* 2 (1964): 177–86.

nineteenth century and with which it is still associated today are intriguing questions.

Some answers to these questions might be found in other stories from the Serat Kandha literature of the sixteenth-century *pasisir* culture of the north coast cities, as Islam was making its accommodation to the remnants of the Shaivite-Buddhist culture of the inland Majapahit kingdom. Certainly the mystical tradition, which has survived under the rubric *sastrajendra*, was not brought to Java by the entry of Islam. Rather the term represents the blending of Shaivite-Buddhist and Islamic Sufi[82] mysticism, which enabled Islam to be intertwined with the Indic local traditions of sixteenth- and seventeenth-century Central Java. Johns argues that Sufism was an important category in Indonesian history and social life between the thirteenth and eighteenth centuries until the rise of Wahhabism (ca. 1800). He believes that the Sufi were the ones who brought Islam to Java and that their effectiveness lay in their ability and willingness to use elements of the non-Islamic culture in order to make Islam acceptable.[83] The shadow theatre may well have served as a vehicle for this process. Pigeaud has commented on the present-day practice of devout Muslims staying away from *wayang* performances: "Earlier this must have been otherwise, for it is said that some of the walis, who brought Islam to Java, made *wayang* puppets and performed as puppeteers themselves."[84]

In the shadow puppet theatre repertoire, the term *sastrajendra* has come to represent esoteric knowledge, and the characters Pandu and Bima of the later Mahabharata cycle of stories also possess this secret doctrine in the *lakon* (stories) Sena Rodra and Pandu Papa.[85] The meaning of the term, however, is far from clear. A teacher from the puppeteering section of the Academy in Solo admits:

Because there has never been a clarification about the contours or the contents of the *sastrajendra* in the Lokapala text, the result is the mushrooming of various

82. A Sufi is an Islamic mystic or holy man. Sufi propagated a wide array of Islamic teachings as Islam spread east from Mecca reaching even the southern Philippines, but Sufi are most commonly associated with the most esoteric doctrines of Islamic mysticism.

83. Johns, "Muslim Mystics and Historical Writing."

84. Th. Pigeaud, *Javaanse Volksvertoningen*, p. 103.

85. Drewes, "The Struggle Between Javanism and Islam," p. 335 n. 4; Kats, *Het Javaansche Tooneel I*, p. 296.

interpretations among the Javanese people in the past and the reverberations of this can still be felt today.[86]

Puppeteers and scholars associate the interpretations of the Arjuna-sasrabahu story that are enacted in the shadow play tradition with Sindusastra's *Serat Lokapala*, a *macapat* poem written in 1829. This telling of the story differs from the earlier texts of the Yasadipuras, and Poerbatjaraka contends that Sindusastra's work is based on the Serat Kandha traditions rather than on the *kakawin* tellings of the story.[87] Murtiyasa found that the puppeteers he interviewed in the areas around Solo all associate the *lakon* Alap-alapan Sukesi (The Marriage of Sukesi) with the Sindusastra text.[88] Javanese mystics today can still recite the verses from the Sindusastra text that are connected with the *sastrajendra*. The two most important verses can be translated very roughly as follows.

The *sastrajendrayuningrat*
Is able to liberate all beings
Beyond that which can be spoken
In knowledge there is no equal.
Conquered by this noble teaching,
The end of knowledge,
Demons, giants, and ogres,
And the creatures in the mountain woods,
If they know the meaning
Of the *sastrajendra*

They will be liberated by the gods.
Reaching the perfect death,
Their souls take on human qualities,
Incomparable humans.
If they know this teaching,

86. B. Murtiyasa, "Tinjauan lakon Alap-alapan Sukeksi dalam pakeliran padat susunan Soemanto" (Surakarta: Akademi Seni Karawitan Indonesia, 1981), p.34.

87. R. Ng. Poerbatjaraka, *Kapustakan Djawi*, p. 149. Cf. Sunardi D. M., *Arjuna Sasrabahu* (Jakarti: Balai Pustaka, 1982).

88. Murtiyasa, "Tinjuan lakon Alap-alapan Sukeksi dalam pakeliran padat susunan Soemanto," p. 17. In *Het Javaansche Tooneel I*, p. 182, Kats gives a summary of the story of Sukesi and Wisrawa. He then refers the reader who wishes further detail to the work of Sindusastra "waarmee de inhoud van de lakon's in hoofdzaak overeenstemt."

They become one with the gods at death,

The noble gods.

Thus Prabu Sumali

Heeding his heart,

Searched for the meaning of this teaching.[89]

While these are the passages from the Sindusastra text associated with the *sastrajendra*, they only describe the power of the mystical teaching. The knowledge contained in the teaching is not explained. Herein lies the power and permeability of mystical teachings; they always remain open to new interpretations.

The shadow theatre links poetry and performance and court and village traditions of the story of Rahwana's birth by its emphasis on the *sastrajendra*. Speaking of the mystical teaching *sastrajendra*, Murtiyasa says that he has never seen a puppeteer explain exactly what this teaching is.[90] Usually puppeteers describe the action of the story in rhythmic prose recitations set to music, and sometimes they use phrases from Sindusastra's *Lokapala*. Murtiyasa quotes a local authority on the Solonese shadow theatre, R. Ng. Samsudjin Probohardjono, who explained that each puppeteer interprets the *sastrajendra* according to his or her own inner beliefs or mystical leanings. The puppeteer Ki Gandawajiran from the village of Boyolali defined the *sastrajendra* as a magical charm with the power "to exorcise all forms of defilement in the world" ("Sastrajendra punika lak saged nglebur sekathahing sukerta . . .").[91] In the Sindusastra tradition of the story of Sukesi and Wisrawa, Sumali actually wants to be taught the *sastrajendra* because he believes it will exorcise his demonic qualities and allow him to be reborn as a human instead of an ogre (*raksasa*). This interpretation of the *sastrajendra* as magical charm rather than mystical teaching is another connection between shadow play traditions and the Lokapala and Serat Kandha texts.[92]

89. A memorized variant of this text was recited to me by the mystic and Hindu leader Ki Hardjanta during the summer of 1990. A recorded text in Sinom metre is found in R. Ng. Sindusastra, *Serat Lokapala*, vol. 1, 2d ed. (Batavia: Bale Pustaka, 1936), pp. 26–27. Ki Hardjanta also helped me to translate these passages.

90. Murtiyasa, "Tinjuan lakon Alap-alapan Sukeksi dalam pakeliran padat susunan Soemanto," p. 39.

91. Interview with puppeteer, 22 May 1984.

92. The interpretation of *sastrajendra* as a magical charm brings to mind the performances that are held on Gunung Kawi in East Java, often by Chinese-Indonesians

Hearing Islamic Voices

The mystical explication of the *sastrajendra* as an example of the inappropriate revelation of the oneness of man and god is found in the texts of the Yasadipura's, and represents one possible interpretation of the term held by the court elites. And yet, many puppeteers from the villages, often those who had some association with the courts in their youth, share this court understanding of the term, and believe in the mystical tradition to which the term refers and which the Yasadipura's were trying to limit.[93]

The Islam Controversy in Javanese *Wayang*

Yasadipura i tried to limit the heterodox mystical tradition that must have been widespread in the Javanese countryside of the late eighteenth century. Yet Yasadipura i is also the author of a text of the Dewaruci story, the quintessential text which promulgates the Javanese pantheistic belief in the absolute identity of man and god.[94] Thus Yasadipura's identification of Wisrawa with such figures as Seh Siti Jenar indicates a belief in the heterodox traditions but an aversion toward the improper revelation of these beliefs. Yasadipura i, an Islamic force at the court, showed his identification with Islam while maintaining his belief in Javanese traditions. The improper revelation of mystical knowledge became associated with sexual power in the texts of the Yasadipuras, and both indiscretions became punishable. In their control over the meaning of *sastrajendra*, the puppeteers were powerful figures whose performances could either sup-

---

seeking to increase their fortunes. These performances generally have no audiences, and the hosts are hoping to receive a boon or blessing for their sponsorship or are giving thanks for a boon they have already received. *Sastrajendra* interpreted as a boon also connects to the dispensing of *wahyu* or boons in many *wayang* stories. What these examples underscore is the plasticity of the *sastrajendra*.

93. In Solo in 1983, Nancy Florida had a storyteller perform the legend of Seh Siti Jenar, who had been put to death for revealing mystical knowledge to the uninitiated. A puppeteer, whose family had strong connections with the Solonese courts in the past and present, said that he thought Florida was "terlalu berani" or "too bold" in holding a performance for the purpose of bringing the Siti Jenar story to the public's attention. He said that he himself was a follower of Siti Jenar, but that he would not want to make that public, so he chose not to attend the event.

94. A. Johns, "From Buddhism to Islam," p. 48. See also P. J. Zoetmulder, *Pantheism and monism in Javanese Suluk literature: Islamic and Indian mysticism in an Indonesian setting*, edited and translated by M. C. Ricklefs (Leiden: KITLV Press, 1995).

port or subvert the position of the courts. Some nineteenth-century Javanese rulers reflected Yasadipura i's ambivalence. Although they believed
in the power associated with mystical knowledge, they were strongly
influenced by Dutch colonial ideas and wanted to limit the power of rural
Islamic *kyai* (teachers), whom they and the Dutch saw as a threat.[95]

While the *sastrajendra* could be interpreted in Islamic mystical terms,
the ability of a *dhalang* in days past to convincingly explicate the *sastrajendra* according to his or her own mystical beliefs was a mark of power.
Dhalang were respected and feared for their command of mystical knowledge. Training for aspiring puppeteers consisted mainly of mystical exercises assigned to them by their parents or other relatives. Although
some contemporary writers insist that Islamic imagery and belief do pervade the *wayang* tradition,[96] these Islamic elements are difficult to find. In
fact, older *dhalang* today relate that the *wayang* is not an appropriate
vehicle for sectarian religious teachings—possibly an idea they learned
from Dutch scholars. Rather they stress Javanist mystical exercises that
associate ascetic practices with the acquistion of power.

In this chapter, I have documented a stage in the history of the coming
of Islam to Java. The synthesis of Javanist mystical traditions and Islamic
teachings discussed here was to prove less and less acceptable to those
segments of the Central Javanese population most directly under colonial
control as time went on. For most Javanese, Islamic teachings remained a
possible path to spiritual power that meshed well with their *kejawen* beliefs. In shadow play performances each puppeteer could interpret the

95. Although these literary and dramatic works document an early stage in the
transfer of authority from Hindu-Buddhist to Islamic models, Ricklefs commented on
the literary texts produced in elite Javanese circles in the latter part of the nineteenth
century which reject Islam as being a religious tradition foreign to Java. He then
concludes: "Whether these texts from the earlier and later nineteenth century spring
from two different groups among the elite, or whether (as this writer [Ricklefs] suspects)
they reflect a positive growth of a commitment to Islam in elite circles which was
stopped short and reversed by the more zealous Muslim proselytizing of the latter years
of the century, cannot be known on present evidence." See "Six Centuries of Islamization in Java," p. 117. In the next chapter, I discuss the argument that the Dutch distrust of
Islam as a rallying point for anti-Dutch movements put pressures on Javanese elites to
turn away from Islam.

96. H. E. Zarkasi, *Unsur Islam dalam Pewayangan* (Bandung: P.T. Alma'arif 1977), I. S.
Mulyono, *Asal-usul, Filsafat dan Masa Depannya* (Jakarta: Gunung Agung, 1975), and
Tripama, Watak Satria dan Sastra Jendra (Jakarta: Gunung Agung, 1978).

sastrajendra in his or her own way. Today in Java most puppeteers and mystics associate the *sastrajendra* with *kejawen* mysticism rather than Islamic traditions.[97] What was most Islamic about the nineteenth-century interpretations of the story of Rahwana's birth was the association of Wisrawa with figures like Seh Siti Jenar.[98] By distinguishing between the belief in the mystical oneness of human and god and the public expression of that belief, the Javanese equated their understanding of *wadhah* (vessel) and *wiji* (seed) with Islamic distinctions between outward behavior and inward conviction. Thus, in their acceptance of Islamic belief, Javanese literati molded Islam to suit their own purposes. While Yasadipura I sided with the *ulama* (those learned in Islamic teachings), who believed that good external behavior was a necessary part of Islamic religious life, he maintained that the essence of Islam was contained in the Dewaruci story, one of the clearest statements of Javanist mystical teachings.[99] Some Javanese today discredit Yasadipura for undermining Javanist traditions.[100] By textually punishing Wisrawa for improper revelation of mystical knowledge, Yasadipura I symbolized the accommodation of Islamic authority to Javanist beliefs.

Although I return to the story of Sukesi and Wisrawa in chapter 5, the next chapter focuses on several nineteenth-century phenomena that combined to reorient the religious and intellectual life of many Javanese: more orthodox forms of Islam, increasing European faith in science and progress, and the pressures of colonial economic policies. By the conclusion of the Java War in 1830, the Dutch had secured their control over Javanese rulers and realms. As unrest continued to simmer in the Javanese countryside, ideas of progress, secular history, and scientific investigation filtered

97. Articles about the *sastrajendra* have continued to appear in Javanist publications since Independence. See, for example, the articles on *sastrajendra* in the magazine *Pandjangmas*, tahun 3, no. 10 (1955): 11, and tahun 4, no. 2 (1958): 13. More recently, there was an article on *sastrajendra* in *Gatra*, a new name for the older publication called *Warta Wayang*, in issue no. 7 (1985): 15–23. Most of these publications connect the *sastrajendra* with Javanist mystical beliefs associating sounds with mystical points within the body.

98. Although the view that the transmission of mystical teachings should be carefully controlled is found throughout the Islamic world, many Javanese of other religious persuasions, as well as Balinese, believe that the mystical path is fraught with danger. The idea of the dangers of the left-handed path—the quick path to enlightenment in one lifetime—is also a common theme in tantric Buddhism and Hinduism.

99. Soebardi, *The Book of Cabolek*, pp. 42–43.

100. Oral communication from Ki Hardjanta, 15 July 1990.

through the thought-worlds of the Dutch administrators, whose control over Java penetrated to deeper levels throughout the century. These European ideas influenced the ways the Dutch viewed this society that was so different from their own. In the latter part of the nineteenth century, Orientalism appeared in Java as Dutch scholars became fascinated with Java's ancient Indic heritage. The Dutch colonial government, however, continued to see Javanese Islam and the passions it could ignite as inimical to their rule. Reverberations of the Islamic Wahhabi movement from the Middle East, which called for a purification of Islam, had made the doctrines of Sufi mysticism less acceptable among those who adhered to stricter Islamic beliefs by the second half of the nineteenth century. In the twentieth century, the Javanese Islamic Reform movement attempted to fill the place of mystical teachings with scriptural studies, reflecting the Islamic usages to which some Javanese put the new attitudes toward narrative traditions that they had adopted in their interactions with Dutch scholars and administrators. The coincidence of the Dutch scholarly fascination with the "Hindu-Javanese" heritage of Ramayana and Mahabharata traditions and the Dutch efforts to suppress and discredit Islam in Central Java led to the creation of new vehicles for the stories in the late nineteenth and early twentieth centuries.

2 Colonial Discourse and Javanese Shadow Theatre

As a small example of this [i.e., Javanese exegesis], an explanation of [the name] Suyudana (Sanskrit: Suyodhana) can serve . . . : "First the title king Suyuddhana: *suyud* [submission] from *papingil* [demeanor], *dana* meaning gift; all the Kurawa submit [to him] and embody one kingdom; many are the gifts that the king of Ngastina bestows, with generosity gifts are given, good or bad it's okay." *Ex uno disce omnes!*[1]—G.A.J. Hazeu on *jarwa dhosok* (Javanese exegesis)

Carangan contains the root cang, cong etc. that expresses "slanting, awry, protruding . . ." so *carang* means "little protruding branches from a tree, where the leaves grow"; and *carangan* means "branching, a thin outgrowth from the main branch." *Jejer* and *carangan* are thus here technical names taken from the same image—quite accurately—the straight trunk and its small protruding branches.[2]—G.A.J. Hazeu explaining the meaning of *carangan*

Hazeu's readings of *jarwa dhosok* and *carangan* capture the very different thought-worlds that Javanese puppeteers and Dutch commentators inhabited well into the twentieth century. Each explanation seems perfectly logical within its own setting, yet strange to those unfamiliar with the rules of its context. To Dutch scholars in the latter part of the nineteenth century, *jarwa dhosok* or *wayang* exegesis, an essential part of every *wayang* performance that shows the cleverness of the puppeteer through his or her ability to execute creative wordplay, seemed incomprehensible and ludicrous.[3] To a puppeteer unfamiliar with Dutch philology,

1. G.A.J. Hazeu, *Bijdrage tot de Kennis van het Javaansche Tooneel* (Leiden: E. J. Brill, 1897), p. 102 n. 3. This Latin quote is from the Aeneid II.65. It refers to an incident in the Trojan War where Sinon helps to betray the Trojans. The full quote reads: "Crimine ab uno disce omnis." Roughly translated this would mean that a crime from one thing teaches us about all. The tone of the Latin quote is definitely pejorative. Thanks to A. L. Becker and Andrew Becker for helping to discover the source of this quotation.

2. Ibid., p. 122 no. 2.

3. The best discussions of *jarwa dhosok*, folk etymologies or Javanese exegesis, are found in Becker, "Text-Building," and W. Keeler, "On Javanese Interpretation: A Scene from a Wayang," in *Writing on the Tongue*, ed. A. L. Becker, Michigan Papers on South

Dutch scholarly explanations and interpretations of Javanese words might seem equally odd. This chapter traces the development of Dutch colonial discourses on *wayang* theatre that arose in nineteenth-century Java and several Javanese responses to them. Javanese patrons, poets, and performers were exposed to Dutch ways of thinking in their contact with Dutch administrators and scholars in the latter part of the nineteenth century. In the twentieth century, expanding travel, technology, and communication diluted the Dutch participation in this process, and Javanese intellectuals began to realize that these new ways of thinking were a feature of European modernity rather than exclusively Dutch.

The European privileging of "authentic" texts and written histories slowly began to influence the ways in which Javanese authors and performers thought and wrote about their Mahabharata and Ramayana stories. Dutch scholars, missionaries, and administrators, as bearers of these European attitudes, helped to unsettle the Islamic associations of the *wayang purwa*, discussed in the previous chapter, by their efforts to connect Javanese "copies" of Ramayana and Mahabharata stories to their supposed non-Islamic Indian "originals." The scholars sought to create a corpus of written texts from the oral performances, and many tended to discount the dynamic ability of poets and puppeteers to create new tellings of the stories, for example the so-called *lakon carangan* or branch stories. The scholars wanted to discover or reclaim "authentic" Javanese traditions and began to see the puppeteers as the bearers of ancient "Hindu-Javanese" literary traditions that had degenerated over the centuries. Starting in the mid-nineteenth century, Dutch and Eurasian men of letters devoted themselves to the production and analysis of written versions of the shadow theatre plays.[4] In the same period, Javanese authors produced new texts like the *Pustaka Raja Purwa* of Ranggawarsita and the *Serat Sastramiruda* of Kusumadilaga. These texts provoked two very

---

and Southeast Asia no. 33 (Ann Arbor: University of Michigan Center for South and Southeast Asian Studies, 1989).

4. C. Hooykaas, in "Javaansche uitgaven van Volkslectuur (Bale Poestaka)," *Djawa* 12 (1932): 93–115, noted that the Bale Poestaka alone had published 146 *wayang* texts by 1932. See Kenji Tsuchiya, "Javanology and the Age of Ranggawarsita," for his thought-provoking discussion of the simultaneous birth of Javanology, the scientific study of Java, and the death of the Javanese *pujangga* tradition, the legacy of court poets and poetry.

Colonial Discourse and Shadow Theatre

different responses in the Dutch scholarly world of the late nineteenth century.

Many Dutch scholars and others interested in documenting Javanese literary and dramatic traditions focused excessive attention on the small percentage of Ramayana and Mahabharata texts within the larger Javanese manuscript tradition, resulting in the exaltation and philological reproduction of a certain portion of Javanese literary traditions as "Hindu-Javanese" art, to be distinguished from Islamic story cycles, *pesantren* (rural Islamic schools) traditions, and other genres of Javanese literature. In his *History of Java*, Raffles devoted forty-seven pages to the Mahabharata, sixty pages to Hinduism and Buddhism, and only four pages to Islam, the religion of Java.[5] During his years in Java, Raffles became a member of the Batavian Society of Arts and Sciences (*Bataviaasch Genootschap voor Kunsten en Wetenschappen*, established in 1778), whose primary attentions were devoted to pre-Islamic art and archaeology until the end of the colonial period.[6] Raffles set directions in the study of Javanese arts and culture that many Dutch scholars were to follow in the later nineteenth and twentieth centuries.

As an important step toward revealing this Dutch scholarly suppression of Islam and Islamic texts, Florida's catalogue indicates that of the 1,450 manuscripts in the archives of the Kraton Surakarta, only seventeen of the texts can be considered part of the corpus of the rewritings of Ramayana and Mahabharata *kakawin* texts of the late eighteenth-century Central Javanese literary Renaissance.[7] However, I counted at least 465 titles that are clearly connected to various genres of Javanese Islamic

---

5. Raffles, *History of Java*; K. A. Steenbrink, *Dutch Colonialism and Indonesian Islam*, pp. 73–74.

6. Steenbrink, *Dutch Colonialism and Indonesian Islam*, p. 59.

7. Florida, *Javanese Literature in Surakarta Manuscripts*, 1:234–38. See Florida's excellent introduction to this catalogue of manuscripts in the library collections of the Kraton Surakarta. Florida also notes (ibid., pp. 17, 19) that in the manuscript collections of the Mangkunagaran—the minor Solonese court much more closely connected to and trusted by Dutch scholars and administrators—a large portion of the collection is devoted to various renderings in the style of Ranggawarsita's *Pustaka Raja* texts. Of these, many of the texts are *Pustaka Raja Madya* tales, the stories that follow the Bratayuda War and whose production was encouraged by if not actually undertaken by Mangkunagara IV. Florida's catalogue of the Mangkunagaran manuscripts is forthcoming from the Cornell Southeast Asian Program Publications Series.

literatures, and this is without including *kejawen* texts, many of which are also clearly Islamic, or the many Pustaka Raja texts, which are also embedded in Islamic thought-worlds. The Dutch scholarly and political desires—and these are not easily separated—to minimize the importance of Islam in Java help to explain the increasing Dutch interest in shadow theatre traditions, especially those that retold Ramayana and Mahabharata stories, from the end of the Java War until World War II and the Revolution brought down the Dutch regime.

By the early twentieth century, Javanese shadow theatre had begun its transformation into the refined tradition nurtured by Dutch-educated Javanese nobility, Ethici,[8] and Theosophists, who will be discussed in chapter 3. Evidence from the nineteenth century, however, indicates that most Dutch missionaries, scholars, and civil servants saw the shadow theatre tradition as degenerate, decadent, and coarse, although several saw the possibility for its aesthetic and moral uplift and development. In contrast to *wayang kulit* (shadow theatre) and *wayang wong* (human theatre) traditions that were consciously cultivated in the Central Javanese courts in the twentieth century, nineteenth-century authors describe an earthy village tradition that appealed to village audiences. Dutch attitudes toward Javanese performances, literature, and history changed over the course of the nineteenth century as Dutch men of letters had increasing contact with Javanese authors and performers.

Scholars, Texts, and Performances

As is common in societies with restricted literacy, poetic texts in Java often turned into performances that were heard by many who could not read; in turn, literacy in Javanese script did not always indicate familiarity with large numbers of written sources. Even in the 1980s, many of the shadow puppeteers I interviewed, who claimed that their fathers and grandfathers were literate in Javanese script, responded that their families may have

8. The Dutch Ethici were followers of the Ethical policy advocated at the turn of this century by a number of liberal Dutch administrators and scholars who felt the colony was being run purely for Dutch profit at the expense of the Indies peoples. The Ethical policy shared some of the goals of the French *mission civilisatrice*, the desire to help "elevate" the native peoples through access to European-language education.

owned only one handwritten book that was often read aloud. Certain court texts had a sacral quality which enhanced their power whether they were frequently read or recopied for future preservation. Books were regarded as heirlooms (*pusaka*) as well as works of literature.[9]

In Javanese society, manuscripts were part of the oral tradition in that they both documented and enriched it. Both Hazeu and Pigeaud compared the Serat Kandha written traditions, discussed in the previous chapter, with the orally performed shadow plays.[10] In many cases the two traditions were quite similar because the authors of the Serat Kandha stories and the performers of the *wayang* plays were drawing upon the same narrative traditions. At that time the *wayang* tradition and the poetic rewritings of Ramayana and Mahabharata stories produced at the Javanese courts, sung aloud in *tembang* verse and read privately, were both highly stylized and able to process and disseminate cultural information that was passed from generation to generation.[11] Rather than seeing a disjuncture between performance and text, performances of written or oral texts were common entertainments in early nineteenth-century Java.[12]

Although members of the voc had generally ignored Javanese arts and culture, during the brief British interregnum on Java (1811–16) Raffles and Crawfurd included accounts of the *wayang* theatre in their encyclopedic

9. For an insightful discussion of manuscripts as *pusaka*, see Florida's forthcoming catalogue of the Mangkunagaran manuscripts. Even today certain palace manuscripts are felt to be powerful (*bobot, sakti*). One of my Javanese assistants, from a large family of puppeteers, came back with a bad headache after copying a few pages from a Kraton Solo manuscript of the *Pustaka Raja Purwa*. She attributed the headache to the *sakti* (power) of the text.

10. Hazeu, *Bijdrage tot de Kennis van het Javaansche Tooneel*, p. 128 n. 2; Pigeaud, *Literature of Java*, 1:140.

11. Sweeney, in "Literacy and the Epic in the Malay World," discusses his distinctions between stylized and nonstylized literary traditions as a way of upsetting the dualistic distinctions between oral and written textual traditions. Stylized traditions can refer to performances as well as written poetic texts. Sweeney suggests that authors used various methods of stylization as a way of preserving important societal information for transmission to future generations.

12. Day, in "Meanings of Change in the Poetry of Nineteenth-century Java," pp. 40 ff., supports this argument for the intertwining—perhaps even the unimportance of distinguishing—between written text and oral performance. Day refutes the ideas of scholars who have argued that meaning is somehow secondary to form or sound. Sound and sense are mutually productive, and it is both patronizing and inaccurate to argue that "meaning" is less important for Javanese authors and audiences than it is for European ones.

descriptions of cultural life in Java.[13] These descriptions are important because they both predate the period of wide Dutch interest in Javanese poetic and performance traditions and indicate that British administrators did not associate the *wayang* tradition with court art or "high" art.[14] In his discussion of shadow theatre, Crawfurd concluded:

From this account of the Javanese drama, it will easily be seen that a play or piece is not intended to be a skillful and interesting representation of the real business of the world, or of human passions, enjoyments, and sufferings, but the simple and artless relation of a common tale. . . .[15]

Raffles was slightly kinder:

The interest excited by such spectacles, connected with national recollections, is almost inconceivable. The eager multitude will sit listening with rapturous delight and profound attention for whole nights to these rude dramas. By means of them, the lower class have an opportunity of picking up a few *Kawi* terms, and of becoming acquainted with the ancient legends of the country.[16]

After these publications of Raffles and Crawfurd, and the end of the Java War (1825–30), Dutch and Eurasian scholars in Java and Holland became more interested in Ramayana and Mahabharata traditions, whether the extant literature in Old Javanese, the new Javanese poetic adaptations of the older poetry, or the shadow theatre traditions. As more Dutch scholars discovered that the Javanese had ancient literary traditions that could be traced back to the once glorious but now fallen Sanskritic culture of India, it raised the status of these traditions in Dutch eyes, but it also led many Dutch scholars to believe that the Javanese literary works were decadent copies of textual traditions that had originated in India. Starting in the mid-nineteenth century, Dutchmen began to compare Javanese tellings of Mahabharata and Ramayana stories with Indian tellings and to

13. Raffles, *History of Java*; Crawfurd, *History of the Indian Archipelago*.

14. As noted above, Raffles did rely upon the work of earlier Dutch scholars in his own monumental work. But D. E. Weatherbee's evidence that Raffles relied on earlier Dutch sources only confirms the point that eighteenth-century Dutch scholars did not have a high opinion of the shadow theatre. See D. E. Weatherbee "Raffles' Sources for Traditional Javanese Historiography and the Mackenzie Collections," pp. 63–93.

15. Crawfurd, *History of the Indian Archipelago*, p. 128.

16. Raffles, *History of Java*, 1:377.

Colonial Discourse and Shadow Theatre

speculate about the many differences they found.[17] In general the scholars considered the Javanese tellings to be corrupt.[18] These Dutch scholars, having been trained in philological traditions where ideas of accuracy and authenticity were highly valued, believed that the Javanese had misinterpreted the Indian myths and had distorted them by inserting all sorts of extraneous material into the main plots of the stories.[19] Hazeu expressed a

17. A. B. Cohen Stuart, "Brata-Joeda, Indisch Javaansche heldendicht," *Verhandelingen van het Koninklijk Bataviaasch Genootschap van Kunsten en Wetenschappen* 27 en 28, 1860, and *Serat Bratajoeda djarwa sekar macapat*, 2d ed. (Semarang: n.p., 1877); Hazeu, *Bijdrage tot de Kennis van het Javaansche Tooneel*, and "Het Oud-Javaansche Adiparwa en zijn Sanskṛt-origineel," *Tijdschrift voor Indische Taal-, Land- en Volkenkunde uitgegevan door het Bataviaasch Genootschap van Kunsten en Wetenschappen* 44 (1901): 289–357; A. Juynboll, "Drie boeken van het Oud-Javaansche Mahabharata in Kawi-tekst en Nederlandsche vertaling, vergeleken met den Sanskrit-tekst" (Ph.D. diss., Leiden, 1893), and "De verhouding van het Oudjavaansche Udyogaparwa tot zijn Sanskrit-origineel," *Bijdragen tot de Taal-, Land- en Volkenkunde* 69 (1914): 386–418; Kats, *Het Javaansche Tooneel I*; H. Kern, "Bijdrage ter verklaring van eenige uitdrukkingen in de wayang-verhalen Palasara en Pandu," *Bijdragen tot de Taal-, Land- en Volkenkunde* 16 (1869): 1–23, and "Eene Indische Sage in Javaansch Gewaad," *Verspreide Geschriften* 10 (1876): 171–211; Ch. te Mechelen, "Een en ander over de Wajang," *Tijdschrift voor Indische Taal-, Land- en Volkenkunde uitgegeven door het Bataviaasch Genootschap van Kunsten en Wetenschappen* jaargong 25, 1879.

18. L. Serrurier, *De Wajang Poerwa: Eene ethnologische studie* (Leiden: E. J. Brill, 1896), pp. 28–31.

19. W. H. Rassers, in *Pandji, the Culture Hero*, summarized the opinions of the early generation of Dutch scholars who wrote about the *wayang*. "The conclusion, indeed, appeared to be that the Javanese drama, in so far as it makes use of foreign material— and in which *lakon* is that not more or less the case?—consists largely of an accumulation of misunderstandings, and is a product of the most unsystematic confusion" (p. 111). In his introductory apology for the confused state of "De Lakon Arimba," which he summarized and presented in Javanese script, G.A.J. Hazeu concluded: "Thus if one desires to sort out the Indian and the authentic Javanese elements from the chaos of present-day Javanese literature, an accurate reading of this epic [the Harivaṃça] is an urgent need too." "De Lakon Arimba," *Bijdragen tot de Taal-, Land- en Volkenkunde* 49 [1898], p. 370. In similar fashion, British scholars thought that regional Indian versions of Ramayana and Mahabharata tales had much spurious material and that most Indian texts were filled with unnecessary later additions. One response to these European philological concerns was the somewhat arbitrary production of critical editions of the Sanskrit epics which was begun in Poona, India, by the German-trained Indian philologist Vishnu S. Sukthankar in 1919. See Bruce M. Sullivan, *Kṛṣṇa Dvaipayana Vyasa and the Mahabharata: A New Interpretation* (Leiden: E. J. Brill, 1990), pp. 13 ff., for a discussion of German and English efforts to cut away the unnecessary cultural accretions in the Sanskrit epic texts.

version of these attitudes toward Javanese texts by his amazement at how the Javanese could have preserved their wild misconceptions in written as well as dramatic traditions.

It is understandable that at present the strangest confusions arise, that the old stories have undergone complete metamorphoses from the poor work of incompetent 'interpreters', that incorrect interpretations give rise to the grossest misconceptions, and also frequently to entertainingly fictitious stories. That is why—as Prof. Kern says—the grossest of these metamorphoses, misconceptions etc. are in fact *not* the consequence of imperfect oral transmission by the folk, but arise from *bungled written* texts. Thus "the running wild [lit. sinking back into savagery] comes from the books."[20]

What strikes the reader of this quote most forcefully is the juxtaposition of words used to describe Javanese traditions: confusion, incompetence, fictitious, gross misconceptions, and finally, the "sinking back into savagery" that typifies the evolutionary thought of the late nineteenth century. And Hazeu, as a follower of the Ethical Policy, was the most forgiving of the Leiden-educated scholars when it came to evaluating Javanese literary traditions. He was also particularly sensitive to the intricate connections between the written and oral traditions.[21]

Although Javanese Mahabharata and Ramayana tales had been inscribed in manuscripts and performances for centuries, the deepening Dutch interest in Javanese literature and drama introduced certain Javanese authors to the idea that their stories were not original and forced upon them the realization that they were even misconceived. Dutch efforts to document Javanese literary and performance traditions began to have an inevitable effect upon those traditions. An early development in the mixing of Dutch and Javanese intellectual worlds was the establishment in 1832 of the Institute for Javanese Language in Surakarta (Het Instituut voor de Javaansche Taal de Soerakarta) whose main purpose was the training of Dutch civil servants in Javanese.[22] The Dutch scholar Ge-

20. Hazeu, *Bijdrage tot de Kennis van het Javaansche Tooneel*, p. 148. The text of Kern's to which Hazeu refers is *Eene Indische Sage in Javaansch gewaad*, first published in *Verslagen en Mededeelingen der Koninklijke Akademie van Wetenschappen Afd. Letterkunde* 9 (1876), and the quote is from p. 29.

21. Hazeu, *Bijdrage tot de Kennis van het Javaansche Tooneel*, pp. 145–46, and *Oud en nieuw uit de Javaansche letterkunde* (Leiden: E. J. Brill, 1921).

22. See C. Fasseur, *De Indologen: Ambtenaren voor de Oost 1825–1950* (Amsterdam:

Colonial Discourse and Shadow Theatre

ricke and the Eurasians Winter and Wilkens, who took an active part in the literary activity of the mid-nineteenth-century Javanese courts, had an enduring impact on the Javanese authors of that period.[23] Having been given some training in the traditions of Dutch philology, Winter and Wilkens were Gericke's main informants in his work on the production of a Javanese-Dutch dictionary to facilitate Bible translation and provide scholarly access to Javanese culture. While students at the Institute for Javanese Language spent six hours a day in class studying the Javanese language, they also attended a *wayang* performance once a week.[24] Fasseur notes that the Dutch students had contacts with the Solonese *kraton* and became conversant with court culture.[25]

Wilkens made major contributions to the famous Javanese-Dutch dictionary of Gericke and Roorda, spent three years of his life in the Netherlands as an assistant to the Leiden scholar Taco Roorda, and taught at the Institute for Javanese Language in Surakarta.[26] This Eurasian scholar, who wrote treatises on the shadow theatre tradition and on Javanese history, set an example for Javanese authors by producing the first printed version of a shadow theatre play complete with the puppeteer's songs, descriptions in rhythmic prose, and dialogues.[27] But I question to what extent authors like Wilkens were documenting existing traditions, or whether they were shaping the traditions they documented through their own judgments about the materials at hand.

Speaking about his published *wayang lakon*, the *lakon* Pregiwa in Javanese script with Dutch translation, Wilkens said the *lakon* was told to him

Uitgeverig Bert Bakker, 1993), pp. 55 ff., for a new discussion of the Dutch attempt to train its civil servants in Javanese language and culture in Solo after the Java War.

23. See E. M. Uhlenbeck, *A Critical Survey of Studies on the Languages of Java and Madura* ('s Gravenhage: M. Nijhoff, 1964); H. Kern, "Taco Roorda" (1928), in *Honderd Jaar Studie van Indonesie 1850–1950: Levensbeschrijvingen van Twaalf Nederlandse Onderzoekers*, ed. Koninklijk Instituut voor Taal-, Land- en Volkenkunde (Den Haag: Smits, 1976); H. Kraemer, "Het Instituut voor de Javaansche Taal te Soerakarta"; and Tsuchiya, "Javanology and the Age of Ranggawarsita," for more on the Dutch and Eurasian scholars in nineteenth-century Java.

24. Kraemer, "Het Instituut voor de Javaansche Taal te Soerakarta," pp. 270–73.

25. Fasseur, *De Indologen*, p. 63.

26. For more information on Wilkens, see Kraemer, "Het Instituut voor de Javaansche Taal te Soerakarta," p. 272; Uhlenbeck, *Languages of Java and Madura*, pp. 50–51; and Tsuchiya, "Javanology and the Age of Ranggawarsita," pp. 80–81.

27. J. A. Wilkens, "Wajangvoorstelling," *Tijdschrift voor Nederlandsche-Indië* 8, no. 2 (1846): 1–107; Pigeaud, *Literature of Java*, 1:248.

by the court *dhalang* Ki Redisuta.[28] In his introduction, however, Wilkens mentioned that he had to omit many of the "platitudes" that never failed to appear in these plays. Even the missionary Carel Poensen, who spent twenty-seven years in Java (1862–89) and wrote extensively on both *wayang* and Javanese Islam, regretted Wilkens's handling of the published *wayang* story. Wilkens had published a *wayang* story,

> . . . the story of Pregiwa, with translation and notes, which he had recorded from the mouth of the court-dalang of Soerakarta, leaving out, however, not only the songs of the dalang (in which the words are indeed quite trivial) but also 'the platitudes, that in the performance would not fail to appear.' *By this omission the example that he had wished to give has not remained a faithful and complete reflection of such a wayang performance,* yet with what he presented, Mr. Wilkens deserves credit; and we would have liked to have seen more wajang-stories published and elucidated by him.[29]

As Wilkens's Javanese text and Dutch translation was the first text of this type to appear in print, Wilkens was establishing the guidelines for a genre of Javanese literature that had previously been known only in manuscripts most often commissioned by the Javanese courts or in the private possession of puppeteers who jotted down outlines of plots to prompt their memories of particular stories.[30] Since Wilkens was considered to be one of the few experts on Javanese language recognized by Dutch scholars in his day, his decisions about what and what not to include were significant for the development of published genres of *wayang* literature. Although poetic and prose Serat Kandha texts and poetic *macapat* texts had transmitted the *wayang* tales in both written and oral as well as stylized and nonstylized forms, the production of both concise and

---

28. Wilkens, "Wajangvoorstelling."

29. Carel Poensen, "De Wajang," *Mededeelingen van wege het Nederlandsche Zendeling-genootschap* 17 (1873): 138–64, at p. 161. Emphasis added.

30. V. M. Clara van Groenendael, *Wayang Theatre in Indonesia: An Annotated Bibliography* (Dordrecht: Foris Publications, 1987), pp. 11–12, notes that Wilkens's text was the first Javanese text of a *wayang* play to be published. Summaries of *wayang* plays were not, however, an invention of Dutch scholarship. The Javanese had been listing the titles of *wayang* plays and giving summaries of them in manuscript form since at least the latter part of the eighteenth century. See Florida, *Javanese Literature in Surakarta Manuscripts,* 7:216–17.

extensive summaries of *wayang* plays in Javanese and their translation into Dutch added numerous texts to the written *wayang* literature.

The Institute for Javanese Language, considered to be a failure,[31] was eventually replaced by the Royal Academy in Delft, set up in 1842 to train Dutch colonial civil servants, and the Royal Academy in Delft in its turn was moved to the University of Leiden in 1864, although a language-training school for civil servants remained at Delft until the end of the century. As Uhlenbeck noted on the move from Delft to Leiden: "From this moment onwards the study of Indonesian languages, history and ethnology became intimately connected with the tradition of the scientific study of Oriental languages for which the University of Leiden was renowned already in the seventeenth century."[32] Thus the orientalist bent of Dutch scholarship on Indonesia—the search for original and "authentic" texts and their translation and explication—was firmly established. At the same time that Dutch scholars and administrators were collecting and preserving Javanese tales, Dutch colonial policies were restructuring Javanese economic, religious, and political domains. A conjunction of scholarly and political domains appears here as the colonial government attempted to suppress Islam and as Dutch scholars began to reproduce "Hindu-Javanese" Ramayana and Mahabharata texts.

Divisions between Secular and Islamic Elites

By 1830, the Dutch were more wary about Javanese Islam than they had been before the Java War. Economic pressures to fill colonial coffers brought the harsh forced cultivation system (*cultuurstelsel*) into the Javanese countryside from 1830 to 1870.[33] The Dutch left the traditional rulers (the *bupati* or regents) in place, hoping in this way to keep the peasants pacified, but made the regents dependent on the colonial government for

31. In *De Indologen*, p. 66, Fasseur notes that G. de Serière, a Dutch civil servant from Banyumas who sent an evaluation of the school to the Governor General in 1838, complained that he found the history of Java no more evident as a subject of study than the *wayang* theatre, which he thought of little use.

32. Uhlenbeck, *Critical Survey*, p. 59.

33. For information on the *cultuurstelsel*, see C. Fasseur, *The Politics of Colonial Exploitation*, and P.B.R. Carey, "Aspects of Javanese History in the Nineteenth Century."

their salaries and their position. Under close Dutch surveillance, the regents were discouraged from identifying too closely with Islam, and by the early twentieth century, the regents were encouraged to turn to Dutch-language education for cultural and intellectual models. Insofar as the Dutch-controlled Javanese administrative corps (*pangreh praja*) followed these rules, they could accrue limited political power and social prestige in the colonial state. At the same time that the status-oriented *pangreh praja* were accommodating themselves to their colonial rulers, they became more and more divorced from the peasants in the Javanese countryside.[34]

Although the Dutch inducted the Javanese administrative corps into their apparatus, they simultaneously repelled and persecuted the Islamic village leaders, the *kyai*.[35] As Kumar notes:

Dutch policy strongly discouraged any link between the aristocracy of the principalities and what may be termed the intellectual leadership of rural Java, the *kyais* and *hajis* whose authority radiated from the rural *pesantren* [Islamic schools] rather than from the *kraton*.[36]

The Javanese *kyai* were Islamic teachers who often ran rural schools (*pondhok* or *pesantren*) which attracted young men in search of knowledge or power. Life in these rural schools revolved around the charismatic figure

34. Carey, "Aspects of Javanese History," p. 84. Although Fasseur, *The Politics of Colonial Exploitation*, is a meticulous study of the continental Dutch politics and policies that put and kept the *cultuurstelsel* in place, he does not devote much attention to the effects of the system on the social and mental worlds of the Javanese people. McVey commented perceptively on how colonial economic and political policies alienated both class relations and religious orientations in the Javanese countryside: "This already marked contrast was greatly intensified in the nineteenth century under colonial rule, when the Netherlands East Indies authorities deliberately set out to estrange the Javanese administrative elite, the *priyayi*, from strict Islam in an effort to remove that religion as a motivational force for their resistance and/or alliance with the masses." R. McVey, "Faith as an Outsider: Islam in Indonesian Politics," in *Islam in the Political Process*, ed. James P. Piscatori (Cambridge: Cambridge University Press, 1983), p. 201.

35. R. Mortimer, "Traditional Modes and Communist Movements: Change and Protest in Indonesia," in *Peasant Rebellion and Communist Revolution in Asia*, ed. John Wilson Lewis (Stanford: Stanford University Press, 1974), p. 102; A. Kumar, "The 'Suryengalagan Affair' of 1883 and Its Successors: Born Leaders in Changed Times," *Bijdragen tot de Taal-, Land- en Volkenkunde* 138, nos. 2/3 (1982): 270.

36. Here Kumar is referring to the special areas of Central Java which included the rival palaces (*kraton*) of Surakarta and Yogyakarta; these were the divisions of the Javanese kingdom of Mataram which the Dutch helped to create in 1755.

of the *kyai*. Students came to study with a *kyai* because of the amount of supernatural knowledge or mystical power he was believed to have accrued through the process of purifying and refining his inner being (*bathin*). Islamic scriptural studies were felt to be useless without the *berkah* or grace of the *kyai* to help elucidate the mysteries of the Arabic texts.

Throughout the course of the nineteenth century, Islamic orthodoxy became associated with lower social status, and the Dutch alliance with the regents insured that in times of stress, oppressed villagers would turn to the *kyai* for guidance and the organization of resistance.[37] As ties between Javanese Islam and the rest of the Islamic world tightened in the course of the nineteenth century, the strength of the *kyai* grew also. Of particular importance were the opening of the Suez Canal and the growth of the KPM (Koninklijke Paketvaart Maatschappij, Royal Mail Steam Packet Company), which turned the pilgrimage to Mecca from a journey of two years into one of two weeks. Carey notes: "In the latter half of the nineteenth century, with the spread of religious revival and the impact of colonial rule, each *pesantren* was turned into a potential source of anti-European and anti-*priyayi* sentiment."[38]

By the early twentieth century, when the colonial state finally decided to give their native administrative corps a Dutch-language education, the estrangement between the modernizing, secular *priyayi* and the old-fashioned rural Islamic peasantry intensified.[39] At this point in the mythological and religious life of Javanese peasants, the war that was necessary to rid Java of the Dutch was as likely to be a *prang sabil*, an Islamic holy war, as the Bratayuda of the Mahabharata tales. According to Sartono, the idea of an Islamic holy war (*jihad*) was imposed upon all Muslims who needed to rid themselves of oppression by nonbelievers as well as to extend the Islamic community and purify the religion.[40]

---

37. Mortimer, "Traditional Modes and Communist Movements," p. 102; L. Castles, "Notes on the Islamic School at Gontor," *Indonesia* 1 (April 1966): 42 no. 27.

38. Carey, "Aspects of Javanese History in the Nineteenth Century," p. 101.

39. Deliar Noer remarks: "To borrow the terminology of Snouck Hurgronje, the Dutch, through education, had indeed been successful in 'emancipating' part of the Indonesian Muslims from their own religion." See *Administration of Islam in Indonesia* (Cornell Modern Indonesia Project Monograph Series, Ithaca, 1978), p. 4.

40. Sartono Kartodirdjo, "Agrarian Radicalism in Java: Its Setting and Development," in *Culture and Politics in Indonesia*, ed. Claire Holt (Ithaca: Cornell University Press, 1972), p. 91.

Wayang Tales and "Hindu-Javanese" Literature

Although the previous chapter described how Islamic mysticism was able
to infiltrate and coopt the Indic authority of the shadow theatre tradition,
Dutch authority never penetrated the domain of the shadow theatre in the
same way. Although Dutch scholars were interested in documenting the
tradition, they did not want to displace the Indic elements of the tradition
with their own authority and imagery. In reaction to the Java War of 1825–
30, when Javanese had risen up against the Dutch under the banner of
Islam, and the bloody Aceh War of the last thirty years of the nineteenth
century, which again saw the "docile" Malays—this time those of north
Sumatra—rallying around Islam as a bulwark against Dutch aggression,
some Dutch scholars and administrators in the late nineteenth and early
twentieth centuries wittingly or unwittingly helped to carve out an area of
Javanese literary culture that was free of Islamic influences.[41] One example
is the plantation manager Karel Frederik Holle, who became an expert on
Javanese, Sundanese, and Malay language and culture. He decided to
manage a tea plantation in Sunda in 1856, helped set up a Teacher Training College for Native Schools (Kweekschool voor Onderwijzers op Inlandsche Scholen) in Bandung in 1865, and was appointed honorary
Advisor for Native Affairs in 1871. Holle attempted to minimize the religious function of the Javanese regents who were head of religious affairs
in their regencies. He railed against regents who took their Islamic duties
seriously, and he recognized the dangers—for the Dutch—of the *haji* and
teachers of Islamic mysticism.[42]

41. S. Supomo, in "The Image of Majapahit in Later Javanese and Indonesian
Writing," in *Perceptions of the Past in Southeast Asia*, ed. Anthony Reid and David Marr
(Singapore: Heinemann Educational Books [Asia] Ltd., 1979), p. 181, suggests that the
scholarly findings of Brandes, Kern, and Krom, which showed Islamic histories like the
Babad Tanah Djawi to be inaccurate, furthered this tendency to nurture a Hindu, rather
than an Islamic, Javanese past. See also Dan Lev's "Colonial Law and the Genesis of the
Indonesian State" in *Indonesia* 40 (October 1985): 57–74, where he discusses the Dutch
appropriation of *adat* or customary law as a bulwark against Islam.

42. *Haji* is a title reserved for those Muslims who have made the pilgrimage to Mecca,
one of the five pillars or requirements of Islam. This discussion of Holle is drawn from
Steenbrink, *Dutch Colonialism and Indonesian Islam*, pp. 78–80. Steenbrink also notes the
pervading fear among Europeans in Java that the natives would rise up and slaughter

Colonial Discourse and Shadow Theatre

Another way to minimize the threat of Islam involved the scholarly attempt to discover the authentic "Hindu" roots of Javanese textual traditions. Late nineteenth- and early twentieth-century Dutch scholars reclaimed the notion of a "Hindu-Javanese" epoch in Javanese history, introduced by Stamford Raffles in the early nineteenth century to refer to that period of Java's past that had seen the adoption and adaptation of so many Indian religious, cultural, legal, and textual traditions.[43] F.D.K. Bosch comments on the ease with which the nineteenth-century scholars concluded that only Hindus could have been responsible for the great artistic remains found on Java:

No wonder that since the days of Raffles those authors in their publications spoke, without further comment, of Hindu art, Hindu society, Hindu civilisation etc., thus expressing that, in the realisation of all this, no others than the Hindus had participated. The only possibility generally admitted of the native population having at least played some part in the creative process, was that the degeneration and debilitation of the formerly noble race of Hindu artists were ascribed to the intermarriage of Indians with Indonesians. This was held to be the clear sign of decay alleged to be noticeable in the later phases of Hindu-Javanese art—a decay which finally resulted in the art entirely vanishing from the island of Java.[44]

---

the Dutch (pp. 81–84). In this light, the so-called Indian Mutiny, which claimed 40,000 Indian and British lives, seemed a warning to the Dutch in the Indies.

43. The term "Hindu-Javanese" is misleading for several reasons: the word Hinduism, itself a nineteenth-century colonial creation, does little more than distinguish a complex array of beliefs and practices in the subcontinent from others that are more clearly Islamic, Buddhist, or Christian; some, but certainly not all, of the influences that came to Java from India could be called Hindu; and, lastly, the separation of local Javanese belief from what was presumed to have come from India is an overwhelming and rather unproductive exercise. Th. Pigeaud said as much based on his extensive research in the 1920s in *Javaanse Volksvertoningen*, p. 32. He objected to the tendencies in most Dutch scholarship to separate court from village traditions and to separate Hindu-Javanese from Islamic traditions, especially after four centuries of Islamic influence in Java. Pigeaud's opinions, however, were always a bit different from the scholarly community in Leiden.

44. F.D.K. Bosch, "The Problem of the Hindu Colonisation of Indonesia" (1946), in *Selected Studies in Indonesian Archaeology*, KITLV Translation Series 3 (The Hague: M. Nijhoff, 1961), p. 5. For an explication of this view, see especially N. J. Krom's *Hindoe-Javaansche Geschiedenis*, 2d ed. ('s Gravenhage: M. Nijhoff, 1931).

The Dutch colonial presence was supposed to counter the internal decay of the Javanese courts in the political realm at the expense of draining away their power and prestige,[45] and some scholar-administrators by the turn of the century hoped that the nurturing of a "Hindu-Javanese" past that included a focus on Mahabharata and Ramayana traditions might diminish the authority of Islam in the social and cultural realms as well as the political one.[46]

Dutch influence on Ramayana and Mahabharata traditions was felt in proportion to the amount of exposure the Javanese had to Dutch ideas and especially to Dutch language. A Dutch-language education radically changed the ways in which these stories were meaningful for Javanese elites while village traditions changed more gradually. In chapters 3 and 4 I explore the results of these transformations; here, however, I suggest that by their focus on non-Islamic stories and by their prolific efforts to document "Hindu-Javanese" traditions, Dutch scholars slowly altered the interlacing of Islamic knowledges and Ramayana and Mahabharata traditions and the ways in which these stories passed on meaningful information. As Sweeney noted for Malay literary traditions: "In carving out the area of Malay discourse to be labeled 'history,' colonial scholars assumed the existence of a boundary between fictionality and referentiality similar to their own."[47] This holds true for the Dutch reaction to the Javanese literary and dramatic traditions as well. Dutch scholars, as part of the colonial fascination with describing and labeling, cut through genre and text with ideas that had been generated in the European scholarly world, ideas that had little meaning within Javanese society. In the same essay, Sweeney argues elegantly against applying these European standards to the Malay traditions he studied:

If, accepting for the sake of argument that the Ramayana and Mahabharata are epic poems, it be proposed that the *Hikayat Seri Rama* and the *Hikayat Pandawa* [i.e., Malay tellings of Ramayana and Mahabharata stories] deserve the appellation

45. Cf. D. J. Steinberg et al., *In Search of Southeast Asia* (New York: Praeger, 1971), p. 147.

46. See Fasseur, *De Indologen*, for a careful study of the increasingly close connections between the civil servants who worked for the colonial government and the rise of Indology at the State University of Leiden.

47. Sweeney, "Literacy and the Epic in the Malay World," p. 25.

Colonial Discourse and Shadow Theatre

"epic" because they are translations of the Hindu epics, one must respond that they are neither translations, Hindu, nor poems.[48]

In Java the situation was a bit different. Poems recounting episodes from the Mahabharata and Ramayana tales *were* written at the Javanese courts in the late eighteenth and early nineteenth centuries, and Javanese authors considered these poems to be reworkings of older poetry that was, albeit rarely, translated from extant Sanskrit works. The Old Javanese poems *were* Indic or at least had been produced at courts where Shaivism, Vishnuism, and Buddhism were major religious traditions. In the nineteenth-century courts, the reworkings of the older poetry had served to legitimize ruling dynasties by linking those dynasties to the glory of the earlier kingdoms. Shaivite, Vishnuite, and Buddhist ideas were intertwined with Islamic mystical conceptions that never entirely negated the earlier beliefs. Sweeney's dissatisfaction with the word *epic*, however, would also apply to Javanese Ramayana and Mahabharata traditions. Rather than "epics," most Javanese considered the *wayang* plays that were the main vehicles for the transmission of Ramayana and Mahabharata tales to be *crita* or stories, and, in nineteenth-century Java, *crita* and *babad* (chronicle/historical text) were not far apart.

Pigeaud has commented upon the increasing Javanese tendency to associate myth and history by arranging the mythic shadow play stories in chronological order.

In the course of time wayang plays were arranged in chronological order as if they were descriptions of episodes of a history. In the flourishing renaissance period of Surakarta literature, in the nineteenth century, the tendency of associating mythic and epic wayang play literature with history grew particularly strong. Its beginning was already visible in the Pasisir period.[49]

Post-Enlightenment European ideas of a scientific, linear history that was considered to be an objective approximation of reality differed from certain Javanese perceptions of the past in which histories were written, sung, and told for aesthetic, didactic, and political purposes.[50] The way

48. Ibid., p. 26.
49. Pigeaud, *Literature of Java*, 1:140.
50. C. C. Berg, "The Javanese Picture of the Past," in *An Introduction to Indonesian*

that Javanese authors arranged the Ramayana and Mahabharata stories in what they believed to be chronological order more closely approximated the way that Islamic scholars had arranged the *hadith* (oral traditions about the Prophet) to produce their early historical texts.[51] Since many Javanese considered these stories to be tales of the ancestors of the Javanese nobility,[52] it is not surprising that as Javanese literati were exposed to Dutch conceptions of history, their perceptions of the Ramayana and Mahabharata tales as a form of Javanese history would be strengthened rather than diminished.

The relations between myth and history in Dutch and Javanese intellectual worlds in the mid-nineteenth century can be studied as a microcosm of colliding worldviews. Raymond Williams observed the post-Renaissance European transformation of historical and literary domains and noted that "The 'national literature' soon ceased to be a history and became a tradition."[53] It is just this process that was taking place in nineteenth-century Java. In the era of dialectical materialism and social Darwinism, Dutch scholars were documenting Javanese traditions in an atmosphere where history was seen as a linear trajectory moving from the past into the future. Along with such linear conceptions of history, discourses of progress, profit, and natural selection were soon to form the rationale for expanding the imperial project in economic and intellectual domains. The *cultuurstelsel* (cultivation system) of the mid-nineteenth century (1830–70) had turned the Indies into a successful profit-making venture, and during this period the Dutch began to move out from their strongholds in Batavia, Priangan, the *pasisir* and other parts of Java into Sumatra, the Celebes, and Kalimantan. History became an evolving destiny that posited the highly evolved Dutch as the "natural" rulers of the Indies and the less-evolved Javanese as their natural subjects.

In support of Dutch claims to superiority was the obvious Javanese lack

Historiography, ed. Soedjatmoko (Ithaca: Cornell University Press, 1965); cf. M. C. Ricklefs, *Modern Javanese Historical Tradition* (London: University of London, School of Oriental and African Studies, 1978).

51. Cf. D. Henige, *Oral Historiography,* pp. 11–13. Pigeaud, *Literature of Java,* 1:39, notes that Islamic concepts of continuity may have "sharpened" the historical views of *pasisir* authors of the Serat Kandha tales.

52. Hazeu, *Oud en nieuw uit de Javaansche letterkunde,* p. 6; Poensen, "De Wajang," p. 159.

53. R. Williams, *Marxism and Literature* (Oxford: Oxford University Press, 1977), p. 51.

Colonial Discourse and Shadow Theatre

of proper written histories, although the Javanese were certainly the most "advanced" of the societies that the Dutch encountered and conquered in the archipelago.[54] All that the Javanese had were myths, in Dutch scholarly eyes, and the myths were Indian to begin with. Moreover, the Javanese had not even understood the myths correctly. They were all confused, and Dutch philology was needed to sort them out.[55] A succinct example of these views was voiced by the missionary Poensen in 1873 in his speculations on the origins of the shadow theatre.

So we would then obviously come to the Hindoe's, and we are certainly closest to the truth if we assume that with their help and under their guidance the first wajang-performance took place in Java. The idea for this may have been inspired from what was available, and their own mythological history offered the material for the lakon [plays]. Who knows whether they just wanted to keep alive in this way the memory of their great heroes and gods from the Mahabharata and Ramayana among their children and grandchildren in Java who never set foot on mainland Asia; and how in the course of time, with the degeneration of the Hindoe descendants and their blending, to a greater or lesser extent, with the native population of this island, the stories themselves were also more or less changed; so that finally in the consciousness of the people, the real origin was lost, and Java was made the theatre where all those histories had once taken place; similarly nowadays the average native sees in the wajang stories nothing other than so many parts of his ancient native history.[56]

Poensen's remarks suggest that for the Javanese, *wayang* stories may indeed have been seen as preserving the stories of the Javanese past. The connections that some Javanese made between Mahabharata stories and history even had precedents in India, where this particular story cycle was seen by many Indians as *itihasa* or history.[57] In addition to Ramayana and

54. Hazeu, in *Oud en nieuw uit de Javaansche letterkunde*, p. 4, summarizes the opinions of J.L.A. Brandes, "Iets over een ouderen Dipanegara in verband met een prototype van de voorspellingen van Jayabaya," *Tijdschrift voor Indische Taal-, Land- en Volkenkunde uitgegeven door het Bataviaasch Genootschap van Kunsten en Wetenschappen* 32 (1889): 368–430, who argued that the Javanese *babad* or chronicles should be seen as handbooks of Javanese literature with occasional historical facts thrown in here and there.

55. Tsuchiya, "Javanology and the Age of Ranggawarsita."

56. Poensen, "De Wajang," pp. 143–44.

57. Sullivan, *Kṛṣṇa Dvaipayana Vyasa and the Mahabharata*, p. 6 n. 24. In India, the Ramayana and the Mahabharata were considered to be *smṛti* rather than *śruti*, the

Mahabharata tales as histories/stories of the ancestors, Javanese literati also wrote court chronicles or *babad* for specific purposes.[58] Court chronicles, usually composed in poetic form, and shadow plays were shaped and stylized, showing that both were considered important vehicles for the preservation of knowledge. The idea of written prose histories describing "ordinary" events was not necessarily new for the Javanese; rather it may have been that they were not considered valuable or worthwhile. But the wretchedly poor Javanese court poet R. Ng. Ranggawarsita, who served as translator and *vraagbaak* (walking encyclopedia) for several Dutch scholars in Solo in the mid-nineteenth century, may have thought that he would impress the Dutch, and be reimbursed for his efforts, if he produced written prose histories, full of dates, that linked the ancient tales to the more recent Javanese past.

The different boundaries between myth and history in Javanese and Dutch intellectual worlds, and Dutch scholarly identifications of history with "objectivity" and prose writing, become clear by the end of the nineteenth century in the Dutch rejection of Ranggawarsita's magnum opus on Javanese history, the *Pustaka Raja*[59] or Book of Kings. The multi-

---

Sanskrit words for, respectively, that which was remembered and that which was revealed. In addition, the Mahabharata was considered *itihasa* ("thus it occurred"), the Sanskrit word for story or history, and the Ramayana was *caritra*, the Sanskrit word for the adventures or exploits of a hero. Monier Monier-Williams, *Sanskrit-English Dictionary* (1899; Delhi: Motilal Banarsidass, 1976), p. 389.

58. Berg, "The Javanese Picture of the Past." See also Ricklefs, *Jogjakarta under Sultan Mangkubumi*, and his *Modern Javanese Historical Tradition*.

59. For the study of Javanese Ramayana and Mahabharata tales, the *Pustaka Raja Purwa* texts are the most significant part of Ranggawarsita's work. However, the first 730 years of Ranggawarsita's history, which contain the Ramayana and Mahabharata tales until the end of the Bratayuda War, are followed by the *Pustaka Raja Madya* texts, which bring the history to the solar date of around 1100, and finally the *Pustaka Raja Puwara* texts, which fill in the years up to at least the fall of Majapahit in the conventional Javanese year, and Ranggawarsita's solar year, of 1400. All these texts together make up Ranggawarsita's *Pustaka Raja* corpus. The series is preceded by the *Serat Paramayoga*, which gives genealogical information and creational stories of the founding of human populations in Java. See Day, "Meanings of Change in the Poetry of Nineteenth-century Java," pp. 220–32; G.W.J. Drewes, "Ranggawarsita, the Pustaka Raja Madya and the Wayang Madya," *Oriens Extremus* 21 (1974): 199–215; Florida, *Javanese Literature in Surakarta Manuscripts*, 1:154–64; and Pigeaud, *Literature of Java*, 1:170–71. Although Ranggawarsita is credited with the authorship of the *Pustaka Raja* in the mid-nineteenth century, the texts were reinscribed many times during the late nineteenth and early twentieth centuries. The texts I have looked at most carefully, which were kindly photo-

volumed Javanese texts, which the ruler of the lesser court in Surakarta, Mangkunagara ɪᴠ, proclaimed to be both authentic and ancient, were eventually scorned as spurious by the Dutch scholars of the Bataviaasch Genootschap,[60] who had decided that the texts were neither authentic nor ancient. The texts were Javanese, of course, but they were considered to be polluted by Ranggawarsita's misunderstandings, or mimicry, of European conceptions of history. Poerbatjaraka, the first Javanese scholar to receive a degree in Javanese literary and historical studies at Leiden (1926), was also contemptuous of Ranggawarsita's monumental work. In his survey of Javanese literature, Poerbatjaraka comments:

The Pustaka-radja book is basically concocted from books of wajang plays [*lakon*] based on stories that R. Ng. Ranggawarsita heard from his friends, and tales that already existed at that time. All of that was changed around and expanded by R. Ng. Ranggawarsita himself according to his own whims.

Although those are the facts, in short the Pustaka-radja book in large part contains just NONSENSE [*OMONG-KOSONG*] from R. Ng. Ranggawarsita.[61]

Dutch scholars were so disappointed with these texts that they have never been translated, summarized, or given the critical apparatus accorded to so many other ancient and a few modern Javanese texts, especially those that retold the Mahabharata and Ramayana stories. Rang-

---

copied for me by the librarians at the Radya Pustaka library in Surakarta, were published by N. P. Voeren H. Boening, Ngayogyakarta, in 1906. Ki Padmosusastro is the person who either inscribed the texts or "validated the literature by the criteria of the Serat Paramasastra (*kaesahaken kasusastranipun awewaton Serat Paramasastra*)."

60. Day, "Meanings of Change in the Poetry of Nineteenth-century Java," pp. 185–89.

61. R. Ng. Poerbatjaraka, *Kepustakaan Djawa* (Djakarta: Penerbit Djambatan, 1952), pp. 186–87. In the Javanese language edition of his book (also published by Penerbit Djambatan in 1952), Poerbatjaraka mentions that Ranggawarsita's "friends" were Dutch, and elsewhere in the book he mentions C. F. Winter and Cohen Stuart. Poerbatjaraka notes that these books by Ranggawarsita were published in Javanese script twice: the first time by H. Buning in 1884, the second time in 1906 (p. 187). E. M. Uhlenbeck expands on this by noting that the books were published in nine volumes between 1884 and 1906, and a second edition in eight volumes was published between 1904 and 1908. Uhlenbeck laments that there are no plans to publish "these important documents of Javanese historiography," by which one must assume he meant to publish them in latin script or translate them into Indonesian for a wider audience. *A Critical Survey of Studies on the Languages of Java and Madura*, p. 130.

gawarsita's *Pustaka Raja Purwa*, like the earlier Serat Kandha texts, saw the Mahabharata and Ramayana stories as intermediary episodes between cosmogonic Islamic genealogies and the tales of historical Javanese kings. What Ranggawarsita had done was to give both solar and lunar dates— dates that differed by only about twenty-two years, resembling the relationship between the solar Gregorian Calendar and the lunar Javano-Arabic one—to all these episodes, as though they had really happened in a very distant pást. In addition to the chronogram style of dating familiar to Dutch scholars from Old Javanese poetic texts—and considered to be "authentic"—he more or less created his own dating system. He also retold the *wayang* tales, and many other tales as well, in prose rather than poetry. The *Pustaka Raja* texts, in fact, reflect a concern with dates that in turn mirrors or mimics what may have seemed to this mid-century Javanese intellectual to be a Dutch scholarly obsession with dates. By giving fictive solar and lunar dates, older-style *candrasengkala* (chronograms), and even Javanese seasonal dates to each event in his chronologies, Ranggawarsita discredited or put into question all dates in his distinctive methodological and literary world.

Ranggawarsita's method seems to have touched on an area of Dutch intellectual sensitivity as the Dutch Indologists themselves were busily establishing boundaries between Javanese myth and history. Ranggawarsita spent a lot of time with C. F. Winter and Wilkens as well as with J.F.C. Gericke, A. B. Cohen Stuart, and Palmer van den Broek. Is it conceivable that Ranggawarsita understood so little about Dutch philology—for which he served as "*de* vraagbaak bij uitnemendheid"[62] (*the* walking encyclopedia par excellence)—that he failed to realize that his work might not fit within the boundaries of European conceptions of history? I suggest that it makes as much sense to see Ranggawarsita's Book of Kings as a kind of grand spoof on Dutch historical and philological methods as it does to see it as either a confused synthesis of Javanese history and myth or a failed attempt at European historical writing.[63] The work of Dutch scholars like

62. This expression, from the Dutch scholar-administrator G.A.J. Hazeu, *Oud en nieuw uit de Javaansche letterkunde,* p. 19, was also quoted in an essay on the *wayang* theatre by Poerwoto Prawirohardjo, "Kesoesasteraan Indonesia Djawa" in the Indies intellectual journal *Poedjangga Baroe* 1, no. 8 (Pebroeari 1934): 256–59.

63. Florida's essay, "Reading the Unread in Traditional Javanese Literature," proves that Ranggawarsita had a sharp sense of humor as well as cynical ideas about achieving wordly fame. Day, in "Meanings of Change in the Poetry of Nineteenth-century Java,"

Colonial Discourse and Shadow Theatre

Hazeu and retired *ambtenaren* (civil servants) like Humme, discussed below, shows that Ranggawarsita may have had good reason to believe that
the many Dutchmen around him were also engaged in the project of dating
and writing down Javanese mythological tales. In his own explanation of
how the texts were compiled, Ranggawarsita described how King Aji
Jayabhaya of Kadhiri, a historical king from the mid-twelfth century, sent
his scholars out to collect data by compiling and comparing older histories
and genealogical data.[64] These may have been the historical methods to
which Ranggawarsita had been introduced by the Dutch scholars in Solo
when they sent him out into the villages to collect and record shadow play
stories.

   Although Pustaka Raja texts were copied and recopied in the nineteenth and twentieth centuries,[65] most Dutch scholars have turned their
backs on this genre of *wayang* texts.[66] Despite the Dutch reaction, the
Pustaka Raja texts were printed in a variety of editions, and they lived on
in the world of the shadow theatre as "the" authoritative texts that both
validated and enriched shadow play traditions. Javanese intellectuals and
puppeteers came to consider Pustaka Raja texts to be the major source
(*babon*) of shadow theatre plays by the first decades of the twentieth
century.[67] Contemporary puppeteers from Solo and the surrounding vil-

pp. 225–32, summarizes Dutch attitudes toward Ranggawarsita's *Pustaka Raja* and suggests that the texts can best be understood within prophetic genres of Javanese writings.
In several personal communications in July 1995, Alan Feinstein helped to clarify many
of these issues for me.
   64. Padmosusastro, *Serat Pustaka Radja Purwa*, vol. 6 (Ngajogjakarta: N. P. Voeren H.
Boening, 1906), p. 1; Day, "Meanings of Change in the Poetry of Nineteenth-century
Java," 223–24.
   65. Florida, *Javanese Literature in Surakarta Manuscripts*, 1:154–72.
   66. If one looks through Clara van Groenendael's very useful bibliography of mostly
Dutch, English, Javanese, and Indonesian scholarship on the *wayang* theatre (*Wayang
Theatre in Indonesia: An Annotated Bibliography*), out of 564 entries she does not mention
one *Pustaka Raja Purwa* text, although she makes one or two references to the existence of
these texts, and their author Ranggawarsita. In contrast, both Pigeaud (*Literature of Java*,
1:170–71) and Florida (*Javanese Literature in Surakarta Manuscripts*, 1:154–72) list numerous editions of these texts, showing that Javanese considered them important
enough to copy and recopy over many decades. Florida's listings, drawn as they are
from extant manuscripts in collections in Java rather than Leiden, are the most authoritative source for the influence of these texts.
   67. Poerwoto Prawirohardjo, "Kesoesasteraan Indonesia Djawa," *Poedjangga Baroe* 1,
nos. 6, 7–12 (1933–34).

lages, familiar with modern educational priorities, assert that the stories they perform are recorded in these great texts—most of whose extant versions live in palace libraries—although many puppeteers may never have seen the texts. The relationship between Ranggawarsita's *Pustaka Raja Purwa* and the stories of the shadow puppet theatre will be discussed in detail in chapter 4.

This struggle in colonial Java between indigenous and Dutch historical conceptions reflected the increasing Dutch need to redefine the boundaries of Javanese historical writing to fit within certain Dutch evolutionary worldviews. If the Dutch decided what was and what was not Javanese history, they were, in effect, colonizing Javanese intellectual as well as geographical domains. Shadow tales could not be history because they were obviously myths, and post-Enlightenment European scholars were engaged in a scientific project of distinguishing myth from history. Ranggawarsita's works were dismissed *because* he refused to accept the colonial categories of his day. But when the shaping and writing down of Javanese Ramayana and Mahabharata traditions coincided with the rise of Dutch Ethnology, scholarly views of the connections between these stories and history began to change. In 1877, a Chair of Geography and Ethnology of the East Indian Archipelago was established at Leiden.[68] Instead of the mid-nineteenth-century dismissal of the connections between myth— as represented in the shadow theatre repertoire—and history, by the 1890s the shadow theatre came to be seen by Dutch ethnologists as a rich source of ancient "Hindu-Javanese" traditions.[69] Although Dutch scholars had reacted negatively to Ranggawarsita's Book of Kings, a second mid-

68. P. E. de Josselin de Jong, *Structural Anthropology in the Netherlands: A Reader* (The Hague: M. Nijhoff, 1977), p. 4.

69. In her dissertation on Yogyanese *wayang wong—wayang* theatre with human actors—Jennifer Lindsay suggests that the evolutionary and racialist thinking of the late nineteenth and early twentieth centuries made the Dutch scholars appreciate "pure" traditions more than syncretic ones. In the world of music that Lindsay describes, this meant that the Javanese *gamelan* would be valued more highly than the Portuguese-influenced *kroncong* music popular in Batavia, especially among Eurasians. "Klasik Kitsch or Contemporary: A Study of the Javanese Performing Arts" (Ph.D. diss., University of Sydney, 1985), p. 10. If we extend Lindsay's argument to shadow theatre traditions, it could account for the marked Dutch preference for what they considered the trunk stories, *lakon jejer*, over the branch stories or *lakon carangan* of the repertoire. Certainly many Dutch colonial scholars deplored the Javanese deviations from what they considered to be the "authentic" Indian Ramayana and Mahabharata stories.

Colonial Discourse and Shadow Theatre

nineteenth-century text fared better in the Dutch scholarly world because it linked the shadow theatre to the Javanese courts.

The influence of the European search for origins and chronologies was evident in the *Serat Sastramiruda* of B.K.P. Kusumadilaga, the son of K.G.P. Adipati Arja Mangkoeboemi and grandson of Pakubuwana III.[70] This text gave a supposed chronological history of the development of the *wayang* theatre, connecting that history with the courts by documenting the creation of new puppets by various rulers from Java's past, and set up certain standards for the musical and poetic fragments that are woven into each performance.[71] I have already shown in the previous chapter that it was not uncommon to attribute the ability to perform a shadow play to rulers of the Javanese realm, yet the surviving evidence also points to strong village traditions. Perhaps scholars need to question the vision

70. Soeharda Sastrasoewignja, in "Hal Wajang Poerwa dan Djalan-djalan oentoek Memperbaharoeinja," *Poedjangga Baroe* 2, nos. 1–4 (1934–35), supplies the information on Kusumadilaga's connections to PB III (p. 193). When I was living in Leiden in 1982, I purchased a copy of te Mechelen's *Drie-en-Twintig Schetsen van Wayang-Stukken* (1879) that presumably had belonged to G.A.J. Hazeu, Dutch Adviser for Native Affairs in the early twentieth century and a scholar of Javanese *wayang* literature. On the front page of this book that bears Hazeu's name is a note that says the *lakon* or *wayang* stories were originally collected by Kusumadilaga. The note also mentions that the *dhalang* of the *lakon* was named Sastramiroeda. Since 1982, I have come across several other books imprinted with Hazeu's stamp and filled with presumably his handwritten notes. The most interesting is a copy of his dissertation, presently owned by the University of Michigan Library, that is filled with handwritten notes that seem to be plans for a revised edition of the work. I believe that these notes, in the same handwriting as the other two books I have seen, are the notes of Hazeu himself. A contributing factor to this assessment is the generally low regard bestowed upon Hazeu by the Indonesianist and Javanist scholars at Leiden. In March of 1993, I was told by Professor Hendrik Maier, Chair of Malay and Indonesian Languages at Leiden, that Hazeu was not considered important enough by Maier and A. Teeuw to include in their edited work *Honderd Jaar Studie van Indonesie 1850–1950 Levensbeschrijvingen van twaalf Nederlandse onderzoekers* (Den Haag: B. V. Drukkerij en Uitgoverij Smits, 1976), which gathers the obituaries of the most famous and well-respected of the Leiden scholars like Roorda, Brandes, Snouck Hurgronje, Krom, and van Vollenhoven. Hazeu snuck in anyway; he wrote the obituary for his mentor H. Kern.

71. K.P.H. Kusumadilaga, *Serat Sastramiruda* (Jakarta: Proyek Penerbitan Buku Sastra Indonesia Dan Daerah, Departemen Pendidikan & Kebudayaan, 1981); a different edition of this work was first published in *Bramartani* 1877–78. J. J. Ras, in "The Historical Development of the Javanese Shadow Theatre," *Review of Indonesian and Malaysian Studies* 10 (1976): 58–60, gives a summary of the contents of this text and its connections with historical Javanese rulers. I cite passages from the text in the next chapter.

of the development of the shadow theatre tradition that this court text portrayed.

Kusumadilaga and Court Performance Traditions

Many Javanese written traditions are connected with the courts of Central Java, and evidence that will be presented below suggests that village traditions of the shadow theatre were not very different from the court traditions of Central Java before the twentieth century. Dutch scholars who have investigated the history of the shadow theatre and argued for a dominant court performance tradition usually relied on their own interpretations of the *Sastramiruda* for their information.[72] The *Sastramiruda*, however, is a court text, and one produced for very specific purposes. The *Sastramiruda* was written in approximately the same period as the *Pustaka Raja Purwa* by a nobleman with much more elevated court connections than Ranggawarsita. If the *Pustaka Raja Purwa* was assumed to be fictional, why should the information in the *Sastramiruda* be accepted at face value? I see the writing of the *Sastramiruda* as an attempt by Kusumadilaga and his colleagues and friends at the court of Surakarta in the second half of the nineteenth century to satisfy Dutch scholarly standards for the future of the shadow theatre tradition and to attempt to place village performance traditions under the textual domination of the Solonese courts.

Looking at other scattered sources that document the Javanese past, there is little evidence of a preeminent court performance style, or even mention of refined court performances, before the late nineteenth century. I noted in the previous chapter that the *Nagarakertagama* from the fourteenth century never mentions shadow theatre performances at court.[73] The *Serat Babad Nitik Mangkunagaran* (1780–91), the diary of a female

72. L. Serrurier, *De Wajang Poerwa: eene ethnologische studie* (Leiden: E. J. Brill, 1896); G.A.J. Hazeu, *Bijdrage tot de Kennis van het Javaansche Tooneel*; Th. Pigeaud, *Javaanse Volksvertoningen*; Ras, "The Historical Development of the Javanese Shadow Theatre"; V. M. Clara van Groenendael, *The dalang behind the wayang*. Ras, in "The Historical Development of the Javanese Shadow Theatre," pp. 71–72, notes that the Surakarta style of shadow theatre performance was a product of attention devoted to the performing arts at the courts of the Susuhunan and the Mangkunagaran in the nineteenth century.

73. Th. Pigeaud, *Java in the Fourteenth Century*, vol. 4 (The Hague: M. Nijhoff, 1962).

Colonial Discourse and Shadow Theatre

soldier connected to the late eighteenth-century court of Mangkunagara I, known for his devotion to Islam, briefly mentions various types of performances held at court in honor of the birthday of the prince.

> Then *ringgit tiyang* [was staged],
> taking turns with *sarimpi* dance,
> and dancers danced before the screen,
> all were petite and beautiful maidens.
> Open-mouthed with wonder was everyone watching,
> the spectators were astounded.
> Then the beautiful female *bedhaya* dance intervened.
> . . . .
> They held entertainment all day long.
> In the late afternoon there was *ringgit* performance
> as well as continuous *taledhekan*.
> In the morning they staged *ringgit* once again—
> the leather puppet show. And also
> blankets were distributed to soldiers.
> At night *wayang wong* dance drama was performed again.
> Then in the morning there were *taledhekan*.[74]

This passage is interesting for several reasons: it shows that even at a Javanese court known for its particular devotion to Islam, Ramayana and Mahabharata stories were frequently performed; also, it indicates that shadow theatre may not have been performed in the all-night performance style common today; lastly, shadow theatre seems to be grouped with performance traditions like *taledhekan*, also known as *tayuban*, a rowdy dance party featuring young male or female dancers for hire, that was certainly not known as high art, rather than with the more refined court dances of *sarimpi* and *bedhaya*.

74. *Ringgit tiyang* is a *wayang* play performed with human actors, *sarimpi* and *bedhaya* are court dances, *taledhekan* are male dance parties where special women are hired to dance and flirt with men, and *wayang wong* is the low Javanese term for *ringgit tiyang*. This passage from the *Serat Babad Nitik Mangkunagaran* was translated by Sumarsam in chapter 1 of his *Gamelan: Cultural Interaction and Musical Development in Central Java* (Chicago: University of Chicago Press, 1995). For further commentary and translations from this interesting diary of a female scribe and soldier at the court of Mangkunagararan I, see A. Kumar, "Javanese Court Society and Politics in the Late Eighteenth Century: The Record of a Lady Soldier, Parts I, II," *Indonesia* 29, 30 (1980): 1–46, 67–111.

In his detailed investigation of court life in Yogyakarta in the same period, the well-respected scholar of seventeenth- and eighteenth-century Java M. C. Ricklefs never mentions a shadow theatre performance held at any of the Central Javanese courts.[75] The Serat Centhini, compiled in the early nineteenth century, describes many shadow theatre performances which take place outside of the courts, except for the Partadewa and Murwakala performances by the dhalang Pandjangmas.[76] The attention devoted to describing these *wayang* performances, however, does show great interest in the shadow theatre among the writers of the text, presumably literati connected to the Kraton Solo. Carey gives the most interesting and complete information on the different types of theatrical performances held at the court of Yogyakarta in the early nineteenth century.[77] He notes that according to the *Babad Ngayogyakarta*,[78] the most popular type of *wayang* performance was *wayang wong*, or plays with human actors, but at the wedding of Sultan Hamengkubuwana IV in 1816, three full-length *wayang kulit* performances were given as well as performances of *wayang gedhog* (Panji stories), *wayang krucil* (Damar Wulan stories using flat wooden puppets), *wayang jemblung* (Islamic Menak stories), *wayang topeng* (masked dance), and *wayang gambyong* (wooden *wayang golek* puppet brought out by a female dancer at the end of a *wayang kulit* perfor-

75. Ricklefs, *Jogjakarta under Sultan Mangkubumi*. In his newest work on Java in the late seventeenth and early eighteenth centuries, *War, Culture and Economy in Java 1677–1726*, pp. 9 and 207, Ricklefs mentions that "higher culture," which included *wayang*, was known at the mid-seventeenth century court of Mataram. He bases this observation on the report of R. van Goens, who traveled to the court of Mataram five times during the years 1648–54, but he does not clarify what is meant by *wayang* or *ringgit* in this period. He also notes that a Dutch Commissioner was entertained by dance and *wayang* (shadow puppet) at the court of Amangkurat IV in 1723. Again, no information is given about what *wayang* was at that time. As usual, *wayang* is accepted as a stable performance genre even though many types of entertainment were grouped under the name of *wayang*, at least in the early nineteenth century. See below.

76. Sumahatmaka, *Ringkasan Centini* (Jakarta: PN Balai Pustaka, 1981); personal communication from Alan Feinstein, 24 May 1995.

77. Carey, *The Cultural Ecology of Early Nineteenth Century Java*, pp. 7–11. For further descriptions of theatrical performances held in Surakarta and Yogyakarta in 1828, see "Journal of an Excursion to the Native Provinces on Java in the Year 1828, during the War with Dipo Negoro," *Journal of the Indian Archipelago and Eastern Asia Series* 1, no. 7 (1853): 1–19, 138–58, 225–46, 358–78.

78. Vol. I, XCVIII 36–39, p. 401.

Colonial Discourse and Shadow Theatre

mance). This list clearly emphasizes that the word *wayang* cannot be used without further qualification. Carey also reports that when the widow of Sultan Hamengkubuwana IV was ill in 1825, she stayed awake and *read wayang* stories for two nights. Although Carey notes that many court figures would try to perform as *dhalang*, he suggests the best *dhalang* often came from the villages.[79] There seems to be a legacy from Hayam Wuruk in the fourteenth century through Pakubuwana IV in the early nineteenth century and up to Soekarno in the twentieth century of the rulers of Java enhancing their reputations and power by showing off their skills with the puppets.

The courts of the eighteenth and nineteenth centuries certainly had their own collections of *wayang* puppets, but these puppets were only supposed to be used by the rulers of the realm.[80] The courts also had special ranks of puppeteers (*panakawan kothak*) who aired (*ngisis*) the puppets once every thirty-five days. The Solonese author/journalist/pub-

79. Carey, *Cultural Ecology of Early Nineteenth Century Java*, p. 10; Carey, "The Role of *Wayang* in the Dipanagara War." Carey, in *Cultural Ecology*, p. 10, discusses the passion of Sunan Pakubuwana III (1788–1820) for both *wayang kulit* and *wayang wong* and how he would sometimes perform as a *dhalang* himself or encourage family members to dance *wayang topeng*. T. E. Behrend, in "The Serat Jatiswara: Structure and Change in a Javanese Poem 1600–1930" (Ph.D. diss., Australian National University, 1987), pp. 258–59, notes that Pakubuwana IV, who ruled in the early nineteenth century, is credited with being interested in *wayang* of all sorts and writing *wayang gedhog lakon*. He also refers to the collection of titles of *lakon* produced by Redi Tanaya, a *dhalang* connected to the courts. Florida, in *Javanese Literature in Surakarta Manuscripts*, 1:217, also mentions Pakubuwana IV's inclination to perform as a *dhalang*. She notes an early nineteenth-century collection of *wayang purwa* plays that were supposedly used by this ruler. On the other hand, Florida also notes (p. 26) that a handful of manuscripts, mostly summaries of *wayang* stories, in the collection of the Kraton Surakarta are signed by village *dhalang*.

80. Raffles, *History of Java*; Ricklefs, *Jogjakarta under Sultan Mangkubumi*. See previous note about rulers using court puppet collections, as well as discussions by Soeharda Sastrasoewignja below. From the available evidence, one might conclude that before the Dutch broke the power of the Javanese elites after the Java War, the noble families retained the services of puppeteers in the areas of Central Java under their control. Since these nobles owed allegiance to the Sultans and Sunans of Central Java, they might be required on occasion to provide the courts with entertainments as well as to entertain in their homes. The puppeteers thus relied on local elites as patrons, and it was the transfer of this patronage to the courts in the late nineteenth century that I am suggesting. Poensen's discussion of the *dhalang* of his day seems to corroborate this idea. He notes the type of services expected from the puppeteers and payments or tax concessions made by the native chiefs to their *dhalang*, in "De Wajang," pp. 204–15.

lisher R. Tanaya recounts his father's disappointment at being given the
rank of *dhalang kesepuhan* (the king's puppeteer) rather than that of *panewu*
(someone with authority over village leaders) in the 1880s.[81] The rank of
panewu was one of the highest held by *dhalang* at the end of the nineteenth
century, and *dhalang* who held this rank generally received a tax-free grant
of land, an appanage, or, after the first decade of the twentieth century, a
salary from the court.[82]

Although some of these *dhalang* with ranks at the court may have
preserved and transmitted oral and written traditions connected with the
shadow theatre, and cared for the court puppet collections, it is unclear
whether they were also skilled performers. Court texts often speak of
dhalang, but some of those called *dhalang* were dance masters, and even
those who received appanages or salaries came originally from the villages
to serve at the courts.[83] Clara van Groenendael mentions a village puppeteer who was called (*ditimbali*) to the court in 1946 to care for the court
wayang puppets, which were still believed to be very powerful (*angker*,
bobot).[84] In Java in the 1980s, the court servant who aired the puppets was a
dhalang, but he could not perform very well; his home, in his words, was
located in the *plosok* (rural area), right outside the city. The other Solonese
dhalang connected to the Kraton Solo in the 1980s was Anom Suroto.
Suroto's popularity among audiences in Central Java and Jakarta made
him eligible to be a court *dhalang*, although he, too, hailed from a village
area outside Solo. In this same way, in the past, famous puppeteers from
the villages would be called to the courts as the courts displayed and

81. Clara van Groenendael, *The dalang behind the wayang*, pp. 84–85.

82. This information comes from Clara van Groenendael, *The dalang behind the wayang*; Augusta De Wit, *Java: Facts and Fancies* (1912; Singapore: Oxford University Press,
1987); and a personal communication on 19 April 1993 from ethnomusicologist Marc
Perlman, a specialist on Central Javanese *gamelan* and *wayang* traditions.

83. Pigeaud, *Javaanse Volksvertoningen*, p. 493; Holt, *Art in Indonesia*, p. 289; Sumarsam, "Historical Contexts and Theories of Javanese Music" (Ph.D. diss., Cornell University, 1992), p. 51 n. 53; Florida, *Javanese Literature in Surakarta Manuscripts*, 7:26. Both
Pigeaud, *Javaanse Volksvertoningen*, p. 58, and Clara van Groenendael, *The dalang behind
the wayang*, p. 89, discusses a passage in *Adatrechtbundel* 23 from 1924 that mentions a
royal decree given to six types of occupations in Yogyakarta allowing these people to
levy a trade tax on other members of their respective trades. The trades mentioned were
dyer, tempe (soybean cake) maker, potter, smith, *tandak* (female dancer) master, and
dhalang. These craftspeople are said to have had the title of *lurah*, a leader or chief of the
trades, with attachments to the royal court.

84. Clara van Groenendael, *The dalang behind the wayang*, p. 80.

Colonial Discourse and Shadow Theatre

tapped the power of the puppeteers, and the reputations of the puppeteers would be enhanced through their association with the courts.

In a series of articles published in the prominent Indies Malay literary
journal *Poedjangga Baroe* in 1934 and 1935, Soeharda Sastrasoewignja recorded the accepted wisdom of the day about the transmission and development of the *wayang purwa* tradition in the nineteenth century.[85] He
states that K. G. Boeminata, the younger brother of Pakubuwana IV
(r. 1788–1820), was in charge of all the arts in the Kraton Solo from the end
of the reign of PB IV into that of PB VII (r. 1830–58). Boeminata was known
as an expert on *wayang* theatre, *gamelan* music, and dance. He commissioned two *kotak* (sets) of *wayang* puppets for the court, the famous Kyai
Djimat set of *wayang kulit* puppets and the Kyai Dewakatong set of *wayang
gedhog* puppets. These are the sets of puppets cared for to this day by the
court *dhalang*. These puppets are considered very sacred and powerful
and are never used because only the ruler is powerful enough to perform with them. According to Soeharda, they were last used by Pakubuwana IV.

Soeharda says that all of Boeminata's knowledge was given to Kusumadilaga, who by these calculations would have been in charge of *kraton* arts
from the death of Boeminata in 1833 until the reign of PB IX (r. 1861–93).
Kusumadilaga supposedly liked to give performances at the *kraton* and the
Mangkunagaran, especially the court of MN IV.[86] Soeharda states that it
was Kusumadilaga who standardized the content of *wayang kulit* performances that lasted for a whole night (*semalam suntuk*).

He arranged the one night style of *wayang* performance, fitting together its parts
with the musical pieces (*gendhing*), the mood songs (*ada-ada*) and the rest of the

85. The information in the following paragraphs comes from Soeharda Sastrasoewignja, "Hal Wajang Poerwa," *Poedjangga Baroe* 2, no. 7 (Januari 1935): 193–96. Soeharda's knowledge is based on a familiarity with Dutch sources, in particular the work of
Hazeu and Rassers, as well as with Javanese sources.

86. Soeharda, in "Hal Wajang Poerwa," p. 195, notes that Kusumadilaga was a
dhalang in addition to being a *poedjangga*, court poet or writer. But when Soeharda
discusses Kyai Redisoeta, he calls him "a real *dhalang*" (*seorang dalang jang soenggoeh-
soenggoehnja*), and records that he was responsible for putting together the story of the
lakon Irawan Rabi (The Marriage of Irawan), which Soeharda says was published by the
Bale Poetaka, although the *dhalang* was illiterate (cf. Clara van Groenendael, *The dalang
behind the wayang*, pp. 85–87). In contrast, Kusumadilaga was a writer and an adapter of
the tradition but not a *dhalang* who performed for compensation.

songs. Although the arrangement and the sequencing were not yet complete, they still remain the basis of the pattern of a *lakon*, just like what is taught at the Dhalang School at the Sriwedari Museum in Solo.[87]

Soeharda goes on to explain that when Kusumadilaga was very old, a man came from the Mangkunagaran court and asked him for all his knowledge—"interviewed him as people say today" ("menginterview, kata orang sekarang")—about *wayang* and *gamelan*. Finally all the knowledge was eventually reshaped for publication and was published in the Solonese newspaper *Bramartani* in 1877 and 1878. The transmission of the knowledge was completed when it all finally appeared in 1930 as a book called the *Serat Sastramiruda*, which has become the "kor'an" for all the *dhalang* of Surakarta and the surrounding areas. Soeharda's discussion is very useful as an understanding of received wisdom about the history of the tradition as told by a Dutch-educated Javanese intellectual in the 1930s.[88] Considering the often volatile relations between the Dutch government and members of the Solonese courts throughout the nineteenth century, the *Serat Sastramiruda* can be seen as part of the Dutch and Javanese struggle to control Javanese literary arts in the late nineteenth century.

The *Serat Sastramiruda* was acceptable to the Dutch scholars of the latter part of the nineteenth century because it did not contest colonial intellectual categories in the way that Ranggawarsita's work did. Rather than attempting to prove the popularly held belief that the *wayang* tales were indeed a type of Javanese history, the *Sastramiruda* gave rules and definitions. Like the Serat Centhini and even the Eurasian language teacher C. F. Winter's *Javaansche Zamenspraken* (1862), in which a Dutch scholar named Tuan Anu or Mr. So-and-So questions a native informant named Gunawan about the literature and customs of Java, the text uses a question

87. Soeharda Sastrasoewignja, "Hal Wajang Poerwa," p. 193.

88. Day, in "Meanings of Change in the Poetry of Nineteenth-century Java," pp. 178–83, interprets the ascendance of Boeminata in the artistic affairs of the Kraton Solo as a kind of turning point in the rise of conservative, Dutch-influenced factions in court politics, particularly when the Dutch placed Pangeran Purbaya on the throne in 1830, after the Java War. For sensitive recountings of the fall of PB VI and his replacement by PB VII, see Florida's *Writing the Past, Inscribing the Future*, as well as Day, "Meanings of Change." For different descriptions of the *Sastramiruda*, see Ras, "The Historical Development of the Javanese Shadow Theatre," and Clara van Groenendael, *The dalang behind the wayang*.

Colonial Discourse and Shadow Theatre

and answer technique. Even more interesting, a telling of the *lakon* Palasara that is included as the second part of the *Sastramiruda* is one of the
three *lakon* that was annotated and published in Holland by Roorda in
1869; it was then freely translated into Dutch by Poensen in 1872 and
summarized in Javanese script by te Mechelen in 1879.[89] It is quite useful to
look at the opening question posed by Sastramiruda to Kusumadilaga in
the text.

First please explain who it was who created the *wayang purwa*, and from whence
comes the custom of ear-piercing for both male and female puppets? And how was
the name *wayang purwa* determined?[90]

Here are two very sweeping questions with a seemingly trivial question
sandwiched in between. The questioner Sastramiruda wants to know who
created the *wayang* and how it received its name. These seem fitting
questions to open a manual that is going to lay out the conventions and the
history of the shadow theatre and discuss other Central Javanese theatrical
traditions as well. But why the non sequitur about earrings? The significance of the question emerges in its answer. Both male and female puppets have pierced ears because King Jayabhaya, the supposed creator of
the *wayang kulit* puppets, took as his model the statues (*arca*) of Indian-
influenced art that displayed clothing styles and jewelry of people from
India (*wong bangsa Hindhu*), thus reconstructing and confirming the association of the shadow theatre with "Hindu-Javanese" plastic arts and
literature.

The *Serat Sastramiruda*, in elaborating the rules or the proscriptions for
courtly *wayang* performances, seemed opportunely to respond to many of
the Dutch criticisms of the *wayang* described below.[91] One of the rules
stated that *dhalang* should not make lewd jokes (*aja bebanyolan ingkang
lekoh*) and they should not bore their audiences. Since raunchy humor is

89. See also Hazeu, *Bijdrage tot de Kennis van het Javaansche Tooneel*, pp. 156–68, where
he attempts to explain the history of the story of Palasara by comparing the text of Roorda
and the *pakem* (summary) of Ch. te Mechelen, "Drie-en-twintig schetsen van wajang-
stukken (Lakon's) gebruikelijk bij de vertooningen der Wajang-Poerwá op Java," *Verhandelingen van het Koninklijk Bataviaasch Genootschap voor Kunsten en Wetenschappen* 40 (1879):
1–437, no. 5 of the 23, with a Sanskrit text of the Mahabharata from Calcutta dated 1834
and a Balinese manuscript found by H. Kern.

90. Kusumadilaga, *Serat Sastramiruda*, pp. 12 and 158.

91. Ibid., pp. 51–52 and 187–88.

the staple of many performances, these rules seem quite contradictory. Several other "rules" that responded to Dutch criticisms include admonitions to the *dhalang* to understand the Kawi words of the *suluk* or mood songs, to be familiar with written texts containing *wayang* lore, and not to change the stories or the order of the stories.[92] As I note in chapter 4, these rules seem not only foreign to the ways in which the puppeteers themselves talk about their traditions, but even inimical to them.

That the *Serat Sastramiruda*, like Ranggawarsita's Book of Kings, was merely the product of its time and not an ancient Javanese text did not seem to trouble the Dutch scholarly community of the late nineteenth century. Even though the *Sastramiruda* dated the puppets by using Ranggawarsita's Javanese chronogram-riddles (*candra sengkala*), the text satisfied the Dutch scholarly search for "authenticity" because it dated the puppets rather than treating the myths as historical events. The *Sastramiruda* also served a useful purpose in perpetuating the Dutch myth of Hindu-Javanese decadence. It recorded the rules that the puppeteers supposedly had forgotten or continually bungled; if the puppeteers followed the rules, the shadow theatre could be returned to its former glory.

To understand this text in the context of later nineteenth-century Javanese society, we might view the writing of it as an attempt by the Solonese courts to tap the power of village puppeteers and to begin the process of reconstructing the shadow theatre tradition that would continue into the twentieth century and culminate in the 1920s with the opening of the court schools for puppeteers. Puppeteers were known for their command of the unseen forces of nature through knowledge of mystical formulas (like the *sastrajendra* discussed in the preceding chapter) and were often called to the courts to commemorate auspicious occasions. By the second half of the nineteenth century, Dutch control had deprived the courts of all their military functions, and most of their political ones, and had directed their energies to elaborate weddings and the cultivation of artistic traditions.[93] The new Dutch scholarly interests, activities, and aesthetic preferences

92. One of Winter's criticisms of the *dhalang* in his above-mentioned *Javaansche Zamenspraken*, 3d ed., vol. 1 (Amsterdam: Muller, 1862), p. 152, was that they failed to understand the words of their *suluk* or mood songs, which were usually taken from Old Javanese poetry.

93. Cf. Day, "Meanings of Change in the Poetry of Nineteenth-century Java"; Pemberton, *On the Subject of "Java."*

Colonial Discourse and Shadow Theatre

gave these artistic endeavors additional prestige in the final decades of the century.

Nineteenth-Century Dutch Descriptions of Javanese Shadow Theatre

Although quite a number of Dutch scholars began expressing their views on the shadow theatre by the mid-nineteenth century, few of them had actually been to Java to witness a shadow play. Hazeu wrote his famous study of the origins of the *wayang* before he ever set foot in Java—although he subsequently spent twenty years there; Roorda never went to Java; Serrurier never went to Java; and although H. Kern was born in Java, his major time in Asia as an adult was spent in India, where he lived for two years. Several of the Dutchmen who actually saw and described the Javanese shadow theatre in the latter part of the nineteenth century were either civil servants like H. C. Humme or missionaries like C. Poensen.[94] But many Dutch scholars felt qualified to comment on the art form that they had never seen. Taco Roorda, for instance, gained his information about Javanese *wayang* from the Eurasians Winter and Wilkens, mentioned above, and from his missionary colleague Gericke. Roorda prefaced his Javanese text of three *wayang* stories with the following opinion:

For knowledge of the language as well as of the morals and beliefs of the Javanese folk the *wajang* stories are surely to be considered of very great interest. The subject of those stories, though, cannot keep the interest of us Europeans, and neither can we find pleasure in the usually insipid and obscene jokes by which the *dhalang* seeks to provoke a laugh from his listeners; but the language that the *dhalang* himself speaks, and the conversations that he has his characters carry on, are a rich source for Javanese language and ethnology.[95]

94. Fasseur, in *De Indologen*, p. 225, notes that both Humme and Poensen were employed in the *docentenkorps* at Delft as language teachers after their return from the Indies. Ch. te Mechelen was another important nineteenth-century observer of *wayang* theatre whose ideas are discussed in chapter 4. He is not mentioned in Fasseur's *De Indologen*, but he seems to have been an independent scholar of Javanese literary arts.

95. T. Roorda, "De lotgevallen van Raden Pandji, volgens de Javaansche wajang-verhalen," *Bijdragen tot de taal-, land- en Volkenkunde van Nederlandsch-Indie*, Niewe Serie, 1863: 1–65. I obtained this passage of Taco Roorda from Poensen, "De Wajang," pp. 160–61, where he quotes several passages from Taco Roorda and other scholars. Although

The missionary Poensen quoted the earlier writings of both Roorda and Wilkens in his interesting study of 1872–73.[96] Poensen's opinions about the *wayang*, based as they were on several years in Java, are particularly useful for gaining an understanding of the workings of *wayang* traditions in the 1860s and 1870s. Although stationed in Kedhiri in East Java, Poensen was familiar with court and urban as well as village puppeteers and had read much of the available literature of the shadow theatre in both Dutch and Javanese. Unfortunately, Poensen's opinion of the *wayang purwa* plays he came to know quite well was not very high.

And we cannot but regret how, especially in the desa [villages], the *dhalang* in general think much too little of this [serious] sort of listeners, and for them and others their recitations are not organized enough; indeed, on the contrary, are way more trivial than serious, insipid and vapid instead of witty and true, and already have fallen far beneath the standards of decency and delicacy. It's also a pity that they [the puppeteers] are not developed or educated enough to study and rework the available materials in such a way that their recitations get more real poetic value, more pleasing coherence and variety of expression. The wajang could become a strong and suitable means of refinement and aesthetic cultivation; now however, for many, they do more harm than good.[97]

Poensen continued:

And look, too, at the prominent lack indicated in those speeches of the *dhalang*. That exaggeration appears in the fables can be forgiven; that impossibilities happen in them is still bearable, but that the art does not exert any efforts in order to communicate spirit, learning, truth, and naturalness to all; portrays its images without nobility or grace and remains estranged from real and pure poetic repre-

---

Poensen gives the citation Roorda, *Bijdragen tot de Taal-, Land- en Volkenkunde*, Niewe Serie, 1863: 1–65, as the source of this quote, I found a slightly different passage in Roorda's "De Lotgevallen van Raden Pandji, volgens de Javaansche wajang verhalen," *Bijdragen tot de Taal-, Land- en Volkenkunde*, zevende deel (1864): 1–65, at p. 65: "Nobody would attribute aesthetic value to it [the Pandji story] because it appears too unnatural, but it is a contribution to the knowledge of the content and purpose of wajang stories, about which people may ask if these [stories] fulfill the role of our theatre for the Javanese or are just puppet shows, and even then puppet shows for grown-up people for whom the most important thing is sensual pleasure."

96. Poensen, "De Wajang," pp. 160–61.

97. Ibid., pp. 152–53.

sentation . . . all of this makes us seek neither aesthetic pleasure nor knowledge in these dramas and regret that they contain no incentives or stimulus even for the people themselves. See, after we have come to learn about the people, all this does not surprise us; the contrary would surprise us much more. Surely the *wajang* also could be a genuine mirroring of the spiritual life of the people, a people without history, insofar as that history has not been written down.[98]

The fact that the Javanese had no written history seemed to be a problem for Poensen, but he acknowledged that they might have had a history which had not yet been written. Poensen even defended the Javanese for their belief that their history was, in fact, told through the shadow theatre tradition and argued that the *wayang* should be of interest even for Dutch writers of Javanese history.

But our credulous native shall indeed not apply [any] critique to them [the stories]. How could all the histories not be truthful? Are they not written down? Are they not told as much in the princely palace as by the lowliest of the King's subjects? And did not father and grandfather know how to tell them in the same way as they are still being recited today? And why would we begrudge the Javanese for allowing themselves to be thrilled by the miraculous?[99]

Poensen then discussed the significance of the plays for patrons and audiences and came to the somewhat startling conclusion that somehow the Javanese had managed to combine their belief in the *wayang* theatre with their religious observances as Muslims.

If the *wajang*-party is a pleasing entertainment for the guest, for the host it usually has a deeper and more serious meaning. The reader, who is quite familiar with the position of people at about the same level of civilization as the Javanese, will not be surprised if we draw his attention to how religious consciousness, or if people prefer, superstition, has also gained control of this play, and how holding a *wajang* performance is viewed as a religious, or rather a pious action.

Poensen admitted after spending years in Java that the Javanese really were Muslims and unlikely to convert to Christianity, although he never believed that Islam could satisfy the real needs of the human soul.[100] He

98. Ibid., pp. 155–56.
99. Ibid., pp. 161–62.
100. Steenbrink, *Dutch Colonialism and Indonesian Islam*, p. 103.

was thus conflicted in his opinions about Javanese Islam. On the one hand he stated:

The Javanese are all (with an unimportant exception) *Mohammedans*. This is what the government says and what the natives themselves say, as well as what reality teaches us . . . and the pesantren and the pilgrimage are continually spreading a better understanding of the true spirit and the essence of the [*sic*] Islam. . . .

Then a few sentences later he qualified these views:

And although they [the masses] continue to live in stupidity, heresy, and poverty, they in fact know, especially in the eastern and southern parts of the island, little more about Islam than the circumcision of the children, fasting, not to eat pork. . . .

But then he returned to his prescient main point:

But all this ignorance and foolishness will gradually diminish, and this is already to be noticed in some classes. The result will be that the masses will become stronger in their Islamic beliefs and its teachings will be better known. In short, the people will become better Mohammedans.[101]

Poensen was, in fact, one of the first scholars to document the distinction which he found the Javanese to draw between *bangsa poetihan* and *bangsa abangan*, the white and red groups of Javanese Muslims, an idea that would be expanded and popularized in American scholarship in the 1960s by Clifford Geertz.[102] Poensen drew a second distinction between the formal or outer life of a people and their inner soul, itself a very Islamic idea. The Dutch in Holland were Christian both inwardly and outwardly, but the Javanese were only Islamic outwardly while their inner soul was really concerned with calling on nature spirits for protection. Even the orthodoxy of the so-called *bangsa poetihan* could be questioned, according to Poensen.

If Poensen's data came from Central and East Java, Humme's work on the *wayang* comes from the western part of Central Java known as Banyu-

101. These last three quotes on Javanese Islam come from *Brieven over den Islam uit de binnenlanden van Java* (Leiden: Brill, 1886, pp. 2–8, 13–17), as excerpted in *Indonesia: Selected Documents on Colonialism and Nationalism*, ed. and trans. by Chr. L. M. Penders (St. Lucia, Queensland: University of Queensland Press, 1977), pp. 242–43.

102. Geertz, *Religion of Java*. The "bangsa poetihan" were what Geertz called *santri* or orthodox Muslims, and the "bangsa abangan" were the so-called nominal Muslims.

mas, or possibly from the western *pasisir* region of Tegal.[103] As a civil servant rather than a scholar, Humme was very apologetic about his translation of the shadow play *Abiasa* that he had been encouraged to undertake by H. Kern. Professor of Sanskrit and Javanese at Leiden, Kern found the manuscript in the Leiden archives and gave it to Humme to work on after the latter returned from his service with the administrative corps in the 1870s with a good command of Javanese.[104]

I referred above to Ranggawarsita's dilemma: he seemed to be doing what the Dutch scholars around him were doing in his attempt to chronicle the *wayang* stories, but his work was rejected as inauthentic. Yet the choice of *lakon* for documentation and translation in the latter part of the nineteenth century shows how several Dutch scholars seemed intent upon putting the "chaos of Javanese literature" into some proper order—in fact, into a proper Indian order. As chapter 4 will show, the boundaries between what came to be known as *lakon pokok* or *lakon jejer*, trunk stories, and *lakon carangan*, branch stories, were flexible and porous. In Dutch scholarly eyes, however, *lakon pokok* were usually the stories most closely connected to Indian tellings of the Mahabharata tales. These also were the stories that the Dutch scholars translated and favored. Dutch frustrations over the Javanese lack of interest in these trunk stories became a fairly consistent theme in Dutch writings on *wayang* from the late nineteenth century into the twentieth century.

Looking at the lists of *lakon* compiled at the Kraton Solo in the early nineteenth century,[105] one sees that there is a varied selection of *lakon*, only a few of which could be designated as trunk stories if I were to accept, for the moment, a definition of trunk stories as those stories closest to Indian tellings of the tales. But in turning to the nineteenth-century Dutch scholarship on the *wayang* repertoire, it is significant that Roorda chose to publish the Javanese text of the *lakon* Palasara, mentioned above in the discussion of the *Sastramiruda*, because it told the story of the founding of

---

103. Cf. Ras, "The Historical Development of the Javanese Shadow Theatre," p. 70 n. 28; Ras calls it a West Javanese *pasisir*-style *lakon*. H. C. Humme, in *Abiåså: Een Javaansch Tooneelstuk*, (*Wajang*), ('s Gravenhage: M. Nijhoff, 1878), p. iv, states that because of the pronunciation of the "a" sound, he believes the text is either from Banyumas or Tegal.

104. Humme, *Abiåså: Een Javaansch Tooneelstuk*, (*Wajang*), p. iii.

105. Florida, *Javanese Literature in Surakarta Manuscripts*, 1:216–20.

the kingdom of Ngastina, setting the historical stage for the events that unfold in the Mahabharata stories.[106] It would seem to be no coincidence that Kern chose the *lakon* Abiasa for Humme to translate since this story follows the story of Palasara in the "historical" progression of tales. And Humme mentioned this in the notes that follow his Javanese text.[107]

Cohen Stuart's reluctantly offered translation of the Modern Javanese *Serat Bratayuda* in 1860, distasteful as it was to him, ultimately showed just how far the Javanese had degenerated from the "correct" tellings of the stories found in Indian or possibly in Old Javanese texts.[108] Although Brandes had argued against an Indian origin of the *wayang*, Hazeu, who reiterated many of Brandes's ideas, was the one who attempted to rehabilitate the shadow theatre tradition by focusing attention on Javanese creativity, although he, too, recognized the degeneration of the tradition.[109] His work was to be widely quoted by Javanese nationalists in the early twentieth century. But Humme, too, who had lived in Java, showed a strong appreciation of the extant tradition.

The *Wajang* remains within the circles of the familiar traditions because the strange and fantastic characters and their actions continue to enthrall and attract the public. [The *Dalang*] takes, therefore, an episode or a fragment from favorite fantasy-stories as the basis of his performance, observing the main traits of the most important characters and the main features of the important happenings, and then takes the freedom to embroider them a bit. Many *Dalang* faithfully follow what they have seen and heard from their colleagues or read themselves in *Lakon*. This perhaps is more a result of a lack of spirit and inventiveness than from conscientiousness.[110]

106. T. Roorda, *De wajang verhalen van Pala-Sara, Pandoe en Raden Pandji, in het Javaansch, Met aanteekeningen* ('s Gravenhage: M. Nijhoff, 1869). In Hazeu's dissertation of 1897, he also chose to devote 34 of roughly 190 pages of his text to a summary and discussion of the *lakon* Palasara, following the method put forward by his major professor H. Kern in the latter's "Eene Indische sage in Javaansche gewaad," for comparing Javanese tellings to their Indian "originals."

107. Humme, *Abiâsâ: Een Javaansch Tooneelstuk*, (*Wajang*), p. 77.

108. Clara van Groenendael, in *Wayang Theatre in Indonesia: An Annotated Bibliography*, p. 12, notes that Cohen Stuart began the tradition of comparing Javanese copies to Indian "originals" that was to continue for half a century.

109. J.L.A. Brandes, "Een Jayapattra of Acte van een Rechterlijke Uitspraak van Çaka 849," *Tijdschrift voor Taal- Land- en Volkenkunde* 32 (1889): 123–24; Hazeu, *Bijdrage tot de Kennis van het Javaansche Tooneel*.

110. Humme, *Abiâsâ: Een Javaansch Tooneelstuk*, (*Wajang*), p. 88.

Colonial Discourse and Shadow Theatre

He finally concluded on a positive but somewhat defensive note:

But that is exactly why I find the study of the *Wajang* so useful, because they introduce to us, besides the wealth of language patterns and unique expressions, the taste of the Javanese people through the poetic, humorous, and coarse fantasies of the *Dalang*.

People should not be too precise in their judgment of the *Wajang*'s absurdities and contradictions: those really don't mean very much to the *Dalang*.

To balance this brief summary of nineteenth-century Dutch discourses on the shadow theatre, I conclude this chapter by turning to material collected from several older Solonese puppeteers in interviews carried out in the early 1980s. The interviews again suggest that there were few differences between court and village shadow theatre performances before the late nineteenth century.

Javanese Memories of Older Shadow Theatre Traditions

Dutch interest in Ramayana and Mahabharata traditions—and criticism of Javanese written and performed versions of the stories—may have inspired the Javanese elites to refine or rework these traditions, or the nineteenth-century interest in shadow theatre traditions might be a continuation of interest shown by the Sultans and Sunans in both earlier and later times.[111] It was not until the early twentieth century that some Dutch-educated Javanese nationalists accepted nineteenth-century Dutch attitudes toward the shadow theatre tradition—that the tradition was degenerate and needed to be upgraded. From their attendance at the new court schools in the twentieth century, we can see that puppeteers, too, came to accept these beliefs. While both the *Pustaka Raja Purwa* and the *Serat*

111. Florida, *Javanese Literature in Surakarta Manuscripts*, 1:220, notes that B.K.P.H. Hadiwijaya, a son of Pakubuwana X, ordered a village puppeteer named Ki Gondawarsana from Ceper to write prose epitomes of fifteen *wayang* stories in 1928. In this same period, Mangkunagara VII both collected *wayang* stories and then distributed illustrated summaries of the stories in the villages. I mentioned above that in the mid-nineteenth century, Ranggawarsita and C. F. Winter were said to have collected stories from village puppeteers. This point was mentioned in several conversations with the late puppeteer and scholar R. Soetrisna in 1983 and 1984.

Sastramiruda were written in the Solonese courts, data derived from oral interviews with older Javanese puppeteers in 1983 and 1984 suggest that the effects of these texts were not limited to or solely intended for the domain of the courts. Puppeteers who had been connected with the courts in the early twentieth century, and who were heirs to oral testimonies about the late nineteenth century from older family members, paint a picture of frequent interaction between court and village puppeteers during this period. The village puppeteers were also subject to the authority of Kusumadilaga and his ideas for upgrading *wayang*.

Nyi Kenyacarita, who was in her eighties when I was in Java in 1982–84, had been a court *dhalang* in her youth. She had been summoned (*ditimbali*) to the court by Pakubuwana x (r. 1893–1939). Because she was clever, witty, attractive, and female, she was popular at the court and took part in the preparation of *lakon* for court performances. She described the relationship between village *dhalang* and the courts in the late nineteenth century as she had heard about it from her grandparents. She begins by describing how ordinary *wayang* stories were prepared for court consumption.

If something was not refined enough, not good enough, it was built up. Certain parts were decreased and others were supplemented. We were told to create stories. . . . [T]he type of stories from Pakubuwana ix's time were developed in the days of Pakubuwana x. The inferior stories were discarded and the good stories were increased. . . . In the old days, originally it was Penjenengan Dalem Gusti Kanjeng Kusumadilaga who gathered the *dhalang*. On the first day of the month of Sura, *dhalang* were called from near and far, from far and near. They were summoned and invited to a discussion, to analyze a set of stories one by one. This is what Sakri is like, Arjuna is like this, Salya is like that . . . once a year. Then afterwards they would walk home to eat and then come back to listen again, to listen to them again, then they would take another break. There was the expression *"kembul nadhah"* when Kusumadilaga would eat with the simple folk (*wong cilik*), with the *dhalang*. Then when the celebration of the first of Sura was over, those who lived far away would be given some money for their trip home, those who lived close would only get a little money.

My companion, her grandson, pressed her to explain where the *dhalang* had come from. She replied that there were some from as far away as

Banyumas and East Java, as well as those from Yogyakarta and Central Java. She said they would all get together to exchange their knowledge so that they could make their stories better. They would discuss their tellings of the stories. Then she said it was her grandfather who had been summoned to such a session.[112]

I asked other *dhalang* familiar with court life if village puppeteers were ever called to the courts. R. Soetrisna from the village area of Klathen, between Solo and Yogya, who was also a teacher at the Academy in Solo, replied that in the 1930s and 1940s there were court *dhalang* and that *dhalang* were also called from the villages.[113] Familiar with much of the Dutch scholarship on *wayang*, he said that the tradition developed simultaneously in both places, and that there were good court puppeteers and good village puppeteers ("Dados perkembangan menika janipun sareng; dados kraton gadhah dhalang sae, ing jawi ugi sampun wonten dhalang sae-sae"). I asked if *wayang* was a folk art or a court art. He replied that according to history (*manut sejarah*), it was a court art first, although it developed together in both domains. He said there was really only one tradition ("Ning carane siji"). Then Bambang Murtiyasa, an astute instructor from the Academy, said, "According to the manipulations of the historians, it was a court art first because nothing really esteemed could have developed among the people, and because the people who wrote history were from the courts."

We asked the court teacher R. Ng. Samsudjin Probohardjono whether village *dhalang* were punished for performing so-called court *lakon* outside the court.[114] He replied, "There are no writings and I have never heard of [anyone] being punished because this was not really important in the politics of the court authorities. . . . But, if someone criticized the court, this certainly could be punished. If someone made up a *wayang* play about

112. Soeharda Sastrasoewignja, in "Hal Wajang Poerwa," pp. 46–51, supports this argument in his discussion of shadow theatre history. Although he divides performance styles into three groups in the 1930s—*padalangan keraton*, *padalangan dalam kota*, and *padalangan diloear kota* (palace puppeteering, city puppeteering, and puppeteering outside the city), with the first two groups being almost indistinguishable—for the nineteenth century he notes that there was almost no difference between court *wayang* and village *wayang*.

113. Soetrisna, interview, 18 April 1984.

114. Interview, 3 May 1984.

a really bad king, this could also [be punished] but I have never heard or read of a village *dhalang* performing a story that was unusual and being punished." We also asked him if village *dhalang* were called to the courts. He replied that many were, especially if they were famous in the villages. They would be called to the courts and sometimes they would become court *dhalang*.

The information above suggests frequent interaction between court and village traditions in the late nineteenth and early twentieth centuries.[115] Famous village puppeteers would perform at the courts, bringing what they learned at court back to the villages, for even the court *dhalang* did not live at the courts. The informants indicate that by the second quarter of the twentieth century there were good puppeteers in both the courts and the villages; often those considered to be good puppeteers moved between the courts and their homes in the villages. The image arises from the interviews of an incorporation of village traditions by the courts and an attempt to smooth out the village performances, to develop them and make them better. But as Soetrisna noted above, there was only one (performance) tradition.[116]

115. Cf. Clara van Groenendael, *The dalang behind the wayang*, p. 92.

116. Pigeaud, who lived in Java in the 1920s and 1930s, speaks of a "nivellerende invloed" or leveling influence wherein folk traditions were refined in the courts and these refined styles spread back to the villages. *Javaanse Volksvertoningen*, p. 32. He argues for seeing Javanese culture as a whole and argues against drawing sharp distinctions between folk and court traditions. He attributes such distinctions to the imposition of Western intellectualism and Islamic orthodoxy, both coming from outside Java, on indigenous Javanese traditions. In the 1920s and especially the 1930s, however, certain mystical *wayang lakon* probably had esoteric versions reserved for courtly consumption. It is possible that such renderings would not have been well received in the villages, but also that the court authorities did not want these powerful stories to be performed outside the courts as their magical effects may have been thought to be too dangerous. According to the late R. Ng. Martopangrawit (interview, 1983), one such story may have been the *lakon* Semar Kuning, which contained *ilmu pengasihan* or mystical love-magic. This story was also performed outside the courts, according to other puppeteers, but there may have been a special courtly performance style. See also R. A. Sutton, "Change and Ambiguity: Gamelan Style and Regional Identity in Jogjakarta," and P. Choy, "Texts through Time: The Golek Dance of Java," both in *Aesthetic Tradition and Cultural Transmission in Java and Bali*, ed. S. Morgan and L. J. Sears, Wisconsin Monographs on Southeast Asia, no. 2 (Madison: University of Wisconsin Southeast Asia Publications, 1984); they discuss the interaction of court and folk traditions in Javanese music and dance.

Colonial Discourse and Shadow Theatre

Reflections

In the late nineteenth and early twentieth centuries, new ideas and new texts were being cultivated in Java that could replace the fading associations of the shadow theatre with the poetic traditions of ancient Java. The codification of shadow theatre traditions in the second half of the nineteenth century, as the Dutch scholars documented more and more of the repertoire, can be seen as an attempt at canon formation for the art of shadow puppeteering.[117] But the attempt to impose this canon formally upon the performers of the *wayang* tradition by Dutch-educated Javanese nationalists and their Dutch supporters throughout the first half of the twentieth century had unpredictable results. The puppeteers gained access to these new styles and standards through the medium of court schools nurtured by Dutch Ethici in the 1920s. However, as I argue in later chapters, the puppeteers did not always find these new styles useful or usable.

Clara van Groenendael, in 1986, preserved the Dutch scholarly view of the village puppeteers.

The lack of education of many popular dalangs, and as a result their unfamiliarity with the archaic poetic language (kawi), from which the language of the dalang (basa padhalangan) has borrowed a great many elements, had given rise in time to tremendous corruption of the expressions used by the dalang, as well as to all kinds of fantastic explanations of wrongly understood words and phrases.[118]

She believes that the shadow theatre was an elite tradition that became corrupted as it was let out of the courts in the first decades of the twentieth century. I am arguing that shadow theatre was always a vital village tradition that was refined in the 1920s and 1930s in response to criticisms of the tradition by Javanese nationalists and Dutch scholar-administrators and then posited as the essence of a lost high culture.

The *Pustaka Raja Purwa* of Ranggawarsita and the *Serat Sastramiruda* of Kusumadilaga, written under the early influence of Dutch scholarly efforts to document the tradition, fulfilled the need for written texts that could set

117. This observation was suggested to me in November 1994 by Professor Hendrik Maier, Chair of Indonesian and Malay at the State University of Leiden.
118. Clara van Groenendael, *The dalang behind the wayang*, p. 32.

standards for the tradition even though one text was embraced and one ignored by many Dutch aficionados of the *wayang*. As the next chapter shows, the emerging Javanese intelligentsia in the twentieth century, who had the benefit of a Dutch-language education, decided to combine the techniques of European modernity and the vigor of village performance styles to "regenerate" Javanese shadow theatre and the Ramayana and Mahabharata stories it conveyed.

As the first generations of soon-to-be Indies nationalists gained a Dutch-language education in the early twentieth century, they became more conscious of the gulf that separated them from the peasantry at the same time that they realized they needed the support of the peasantry in order to overthrow the Dutch regime. It is in the first decades of the twentieth century, under the collaborative efforts of liberal Dutch scholar-administrators, Dutch-educated Javanese nobility, and Javanese nationalists, that the village-based shadow theatre tradition appeared as a useful vehicle for drawing Javanese peasants away from the increasing influence and knowledge of Islam that the steamship and the opening of the Suez Canal enabled and that rising anticolonial feeling fueled. To combat the *kyai* and the *haji* in the countryside, the shadow theatre tradition, rather than Islam, was touted as the essence of Javanese culture by small but vocal groups of Javanese nationalists and their liberal Dutch supporters. While Dutch scholars may have been the patrons for these efforts by modernizing Javanese, the *priyayi* were consciously using the Dutch to further their own program of shaping an inclusive, secular state in which they, the *priyayi*, rather than orthodox Islamic elites, would eventually assume power. The next chapter shows how the shadow theatre tradition was used to attract the Javanese peasantry into an Indies nationalism that was not dominated by Islam.

3   Failed Narratives of the Nation

or the New "Essence" of Java?

Will the Javanese Nation disappear in the future into an Indies Nation or will it evolve into a young and powerful Nation, which stands independent among the various great and small nations of this world?[1]—Soetatmo Soeriokoesoemo

Nationalism denied the alleged inferiority of the colonized people; it also asserted that a backward nation could "modernize" itself while retaining its cultural identity. It thus produced a discourse in which, even as it challenged the colonial claim to political domination, it also accepted the very intellectual premises of "modernity" on which colonial domination was based.[2]—Partha Chatterjee

The rise and subsequent disappearance of Javanese national consciousness into a pan-Indies nationalism was interlaced with Mahabharata tales, Theosophical thought, and notions of human subjectivity brought to Java in the wake of the early twentieth-century Dutch Ethical policy. Although the autonomous human subject constituted by nineteenth-century European liberalism has been under attack since the emergence of the thought of Marx, Freud, and Nietzsche, the devastation of World War 1—the use of science and technology for human destruction—poignantly questioned the connections between the autonomous human subject and nineteenth-century ideas of progress.[3] Freudian ideas also suggested that individuals were much less in control of an autonomous

1. Soetatmo Soeriokoesoemo, "Het Javaansche Vraagstuk," *Wederopbouw* 1, no. 7 (1918): 4.
2. Partha Chatterjee, *Nationalist Thought and the Colonial World: A Derivative Discourse* (London: Zed Books, 1986), p. 30.
3. For discussions of both Javanese and European disillusionment with science and technology after World World 1, see "De Twijfel van Djanaka," *Wederopbouw* 5, nos. 1–5 (1922): 26–32, probably written by the journal's editor R.M.S. (Soetatmo) Soeriokoesoemo, and see M. Adas, "The Great War and the Decline of the Civilizing Mission," in *Autonomous Histories, Particular Truths: Essays in Honor of John R. W. Smail*, ed. Laurie J. Sears (Madison: University of Wisconsin Center for Southeast Asian Studies, 1993), pp. 101–21. Adas's essay concisely presents some of the ideas from his important book *Machines as the Measure of Men: Scientific and Technological Superiority and Ideologies of Western Dominance* (Ithaca: Cornell University Press, 1989).

"I" than had previously been thought.[4] This chapter shows how the *wayang* tradition became constituted as the "essence" of Java through the interlacing of Javanese and Dutch *mentalités* within discourses of modernity. But, as discussed in the next chapter, new constructions of shadow theatre may have exacerbated rather than eased nationalist tensions and colonial anxieties.

Doubts about progress and autonomous subjectivity were compounded in the early years of the twentieth century when the colonial rulers began to realize the implications of evolutionary theory for their colonies. Education in European languages, available to limited numbers of local elites, made these colonial subjects question their colonial status, bringing both colonial subjectivity and autonomous subjectivity into question. At the very moment that the autonomous subject was fragmenting within through the opening of the unconscious, the theoretical structures that had produced the colonial subject were coming under attack from without. If subjects were indeed autonomous and Darwinian evolution inevitable, then Asians and Africans could also achieve autonomous subjectivity, threatening the rationale for colonial rule or, at least, anticipating its demise. If, on the other hand, autonomous subjectivity was little more than a fiction held together by the will of imperious or imperial egos, colonial hierarchies were also doomed to implode, turning conqueror into victim in the fragmentation of colonial desires. In the early part of this century, colonial communities often masked these mounting fears of disintegration by strengthening hierarchies of racial and ethnic distinctions and by an uneasy paternalism, the masters preferring to see their colonial subjects as children, possibly even bright ones, who in time—maybe decades, maybe centuries—could be prepared to receive the responsibilities of rule.

Looked at in another way, the contradictions of colonial subjectivity posed equally perplexing problems for those colonial subjects newly educated in European languages. As the recipients of Dutch-, English-, or French-language educations, these eager students became subjected to

4. For evidence that the ideas of Freud were indeed circulating in the Indies, see R.M.S. (Soetatmo) Soeriokoesoemo, "Geschiedenis van Java: Gelicht uit het prea-advies van R.M.S. Soeriokoesoemo," *Wederopbouw* 5, nos. 1–5 (1922): 51–56. Although *Wederopbouw* did not have a wide circulation, it shows the dissemination of ideas that were percolating through Dutch-educated Javanese communities in the second and third decades of this century.

the thought-world of the languages they studied. They became constituted as subjects within a world of European ideas where a variety of ideological positions were introduced that disrupted the familiar hierarchies of colonizer and colonized. But at the same moment that colonial subjects were being initiated into the intricacies of European languages and ideologies, they were also exposed to its vulnerability. Postwar European disenchantment with ideas of progress and technology coincided with the rise first of Javanese and then of Indies nationalism, and of other Asian nationalisms as well. As a result, many colonial elites rejected European ideas of subjectivity that did not mesh with their own political ambitions.

Some Asian intellectuals who studied in Europe were aware of the postwar European assault on subjectivity, and different groups of Indies intellectuals responded in various ways to the implications of autonomy for their own views of the world. Was autonomous subjectivity in harmony with Islam? Was autonomous subjectivity in harmony with Javanese ideas of ruler and ruled that had been transmitted over the centuries via oral traditions and reconstituted in Dutch philological editions of ancient Javanese texts? Soetatmo Soeriokoesoemo, one of the most persuasive supporters of Javanese rather than Indies nationalism, argued in 1920 that the European concept of equality might not be in harmony with Javanese worldviews.[5] An intellectual connected to the Pakualaman minor court in Yogyakarta, Soetatmo was willing to accept fraternity (*broederschap*) in his definition of nationalism, but equality (*gelijkheid*) seemed to him a dangerous concept, particularly for the prospects of the *priyayi* class in Java.[6]

5. See Soetatmo's "Theosofie en Javaansch Nationalisme," in *Wederopbouw* 3, nos. 4–7 (1920): 73–77, where he rails against the concept of equality in his somewhat ambivalent attempt to reconcile Theosophical beliefs and nationalist thought. "The first difficulty that a beginner encounters is the word equality. O what misunderstanding has this simple word not already caused! I am even doubtful if the leaders of the theosophical society really understand this word. I have a great inclination to make a proposal to the society to leave out that word entirely." See also M. Djajadiningrat-Nieuwenhuis's recent essay on another contemporary Pakualaman intellectual, "Noto Soeroto: His Ideas and the Late Colonial Intellectual Climate," *Indonesia* 55 (1993): 41–72. Noto Soeroto did not think the parliamentary system was appropriate for Java or the Indies and put forth his own system called Aristo-Democracy.

6. In a different vein and with much greater stakes, in the late 1950s Soekarno began to rail against the tyranny of a parliamentary majority of fifty plus one per cent over the remaining forty-nine per cent. These arguments have become the philosophy that

Colonial subjects responded in different ways to notions of autonomous subjectivity.

Javanese nationalists argued in Dutch over the legacies of the Javanese past and the implications of these constructions of the past for the future of the Javanese state. Classical imagery of scabbards fitting into swords (*warangka manjing curiga*)—one of many metaphors for the union of ruler and ruled—was used to diffuse the possibility of autonomous subjectivity for the Javanese masses, reserving the possibility of subjectivity only for the educated *priyayi*, who felt it was they who had lost the most under Dutch rule.[7] The ruler represented the will of the people—"he" represented and expressed their desires and needs. If the ruler was just, he would address those needs and desires in ways that would be good for the state, for the people, and for himself. The Javanese shadow theatre offered an excellent illustration of this identity between ruler and ruled. Each shadow play began with a scene which reinforced the connections between the prosperity of the realm and the nobility and power of the ruler. Of course, these relations could be mocked by clever and subtle puppeteers—and they often were. But the imagery of rulers and their awesome power over the lives of their subjects was stressed in each shadow play performance.

Javanese nationalists like Soetatmo Soeriokoesoemo blurred the autonomy and agency of individual subjects, claiming the moral high ground over their Dutch masters by suggesting that the needs of the many should outweigh the rights of the individual, unless, of course, the individual was working on a higher spiritual plane that would be incomprehensible to the

---

undergirds the New Order state of Indonesia, where Army leaders insist that democracy as defined in the "West" is not in harmony with the interests of the Indonesian people. Although similarities with several of Soekarno's ideas can be found in the thought of these early twentieth-century intellectuals, Soetatmo and Noto Soeroto were trying to protect the interests of the *priyayi* class. By the late 1920s, Soekarno was seriously engaged with several European ideological positions as he tried to find a synthesis that would fit the challenge of Indies nationalism, but, by the late 1950s, Soekarno's rhetoric had turned definitely against the "West."

7. See Soemarsaid Moertono, *State and Statecraft in Old Java*, for discussions of Javanese kingship and the use of shadow theatre imagery to express the relations between ruler and ruled. A Javanese scholar who grew up with a rich understanding of the world of shadow theatre traditions, Moertono was required by the rules of academic writing to authorize his work with studies on *wayang* by Dutch scholars who might never have seen a *wayang* play.

Failed Narratives or the New "Essence"?

masses.[8] Dutch-educated Javanese intellectuals were influenced by liberal and radical streams of European thought that came into prominence in the Indies and throughout the world in the first decades of the twentieth century at the same time that liberal and mystically inclined Europeans were flocking toward the religions of the "exotic" East. The blending of European and Javanese knowledges gave rise to new ways of thinking and talking about the *wayang* theatre in Java. These modernist vocabularies allowed Javanese intellectuals to use the *wayang* theatre to build a case for Javanese or Indies nationalism in their Dutch scholarly writings, and new ways of talking and thinking about ethnicity and nationality interpellated European scholars and Javanese nationalists as subjects of these new discourses.[9] In the end, the *wayang* tales failed to serve as national narratives just as Javanese nationalism failed, and discourses about the shadow theatre began to pass from Dutch into the Malay language, which was adopted as the vehicle of a rising Indies nationalism.

Theosophy and Javanese Nationalism

There have been a number of scholarly references to the influence of Theosophical thought in the Indies.[10] Not only Soewardi Soerjaningrat (Ki Hadjar Dewantara), but also Tjipto Mangoenkoesoemo, H. S. Tjokroaminoto, and Soekarno came into contact with Theosophical ideas in their

8. See K. Tsuchiya, *Democracy and Leadership: The Rise of the Taman Siswa Movement in Indonesia* (Honolulu: University of Hawaii Press, 1987), chapter 7, and F. Jameson, "Modernism and Imperialism," in *Nationalism, Colonialism, and Literature*, T. Eaglton, F. Jameson, and E. Said (Minneapolis: University of Minnesota Press, 1990), pp. 43–66.

9. The term *interpellate* is used in the work of R. Barthes, L. Althusser, S. Hall, and others and has come into wider academic use by theorists who write about media and mass culture. The word means to hail someone within an ideological frame; the person who is forced to respond to that hailing may remain unaware of the ideological implications that answering the hail entails. See L. Althusser, "Ideology and Ideological State Apparatuses," in *Lenin and Philosophy*, trans. Ben Brewster (New York: Monthly Review Press, 1971), for extensive discussion of the term. Daniel Lev, a scholar of Indonesian law, informed me that the term comes out of parliamentary debates, where it indicates an obligation to respond.

10. Ethnomusicologist Marc Perlman has looked at the impact of Theosophy on the *wayang* repertoire, in "Theosophy in Java and the Re-Indicization of the Wayang Kulit," and Tsuchiya, in *Democracy and Leadership*, has drawn attention to the impact of Theosophy on the major leaders of the early nationalist movement in the Indies.

formative years through their association with the Dutch Theosophist D. van Hinloopen Labberton and his wife. Hinloopen Labberton had taken over as editor of the Dutch Indies Theosophical journal *Theosofisch Maandblad van Nederlandsch-Indië* by 1912 and was president of the Indies Theosophical Society from 1912 to 1923; Tjipto Mangoenkoesoemo and other young nationalist leaders were heavily influenced by the Hinloopen Labbertons and by their Theosophical beliefs.[11]

As a religious movement, Theosophy began in 1875 in America and quickly spread to Europe and Australia.[12] Interestingly, women played a major role in the movement; Helena Blavatsky, Annie Besant, and Alice Bailey were among the most prominent.[13] Blavatsky was said to have

11. Tsuchiya, *Democracy and Leadership*, p. 43. Takashi Shiraishi, *An Age in Motion: Popular Radicalism in Java, 1912–1926* (Ithaca: Cornell University Press, 1990), pp. 122 and 126; Ki Hadjar Dewantara, *Dari Kebangungan Nasional sampai Proklamasi Kemerdekaan: Kenang-kenangan Ki Hadjar Dewantara* (Djakarta: N. V. Pustaka Penerbit "Endang," 1952), p. 227; M. C. Ricklefs, *A History of Modern Indonesia since c. 1300*, rev. ed., p. 165. Tjipto's third and last wife, a Eurasian woman named Vogel, who was both a dedicated Theosophist and a member of the radical Indies Partij, also may have strengthened his interest in Theosophy. Dewantara notes, however, that Tjipto was given a strong Islamic upbringing by his father (p. 227). When the two famous nationalist leaders were living in Bandung in 1913, Tjipto would organize readings every "malam Selasa Kliwon," an evening that occurred once every thirty-five days in the Javanese calendar and that was of particular significance for Javanist religious practice; the readings ranged from the Bhagavad Gita to "Maulid Nabi Muhammad," the *Babad Tanah Djawi*, and stories about the "Wali Sanga"—the nine saints who supposedly brought Islam to Java. See also Tjipto's defense of Pangeran Dipanagara, the Yogyanese prince who rallied the Javanese under the banner of Islam and led the Java War against the Dutch (1825–30), in "Iets over den Javaan, zijn Geschiedenis en zijn Ethiek," a speech he gave to the first Indiers Congress in Semarang 21–23 March 1913, translated in M. Balfas, *Dr. Tjipto Mangoenkoesoemo: Demokrat sedjati* (1952; Jakarta: Penerbit Djambatan, 1957), as "Sedikit tentang si Djawa, sedjarah dan ethieknja," pp. 60–64.

12. My discussion of Theosophy draws on *An Abridgement of the Secret Doctrine*, by Helena Blavatsky (London: Theosophical Publishing House, 1966); *Krishnamurti: The Years of Awakening*, by Mary Lutyens (New York: Farrar, Straus & Giroux, 1975); *The Masters*, by Annie Besant (Adyar, Madras: Theosophical Publishing House, 1912); *A Dictionary of Theosophical Terms*, compiled by Powis Hoult (London: Theosophical Publishing House, 1910), the essay "Theosofische Vereeniging" in the *Encyclopedie van Nederlandsch Indië* ('s Gravenhage: M. Nijhoff, 1932), pp. 391–92; and my own experiences studying and discussing Javanese mysticism in Solo in the early 1970s and early 1980s. The article in *Encyclopedie van Nederlandsch Indië* (pp. 391–92) noted that Mevr. Blavatsky made three trips to Java, in 1853, 1858, and 1883.

13. The role of women within the Theosophical hierarchy is, as usual, a contradictory

channeled many of the teachings from her mystical contact with the disembodied Great (Male) Masters whose task it was to oversee life on this human earth. Leaders of the movement were appointed through psychic contact across continents, particularly between Australia and India in the early twentieth century. When Besant encountered the young Krishnamurti in Adyar, India, in 1909 through her association with C. W. Leadbeater, she was convinced she had found the Spiritual Leader of the new century, and Krishnamurti was adopted by the Theosophists and raised to be the Messiah, a role he rejected as soon as he was knowledgeable enough to do so, to the great disappointment of his mentors.

The Theosophical teachings themselves were a mix of several world religions with an emphasis on tolerance toward all religious practices. Hinduism, Christianity, Islam, and Judaism could all blend in harmony in the Theosophical worldview, although pre-Islamic Hindu and Buddhist teachings were favored.[14] The Ramayana and Mahabharata became key texts for the Theosophists, especially the Bhagavad Gita, which told the story of Arjuna's enlightenment by the god-incarnate Krishna on the battlefield of Kurukshetra. Theosophy, however, was as much a product of social Darwinism as it was of religion; human life was ordered on an evolutionary plane in which the seven Root Races of humanity worked out their path toward perfection. The lost continent of Atlantis played a significant role in Theosophical thought, representing a past stage of human religious and mystical development and the home of the Fourth Root

one. Women like Blavatsky and Besant were very well respected, but they based their power on their ability to channel the thoughts and desires of disembodied male beings. I would suggest that the freedom that women obtained through their association with Theosophy and its many conferences and gatherings might be seen as part of the first wave feminism in the first decades of this century. This is a topic worthy of extended study. For insights into the role women played within the Theosophical movement in India, England, Holland, and America, see M. Lutyens, *Krishnamurti: The Years of Awakening*. Even Kartini mentions in 1902 that she and her sisters spoke to the president of the Theosophical Association, who was willing to initiate them into the practice. See Joost Cote, trans., *Letters from Kartini: An Indonesian Feminist, 1900–1904* (Clayton, Victoria: Monash Asia Institute, 1992), p. 279, cf. p. 267.

14. Florida, in *Javanese Literature in Surakarta Manuscripts*, 1:293, notes an early twentieth-century Javanese Buddhist manuscript (KS 521) in the collection of the Sasana Pustaka of the Kraton Solo that was translated into Javanese from German via Dutch, from an English original. It is the story of the life of the Buddha, first published by Henry S. Olcott, one of the founders of Theosophy, in India in 1881.

Race.[15] Racialist thought was built into Theosophy from the beginning, albeit in a paternalistic and tolerant way: certain races were considered "naturally" more evolved than others just as humans were more evolved than monkeys. Aryans, deriving from ancient Indo-Europeans, were believed to belong to the Fifth Root Race while most Mongoloid peoples, including the Indies natives, belonged to the Fourth. Thus in India, European Theosophists and well-born Indians could mix on equal terms, and Krishnamurti could be groomed as a World Savior, reflecting the way that English and Sanskrit had been discovered in the mid-nineteenth century to belong to the Indo-European language family.[16]

In Java, the situation was a bit different. When Dutch Theosophists encountered Javanese Ramayana and Mahabharata stories, they realized that the Javanese were also heirs to mystical teachings revered by members of their eclectic religious persuasion. But Javanese were not actually Aryans, unless one counted the mixing of ancient Indo-Aryans with local Javanese, whose fruitful union had supposedly produced the great temples of Borobudur and Prambanan. Dutch scholars attributed the present state of Javanese "indolence" and "fanaticism" to the pollution of these early Aryans by Malay blood until most traces of the "higher" race had disappeared.[17] So most Javanese were seen as members of the Fourth Root Race, a race believed to be capable of great development of the heart *chakra*[18]—centered in the feelings—but more limited in their mental development than the members of the Fifth Root Race, the Aryans.[19] In Theosophical thought, all the members of a particular root race did not proceed at the same pace as they matured, and the historical evolution of

15. Hoult, *A Dictionary of Theosophical Terms*, p. 17.

16. Stocking, *Victorian Anthropology*, p. 59.

17. "Rasvershil onder Inlanders," *De Indische Gids* (1912): 123–25.

18. *Chakra*s are centers of power, capable of unfolding, that many Indian religions and philosophies suggest are located in the physical-spiritual bodies of all human beings. There are supposedly seven *chakra*s that run from the grossest at the base of the spine to the most refined at the crown of the head. There are corresponding ideas of physical centers of mystical power in Chinese religion and philosophy also. The root races of Theosophical thought corresponded to the seven *chakra*s.

19. I was informed by several members of the mystical group Sumarah in the early 1970s that the Javanese were members of the Fourth Root Race and could only excel in the development of *rasa* or feeling, while the Euroamericans studying with the group were members of the Fifth Root Race and could perfect the intellect or *budi*.

the root races allowed for the overlapping of members of different root races at different points in time.[20]

When Mrs. C. van Hinloopen Labberton wrote up her thoughts on the Javanese shadow theatre, she believed she saw there the evidence of ancient Javanese contact with higher knowledge. This contact led back to the days of the great Shaivite and Buddhist kingdoms of the pre-Islamic period, when colonies of Indians were believed to have brought their higher civilization to Java. Mrs. Hinloopen Labberton's essay on Javanese shadow theatre, which appeared in English in 1912 and in two Dutch Indies journals in 1921, seems to be one of the earliest published contributions to a discourse that began to speak about the shadow theatre in a new way.[21] Rather than the quaint and degenerate folk art described by nineteenth-century Dutch scholars and missionaries in the previous chapter, the shadow theatre became a vehicle of higher knowledge, a point of access to an ancient and fading wisdom. Just as Dutch-educated Javanese were beginning to become aware of the potential for making Javanese traditions—articulated in Dutch—the basis for Javanese nationalism by the formation in 1908 of the Boedi Oetomo [Glorious Endeavor], the first European-style association in the Indies, young Javanese intellectuals who had watched many a shadow play in their youth were quick to respond to this new appreciation of what had previously been valued as a slightly degenerate remainder and reminder of old-fashioned village ways.[22] Dutch missionaries and scholars in the late nineteenth century had com-

20. Blavatsky, *An Abridgement of the Secret Doctrine*, pp. 168 ff.

21. An English edition of this essay exists that has been given an American library cataloging date of 1912, followed by a question mark, which, I am told, indicates that the cataloger was confident about that date although the date is not given on the publication. It was republished in Dutch in the *Theosofisch Maandblad* in August 1921 and republished in *Wederopbouw* 6, nos. 8–9: 123–45, several months later. V. M. Clara van Groenendael cites an undated publication by Mevr. Hinloopen Labberton titled "The wajang or shadow play as given in Java; An allegorical play of the human-soul and the universe" published in Bandung by Djamur Dvipa. She annotates this publication as "Superficial notes on the wayang theatre of Java and its mystical meaning for the Javanese" in *Wayang Theatre in Indonesia: An Annotated Bibliography*, p. 69.

22. For an extended discussion of the Boedi Oetomo, see Akira Nagazumi, *The Dawn of Indonesian Nationalism: The Early Years of the Budi Utomo* (Tokyo: Institute of Developing Economies, 1972); for a more revisionist look at the organization, see Shiraishi, *An Age in Motion*, pp. xi–xii, 34–35, 38–39, and further discussions throughout the text.

plained about the decadence of the shadow theatre, although they saw its potential for influencing the Javanese masses. Some Dutchmen had distinguished between coarse and uneducated *dhalang* and those with greater knowledge of Javanese literary lore.[23] It was to this latter group that the Theosophists turned for their inspiration.

This new discourse, in which the shadow theatre was seen as a vehicle of higher wisdom, advanced several contradictory propositions: if the shadow theatre was decadent, it could be restored; this restoration could be carried out in "modern" ways through the setting up of schools for the puppeteers; the newly restored tradition could then be used as a vehicle for lifting up the Javanese masses, who were blinded by their attachments to village rituals—like the shadow theatre—and their fanatic but usually faulty understandings of Islam. For those children of lesser *priyayi* who had been given a Dutch-language education in the early twentieth-century Ethical period in Dutch colonial policy, Islam had often been presented by their Dutch teachers as an undesirable and troublesome feature of Javanese life. As noted in the previous chapter, nobility and lesser officials had been cautioned by the colonial government against identifying too closely with Islam throughout the second half of the nineteenth century. A newly constituted *wayang* tradition might help to draw those Javanese peasants who did not yet fully understand Islam toward an identification with older non-Islamic traditions of the past, and a newly refurbished tradition might guide the peasantry successfully into a "modern" future that could displace the poorly understood Islam.[24] From his speeches and writings, it is clear that the nationalist leader Tjipto Mangoenkoesoemo was familiar with the ideas of Hinloopen Labberton about shadow theatre that were being introduced into Javanese and Dutch scholarly and literary discourses

23. C. Poensen, in "De Wajang," *Mededeelingen van wege het Nederlandsche Zendeling-genootschap* 7 (1873): 164, noted: "Let us hope that the time comes again in which the *wajang*-play will undergo a great development because it possesses in form and principle every incentive to contribute powerfully to the moral and intellectual development of the people." See Poensen, "De Wajang," *Mededeelingen van wege het Nederlandsche Zendeling-genootschap* 16 (1872): 208–9, for a discussion of different types of puppeteers.

24. Cf. C. Snouck Hurgronje's comments about the delicate need to introduce Dutch-style education into the Indies without forcing Christian education in the hope that those areas of life untouched by Islam might become more European through his policy of "Association," in Penders, *Indonesia*, pp. 157–64, and in the discussion of Snouck Hurgronje below.

in the first decades of the twentieth century.[25] But an essay written in 1913 by Tjipto shows that it was not just Theosophy that changed the way Javanese thought and spoke about the Central Javanese shadow theatre tradition in the twentieth century.

Education and Exile

Chapter 1 showed how Islam and shadow theatre were closely inter-twined in the early nineteenth century and how these connections came under assault after the Java War. By the late nineteenth century, Dutch scholarship had placed "Hindu-Javanese" literary traditions at the center of what they saw as Javanese culture, and *wayang* was seen as the only remaining vehicle of older traditions that Javanese elites and peasants could still—albeit imperfectly—understand. The Dutch scholars of the latter part of the nineteenth century had devoted considerable attention to translating and annotating as many examples of Hindu-Javanese literature as they could find. But it was not until the second decade of the twentieth century that the *wayang* theatre, through its elevation in Theosophical thought, also became a useful vehicle for the propagation of Hindu-Javanese mythologies that could serve as the content of a Javanist religion or *Agama Jawa*, emptied of Islam, and in the uplifting of the Javanese native (*de opheffing van de Javaansche inlander*). Rather than Dutch colonial rulers or even Dutch scholars, it was Javanese intellectuals themselves who seized the initiative and became the manipulators of *wayang* plays and stories.

Tjipto Mangoenkoesoemo is a well-known Javanese intellectual who was active in the first quarter of the twentieth century.[26] He was one of the

25. In his speech to the Congress for Javanese Cultural Development in 1918 ("Iets over Javaansche Cultuurontwikkeling: Prae-advies uitgebracht voor het Congress 5/6 Juli 1918"), Tjipto talked at length about the Bhagavad Gita and D. van Hinloopen Labberton's ideas that the essence of the Gita remained alive among the majority of the Javanese people. Part of this speech is translated in Balfas, *Dr. Tjipto Mangoenkoesoemo*, pp. 66–71.

26. See Balfas, *Dr. Tjipto Mangoenkoesoemo*; G. D. Larson, *Prelude to Revolution: Palaces and Politics in Surakarta, 1912–1942* (Dordrecht: Foris Publications, 1987); S. P. Scherer, "Harmony and Dissonance: Early Nationalist Thought in Java" (M.A. thesis, Cornell University, 1975); T. Shiraishi, "The Dispute between Tjipto Mangoenkoesoemo and

three founders of the Indische Partij in 1912, which argued for an Indier or Indies rather than a Javanese nationalism; thus Tjipto and Soewardi Soerjaningrat allowed Dutch imperial conquests to circumscribe their nationalist visions. Although known for his embodiment of many of the ideals of refined Javanese manhood—humility, dignity, and subtlety—Tjipto held a vision of the Indies that saw all the different ethnic groups uniting and, by adopting the fruits of European knowledges, founding an independent nation.[27] Shiraishi has elegantly presented the debates over nationalism and culture that Tjipto had with Soetatmo Soeriokoesoemo of the Pakualaman minor court in Yogya, debates that coincided with the founding of the Volksraad or People's Council in 1918 as well as with the founding of the supposedly nonpolitical Java Institute one year later.[28] Shiraishi suggests that both Tjipto and Soetatmo, who—unlike Tjipto—was a supporter of Javanese rather than Indies nationalism, argued from within the worldview of the shadow theatre, in which Soetatmo viewed himself as a *pandita* or sage while Tjipto saw himself as a *satria* or noble warrior.

Kenji Tsuchiya has also discussed these early nationalists in the first decades of the twentieth century in his excellent book on Soewardi Soerjaningrat and the rise of the Taman Siswa, Garden of Learning, Javanist schools.[29] Both Tsuchiya and Shiraishi have set their studies against a background in which the *wayang purwa* theatre assumes a foundational position. The *wayang* in the work of these scholars becomes synonymous with Javanese culture, illustrates basic ideas about Javanese conceptions of power, and marks off the frame—here, literally a stage—on which Javanese discourses of modernity are enacted. But this assumes an unchanging, ahistorical vision of the shadow theatre and its reception by Javanese audiences. I am proposing that the idea of the *wayang* as the essence of Javanese culture was a product of the interlacing of Javanese and Dutch aesthetic visions and intellectual agendas that engendered and were

---

Soetatmo Soeriokoesoemo: *Pandita* vs. *Satria*," *Indonesia* 32 (1981): 93–108; Tsuchiya, *Democracy and Leadership*.

27. Balfas, *Dr. Tjipto Mangoenkoesoemo.*

28. Shiraishi, "The Dispute between Tjipto Mangoenkoesoemo and Soetatmo Soeriokoesoemo." The Volksraad was the first all-male advisory body in the Indies with some pretense to native representation: the new body contained fifteen native members, ten elected and five appointed out of thirty-eight members in all. See Nagazumi, *The Dawn of Indonesian Nationalism.*

29. Tsuchiya, *Democracy and Leadership.*

Failed Narratives or the New "Essence"?

engendered by discourses of empire. It is an idea that was congenial to Dutch scholars and government officials—and often the two groups overlapped—because it displaced attention from the threatening potential of Javanese unification under the banner of Islam that had arisen in 1912 in the form of the Sarekat Islam, the first mass organization in the Indies. For both Javanese and Indies nationalists, positing the *wayang* as the essence of Java and associating the *wayang* with spiritual development and higher wisdom was useful because it allowed the nationalists to use the *wayang* to talk about politics right under the noses of the Dutch.

An example of this blending of Javanese and Dutch knowledges and purposes appears in an article written by Tjipto Mangoenkoesoemo at the end of 1913 in Holland and published in 1914 in *De Indische Gids*, the useful guide to the Indies, published in Amsterdam, which brought together summaries of economic data, book reviews, literary fragments, and opinions written mainly by Dutch scholars, travelers, businesspeople, and administrators. Tjipto's essay on shadow theatre had a special poignancy, as around the time of its writing he was exiled to Holland because of what the colonial government felt were the subversive activities of the Indische Partij and, in particular, the activities of Soewardi Soerjaningrat, Douwes Dekker, and Tjipto.

If it seems strange that a political exile would be asked to contribute to a Dutch publication with close connections to the colonial government, Balfas explains how the Dutch Advisor for Native Affairs, G.A.J. Hazeu, had tried to convince Tjipto to apologize to the colonial government for his political activities and obtain a doctorate in Leiden with a stipend of fifty Dutch guilders a month.[30] Soewardi's famous essay, "Als Ik eens Nederlander Was" (If Only I Were a Dutchman), written to comment on the Dutch one-hundred-year celebration of Holland's release from French domination in 1813, and a series of outspoken articles in the Indische Partij's organ *De Expres* showed the colonial government that several of their subjects were becoming both restless and politically astute. The only way to rid the colony of these unsettling influences was to banish them from Java, and Holland was occasionally used as a place of exile in these closing years of the Ethical period.[31] Less than two months after his arrival

30. Balfas, *Dr. Tjipto Mangoenkoesoemo*, p. 55.

31. See Pramoedya Ananta Toer's brilliant novel *Rumah Kaca* (Glass House) (Kuala Lumpur: Wira Karya, 1990), mentioned in chapter 1, for insights into the colonial

in Holland on 2 October 1913, Tjipto collected both old and new thoughts for the Dutch publication.

In his essay "De Wajang," Tjipto positioned himself both inside and outside the worldview of the *wayang* world and began to speak about the shadow theatre in a new way.[32] It is certainly true, as Shiraishi has argued, that Tjipto saw himself as a Javanese *satriya* (noble warrior).[33] But his trip to Holland also allowed him to see the *wayang* from a new vantage point. Speaking about the *wayang* from Holland, Tjipto became the *dhalang*, began the journey that Pramoedya called "freeing oneself from the grip of that *wayang* world," and used the techniques of the *wayang* for his own nationalist purposes. He deftly lulled the Dutch readers of his essay as he presented first the ethnographic and then a mystical Theosophical discourse on *wayang*, with images of Higher Beings, inner lives, pain, and suffering.

In [the *wajang*] the Javanese has embodied a good part of his philosophical and mystical insights; he has put into words his inner life. No wonder, then, that even in the *dalem* [villas] of the highest aristocrats, as in the poorest *kampung* [neighborhood] homes, it has become a beloved folk play. Old and young spend their hours with pleasure listening to the words of the *dalang*, following him in his stories about gods and kings, about princes and ksatriya [warriors], how they suffer and conquer, falling captive to their passions, becoming slaves to it, and finally, however, coming out of the battle victorious. The *wajang* is a purely Javanese creation and was already being performed at the court of Daha around the year 800, being revised around 1500 by Sunan Kali Djaga, the Islamic missionary [*zendeling*]. Exactly because it is a Javanese creation, through it one can learn a great deal about the inner life of the Javanese. The Netherlands Indies branch of the Theosophical Society did a good job of putting on [the play] Sakuntala and writing down the results of the research.

This passage shows two important things: Tjipto had read the Dutch scholarship on the *wayang*, especially Hazeu's ideas about the Javanese

---

government's thinking about the rise of national consciousness in this period; the collected translations on nationalism in Penders, *Indonesia*, pp. 177–348; and, for the most impressive statement to date, Shiraishi, *An Age in Motion*.

32. *De Indische Gids* 36, no. 1 (1914): 530–39.

33. Shiraishi, "The Dispute between Tjipto Mangoenkoesoemo and Soetatmo Soeriokoesoemo."

Failed Narratives or the New "Essence"?

origins of the *wayang*, and he praised the Theosophical Society's influence and efforts to endow the *wayang* with new mystical meanings.

Behind [the *blencong*] the *dalang*, the performer, will take his place. The Javanese sees in him the source of all life, because without him, no matter how artistically designed, the wajang puppets will never come to life. The Javanese proverb: *wajang manut dalang* [the wajang follows the dalang] adequately expresses how he regards them. What this relationship represents precisely is the image that the Javanese has of his relationship to the Unknowable, the Power-source, without which no life is possible here on earth. Our eye can only observe the sun that gives color to our earthly life; that is the visible source of all life here on earth.

But behind that hides one even Mightier, an unknown Beginning, a Divinity, without whom "not even a bird falls from on high." All, everything, is dependent upon that unknown Beginning, without whose will "not even a hair shall be touched." Just as the wajang follows [*manut*] the dalang, so the creature follows [*manut*] the Source of Life; this [Source] shall determine the role that humankind has to fulfill here on earth.

Here are the origins of what will become the scholarly judgments about the Javanese *wayang* in the twentieth century: *wayang* is the essence of Javanese culture and a window through which the outsider can peer to understand the Javanese "soul." Tjipto also reinscribed the metaphor of Hidden Power coming to life through the puppeteer, as the puppets come to life in performance. Earlier Javanese beliefs connected the *wayang* with Sufi mystical teachings, as discussed in chapter 1. What seems to be taking place here is a displacement of *wayang* mysticism and a rephrasing of it in non-Islamic terms. In the 1920s and 1930s, this Hidden Power came to be interpreted in "Hindu-Buddhist" religious-mystical terms because of Theosophical influence. In the 1950s and especially the 1960s, the Hidden Power was interpreted in the partisan political terms of that period.[34]

Tjipto also described the *wayang* as a good ethnographer would, show-

---

34. The interpretation of the *dhalang* as the political power behind the puppet is one that is centuries old. M. C. Ricklefs notes how, in the *Babad Kraton*, written at the court of Yogyakarta in 1777–78, the author(s) describe complex negotiations among the Javanese notables at the court of Amangkurat II in the 1680s, and one of the nobles, Anrangkusuma, is supposed to act like a shadow puppet (*ringgit*, *wayang*) to conceal the movements of the Javanese monarch in *War, Culture and Economy in Java*, p. 92.

ing how it can be decoded to yield "meaning." He gave his Dutch readers access to "the Javanese way of thinking."

It is the never-ending battle of light against darkness. In the Javanese way of thinking, people compare that to the battle of good spirits against the evil ones. As the daylight fades away, when the darkness creeps over the land, that is the time for the evil spirits to come out. In the musical overture people hear that clearly indicated: the mellow and soft opening notes increase in ferocity, just as the fierceness of the passions of the evil spirits increases more and more as the evening progresses.

But then he used the *dhalang*'s talent for creating *lakon pasemon* as allegories to allude to the political situation in the Indies. As he described the scene where the *dhalang* can slip in criticisms of the government, Tjipto slipped in his *own* criticism of the government.

The three clowns, Semar, Gareng, and Petroek, make funny faces and give the dalang the opportunity to keep the audience awake with quips and jokes. At the same time the three clowns give the dalang the opportunity to speak out about the happenings of the day. One often hears, then, his judgments of government measures poured out in comical form. One hears him complain in joking ways about the heavy fate of the Javanese under the Government of the so paternally minded white Dutchmen.

That all has the value of an intermezzo. It serves at the same time to drive the sleep out of the eyes of the listeners and spectators and to make sure that the wajang party does not become bored as would be possible with a story that is stretched out for a whole night.

Tjipto presented an astonishing fait accompli in which every *wayang* performance provided *dhalang* with the opportunity to criticize the colonial government. He conjured up an image of Java in which thousands of imaginary puppeteers were constantly criticizing the "fate of the Javanese under the Government of the so paternally minded white Dutchmen." But then Tjipto slipped back into his role of neutral ethnographer. All this was only an intermezzo, something understandable to all the readers of his essay. It was just a technique used by the puppeteers to keep their audiences awake in the wee hours of the night.

It becomes obvious to the reader of this article that Tjipto saw the Dutch

Failed Narratives or the New "Essence"?

The Pandhawa hero Bima (left) with the clown-servant Semar and his sons Petruk and Gareng.

as the *danawa* (ogre), the *raksasa* (demon), and the *wong sabrang* (foreigner)—all *wayang* characters—whom the *satriya* had to fight. These *wong sabrang* came to Java because they dreamt of the beauty of a Javanese princess, a symbol perhaps for the beauty of Java, which the Dutch came to rape and pillage. Not until the *raksasa* are killed, Tjipto said, not until the land is returned to the children of the ancestors, will Java be at peace again.

The army of the foreign king made up of ogres had set up their camp right in that forest [where the ksatrya was walking alone]. A meeting with the ksatrya cannot be prevented. The ksatrya, requested to turn back, replies that he would rather die than interrupt his trip. A battle erupts, a battle between the lone ksatrya and the entire army of *danawa*, one against many, against all.

It does look like a fairy tale, the story of the dalang. The little ksatrya against the monstrous ogres, great in number. And do we not see this in real life occurring again and again? Do we not see it often happen that the little man, fortified by the spirit that lives in him, dares to take on the task that under shallow consideration one would think far beyond his powers?!

There is a wonderful example of Tjipto's creative use of hybrid language in this passage: "de reusachtige danawa," or the monstrous monster, is the enemy of the noble *satriya*; he has combined Dutch and Javanese in such a way that his meaning is clear in either language. In the *lakon* that Tjipto was creating, there was no mention of the Korawa, the main enemies of the Pandhawa heroes in most of the stories. Tjipto created a new telling of the Mahabharata stories in which the Korawa and Pandhawa heroes could unite to rid Java of the *wong sabrang*, the Dutch. The Pandhawa and Korawa were all cousins and all *satriya*; they all shared the same moral code, the same love for the fatherland.

Tjipto used his exile in Holland to continue his struggle against the Dutch, and the Dutch allowed him to use the *Indische Gids*, their own Indies Guidebook, as a forum for his nationalist cause. Even with his mastery of Dutch, he continued to use Javanese words, to compel the Dutch to use Javanese words to subvert their own rule. He forced the Dutch to think in Javanese. He closed his essay with the poignant words: "I cannot ignore that the *wajang* made a great impression on me, when I got so far that I could understand it."[35] Tjipto seemed to suggest that he had to go as far as Holland in order truly to understand the *wayang*. He cleverly mocked both Theosophical and Dutch scholarly discourses on *wayang* as he realized that his exile to Holland allowed him to get out of, and thus, in a sense, further into, his own understanding of what it meant to be Javanese. His trip to Holland opened his eyes to colonial visions of the *wayang* through which he could clearly see Javanese traditions as "culture." He began to see the *wayang* as subject, rather than being subject to its powers.[36] Although Tjipto was later to become known for his dismissal of Javanese culture as a mystification of the masses, he first learned how to use the *wayang* for his own purposes. In contrast to his compatriots in the early nationalistic movement, Tjipto's increasing politicization meant that he was forced to spend many years of his life in exile—far away from Central Java—as the

---

35. Tjipto, "De Wajang," *De Indische Gids* 36, pt. 1 (1914): 539.

36. Shiraishi, in "The Dispute between Tjipto Mangoenkoesoemo and Soetatmo Soeriokoesoemo," p. 104 n. 36, notes that in 1927 Tjipto began to speak of "het Volk," or the people, becoming the subject rather than the object of the times. Shiraishi suggests that Tjipto had already begun to see the people as subjects rather than objects of history in his debates with Soetatmo in 1918.

Failed Narratives or the New "Essence"?

1920s and 1930s brought more repressive colonial governments to power.[37] Those nationalists who turned their efforts to the enrichment of education and the reconstitution of Javanese "culture" were able to realize some of their visions through the setting up of schools that translated Javanese traditions into languages of modernity.

Javanese-Dutch Shadow Theatre Discourses

Among those Indies intellectuals who channeled their nationalist zeal into a reevaluation of Javanese history and artistic expressions, Soetatmo Soeriokoesoemo remains a figure whose historical importance has often been overshadowed by the failure of Javanese nationalism.[38] The contradictions and insights of his arguments—his harsh criticisms of much of what Europe had to offer the Javanese—and his efforts to reinterpret Javanese traditions as high culture make him an important figure in the study of the changing ways in which Javanese and Dutch spoke about the *wayang* tradition. As a strong supporter of the elevation of the Javanese arts, Soetatmo frequently used characters from the *wayang* stories to illustrate his arguments. He also republished in 1921, in his journal *Wederopbouw*,

37. For a very sympathetic study of Tjipto's life and latter years, see Balfas, *Dr. Tjipto Mangoenkoesoemo.*

38. Shiraishi, in "The Dispute between Tjipto Mangoenkoesoemo and Soetatmo Soeriokoesoemo," and Tsuchiya, in *Democracy and Leadership* (pp. 36 ff.), offer excellent insights into Soetatmo's thinking on the confluence of political and cultural issues. A. Reid, in "The Nationalist Quest for an Indonesian Past," in *Perceptions of the Past in Southeast Asia,* ed. A. Reid and D. Marr (Singapore: Heinemann Educational Books [Asia] Ltd., 1979), pp. 281–86, discusses Soetatmo's thought in his essay on various nationalist reconstructions of the Indonesian past. R. McVey, "Taman Siswa and the Indonesian National Awakening," *Indonesia* 4 (October 1967): 128–49, at p. 131, mentions that Soetatmo was a Buddhist and a leader of the radical faction of the Boedi Oetomo. Both Tsuchiya (p. 55) and McVey (p. 131 n. 2) mention that Soetatmo was a leader of the Yogyanese Selasa Kliwon Society, a group of Javanese nationalists and followers of the mystical teacher Pangeran Soerjomentaraman; the group met a number of times in 1921 to further their aim of promoting the happiness "of self, of nation, of mankind." See M. Bonneff, "Ki Ageng Suryomentaraman, Javanese Prince and Philosopher (1892–1962)," *Indonesia* 57 (1994): pp. 49–70 [orig. in *Archipel* 16 (1978): 175–203]. Whether a Buddhist, a mystic, or both, Soetatmo's essays in *Wederopbouw* indicate that he was both influenced by and critical of Theosophist thought.

Mrs. C. van Hinloopen Labberton's essay on *wayang* mentioned above. Soetatmo's prefatory remarks to this essay are interesting in themselves.

Among the Westerners it is as a rule the theosophists who can provide an entrance to the inner life of the Javanese. There are many examples where a Javanese who would not let a stranger see what was going on in his innermost soul will pour out his heart to a Western theosophist. This is because the Western theosophist himself will spare no pains to be able to understand the thought life of his brown brothers. And we Easterners are such a pushover for a kind heart.

Soetatmo's comments here are both mocking and insightful. He told his readers he was not a dedicated Theosophist, although he was characterized as a "fanatic mystic" in the pages of *Wederopbouw*, possibly by himself.[39] That he was both critical of Theosophy and influenced by it is clear, as is his hostility to Islam.[40] More interesting, however, is the complex Javanese-Dutch hybridity of Soetatmo's thought. He was a major critic of European actions and ways of thinking even as he positioned himself within colonial discourses. As an intellectual who consistently juxtaposed European "science" against Javanese "tradition," Soetatmo argued vehemently for a mythical return to a world constituted within myth, and he used the scientific reasoning learned from his Dutch education as a tool to defend his reconstruction of Javanese traditions and to criticize Dutch science. One particularly poignant argument appears in his defense of Javanese history. If he was to accept the "Western" evaluation of Javanese historical texts—the *babad*—as the worthless products of uncontrolled fantasy,[41] then he would have to make his ancestors into liars or charlatans. He mentioned the supposed meetings of Panembahan Senapati and Sultan Agung, past rulers of Java, with the mythical Queen of the South Seas, the famous magical weapon of Ki Ageng Mangir, and Ki Ageng Solo,

39. See Soetatmo Soeriokoesoemo, "Theosophie en Javaansch Nationalisme," for insights about his relationship to Theosophical thought. In another essay titled "Geschiedenis van Java," the editor, who may be Soetatmo himself, says that he is reprinting a talk given by the "fanatic mystic" Soetatmo Soerio Koesoemo.

40. Soetatmo Soeriokoesoemo, "Een beschouwing over de vormen der overheersching," *Wederopbouw* 2 (1919): 76–77. Soetatmo's feelings about Islam as an Arabian import to Java are captured in this passage from Soetatmo, translated by Anthony Reid in "The Nationalist Quest for an Indonesian Past": "The beginning of this [foreign economic] domination was only made possible by the confusion which Islam introduced into the original conception of life of the Javanese people" (p. 286).

41. "Geschiedenis van Java," p. 51.

who had conquered lightning and thunder. How were Javanese supposed to regard these stories of their ancestors?

We make our elders and ancestors into liars, those who have left us these traditions, if we dare to doubt for a moment what they in their beliefs acknowledged.

A child of a liar—the nobility of the intellect resists this. No, if we in the twentieth century can no longer believe in supernatural powers, then we hold ourselves to that and let it rest, but we have to postpone our judgment about the miracles of the past because the honor of our ancestors is at stake.[42]

This is where the Theosophist reevaluation of the *wayang* theatre provided such crucial support. Perhaps the *babad* could not be rescued from the past, but because of its connections with ancient India, the shadow theatre could. Mrs. Hinloopen Labberton helped to set in motion a discourse in which the shadow theatre could be used to validate a reconstructed "Hindu-Javanese" religious tradition by becoming the essence of it, but Soetatmo had to weed out the excesses of Hinloopen Labberton's Theosophist thinking by ignoring the weaknesses of her understanding of Javanese literary and religious traditions. Soetatmo carefully introduced her ideas to the readers of his journal.

One of the examples where a Westerner has succeeded in penetrating into the psyche of the Native (Inlander), we find in the article of Mevr. C. v. H. Labberton. . . .

The Javanese still give far too little attention to the deep meaning of the wajang. The writings that thus far have appeared contain only stories about the wajang.[43]

Soetatmo was ambivalent toward the Javanese reception of *wayang* theatre and European scholarship about it. He criticized educated Javanese for not appreciating the "deep meaning" of their own artistic tradition. But Dutch scholars are then criticized for devoting their attentions merely to recounting, documenting, and writing down the stories. Mrs. Hinloopen Labberton, Soetatmo argued, provided the proper way of approaching the *wayang* theatre by her focus on the underlying meaning of the stories—even though that meaning might have been unfamiliar to

42. Ibid., p. 56.
43. "De Wajang of het schaduwenspel," in *Wederopbouw* 4, nos. 8–9 (1921): 121–45. Soetatmo Soeriokoesoemo introduces the work of C. van Hinloopen Labberton in the first few pages of this essay.

many Javanese—and she attached the stories to ancient wisdom and Theosophical teachings that honored the Bhagavad Gita as the statement par excellence of these teachings. Soetatmo explained:

If people want to understand the meaning there then they must allow themselves to trust the so-called language of symbols.

To the best of our knowledge, a few young men who by their study have "un-learned" the Eastern manner of thinking are trying to understand the meaning of the wajang.

When we join in trying to make the wajang play understandable to young people, we are proceeding from the conviction that with the disappearance of this play, the Javanese will cease to be a civilized people.

Often we are criticized if we would *allow* our people *to remain* at the same stage where they now stand. And then, as an example, is cited our zealousness about the wajang and our respect for other arts of our people. We are not thought capable of being a new nation with a new culture to create. We ourselves are aware of it; that is something. Our art will be transformed, too, and already we are eager to retain that art as we have received it from our ancestors, because we have not yet created anything new. We will be very grateful if our wajang is not exchanged for the cinema.

Thus our art will change, but we hope that the change will be for the better.

This is the crisis of Soetatmo's argument and the quandary in which he found himself enmeshed. The Javanese have obviously been criticized by the Dutch for wallowing in the fantasies of the *wayang* world, but they have nothing yet to replace it except the unacceptable Islam. Without the *wayang*, the Javanese would cease to be a civilized people.[44] Soetatmo felt pulled apart by the paradoxical urge to protect the tradition as it had been received from the past, even though he sensed that the demands of the times would require the ancestral traditions to change. This problem was

44. The failure to be considered a civilized people could have dire consequences. Stocking, in his historical study of Victorian Anthropology, notes the intricate inter-weavings between anthropological, evolutionary, and colonial discourses and, in particular, describes the call for the massacre of uncivilized peoples at the meeting of the British Anthropological Society in 1866 after the reading of a paper titled "The Negro and Jamaica." See *Victorian Anthropology*, p. 251.

Failed Narratives or the New "Essence"?

reflected in the efforts of Soerjosoeparto, the future Mangkunagara VII, and liberal Dutch scholars and administrators like Hinloopen Labberton and Hazeu, as they set up the Java Institute in the second decade of the twentieth century.

Dutch Scholar-Administrators and the *Wayang* Theatre

In the early part of the twentieth century, liberal Dutch scholar-administrators like Snouck Hurgronje, Hazeu, Rinkes, and Kern were active in supporting the effort to train Javanese lower *priyayi* in Dutch language and administrative techniques in order to turn their political aspirations away from the growing strength of Islam. It was C. Snouck Hurgronje, the first Dutch Adviser for Arabian and Native Affairs at the turn of the century, who had developed a policy in northern Sumatra (Aceh) of combatting Islam by bolstering *adat* or local traditions. Snouck urged the Dutch government to support and nurture those elements of society that were least under the sway of Islamic "fanaticism," including the *adat* chiefs and the Javanese *priyayi* elites.[45] Most importantly, Snouck's vision for the Indies included a policy of educating the Indies peoples. Snouck believed it was only through the introduction of Dutch-language education and European lifestyles that a strong and lasting bond could be forged to link the Dutch and Indies societies together. Following Snouck in the role of Adviser for Native Affairs over the next twenty years were G.A.J. Hazeu (1906–12), D. A. Rinkes (1913–16), and R. Kern (1920–22, 1923–26).[46]

It was not only the Dutch scholar-administrators who realized that Dutch education should be made available to the colonized peoples, but also Javanese and other native elites, who began to perceive power and prestige to lie in the mastery of new kinds of knowledge. With the found-

45. H. Benda, *The Crescent and the Rising Sun* (The Hague: W. van Hoeve, 1958), pp. 20–31; Snouck Hurgronje (1911) in Penders, *Indonesia*, pp. 157–65; H. Sutherland, *The Making of a Bureaucratic Elite: The Colonial Transformation of the Javanese Priyayi* (Singapore: Heinemann Educational Books [Asia] Ltd., 1979), pp. 38–39.

46. See Sutherland, *Bureaucratic Elite*, pp. 38–39, for a discussion of Snouck Hurgronje's ideas and the reactions of the conservative Dutch Binnenlandsch Bestuur (Civil Service) men, who thought that Snouck and his successors were too liberal and too friendly with the "natives."

ing of the Hollandsch Inlandsche Scholen in 1914 for children of the royal families and other *priyayi*, or elite Javanese, Javanese was secondary to Dutch in the school curriculum, and in the ensuing years, Dutch-educated Javanese *priyayi* began to lose their ability to speak the refined levels of Javanese.[47] As modernizing Javanese began to turn their energies to the acquisition of European and scientific knowledges, and to demand a larger voice in the rule of the Indies, Dutch scholar-administrators and Javanese *priyayi* attempted to bolster the position of the *wayang* tradition among the newly educated groups by linking European aesthetic prefer-ances to the evaluation of the tradition. If the stories were more organized, if the aesthetic standards were raised, perhaps the power of the tradition could divert the attention of Javanese peasants from more threatening pursuits brought about by increasing resistance to the Dutch regime and the growing strength of Islam as a rallying point for nationalist feeling.

One example of the mixing of Javanese and Dutch knowledges and its impact upon the shadow theatre tradition is the Congress for Javanese Cultural Development held in Surakarta, on 5–7 July of 1918. The idea for such a Congress came from a combination of Dutch and Javanese sources. In Batavia, a preliminary committee was convened by the The-osophist C. van Hinloopen Labberton to discuss the Javanese language. The committee members included the Dutch scholars and administrators Dr. F.D.K. Bosch, Dr. B. Schrieke, the Adviser for Native Affairs Dr. Hazeu, and the Dutch-educated Bantenese Dr. Hoesein Djajadiningrat. They sought to make Mangkunagara VII (r. 1916–44), ruler of the minor court in Solo, chairman of the new committee.

But efforts to hold a conference concerned with Javanese cultural de-velopment also came from members of the Solonese branch of the Boedi Oetomo (Glorious Endeavor), mentioned above as the first Indies associa-tion organized along European lines. In 1914, members of the Boedi Oetomo had formed the Committee for Javanese Nationalism and, under the patronage of Soerjosoeparto, the Mangkunagara to be, had begun to publish the periodical *Wederopbouw* (Reconstruction) discussed above, which argued for the rehabilitation of Javanese culture.[48] The Batavia

47. See J. J. Errington, *Language and Social Change in Java*, Ohio Monographs in International Studies, Southeast Asian Series, no. 65 (Athens, Ohio: University of Ohio Press, 1985), pp. 47–48.

48. For more information on this Congress, see Shiraishi, "The Dispute between

Failed Narratives or the New "Essence"?

group decided to let the Solo group take the initiative for the Congress, which was subsequently held in July, a few months after the first meeting of the Volksraad.[49]

At the Congress, debates were held over the future of Javanese culture. Although Tjipto could see no use for Javanese culture as an instrument to achieve independence for the Indies, Soetatmo, who had first formed the Committee for Javanese Nationalism, distinguished between the moral "upbringing" (*opvoeding*) of older Javanese culture and the Western concept of "upbringing," which was based solely on intellectual means.[50] By reviving the Javanese concept of moral *opvoeding*, Soetatmo saw the possibility of guiding the Javanese safely out of what Ranggawarsita had named the age of madness (*zaman edan*) into an age of progress by attaching European science and technology to Javanese tradition. Soetatmo felt that out of Java's glorious past only the *wayang* tradition remained as a reservoir of Javanese wisdom, which held the key to the future moral education of the Javanese. While Dutch scholar-administrators may have thought the *wayang* tradition could be a distraction from anti-Dutch groupings around Islam and nationalism, Soetatmo saw the *wayang* as a way to help rehabilitate Javanese arts and tradition and give authority to the notion of a Javanese nationalism.

Soon after the Congress, political developments in the Boedi Oetomo and a rising interest in the potential of Javanese culture for moral education were to lead to the establishment of the Java Institute in 1919.[51] Its aim

Tjipto Mangoenkoesoemo and Soetatmo Soeriokoesoemo"; Nagazumi, *Dawn of Indonesian Nationalism*; and "Congres voor Javaansche Cultuur-Ontwikkeling," in *Djawa* 1 (1921): 313–17, reprinted from *De Locomotief*.

49. It is interesting to note the overlap between the Committee for Javanese Cultural Development and the Volksraad: Javanese who were involved in both organizations included Dr. Radjiman (personal physician to the Sunan of Solo), Sastrowidjono of the Boedi Oetomo, Mangkunagara VII, and Tjipto Mangoenkoesoemo of the radical Indische Partij. In August of the following year, the Java Institute was officially established to encourage the scholarly study of Javanese culture, and the governing board of the Institute resembled the native participation in the Volksraad even more closely: included in both organizations were the regent Koesoemo Oetojo, Sastrowidjono, Mangkunagara VII (who was the honorary chairman), and Tjokroaminoto, the famous leader of Sarekat Islam, as well as Hoesein Djajadiningrat, who was to become the son-in-law of Mangkunagara VII and whose brother sat on the Volksraad.

50. Shiraishi, "The Dispute between Tjipto Mangoenkoesoemo and Soetatmo Soeriokoesoemo," pp. 98–99.

51. Right after the Volksraad was authorized in 1917, the Boedi Oetomo decided to

was to further the development of indigenous (*inheemsche*)[52] culture, in the broadest sense of the word, of Java, Madura, and Bali by means of congresses, exhibitions, recitals, readings, courses, competitions (*prijsvragen*), and writings.[53] The board members of the Institute were again a mixture of Dutch scholars and administrators, Javanese elites, and Indo-Europeans. The language of scholarly debate for the Java Institute and its publication *Djawa* was Dutch because this was the language in which the newly educated elites had learned to think about their arts and history.[54] By the end of the 1920s, Malay would begin to replace Dutch as the language of an Indies nationalism.

At a meeting of the Java Institute in Yogyakarta in 1921, a Javanese *wayang* aficionado named Soetopo[55] gave an address in Dutch in which he presented a list of propositions to the Institute.[56] Soetopo noted a deterioration of the *wayang* in the leading Javanese artistic circles. Because of the demands of the performance, most had degenerated into banal presentations of the same warlike episodes about some princess, trite waggery, and

---

take a more open attitude toward Islam by supporting mosques and *pesantren* (Islamic village schools) education in order to gain more popular support so they would have better representation on the Volksraad. Dr. Radjiman was firmly against this and argued for the influence of Hindu-Buddhist culture. The Boedi Oetomo finally voted in favor of religious freedom rather than for support of Islam. This debate might be seen as a background for the establishment of the Java Institute. See Nagazumi, *The Dawn of Indonesian Nationalism*, pp. 115–16.

52. As a result of the Ethical turn in Dutch-Javanese relations, the pejorative Dutch term *inlander* for native was changed to the more neutral *inheemsche* (indigenous) in the 1920s (Abu Hanifah, *Tales of a Revolution* [Sydney: Angus & Robertson, 1972], p. 31 n. 34).

53. *Djawa* 1 (1921): 65–66.

54. In 1923, the periodicals *Poesaka Djawi* and *Poesaka Soenda* were founded, the former published in Javanese script and the latter in roman script, to make a number of the essays from *Djawa* available to Javanese and Sundanese who could not read Dutch. The periodicals also published original essays. See *Encyclopedië van Nederlandsch Indië* (1932), pp. 182–83.

55. It is likely that this Soetopo, the author of these comments, was R. Soetopo Wonobojo, editor of the newspaper *Boedi Oetomo*, which was issued, at various times, in Dutch, Javanese, and Malay language editions. He later became a member of the Supreme Board of the Taman Siswa educational movement. For information about Soetopo, see Abdurrachman Surjomihardjo, "National Education in a Colonial Society," in *Dynamics of Indonesian History*, ed. Haryati Soebadio and Carine A. du Marchie Sarvaas (Amsterdam: North Holland Publishing Company, 1978), p. 287.

56. Soetopo, "De behoefte aan intellectueele dalangs in verband met de ontwikkeling van het wajangspel," *Djawa* 1 (1921).

Failed Narratives or the New "Essence"?

long-winded homage arguments about kings and realms. Soetopo went on to say that the puppeteers, because of their education and environment, were too much the servants of those who paid for the performance, and thus they were not able to develop the story and characterization appropriately. He noted that puppeteers lacked schooling and thus had to depend on the performances of other puppeteers (i.e., the oral tradition) to learn their trade. He also commented regretfully on the lack of *wayang* art critics, who might be able to maintain or demand proper standards.

Soetopo advocated the formation of a school to train puppeteers, musicians, and singers, and he thought that the graduates of the native schools, which used European techniques but taught in Javanese, might be good candidates to become puppeteers because they had learned the proper command of the Javanese language. Finally, Soetopo urged that the *dhalang* should become thinkers, knowers, and therefore leaders, who could awaken the slumbering masses from their unconsciousness; the *wayang* then would not only breed philosophical thinking but also inculcate the kind of thinking that leads to a better understanding of great world events. It is in this light that the first schools for *wayang* puppeteers were opened in the 1920s and 1930s.[57]

The Opening of the Court Schools

Recent scholarship has cited 1923 as a turning point in the development of the *wayang* tradition in the twentieth century because the court school Padhasuka was founded, the elite court tradition was supposedly opened up to the village *dhalang*, and the government began its efforts to erase the differences beween court and village performances.[58] But my investiga-

57. The first court school for *wayang* puppeteers was Padhasuka, opened in 1923 under the auspices of the *kepatihan*, the Solonese *kraton* residence of the *patih*, the palace official most closely linked to the Dutch colonial regime. In 1925 Yogyakarta followed with the opening of Habiranda under the authority of Hamengkubuwana VIII and at the promptings of the Java Institute; then the Mangkunagaran in Solo followed by opening its own school PDMN (*Pasinaon Dhalang ing Mangkunagaran*) in 1931.

58. Clara van Groenendael, *The dalang behind the wayang*, pp. 30–36; McVey, "The Wayang Controversy in Indonesian Communism," p. 50 n. 70. Both Clara van Groenendael and McVey make valid points about this period. Clara van Groenendael among other things mentions how the stress at the court schools was on technical expertise

tions show this to be more complicated. What happened in 1923 was the culmination of a process that had begun in the late nineteenth century under the influence of Prince Kusumadilaga. There was a new consolidation of traditions and the setting of new standards for *both* court and village performances. Poetic texts from nineteenth-century poetry in modern Javanese were substituted for many of the sung *suluk* in Kawi, which could not be readily translated by court or village performers. Certain musical pieces were prescribed for use in certain scenes and in a certain order. The position of the *pesindhen*, female singer, was set inferior to the *dhalang* (contrary to the current practice in West Java), and the three musical *pathet*, modes, were standardized for progressive development throughout the *wayang* night.

According to three performers who were knowledgeable about court traditions (the late R. Ng. Martopangrawit, R. Ng. Samsudjin Probohardjono, and the late R. Soetrisna), before 1923 court performances were as unpredictable as village ones. When asked if the *wayang* performances at the court were good, the best thing Martopangrawit, a musician who served at the Kraton Solo in the 1930s and 1940s, could say was that they were *"teratur,"* or orderly; the *suluk* were orderly and the movements were orderly.[59] Probohardjono, an intellectual attached to the Kraton Solo in 1953 to teach about *wayang*, said that the situation at court was disorganized before the founding of Padhasuka, when regulations were established. He noted how the puppeteers had to use a particular song in the beginning of the *wayang* night. "At the beginning of *pathet nem*, you had to memorize '*Leng leng ramyaningkang,*' you couldn't deviate from '*leng leng ramyaningkang.*'"[60] The Dutch scholar Th. Pigeaud, who lived in Central

rather than mystical power; McVey explains how upgrading wayang to courtly tastes expands the cultural space controlled by the political center. Of course, in this period the political center was Dutch rather than Javanese.

59. It is in the 1930s that tellings of certain stories may have been forbidden to be performed outside the courts. See Clara van Groenendael, *The dalang behind the wayang*, p. 91. Yet even in the 1930s, when Mangkunagara VII and Kusumadiningrat of the Kraton Solo collected *wayang* stories to be published by Bale Pustaka, the stories were collected in the villages (ibid., p. 87). The information cited here usually comes from interviews carried out by me and one or another of my Academy colleagues.

60. Interview, 30 May 1984. "Leng leng ramyaningkang" are the words of the first *suluk* sung by the puppeteer at the beginning of a performance. Most written guides of *wayang* also prescribe this *suluk* for opening an evening's performance. Probohardjono's

Failed Narratives or the New "Essence"?

Java in the 1920s and 1930s, used to watch the training of village *dhalang* at the court of Mangkunagara VII. Palace teachers taught mostly puppet movements, but the village *dhalang* also had to memorize fixed passages (*kanda*) describing certain characters and settings.[61]

Some Javanese today do not understand what goes on in the first hour of the *wayang* night. The first scene, the *jejer*, which always takes place in a royal court and uses various levels of Javanese, is also the scene that was taught most rigorously in the court schools. The elevation in importance of this scene in the latter part of the nineteenth and early twentieth centuries may be seen as a feature of the new court performance tradition, which naturally emphasized the importance of court protocol. In comparing written versions of *wayang* stories recorded by Dutch scholars and administrators in the nineteenth century, it appears that the performance of this scene was affected by the written documents. In Humme's 1878 publication of the *lakon* "Abiasa" discussed in chapter 2, the opening passage or *janturan* can be compared with the *janturan* from the *lakon* "Pregiwa," recorded by Wilkens in 1846, and the *janturan* from the *lakon* "Kartawi-yaga" recorded by te Mechelen in 1882.[62] Although there are similarities between the three nineteenth-century *janturan*, Wilkens's and te Mechelen's Solonese *janturan* are much more elaborate than Humme's *pasisir* text. Not only is the opening passage much longer, but the language is more ornate, describing in detail the beauties of the court and the glory of the king.[63] In comparing the nineteenth-century Solonese *janturan* with

explanation indicates that before the opening of the schools, puppeteers had more flexibility in their choice of this opening song.

61. Interview in Holland, 15 April 1982.

62. The *lakon* recorded by Wilkens, as noted in the previous chapter, came from the mouth of the [illiterate] court *dhalang* in Solo. The *lakon* recorded by te Mechelen supposedly came from an illiterate Solonese court *dhalang* also.

63. In his doctoral dissertation, Peter Wilhelm Pink also compared *janturan* from nineteenth-century texts with contemporary usage and came to similar conclusions. See his *Gathut Kaca nagih janji; Gathut Kaca fordert die Ein ösung eines Versprechens* (Berlin: Reimer, 1977). Although it is brief, the *janturan* from the *lakon* "Abiasa" still mentions that the *kraton* is between the sea and the mountains in Humme, *Abiåså, Een Javaansch Tooneelstuk*, [*Wajang*], p. 6. Thus J. J. Ras is probably correct in arguing that a New Javanese shadow theatre must have been formed in the cities of the *pasisir* in the sixteenth century in "The Historical Development of the Javanese Shadow Theatre," p. 60. I am suggesting that the traditions which may have come to Central Java from the *pasisir* in the seventeenth and eighteenth centuries may have been refined in the courts

those from the *lakon* "Irawan Rabi,"[64] which was used to teach the new court tradition in the schools of the 1920s, it appears that they are almost identical.[65] Generations of puppeteers have performed this scene the way it was taught at the court schools and the way it was recorded in the first Dutch transcriptions of the tradition.

The year 1923 may actually mark the sharpening of distinctions between court and village *wayang* traditions, rather than an end to the period when the traditions were distinct. The court style was first outlined in the mid-nineteenth century, when Kusumadilaga produced the *Serat Sastramiruda*, setting out the rules for "correct" performances. It was in the court schools that were established in the 1920s that the court *wayang* tradition was really created, and it can be interpreted as a creative Javanese adaptation to Dutch scholarly attitudes and the aesthetic preferences of Dutch-educated Javanese.[66] This so-called court tradition came to be seen as something separate from a popular tradition, and village *dhalang* who had studied at the court schools discovered that the styles they were learning in the courts did not always please non-court audiences. They came to understand that the techniques they learned at the court schools might be more appreciated by elite Javanese and Dutch audiences than *kampung* or village ones.

In contrast to what the Dutch-educated overseers of the tradition may have expected, as the Javanese puppeteers read written versions of the plays and began to question the authority of their fathers, they became less subject to the tradition's power and influence. While the court schools at first reinforced traditional beliefs, they did so using the techniques of modern education; they emphasized written materials, notation, and memorization. One educated Javanese puppeteer whom I interviewed in

---

in the nineteenth century and not much earlier. It was also after 1830 that the principalities were cut off from artistic influences emanating from the *pasisir* as the Dutch took over the administration of Java.

64. M. Ng. Nojowirongko, *Serat tuntunan pedhalangan caking pakeliran lampahan Irawan Rabi*, Jilid I/II, III/IV (Surakarta: Akademi Seni Karawitan Indonesia, 1976).

65. When we compare these nineteenth-century Solonese *janturan* with *janturan* recorded from *dhalang* performing in Solo and the surrounding areas in 1984, we find that almost all Solonese *dhalang* and many from other parts of Java are still reciting the nineteenth-century text.

66. For extensive information about the history of the court schools in Surakarta and Yogyakarta, see Clara van Groenendael, *The dalang behind the wayang*.

Failed Narratives or the New "Essence"?

Solo in 1984 had a reputation for being very knowledgeable about the *wayang* tradition. His father had performed at the Solonese courts around the turn of the century. When I asked him what was the source—the *babon*—of the *wayang* tradition, he replied that the real, authentic tradition resided in the *wayang* plays collected and published by te Mechelen under the auspices of the *Bataviaasch Genootschap* in 1879. He felt that the "authentic" tradition resided in a Dutch-published Javanese text rather than in the hearts and minds of Javanese performers.

For a small group of Dutch-educated Javanese, 1923 can be used as a symbolic date to mark new ways in which these intellectuals understood their own *wayang* traditions. It is in this period that Dutch-educated Javanese came to believe that the *wayang* tradition needed to be cleaned up, the stories needed to be organized, and correct versions of them needed to be taught.[67] These Javanese began to perceive power and prestige to lie in the mastery of new kinds of scientific and literary knowledge. For the Javanese elites and their Dutch rulers and colleagues, the schools were also a way of controlling the power of the puppeteers,[68] something that the courts had been trying to do for centuries and that the government in Jakarta is still trying to do.

As modernizing Javanese elites began to lose interest in the *wayang* tradition as a source of authority and turned their energies to the accumulation of European or scientific knowledges, Javanese nationalists as overseers of the tradition responded to this threat by applying Dutch scholarly values to the uplifting of the shadow theatre.[69] If the stories were

67. McVey, "The Wayang Controversy in Indonesian Communism," p. 39, notes that the opening of the court schools denied the *dhalang*'s claim to a special relationship with the spirit world. The opening of the schools did not deny this relationship, but the relationship no longer brought the puppeteers power and respect in educated circles. In the villages to this day, *dhalang* are respected for their abilities to control the unseen forces of nature. At the schools, *dhalang* were respected for their command of artistic technique rather than their mystical accomplishments. See Clara van Groenendael, *The dalang behind the wayang*, p. 36.

68. Cf. McVey, "The Wayang Controversy in Indonesian Communism," p. 50 n. 72.

69. J. J. Errington, in *Language and Social Change in Java*, pp. 47–48, argues that the Javanese "speech level system" probably underwent a "compensatory prescriptive elevation" as many educated Javanese opted for mastery of languages other than Javanese, sometimes to offset their humble birth. See also R. McVey, "Taman Siswa and the Indonesian National Awakening," p. 129. I suggest a similar development in the *wayang* tradition.

developed and organized, if the musical pieces were written down, if the aesthetic standards were raised, if the obscene jokes and allusions were removed, perhaps the power of the shadow theatre, and the future of Javanese nationalism, could be insured.

Theosophy and Shadow Theatre

Even though, as the next chapter shows, many puppeteers ignored the *wayang* schools, the decision to open court schools to teach the puppeteers how to upgrade their performance styles certainly marked how Dutch-educated Javanese elites had adopted Dutch scholarly evaluation of their shadow theatre traditions. But I noted at the beginning of this chapter how Theosophical ideas had offered the possibility of elevating the *wayang* by seeing in it the remains of ancient mystical wisdom and the teachings of the Indian Bhagavad Gita. If Mrs. Hinloopen Labberton was indeed the first to articulate this new way of speaking about the shadow theatre as early as 1912, her ideas can be traced in the thought of Soetatmo and in the famous 1930s text of Mangkunagara vii, the elegant Javanese prince so admired by Dutch intellectuals.

We are taught that there are seven keys which unlock the secret gate of knowledge. Can it be possible that one of those keys unlocks the true meaning of the *Bharata Yuddha* (Great War) and the *Kurukshetra* in the *Lakon Purvo* (Epic of Purvo)?[70]

This opening by Mrs. Hinloopen Labberton shows immediately that she was on much surer ground in her knowledge of Theosophical thought than in her knowledge of the *wayang*, here awkwardly called "The Epic of Purvo." She tells us that she had lived in India and heard about the existence of a shadow theatre there, but had unfortunately never seen it.[71]

70. This and the following quotations are from Mrs. C. van Hinloopen Labberton's English language publication titled *The Wayang or Shadow Play as Given in Java* discussed in n. 21. As noted above, the publication has no date or place of publication but a cataloging date of "1912?" [*sic*]. The article is almost identical with the one published in *Wederopbouw* 4, nos. 8–9 (1921): 123–45. The Dutch edition, however, is illustrated with drawings of *wayang* puppets and intricate Theosophical charts, one of which is reproduced below.

71. For reasons connected with the caste prohibitions of Brahmins and other high-caste Indians, the shadow theatre of India remained virtually unknown until it was

Failed Narratives or the New "Essence"?

But even in these few lines, Hinloopen Labberton established the major connections that would designate the scholarly discourses about *wayang* in the twentieth century: she linked the shadow theatre of Java, the Bhagavad Gita, and secret knowledges framed in Theosophical jargon. What remained outside her discussion, of course, was Javanese Islam. She went on to note that the *wayang* had become a part of the "racial" life, as well as the moral life, of the Javanese. Expanding on this theme, she concluded: "As the Javanese race is now probably in its decadence, the new forms that have been added to the Wayang are much inferior to the originals."[72]

This discourse of decadence, degeneracy, and the nonoriginary quality of the *wayang* resonated with the late nineteenth-century Dutch scholarly discourse. But the Dutch scholars whose works were cited in the previous chapter never felt that the *wayang* could unlock very much except obscene humor and insipid dialogue, which were useful mainly for learning about Javanese language, customs, and linguistics. In figure 1, Hinloopen Labberton links the Mahabharata characters in intricate, esoteric drawings and symbols that highlight her racialist arguments. In the accompanying text she focused on several different parts of the tradition, beginning with the light of the *blencong*.

This light is the symbol of consciousness, and this consciousness is eternal for all periods of growth; without that light there would be no shadows. . . . However, here and there an individual in the masses begins to be conscious, and he only is able to begin to understand the laws of evolution.

Without this light the people of the races could not evolve. Without the Dalang

---

finally "discovered" and written about in the 1930s by English scholars. The use of leather puppets, according to one theory, made the performers ritually unclean. This reluctance of Indians to talk about the shadow theatre paved the way for Dutch scholars like Brandes and Hazeu to posit Javanese origins for the shadow theatre. Scholars now assume that the shadow theatre came to Java from India along with a great wealth of religious and narrative traditions. See Ras, "The Historical Development of the Javanese Shadow Theatre," for a discussion of shadow theatre origins, and S. H. Blackburn, "Epic Transmission and Adaptation," for a discussion of shadow theatre in Kerala. Sears, "Rethinking Indian Influence in Javanese Shadow Theatre Traditions," reassesses the arguments for Indian origins of Javanese shadow theatre traditions.

72. As another example of this racialist interpretation of the Mahabharata characters, Hinloopen-Labberton notes in "The Wajang or Shadow Play," p. 12, that Arjuna "stands for the Aryan Race, as well as mankind, also the Javanese race."

Bhisma Drona

Doeryodhana
Doeryodhana is de uitkomst van het karma van het Ras
(*Doeryodhana* is the result of the karma of the Race).

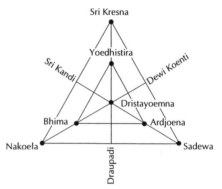

*Figure 1. Theosophical diagrams of
Mrs. Hinloopen Labberton, from
Wederopbouw 4, nos. 8–9 (1921).*

there would be no play; the shadows would drag out an inactive life 'til the oil was exhausted and the light extinguished. . . .

The link that connects the parts in the Wajang Play is Shri Krishna's work.

Her focus on the light, the oil lamp or *blencong*, was also found in Tjipto's essay in *De Indische Gids* mentioned earlier. Tjipto spoke, too, of the light-giving lamp, representative of the sun, "without which the whole earth would be stagnant, just as on the screen no representation is possible without the life-giving and light-giving blentjong."[73] This discourse is produced, of course, by the combination of Theosophical and Javanese knowledges. Hinloopen Labberton could not have spoken about the *wayang* if she had not received her information from Javanese sources. She then took that knowledge and filtered it through her Theosophical world-view (see figure 1). But Tjipto eliminated the racialist thought that perme-

73. Tjipto, "De Wajang," p. 532. Cf. Zoetmulder, *Pantheism and Monism*, ch. 10.

Failed Narratives or the New "Essence"?

ated Hinloopen Labberton's work. He took and used only that knowledge that would be useful for his nationalist purposes.

Although Tjipto erased the racialist thought, he accepted the mystical discourse of coming to awareness that the performance of a good *dhalang* could bring. "How exact is his insight, how philosophical his thought that the use of the sense organs brings a certain pain, and only through this can people become conscious of living in a World of Oppositions."[74] For Tjipto these oppositions often moved out of the world of *wayang* into the contradictions of the colonial experience. But the Theosophical emphasis on the god Kresna and the Bhagavad Gita also surfaced in Tjipto's later thought. In a 1918 speech, he addressed the conflict between Javanese and Indies nationalisms. He also noted that the distinguishing feature of the popular folk play, the *wayang*, was the Bhagavad Gita, even though, according to Tjipto, the Javanese *wayang* did not have a *"pakem"* or stable tradition connected to that text.[75] Then Tjipto said, relying on the opinion of D. van Hinloopen Labberton, the Dutchman who headed the Indies Theosophical Society from 1912 to 1923, that the essence of the Bhagavad Gita is alive in a qualitative way among a large proportion of the Javanese people. Authorizing his remarks with the opinions of Hinloopen Labberton, Tjipto proceeded to give a sketch of the spiritual life of the Javanese.

Tjipto described the subject matter of the Bhagavad Gita: Arjuna is on the battlefield of Kurukshetra with his charioteer Sri Kresna, incarnation of the god Wisnu. Arjuna loses all his will to fight when he sees his

74. Ibid., p. 535.

75. Unfortunately, the Dutch text of this 1918 speech, and those of R.M.S. Soeriokoesoemo, A. Muhlenfeld, and J. B. Wens, published as a special issue of *Wederopbouw* under the title "Javaansch of Indisch Nationalisme," does not yet seem to be available in America, at least in the several sets of IDC microfiche from various universities that I have seen. The microfiche for the first year of *Wederopbouw*, in which these speeches are collected, contains only the first sixteen pages, with a note that the fiches will be sent when they are filmed. The second year is blank also, except for about forty-five pages. Thus, I am working from Balfas's translation into Indonesian of (part of?) Tjipto's speech on Indies nationalism in *Dr. Tjipto Mangoenkoesoemo*, pp. 66–71. Balfas translates Tjipto as saying that the Bhagavad Gita is a part of the Mahabharata "yang tidak ada pakem kita" (p. 67). Roughly translated into English, this means there is no stable oral or written Javanese text of this work. In the following chapter, I analyze the Javanese concept of *"pakem."* The discussion of Tjipto's speech that follows is drawn from Balfas's Indonesian translation of the Dutch text.

relatives arrayed against him on the battlefield.[76] Tjipto then made a surprising detour. Rather than continuing with the teachings of the Gita—nonattachment to the fruits of one's actions—Tjipto uses the story to illustrate to his audience the nobility of the character of the Javanese people. Challenging the misguided image of polytheistic lazy natives that the Javanese were in Dutch eyes, Tjipto asked how a people could not be thought virtuous who valued this story of Arjuna, a man so noble that he would rather die than kill even one of his beloved relatives, a man with such compassion for his enemies. Once again, Tjipto took an element of Indian Theosophical thought and reinterpreted it, using it for his own purposes.

Tjipto's speech went on to compare Arjuna's reluctance to fight with Dipanagara's reluctance to kill anyone in the Java War. But what is most striking about the speech, and reappears continually in the writings of Dutch-educated Javanese, is the effort to refute Dutch ideas that see the Javanese as polytheistic immoral humans who will not be able to evolve properly until they become monotheistic. Tjipto showed his understanding of European evolutionary thought when he compared the Javanese notion of a *Goden hierarchie*, a hierarchy of gods, to what existed everywhere on earth:

A certain gradation of progress achieved in levels that rise gradually from the Hottentot to the races of Heroes, in ancient and recent history, Heroes in spiritual as well as intellectual fields, and on the field of battle.

But then, Tjipto argued, the Javanese believe in one Supreme Being who rules over this evolutionary span from the lowliest to the highest. The Dutch do not have to think that the Javanese worship every stone that looks a little strange or any tree that appears slightly eerie, a reference to village practices that included giving offerings to trees where village guardian spirits were believed to reside.

Tjipto concluded his remarks on *wayang* and Theosophy by citing ex-

76. The very Indian character of Tjipto's telling of the story of the Gita is illustrated by his calling Kresna *"gembala sapi"* or cow-herder. The stories of Kresna's life as a naughty young child and the perfect lover to each of the hundreds of cow-maidens or *gopi* are not well known in Java. But in new comic book tellings of Mahabharata stories, discussed in chapter 7, Indian stories of Kresna's youth, minus the sexual dalliances, are being retold.

Failed Narratives or the New "Essence"?

amples from the Old Javanese *Niti Sastra*, again to show that the Javanese were not degenerate and had long had high ethical standards. In this text the king is supposed to know the trials and tribulations of his subjects, help them in times of need, and reward them in the face of battle. Tjipto compared this model behavior of the ancient king with the contemporary *dhalang*. In this way Tjipto both accepted and recontextualized the Theosophical interpretation of the *dhalang* as "the leader of the race" into a leader who helps to bear the suffering of the people and stands out in times of crisis and humbly retreats when happiness and success overflow. Once again we see here a blending of Javanese and Theosophical knowledges to produce new ways of seeing Javanese practices and Javanese beliefs.

On the other hand, Tjipto's colleague and intellectual opponent Soetatmo Soeriokoesoemo blended Theosophical discourses about the shadow theatre in *Wederopbouw* for his very different goal of renewing Javanese culture and making it the essence of Javanese nationalist ideals.

Whoever has a good understanding of the wajangplay [*wajangspel*], of its meaning and knowledge, is surprised and moved by the striking likeness there with the outside world, a world of appearance and illusion in which the fragments of Truth play their assigned role with admirable devotion. . . . [*sic*] according to the plan of the Teacher, the Dhalang.

Beautiful is the wajangplay without argument!

And in order that the new generation, whose gaze is clouded more or less by a western-schooled intellect, could also profit from the beauty of this sacred, national play, I will attempt here with the help of their imagination, to illuminate that wajang as clearly as possible for them, with the (lively) [*sic*] light of the "blentjong."[77]

Once again the elements of the discourse on the shadow theatre appear that have become familiar from the writings of Tjipto and Mrs. Hinloopen Labberton: the stress on the *dhalang* as a wise teacher, the importance of the oil lamp or *blencong*, and the high and sacred value of the tradition. Soetatmo, too, did not just accept the received wisdom; he inserted his

77. Soetatmo, "Het Heilige Schrift in beeld. De Wajang," *Wederopbouw* 6 (1923), pp. 30–39.

own agendas into the discussion. As noted above, Soetatmo was troubled by the tendency of Javanese youth to turn away from their "traditional culture" and replace it with the scientific modernity provided by their Dutch-language education. But Soetatmo goes even further and calls the *wayang* a "sacred, national play" ("gewijde, nationalespel"). But the *wayang* can only be a national play in a nation whose boundaries coincide with the island of Java.

Soetatmo was calling out to the Javanese youth to come back to their shadow play. He hoped to reconstitute them as subjects of the play within the new discourses of the 1910s and 1920s that had elevated the village tradition of the past into the sacred essence of the Javanese nation's future. In Tjipto's essay, which he wrote in Holland and published in *De Indische Gids*, Tjipto was attempting to constitute his Dutch audience as subjects of the *wayang* to bring the inequities of the colonial relationship to their attention. Soetatmo's task seems more daunting, more ambitious, and more poignant; he was arguing for the very existence of the Javanese nation.

The gamelan on such a wajang-evening, announcing the beginning of the performance through the power of its reverberations, invites You with charming notes, Your own being, your highest Self to seek in this dusky realm of shadows. Thou would find thyself inscribed there. Your will be done, your plan fulfilled. And more can you draw from it. The gamelan whispers to you that you yourself are the "gending."

Sa gendingipoen [the melody]. . . . Thou shalt not seek in vain.

In this passage I have tried to capture the flavor of Soetatmo's ornate religious style, his quirky choice of words, and his high drama. He was speaking very clearly to the educated youth of Java and said earlier in the essay that if they failed to understand his words, it was their fault as much as his. He could only do his best in this language that was not his own, but they, too, had to strive to understand his meaning.

The receptivity of your heart is brought about by Yourself; no one can offer You a helping hand. The opening of the gate lies in your power, because the key is in your hand, the golden key, that will allow you to enter the hidden worlds of the East.

After their long journey through the discipline of European "science," which Soetatmo often juxtaposed against Javanese "tradition," young Javanese needed to be, as it were, reinitiated into their own culture. Because of their Javanese ancestry, they had the power to relearn their own culture, which they had supposedly lost through their European training. But, like any other traveler to Java, they had to find the key that would open up the mysterious world of the East that they had lost. In Soetatmo's larger argument, however, he made a sweeping reversal: he made the educated children of elite Javanese aware of a lack. No longer at the center of their "culture," they had become marginal to it. At the center of Java, of Javanese nationalism, was a mysterious essence that could only be unlocked with a secret key—a key forged by European Theosophists— and this essence was concealed in the shadow theatre.

Some of Soetatmo's other writings help to fill in his argument, because the argument connects shadow theatre, Theosophical teaching, nationalism, and the fate of the children of mixed Javanese-Dutch ancestry. In a 1920 essay on Theosophy and Javanese nationalism, Soetatmo had tried to reconcile the teachings of Theosophy with his vision of a Javanese nation-state.[78] It is here that he first posited the Javanese folk at the center of his vision and the Dutch-educated Javanese on the margins.

Javanese nationalism is based on Javanese individuality, on Javanese personality, and acquires a whole other meaning than the nationalism of the West, which comes from the love of the fatherland. Javanese nationalism is the inevitable color of Javanese culture and thus cannot possibly be in contradiction with Theosophy, which here must signify the "divine." The highest nationalism can only be perceived in the nature of things, understood and felt through those [things] that have penetrated to the heart of Javanese culture.

This can be illustrated by an example. Firstly, the dear Javanese from the kampung[79] feels by intuition in his heart that he is Javanese. He understands nothing of the powerful operation of Javanese culture; still he lives this culture without understanding it. Compare that with a cultivated Javanese who since childhood has enjoyed his upbringing in Europe; he then can perhaps truly say that he is Javanese with the knowledge that he was born from Javanese parents, but the feeling of the kampung Javanese is strange to him.

78. "Theosofie en Javaansch Nationalisme," pp. 73–77.
79. *Kampung* usually refers to a village but can also refer to an urban neighborhood.

Soetatmo linked the concepts that he needed to express his ideas of what the basis for Javanese nationalism must be: Javanese culture, the authentic—but unaware—Javanese village people, and a Theosophical appreciation of racially and spiritually constructed hierarchies. This marks the rise of a discourse which celebrates rather than laments the construction of Javanese subjectivity as different from European subjectivity—a discourse that is racially constructed but on Javanese rather than Dutch terms. Theosophical hierarchies become useful here, for on the spiritual planes posited within Theosophical thought, Europeans and Javanese can meet and be in harmony. But on this human earth, Javanese blood becomes the raison d'être of the Javanese nation state.

There is one last essay that ties up this argument about the importance of the shadow theatre within Soetatmo's thought. In the very first issue of *Wederopbouw*, Soetatmo had published an essay called "Het Javaansche Vraagstuk," or "The Javanese Question."[80] In this essay Soetatmo introduced many of the ideas that he would continue to espouse in his pursuit of Javanese nationalism. The position in the Indies of the people of "mixed blood" was obviously something Soetatmo had thought deeply about. The conclusions he came to illustrate the ambivalent nature of Soetatmo's thought, where he could appear as radically conservative or progressively liberal at the same time.

People will object that it is also egoistic of me not to think about the lot of the small group of Indiers of mixed blood.

I ask myself then: Why can they not dissolve themselves into us? Why must they unconditionally bear the nationality of the father, of the man? Is that of the woman so much less, so insignificant that it is impossible for them to think of it and they prefer to create a new nationality, namely the Indian, even in the case where they no longer wish to bear the nationality of the father? The question would have been solved if our half-brothers themselves were not ashamed of the nationality of the woman and valued it, a shame finally that is out of place and without any basis.

Soetatmo attempted to uplift the native mothers along with his rehabilitation or reconstruction of Javanese culture. Although the rights of women were not foremost in his mind, he was asking why the children of mixed blood always put their Dutch fathers over their Javanese mothers. In this

---

80. *Wederopbouw* 1, no. 1 (1918): 4–7.

Failed Narratives or the New "Essence"?

case, Soetatmo was willing to accept all those who would call themselves Javanese; even a little Javanese blood would suffice.

In his efforts to lift up the Javanese, to make Javanese proud of their heritage, Soetatmo needed role models to show the nobility of the Javanese people. For a brief moment, there is an overlap between Soetatmo's thought and that of Tjipto as they both sought to reclaim the ethical basis of the Javanese in the face of Dutch beliefs about the immorality of the Indies natives. And again for both of them, role models from the *wayang* proved useful. Rather than choosing the Theosophical Arjuna of the Bhagavad Gita as Tjipto did, Soetatmo chose the Arjuna that Javanese knew from the shadow theatre—the delicate mystical hero who fights with greedy and uncontrolled *raksasa* (ogres) in every play. Arjuna not only served as the model for the Javanese nobility but also as a suitable role model for the Javanese youth whom Soetatmo wanted to construct as the subjects of his discourse.

Ardjoeno, the adventurous hero of the youth, with his ever-inspiring inclinations to asceticism, the mystical hero of the searching philosopher, recalls for You the image of the perfect Ksatriya with his rhythm of voice and action. He is courteous in every respect, fine and noble in word and deed. He is courageous like no other. I only have to remind you of the meeting of boeto [ogre] Tjakil with Ardjoeno, the inimitable liveliness and activity in voice and gesture of the first and, as a worthy opponent, the beautiful and still figure of Ardjoeno, who later with one movement of the hand calmly invites the boeto to quiet down and then taunts him directly with the words: "Boeto hendi dangka moe [lit. what cave of corpses are you from] . . . !"

You see there the characterization of the ungovernable, greedy man with his attitude of cunning fickleness, drunk with delusions of power and trusting only in the power of his arms and the sharpness of his teeth, said in a modern style, trusting in the power of violence and the point of the bayonets. Then you find in the immobile Ardjoeno the type of calm and orderly ksatriya with his immovable will and unequalled courage, a courage that he calmly displayed in his simple question: "Boeto . . . hendi dangkamoe . . . !"[81]

In Soetatmo's story, however, it is harder to fix with certainty the models for his *wayang* characterizations. The "greedy, ungovernable man"

81. Soetatmo, "Het Heilige Schrift in beeld," pp. 31–32.

*The refined hero Arjuna (Ardjoeno)
fights with ogres and demons in
many shadow plays.*

may have referred to Indies natives from the other parts of the Dutch
colonial state or even to Javanese who had accepted European values,[82]
although most likely the "greedy man" referred to the Dutch themselves.
Soetatmo's story was both simpler and more complex. All who were not
Javanese had the propensity to act like the ogres of his story, but his
mystical thinking would lead him to rehabilitate those who believed in the
evolutionary potential of the human soul. Again, the contradictory nature
of Soetatmo's thought allows his words to be read and interpreted in
various ways. He finally elevated the *wayang* to encompass all religious
teachings.

82. Anthony Reid has translated a revealing passage from Soetatmo's essay "Gewijd
aan mijn Kameraden in 'Insulinde'," published in *Wederopbouw* 1 (1918): 9: "So you stay
in Sumatra, and you there in Ambon. Only in this way will our friendship be long
preserved. If we live in the same house and conduct our housekeeping jointly, no good
can be expected from that. Our tastes now differ; our culture is absolutely different"
("The Nationalist Quest for an Indonesian Past," p. 283).

Failed Narratives or the New "Essence"?

A conversation between buta *Terong (the eggplant demon at left) and* buta *Cakil (boeto Tjakil), who fights with Arjuna.*

The point of the teachings and moral lessons from the Bible and the Koran are found again there in the stories of Rama and the Maha-Barata. You can think of no philosophical work of any meaning that the wajang does not also know.

The convoluted and contradictory arguments of Soetatmo finally culminated in an elevated vision of the *wayang*, drawing inspiration from the Theosophical, evolutionary, and even racialist thought of his day. But the sophisticated scholar-soldier-ruler Mangkunagara VII would again pick and choose from this thickening discourse those elements that were useful for his vision of a more inclusive—and more hybrid—Indonesian future.

Mangkunagara VII and Colonial Discourse

Before he was elevated in 1916 to the position of Mangkunagara VII, the head of the minor ruling house in Solo, Soerjosoeparto was one of only two Javanese to have served as an officer in the Dutch army in World

War I.[83] He had interrupted his literary studies at Leiden to join the army but was recalled to Java in 1915 when it became known that Mangkunagara VI wished to abdicate and Soerjosoeparto was one of two eligible contenders to replace him. He also served as the national chairman of the Boedi Oetomo from August 1915 until he accepted the position of Mangkunagara VII in February 1916 by signing away much of the authority of his position to the colonial government.

It is clear that he had to give up his nationalist activities when he acceded to the throne. In comparison to the then-reigning Pakubuwana X (r. 1893–1939) of the Kraton Solo, a mysterious anti-Dutch figure,[84] whether Mangkunagara VII is seen as the model modernizing ruler or as a Dutch collaborator, he has had an enduring impact on the interpretation of the Javanese shadow theatre by Dutch and other foreign observers since the publication of his essay on shadow theatre in 1933. To conclude this discussion, I place that essay within the changing discourses of Javanese shadow theatre that I have been tracing from the nineteenth into the late twentieth centuries. A close reading of his text can show what was new in Mangkunagara VII's text and what he took from his Dutch and Javanese predecessors.

In the following essay, which except for certain additions remains the same as my reading of last December 1, have I dared to lift a small tip of the veil, to explicate how the wayang encompasses and keeps hidden the secret Javanese knowledge of the deepest meanings of life.[85]

---

83. This brief summary of Mangkunagara VII's life is drawn from Larson, *Prelude to Revolution*, pp. 59–75. There remains no in-depth study of the life and influence of this very important Solonese ruler although one gets a rather intimate view of him in his daughter Partini's autobiography. See *Partini: Recollections of a Mangkunagaran Princess*, as told to Roswitha Pamoentjak Singgih (Jakarta: PT Djambatan, 1986). Nancy Florida is publishing a catalog of the holdings in the Reksa Pustaka library, the library of the Mangkunagaran Palace. Mangkunagara VII's essay on shadow theatre "Over de wajang-koelit (poerwa) in het algemeen en over de daarin voorkomende symbolische en mystieke elementen" was first published in 1933 in *Djawa* (vol. 13 pp. 79–95), the journal of the Java Institute. It was translated by Claire Holt in 1957 as *On the Wayang Kulit (Purwa) and Its Symbolic and Mystical Elements* and published as Data Paper 27 by the Southeast Asia Program of Cornell University.

84. For an intriguing and insightful study of this ruler that paints him as a subtle and controversial anti-Dutch figure, see Pemberton, *On the Subject of "Java."*

85. Holt's translation, *On the Wayang Kulit*, only gives brief excerpts from the Mangkunagara's preface to his essay (p. 1). I have made slight changes in Holt's rendering of one sentence of this passage: "Met de volgende verhandeling, welke behoudens enkele

Failed Narratives or the New "Essence"?

Mangkunagara VII originally gave his talk on 1 December 1932 to the Solonese Cultural-Philosophical Study Circle, a group of Dutch, Eurasians, and Javanese who, as Claire Holt tells us, were "philosophically oriented intellectuals and professionals" and met monthly for discussions. Like Soetatmo, Mangkunagara VII adopted a Dutch orientalist approach to Java as exotic and mysterious. Mangkunagara VII also said in his short foreword that it was the "great national duty" for those who loved the Javanese folk to accommodate the perhaps not yet consciously felt but nonetheless existing need of prominent Javanese minds for deepening the inner life. So Mangkunagara VII also saw among "prominent Javanese minds" a lack—a lack in their inner life. It was to fill this lack that he dared to lift the veil. But here is the contradiction: why would the prominent Javanese minds not have been able to lift the veil for themselves? Was he not, in fact, lifting the veil for his Dutch listeners and readers, those who really lacked what Java had to offer and whose need he would fill through his explication of the shadow play? Yet he said that he dared to lift the veil so that the bond with the core of "our entire folklife," of which the *wayang* was a highly important and distinguished expression, would not be broken. Leaving this contradiction in mind, the text continues:

Therefore, the wayang stories, though based on the Indian epics, may be regarded in their Javanese form as creations of our poets and thinkers and as manifestations of a very special and a very high culture.[86]

Mangkunagara jumped right into the very contentious argument of origins discussed in the last chapter. Although Brandes's and Hazeu's thesis of indigenous origin for the *wayang* had recently been contested by Krom, Mangkunagara chose to ignore Krom and to focus on Rassers's new work on the origins of the Javanese drama,[87] even citing Rassers's support

toevoegingen hetzelfde inhoudt als mijn lezing van den 1sten December j.l. heb ik gewaagd een tipje van de sluier op te lichten, als hoedanig de wajang de geheime Javaansche wetenschap omtrent de diepste bedoelingen van het leven omhult en verborgen houdt" in Mangkunagara VII, "Over de wajang-koelit," p. 79.

86. Unintentionally Holt seems to have left out a few words in her translation of this passage. The text reads "een zeer bijzondere en een zeer hooge beschaving." I have added the missing words to Holt's translation. See "Over de wajang-koelit," p. 80.

87. J.L.A. Brandes, "Een Jayapattra of Acte van een Rechterlijke Uitspraak van Çaka 849"; Hazeu, *Bijdrage tot de Kennis van het Javaansche Tooneel*; N. J. Krom, *Hindoe-Javaansche Geschiedenis*, 2d ed.; Rassers, *Panji, the Culture Hero*. Rassers, of course, had never been to

of the ideas of Brandes and Hazeu. By positing the *wayang* stories as the creations of Javanese poets and thinkers despite their rootedness in Indian stories, a link that he certainly did not want to break, Mangkunagara vii authorized his own ideas with the latest Dutch scholarship. Moving deftly from the scientific to the philosophical, Mangkunagara once again supported his ideas with this scholarship. In addition to the work of Rassers, he cited the work of Dr. K.A.H. Hidding, who also argued, in *Tijdschrift voor Indische Taal-, Land- en Volkenkunde*, a major Dutch scholarly periodical, that the *wayang* should be a type of initiation for its spectators into "the secrets of earthly existence."[88]

Warming to his subject, Mangkunagara vii then introduced the ideas of R. M. Ir. Sarsita, who had lectured to the same group in May of 1932.[89] What Sarsita had established was the very important distinction between magic and mysticism: magic was equated with superstition and a low level of evolution while mysticism resonated with the higher discourses of Theosophical thought.[90] Sarsita argued that every *wayang* performance illustrated the victory of the mystical over the magical, and Mangkunagara used Sarsita's argument to show the high status of the *wayang purwa*. For Mangkunagara's last authorization, as he slowly guided his audience from scientific to mystical interpretations of the *wayang*, he offered the poetic insights of R. M. Noto Soeroto, a member of the Pakualaman nobility mentioned above, whom he had come to know in Holland and who also had served in the Dutch army.[91] It is in the poetry of Noto Soeroto that the deep interlacing of Javanese and Dutch knowledges appears. Noto Soe-

---

Java. What he did was to overlay a synchronic structuralist argument on the long-debated diachronic question of origins. Although Mangkunagara uses Rassers to support the argument for an indigenous origin, my reading of Rassers sees him sidestepping the question of origins altogether.

88. "De beteekenis van de Kekajon," *Het Tijdschrift voor Indische Taal-, Land- en Volkenkunde, uitgegeven door het Koninklijk Bataviaasch Genootschap van Kunsten en Wetenschappen* (1931).

89. The initials "R. M." stand for Raden Mas, showing that the speaker had claims to the ranks of Javanese nobility; his title of Ir. or engineer, showed his European scholarly credentials.

90. R. M. Ir. Sarsita also discussed the interpretation that compares every *wayang* play to the life cycle of human beings as they pass from childhood to old age, equating the musical and dramatic progression of the *wayang* night with the acquisition of knowledge.

91. See M. Djajadiningrat-Nieuwenhuis, "Noto Soeroto."

roto achieved some fame in Holland for poetry that he wrote in Dutch—poetry radically different from older Javanese poetic practices that relied on intricate rhyme schemes. The image of the young Javanese noble studying law in Leiden and pouring out his longing for his ancestral traditions in Dutch unrhymed verse is an illustrative one—probably as representative of the hybrid intellectual worlds of the period as Mrs. Hinloopen Labberton's enchantment with the "Epic of Purvo." As Noto Soeroto wrote:

Thus mirror yourself in my play, Oh Man, and know yourself! On the battlefield of your own heart will the grim war rage between friends and relations. Play then the demon as befits a demon, and play the nobleman as proper for a noble.

This bit of poetry from Noto Soeroto's "Wajang-liederen" (Wayang Songs), quoted by Mangkunagara VII,[92] is revealing for what it tells about the thought-world of the author. Noto Soeroto in this passage showed his familiarity with the Bhagavad Gita by stressing the teachings of Krishna to Arjuna, where Krishna alleviates Arjuna's doubts about killing his cousins and teachers by explaining that each person is born into a certain caste and must fulfill the duties of that caste. Arjuna has been born into the warrior caste and must fulfill his duties as a warrior; that is his Dharma.[93] Thus Noto Soeroto's admonition to act according to one's station in life, whether demon or noble, may have suited Mangkunagara's efforts to connect the *wayang* with the noble Indian text, as well as with Dutch poetry and, finally, even the essence of European "culture." In the next passage, Mangkunagara VII argued that Noto Soeroto's poetry clearly linked the wisdom of the *wayang* to the philosophical views of Plato, who also "regards this world as a reflection of the world of ideas." The wisdom of the *wayang* had now been elevated to Platonic Heights.

Having established the firm credentials of the shadow theatre through

92. Mangkunagara, "Over de wajang-koelit," p. 82; translated by Holt, *On the Wayang Kulit*, pp. 4–5.
93. Cf. Soetatmo Soeriokoesoemo "Het Heilige Schrift in beeld. De Wajang": "But you shall not find a raksasa in Praboe [King] Rama, nor on the other hand a Ksatriya in Rahwana." In his *Catalogus van boeken en tijdschriften uitgegeven in Nederlandsch Oost-Indie van 1870–1937* (Amsterdam: Swets & Zeitlinger, 1966), G. Ockeloen notes that D. van Hinloopen Labberton published a translation of the Bhagavad Gita (*Heilandslied*) in Dutch in 1913. The Ockeloen citation comes from Perlman, "Theosophy in Java," p. 7 n. 12.

citations from the work of other authors, Mangkunagara VII felt ready to present his own views. He argued strongly for both an ancient and an indigenous past for the *wayang purwa*, offering a synthesis of the Dutch debates by suggesting that dramatic traditions and stories coming from India in ancient times probably blended with a preexisting Javanese rite of ancestor worship—a view that many might adhere to today.[94] More importantly, however, was the Prince's argument that every shadow theatre performance is an exercise in *semadi* or meditation, and he illustrated this argument by his explication of two *lakon*, the Arjuna Wiwaha (or Ciptoning) and the Dewa Ruci stories.

I noted in chapter 1 how the Dewa Ruci story was connected in the early nineteenth century with Islamic Sufi mysticism, but Mangkunagara VII made only the briefest reference to his clear knowledge of the Islamic interpretation of this story. He referred his readers to a Javanese book titled "Soeksma Poesara" by a certain Dr. Bavinck—a Eurasian or Dutch scholar?—"who introduces *under other names* the well-known Arabic conceptions of Aluamah, Amarah, Supiah, and Mutmainah."[95] Here Mangkunagara showed intimate knowledge of the very Islamic interpretation of the Dewa Ruci story through the association of the colors red, yellow, black, and white with human emotions and the fight between reason and passion (*akal* and *nafsu*) that lies at the heart of much Sufi mysticism.

But Mangkunagara VII preferred to "lift the veil" only partially; he did not dare to tell his audience what most Javanese Muslims knew—that Islamic as well as "Hindu-Javanese" interpretations could be used to explain the *wayang* in mystical terms. Even his description of Arjuna's *semadi* or meditation, supposedly taken from a recitation of a *dhalang*[96] and translated into Dutch, can be read in Islamic terms.[97] But Mangkunagara VII did not want to draw the attention of his Dutch listeners to Islam, and his Javanese listeners would not need to be reminded. If there were hidden meanings in Mangkunagara VII's text, they pointed to the unspoken presence of Islam, rather than the nationalist messages of Tjipto or

94. Cf. Ras, "The Historical Development of the Javanese Shadow Theatre," and Sears, "Rethinking Indian Influence in Javanese Shadow Theatre Traditions."

95. Mangkunagara, "Over de wajang-koelit," p. 87 (emphasis added).

96. Ibid., p. 90; Holt translation, *On the Wayang Kulit*, p. 14.

97. When I was in Java in the early 1970s, I was introduced by a Sufi master to mystical exercises that incorporated the very practice described in the *dhalang*'s recitation given by Mangkunagara VII.

Failed Narratives or the New "Essence"?

Soetatmo. But he drew his text to a close with scholarly charts, modeled somewhat after J. Kats's *wayang wong* programs for Dutch audiences and this firm conviction: "In any case every lakon should be regarded as a symbol of mystical action—the practice of semadi."[98] Mangkunagara VII's text of 1933 remains today the definitive statement on the meaning of Central Javanese, especially Solonese, shadow theatre.

The Solonese *wayang purwa* performances held at the court of Mangkunagara VII in the 1930s and the *wayang wong* performances staged at the court of Sultan Hamengkubuwana VIII (r. 1921–39) of Yogyakarta were produced for hybrid Javanese and Dutch audiences and fashioned to suit the tastes of those audiences.[99] I was told by the late K.R.M.T.H. Sanjoto Sutopo Kusumohatmodjo, Head of Palace Affairs at the Mangkunagaran palace, that *wayang* performances held at the court in the 1930s were very private esoteric events with limited audiences.[100] The celebration of these performances over others was unique to a particular moment in the intertwining transformations of Javanese and Dutch knowledges. They were neither more nor less "authentic" or pleasing than other performance styles. Rather, they were created in the context of the colonial encounter, and related mystical styles were celebrated again in the 1970s and 1980s even when colonialism had supposedly been swept away.

This chapter has analyzed the rise of new ways of speaking and thinking about the shadow theatre and has explored the emergence of new Javanese subject positions brought into being by Theosophy, exile, and imagination. As Javanese intelligentsias began their journeys out of the thought-world of the shadow theatre tradition, they continued to manipulate its power and influence for their own purposes. Although some of the puppeteers I met in Java had learned the Theosophical interpretations of the *wayang* tradition in the 1930s, the following chapter shows that most puppeteers did not cite mysticism as the main feature of the performance tradition.

98. Kats, *Het Javaansche Tooneel I*; Holt translation, *On the Wayang Kulit*, p. 21.
99. See Lindsay, "Klasik Kitsch or Contemporary."
100. Personal communication, 1983.

4 Javanese Storytellers, Colonial Categories,

Mahabharata Tales

The shape and form of each *wayang* puppet is really strange if looked at objectively: the body faces forward, the arms are long, the face and features like the nose and eyes are not like normal pictures that match up with reality [*natuurlijk*], but are stylized. The stylization is called: *frontaliteit*, namely with a body facing the viewer, like drawings from Egypt.[1]—Soeharda Sastrasoewignja

For example, it used to happen like this in the past. The puppeteer had to ask the host: What would you like to have? Oh, it's a circumcision, then what do you prefer? You like fancy puppet movements, and lots of clown scenes, and not too many speeches. Now, these three preferences symbolize what the puppeteer has to work with. Okay, I'll pick a play that I already know well, one that's really familiar. Now, let's say this familiar play uses the Pendawa characters. Then on the spot I'll make up a story that can attract and please these people.

It's usually easy for me. I'll describe my own experience. Mas Tikno, we'd like the story Sangsang Kencana Anting Retno. Now in this case, I've never heard of that story. Actually I'm rather surprised. Ha, what's this Sangsang Retno Anting story? Well, Sangsang Anting Retno, what could that story be? Then suddenly I get some ideas. Since these people like fancy puppet movements and clown scenes, I'll use a story that highlights those things. So it happens like this. I took a mask play [*topeng*] story but I changed the name of the boon. It's just a starting point. In the first scene, if I'm not mistaken, there's that visitor to the kingdom, but maybe I'll change it to another. That's how it's done in the performances. Most puppeteers who create stories take things from their own imaginations.[2]—Ki Sutikno

The quotes that begin this chapter capture the different ways in which Dutch-educated and village Javanese intellectuals were talking about the shadow theatre tradition in the 1930s and the 1980s. Dutch-

1. Soeharda Sastrasoewignja, "Hal Wajang Poerwa dan Djalan-djalan oentoek Memperbaharoeinja," *Poedjangga Baroe* 2, no. 1 (July 1934): 6. The title of this article—written in Malay with many Dutch words—translates as "Concerning the Shadow Theatre and Ways to Renovate It."

2. Interview, 5 January 1984.

educated Javanese had begun to look at the shadow theatre from outside the tradition, seeing the strangeness of the puppets, especially when compared to European realist or even romantic styles of representation. The writer of the first quotation compared the *wayang* puppets to Egyptian drawings and could find no word in Malay to indicate the way in which he felt the puppets were strange. He finally called the quality he was trying to describe *frontaliteit*, a word that does not occur in Dutch dictionaries— although it technically could—and gives the same sensation as "front-ality" does in English. I have juxtaposed this quote with the words of a successful Javanese village puppeteer speaking in the early 1980s. The puppeteer is explaining how he creates his stories. The two quotations reveal a dissonance that was emerging between the world of many village puppeteers and that of the Dutch-educated Javanese elite. This chapter explores the relevance of the ideas of intellectuals like Soetatmo and Mangkunagara VII in the thought-worlds of village puppeteers.

The new ways of talking about *wayang* performances discussed in the previous chapter led to an increasing separation between elite and folk audiences. Ramayana and Mahabharata stories and the performance practices of village puppeteers were refined in the court schools of Central Java to cater to the tastes of Dutch-educated elites and their Dutch colleagues and friends. If court audiences praised performers for their mystical knowledge, village audiences appreciated puppeteers for their earthy humor, their shamanistic prowess, and their intimate knowledge of village affairs. Although Mangkunagara VII argued that each *wayang* performance symbolized the triumph of the mystical over the magical, village puppeteers were respected more for their ability to manipulate magical than mystical forces, for their ability to heal both physical and psychological wounds, and for their great knowledge of Javanese traditions and genealogical information.[3] In the court of Mangkunagara VII, perhaps,

---

3. Cf. Pigeaud, *Javaanse Volksvertoningen*, p. 368. This is not to criticize Mangkunagara VII's interpretation of the shadow theatre but rather to see it as one among many possible ways of speaking about shadow theatre. Pigeaud, one Dutch scholar who generally argued for seeing the *wayang* as a village tradition, was a bit skeptical about those theories that saw the *wayang* characters as representatives of the powers of the human soul. Reacting to the work of structuralists like Rassers, however, Pigeaud defended Mangkunagara VII's essay: "This doesn't alter the fact that for understanding the present-day Javanese thought-world, it has much more worth than the scientific-ethnological explanation of the Javanese theatre from very old pagan cosmic-mythological ways of think-

Rice paddy in a village outside of Solo.

these same puppeteers would be appreciated for their poetic choice of words, for their ability to create a meditative atmosphere, for their sensitivity to the intrigues of the court, and for their skill at satirizing these intrigues in acceptable ways.

Although the court libraries of Central Java contained texts which told the stories of the shadow theatre, was the information in these texts available to village puppeteers, and how did these texts impinge upon the performance tradition? Although the *wayang* puppeteers used Ramayana and Mahabharata stories, which tellings of these stories did the puppeteers prefer and perform? Scholars have often separated the Javanese stories into trunk and branch plays, but what were the Javanese norms by which these distinctions were measured?

Although European and American scholars have defined key terms in the vocabulary of the Javanese shadow theatre,[4] rarely have these terms

ing, that see the main characters of the wayang-play as representatives or ur-types of a world and society embracing classification system." Ibid., p. 76.

4. Te Mechelen, "Een en ander over de Wajang"; Poensen, "De Wajang"; Hazeu, *Bijdrage tot de Kennis van het Javaansche Tooneel*; Kats, *Het Javaansche Tooneel I*; Holt, *Art in*

A village lane in Central Java.

been presented in the words of the Javanese puppeteers themselves. The separation of Javanese shadow plays into trunk (*pakem*, *baku*) and branch (*carangan*) stories provides an entry point for placing shadow theatre performances within their literary milieu, but scholarly definitions of trunk and branch stories are often inadequate to explain the complex relationships among the various components of the tradition. Although this chapter explores the relationships between trunk and branch stories, between oral and written stories, and between Javanese and Indian ones, most importantly, I show that these relationships remain fluid and dynamic. The stories that are recorded in written texts often document features of the performance tradition, and this is what connects the written literature to contemporary performance practice. The main voices in this chapter are those of the puppeteers as they construct, reconstruct, and reflect upon their traditions. In the last chapter I spoke of the Javanese

Indonesia; Brandon, *On Thrones of Gold*; Ras, "The Historical Development of the Javanese Shadow Theatre." See especially Feinstein et al., appendix to vol. 1 of *Lakon Carangan*, for a survey of definitions of "carangan," "baku," and "pokok," and also Feinstein's introduction to vol. 1 where he analyzes these terms in detail.

connection between *sejarah* (history) and *crita* (story). Here the puppeteers turn *crita* into *lakon* (plot) by weaving tales, rumors, and mystical teachings into all-night performances.

Texts and Performances

Descriptions of *wayang* performances and titles of stories from the late eighteenth century still exist in the court libraries at Surakarta.[5] From the late eighteenth and the nineteenth centuries there are written *lakon*, some put together under Dutch patronage starting in the 1840s, and others copied by hand at royal command for the palace archives. Although I have argued that Dutch literary values and philological biases influenced the production of texts that recorded the *wayang* stories, it is more difficult to assess the influence of Dutch philology on Javanese performance practice. Certainly Dutch scholars intended to preserve the dramatic traditions by documenting them, but have Dutch attempts to make written *wayang* texts more coherent or more poetic or more Indianized carried over into performance practices? Clearly, were it not for the Dutch records, there would be fewer observations and examples of *wayang* traditions from the nineteenth and early twentieth centuries.

The proliferation of written and printed texts over the past 150 years may have kept alive certain stories or parts of the tradition at the expense of other stories, but few *dhalang*, even those called court *dhalang*, had access to these printed texts before the twentieth century. After the opening of the court *wayang* schools in the 1920s and 1930s, texts in palace libraries began to have an ambiguous authority over shadow theatre traditions as Dutch-educated Javanese intellectuals believed written texts contained more "accurate" tellings than the oral transmission of stories that has commonly shaped *wayang* repertoires. Until recently, this authority had mythical status within the community of puppeteers. Some puppeteers had heard of the existence of these palace texts but most had never seen them. In general, puppeteers did not associate knowledge recorded in written texts with performance ability. It was not until the puppeteers

5. See Florida, *Javanese Literature in Surakarta Manuscripts*, 1:214–28.

were exposed to written and printed texts in palace upgrading courses or fine arts schools that their attitudes toward these texts began to change.

Court poets and princes and Dutch and Javanese scholars sponsored the production of written texts that recorded preferred tellings of stories and the writing of handbooks that were intended to assert influence over performance practices. As emphasis was placed on the written documentation of *wayang* texts, the word *pakem* (fixed text) was increasingly used to describe written rather than oral stories. In most Dutch and American studies on the Javanese shadow theatre, *pakem* are described as a genre of written play texts which serve as puppeteer's manuals.[6] The written *pakem* contain brief outlines of the stories in prose form and cannot be used as playscripts. With this emphasis on *pakem* as written texts, Ras traced the history of the *wayang* theatre and suggested that the *parwa* texts mentioned in chapter 1, prose versions of the Mahabharata stories in Old Javanese, may once have been considered as *wayang pakem*.[7] That the poetic *kakawin* texts were used, at times, as *pakem* is indicated by the fact that they are still used in this way in Bali, where the practice of oral recitation (*mabasan*) has kept these texts alive.[8]

There have been many stylistic changes in the written texts associated with the shadow theatre over the centuries. The *parwa* texts that retold Sanskrit-language Mahabharata stories represented early literary efforts of the ancient Javanese kingdoms and were written on palm leaves by court scribes. Their language was Old Javanese mixed with Sanskrit phrases, and the texts indicated some knowledge of both languages. The poetic *kakawin* texts followed, producing more stylized works that may have been used to generate various court performance traditions, with or with-

6. Te Mechelen, "Een en ander over de Wajang," p. 82; Hazeu, *Bijdrage tot de Kennis van het Javaansche Tooneel*, pp. 127–32; Pigeaud, *Javaanse Volksvertoningen*, pp. 367–68; Holt, *Art in Indonesia*, p. 138; Brandon, *On Thrones of Gold*, p. 34; J. J. Ras, *De schending van Soebadra: Javaans schimmenspel*, pp. 101–2.

7. Ras, "The Historical Development of the Javanese Shadow Theatre," p. 57. This could account for the unusual form of the *parwa* texts, which are marked by the insertion of many Sanskrit phrases. Cf. P. J. Zoetmulder, *Kalangwan: A Survey of Old Javanese Literature*, and M. S. Zurbuchen, *The Language of Balinese Shadow Theater* (Princeton: Princeton University Press, 1987). Ancient performers could have used the Sanskrit phrases (Skt. *śloka*) just as eighteenth-century puppeteers used Kawi phrases to give weight to the oral tradition by tapping the foreign language to invoke its authority.

8. Zurbuchen, *The Language of Balinese Shadow Theater*.

out puppets. These texts were copied by hand over the centuries, mostly by the Balinese, and they were totally cast in Old Javanese with no Sanskrit quotations.

The next centuries are hazy, and Ras speculates that it was during this period that a *wayang purwa* tradition in Old Javanese was recast into modern Javanese for the benefit of the *nouveaux riches* elites in the port cities who no longer understood the poetic language of the earlier period.[9] The stories recounted in the Serat Kandha texts, closely connected to oral *wayang* traditions, incorporated and intertwined Javanese and Islamic knowledges. In the *wayang* tradition, passages from Old Javanese *kakawin* texts, used by the *dhalang* for their dramatic and musical mood, were transmitted orally, maintaining loose connections with written texts from the earlier period.

Pakem texts in modern Javanese date from the nineteenth century and generally gave summaries of selected stories.[10] According to usage set in place by Dutch scholars, *pakem* texts were brief prose outlines of stories while *lakon* texts recorded the stories in detail.[11] There are standardized parts in these texts including certain conversations between kings and their retainers, between respected mystical teachers and seekers of knowl-

9. Ras, "The Historical Development of the Javanese Shadow Theatre."

10. Hazeu spoke about the history of the *pakem* and suggested that *pakem* were not known in the so-called Hindu-Javanese time. He noted that Dr. van der Tuuk had not found *pakem* to exist in Bali, where the puppeteers took their stories directly from the older poetry. Hazeu suggested that the first *pakem* were only put together after the literary renaissance of the eighteenth century. It was then that the "Moslem religious zeal" and the long wars lessened the interest in the older stories, and the pressing need for sketches of the older stories began to be felt. "It was thus of concern that the dhalangs, who still recalled the most from the oral traditions, as speedily as possible wrote down what they knew. The dated *pakem* collections, that are known to me, were all put together after A.D. 1800, but this does not prove much because older *serat's pakem* [sic] could have been lost or at least not have found their way to the European libraries." *Bijdrage tot de Kennis van het Javaansche Tooneel*, p. 132. One gets the impression from this last sentence of Hazeu's that he saw all Javanese texts on a journey that lead to a predetermined resting place in Dutch libraries.

11. E.g., Ch. te Mechelen, "Drie-en-twintig schetsen van wajang-stukken (Lakon's) gebruikelijk bij de vertooningen der Wajang-Poerwå op Java," and "Drie teksten van tooneelstukken uit de wayang poerwå," *Verhandelingen van het Bataviaasch Genootschap voor Kunsten en Wetenschappen* 43 (1882): 1–494; A. C. Vreede, ed., "Drie Teksten van tooneelstukken uit de wajang poerwa voor den druk bezorgd door A. C. Vreede," 2de Deel, *Verhandelingen van het Bataviaasch Genootschap van Kunsten en Wetenschappen* 44 (1884): 1–582.

edge, between the clown-servants, and between noble heroes and the ogres they will kill. A. L. Becker diagrammed the plot structure of shadow play performances that he studied and recorded the general scheme of descriptive passage, conversation, and battle, which alternate throughout the night, interspersed with the *dhalang*'s songs and occasional musical pieces.[12] Both written and performed forms of shadow play stories follow this structure, although great deviation is permitted within the various parts of the structure, especially in the performed stories. The writers of *pakem* and *lakon* had the same freedom as the *dhalang* (often these writers were, in fact, *dhalang*) to expand or contract their texts as they chose. *Pakem* were also generated upon the occasion of a performance when programs—outlining the major action of the night's performance—were given to invited guests. This practice originated in the nineteenth century to explain performances to Dutch scholars and administrators; it flourished in the 1920s and 1930s when the Java Institute sponsored various performances for Javanese and Dutch audiences.[13]

Pakem in this sense of written texts have rarely been used by practicing *dhalang*. Over the past one hundred years, written *pakem* and *lakon* have tended toward greater and greater detail, with extended conversations, musical notation, and the mood songs (*sulukan*) of the *dhalang* all included in the text. The most formulaic and standardized parts of the texts are the *janturan*, passages generally chanted by the *dhalang* at the opening of a performance and before certain other important scenes. These passages are descriptive and speak of the beauty and prosperity of the kingdom at hand and the virtues of the ruler to be introduced.[14] Comparison of a number of written texts and transcribed performances shows both diachronic and synchronic similarity on a phrase level rather than a word level. In other words, word order may vary or additional phrases can be added, but there is a high level of standardization in written versions of these passages.

As noted in chapter 2, if we compare *janturan* passages from the first *wayang* texts committed to writing by the Dutch in the nineteenth cen-

12. Becker, "Text-Building."

13. E.g., *Programma van de Wayang-Wong Opvoering in den Kraton te Jogjakarta* (1923); *Programma voor het Congres van het Java-Instituut* (1924).

14. For English examples of several *janturan* translated from written rather than performed *lakon* texts, see Brandon, *On Thrones of Gold*.

tury[15] with transcribed performances from 1984,[16] the degree of similarity is striking. The *janturan* developed and inscribed in Javanese court texts of the nineteenth century were published by Dutch scholars and were then incorporated into the texts used in the court schools which opened in the 1920s. These *janturan* passages from the nineteenth century are still used by literate and nonliterate puppeteers today.[17] Famous passages from other genres of Javanese literature may also be woven into *pakem* much as they can be woven into a night's performance. For example, puppeteers use *wulangan* or mystical passages taken from poetic texts to edify or enlighten those in the audience interested in such teachings. The most familiar *wulangan* come from the "Asta Brata," a section of the nineteenth-century *Serat Rama*, written by Yasadipura I.[18]

One could argue that the production of written *pakem*, particularly documenting Solonese style, has preserved elements of the tradition that might have disappeared from memory.[19] Pigeaud noted that there were

15. J. A. Wilkens, "Wajangvoorstelling"; te Mechelen, "Drie teksen van tooneelstukken uit de wayang poerwå."

16. Feinstein et al., *Lakon Carangan*, vols. 1–3.

17. I mentioned in chapter 3 that the *lakon* Palasara, used in the Javanese court performance manual, the *Serat Sastramiruda*, was one that had been published in several versions by Dutch scholars. In the same vein, the *lakon* Irawan Rabi (Irawan's Wedding), the text used most commonly to teach the puppeteers at Padhasuka, the *dhalang* school connected to the Kraton Surakarta, had begun to receive the attention of Dutch scholars as early as 1880. See H. Kern, "Het Javaansche wajangstuk Irawan Rabi," *Mededeelingen der Koninklijke Akademie van Wetenschappen, afdeeling Letterkunde* (MKAW.L), 2d series 9 (1880): 125–32. This was not, however, a complete *lakon* text, just a summary and notes.

18. See Moertono, *State and Statecraft in Old Java*, Appendix 3.

19. Hazeu argued: "It appears thus that there is more need for the pakem of the wayang purwa lakons than the others, and this is easily explained because (1) *purwa* plays are much more often performed than the others; doesn't the whole *wayang purwa*, the dramatic apparatus as well as the plays, still carry in the eyes of the Javanese a very special character, and (2) one can for the performance of the lakons from the *Panji, Damar Wulan* or *Moslem* tales still consult the New Javanese poetry from which those lakon are borrowed, which is not possible for most of the *wayang purwa* plays, because the [Old Javanese] works, that, in epic style, contain the same stories as these plays today no longer exist or at least are no longer understood: the stories from these lakon were handed down over the centuries almost exclusively in oral traditions, until they were finally written down by later dhalangs in dramatic form. And it is exactly this that gives those pakems from the *purwa* lakons such a special worth." *Bijdrage tot de Kennis van het Javaansche Tooneel*, pp. 137–38. This explanation is hard to accept because many stories from the *wayang purwa* repertoire were written down in modern Javanese poetic forms. In general, however, the nineteenth-century Dutch scholars did not look kindly upon

few *pakem* from Yogyakarta, the other main Javanese center of traditional culture. He surmised that most of the *pakem* were from Solo (Surakarta) because Yogyakarta did not have the famous nineteenth-century court poets that Solo did.[20] Solonese-style shadow theatre differs from Yogya-style in many ways: for example, in musical traditions, *suluk* styles, repertoire, number of battle scenes, puppets, and order of scenes. The textual traditions which are believed to underlie the two repertoires also differ. While most educated Solonese puppeteers cite Ranggawarsita's *Pustaka Raja Purwa* as the source of the Solonese repertoire, Solonese puppeteers suggest that the Yogya puppeteers draw their material mainly from Serat Kandha traditions, whether written or oral.[21] Solonese puppeteers do not cite the Serat Kandha as the source of Solonese traditions.

Although Yogyanese puppeteers may not necessarily be familiar with any written texts connected to the shadow theatre, in contemporary Yogya-style plays, a passage from the *Purwakandha* (i.e., a court inscription of Serat Kandha texts) is often recited at the beginning of each play. Also, I noted in chapter 2 that Raffles equated the name *Pepakem* with a Serat Kandha text in the early nineteenth century. Written *pakem* might also have been scarce in Yogyakarta because Dutch scholars encouraged the Solonese puppeteers to produce written *pakem*.[22] It is over the past thirty years that *pakem* have been written for general audiences as advances in print technology have encouraged the proliferation of all kinds of texts. Most bookshops in Solo today carry at least a few *wayang pakem*, although I never knew any puppeteers who owned one of these texts.

The most recent chapter in the history of written play texts is now

---

these texts. See, for example, A. B. Cohen Stuart's introduction to his translation of a modern Javanese telling of the stories of the Great War, "Brata-joeda, Indisch Javaansch heldendicht."

20. Pigeaud, *Literature of Java*, 1:249.

21. During the reign of Hamengkubuwana V (1822–55), a Yogyanese court text of the Serat Kandha traditions, the *Purwakandha*, was compiled. This became one Yogyanese court text believed to be associated with Yogyanese *wayang* traditions, although most Yogyanese puppeteers have never seen the text, which is housed in court libraries; see Clara van Groenendael, *The dalang behind the wayang*, p. 33. Recently, published paperback versions of the *Purwakandha* have become available in Yogyakarta.

22. Many printed collections of *wayang lakon* were put together under the direction of Dutch scholars. Ch. te Mechelen and J. Kats were two of the most ambitious collectors. See te Mechelen, "Drie teksten van tooneelstukken uit de wayang poerwå," and Kats, *Het Javaansche Tooneel I.*

taking place in the fine arts academies, particularly the Academy in Solo, where students and faculty are creating and documenting new styles of shadow play texts and performances. One example is the *padat* or condensed play, which shortens the all-night performance to one or two hours. The written versions of these plays, called *naskah*, are quite different from traditional *pakem* in that they are actually playscripts intended to be memorized verbatim by the performer. *Padat naskah* differ from traditional *pakem* in both structure and content. I will discuss these new shadow play performances, and their written texts, in the next chapter.

The Major Written Texts Connected with the Shadow Theatre

Although puppeteers might be conversant with the nineteenth-century Javanese poetic literature discussed in preceding chapters, the major texts connected with the shadow theatre tradition were prose retellings of the *wayang purwa* stories. Although the *Serat Sastramiruda* has been widely written about in Dutch and American scholarship on the *wayang purwa*, the puppeteers themselves hardly ever mentioned this text. The most famous written text for Solonese puppeteers is Ranggawarsita's *Pustaka Raja Purwa* (Book of Kings), discussed in chapter 3, which dates from the latter part of the nineteenth century. From what I was told by one scholarly *dhalang* in Java, who had received a Dutch-style education in the not too distant past, Ranggawarsita collected the information for his *Pustaka Raja Purwa* from the tales of village *dhalang*. And he collected the information either in the company of or under the encouragement of his friend and colleague C. F. Winter.[23] This is corroborated by the disdainful comments of Poerbatjaraka quoted in chapter 3.[24] In a sense, Ranggawarsita carried out field research among the village *dhalang* of his day and wrote down the genealogies that had been passed through oral traditions for centuries. The stories included in Ranggawarsita's compendium might serve as an inventory of the stories being performed in the villages at that time. What Ranggawarsita did was to arrange the shadow play stories in a chronolog-

23. R. Soetrisno, personal communication, 1983.
24. Poerbatjaraka, *Kepustakaan Djawa*, p. 181.

ical fashion, along with other Javanese myths and quasi-historical materials, to produce a magnum opus which, in a unique way, documented
the history of Java from the Islamic creation story to the fall of the last
great "Hindu-Javanese" kingdom, Majapahit, at the end of the fifteenth
century.[25]

Although the Dutch scholars of the time were greatly disappointed by
Ranggawarsita's *Pustaka Raja Purwa*, I have suggested that it is more useful
to see the work as a creative adaptation of both Javanese and Dutch styles
of historical writing.[26] Ranggawarsita's mistake, in Dutch eyes, was his
falsified dating system—a creative way to reconcile in tangible form the
intertwining transformations of historical and mythical time that seemed
to preoccupy the thought-worlds of philologically oriented Dutch and
Eurasian thinkers. In the writing of his *Pustaka Raja Purwa*, Ranggawarsita
produced a kind of cognitive dissonance for his Dutch critics. For Dutch
scholars and would-be scholars, the search for a proper ordering of the
stories could be elegantly explained within a world of Dutch philology but
not within the world of Javanese Universal Histories, as these texts came
to be called.

I explained in chapter 2 how, in the nineteenth century, Roorda, Kern,
te Mechelen, and Humme attempted in their published works to order the
wayang purwa stories in a genealogical and historical fashion. The Dutch
scholars and retired civil servants most often chose to translate or to
document the more Indian stories of the *wayang purwa* repertoire, stories
that were not necessarily popular with either Javanese village or palace
audiences. The scholars were attempting to understand the progression of
stories and to match the progression that they found in Java against an

25. Ramayana and Mahabharata tales were arranged chronologically in Ranggawarsita's work as they had been in the earlier Serat Kandha literature. A major difference
was that Ranggawarsita attempted to fill in all the historical gaps, which the Serat
Kandha authors had not thought to do. Drewes, "Ranggawarsita, the Pustaka Raja
Madya and the Wayang Madya," pp. 199–215. Since at least the *pasisir* period, the
Javanese had believed that the action of the Arjunasasrabahu stories, discussed in
chapter 2, had taken place in the distant past, before the action of both the Ramayana
and Mahabharata stories. The shadow play stories were the links that connected the
ancient gods and heroes to the historical Javanese kings.

26. Uhlenbeck considers the work to be Ranggawarsita's conception of a "final
synthesis of Javanese history in the traditional babad-style." *A Critical Survey of Studies on
the Languages of Java and Madura*, p. 130.

"authentic" Sanskrit telling of the Mahabharata from India. In their own way, the scholars and would-be scholars were involved in the same search for order that may have impelled Ranggawarsita to compile his Book of Kings.

In the *Pustaka Raja Purwa* of Ranggawarsita, the story-cycles of Rama, the Pandhawa, and Arjunasasrabahu, about three hundred stories in all, are recounted in simple prose form, *gancaran* in Javanese.[27] The courts of Central Java contain handwritten manuscripts of this work in Javanese script, and other handwritten and printed versions proliferated in the late nineteenth and twentieth centuries. All of the puppeteers that I encountered in the course of my research in the villages surrounding the court city of Solo knew of this work. The Solonese puppeteers acknowledge the *Pustaka Raja Purwa* to be the source (*babon, pakem*), the main trunk (*baku, pokok*), of the shadow play stories, even if most of them have never seen a copy of the text. A few puppeteers had read quite a bit of it, some had only seen a volume here or there, and some had never seen any of it. The testimony of one middle-aged puppeteer, who did not appear to have had much modern-style schooling, supports the idea that Ranggawarsita collected village stories and then rearranged them in his Pustaka Raja texts.

Plays that are considered to be basic [*baku*] and not branch stories [*carangan*] have fixed texts [*pakem*]. The *pakem* are books inherited from [our] ancestors. But the *carangan* plays are the work of the puppeteers who do not have books. . . .

Maybe there are still one or two copies of the book from the Bale Pustaka named Pustakaraja. I do not know if this is *carangan* but I consider it *baku*. According to the stories of my father, these *lakon* are really Mahabharata . . . or Ramayana. But when they reached the Kraton, they were fixed up by the *pujangga* and others who had power at the Kraton, they were changed into the Pustakaraja.

. . . Thus as far as I know what is considered *pakem* is from the Kraton.[28]

27. Behrend, in "The Serat Jatiswara: Structure and Change in a Javanese Poem 1600–1930," p. 191, notes that there are few surviving manuscripts which show evidence of the use of prose for belletristic purposes until the middle of the nineteenth century. There are also manuscript traditions in which the Pustaka Raja Universal History style has been cast in *macapat* poetic meters.

28. Interview with Pak Gandawarangka, 15 November 1983, as excerpted in Feinstein et al., *Lakon Carangan*, 1:441. All the following quotes from the puppeteers were originally in Javanese except when noted.

According to Ki Gandawarangka, the Mahabharata and Ramayana stories that the puppeteers performed were rewritten or reconceptualized in the Kraton by *pujangga* like Ranggawarsita. Thus, for this puppeteer, court tellings became connected to the idea of trunk stories.

Another puppeteer, who was in his seventies in 1984, had different conceptions of Pustaka Raja traditions.

Sometimes there are special branch stories, a branch taken from a branching tree. The tree is ancient wisdom, this wisdom is contained in the Mahabharata, the Pustakaraja, the Lokapala, the Ramayana. . . .

What is from the trunk of the tree, what is the essence of the tree, begins with the Paramayoga, which tells of Nabi Adam up to the gods, then the gods up to the Pandhawa. This is what is called the tree, the branch, the leaf, the flower, the fruit.[29]

Pak Gandasugeng connected the Paramayoga (the introduction to Ranggawarsita's *Pustaka Raja Purwa*) to genealogies that linked Islamic creation stories to the Indic gods, and he connected the rest of the *Pustaka Raja* to genealogies that linked the ancient gods to the Javanese Pandhawa heroes. He saw the Mahabharata, Ramayana, Lokapala, and *Pustaka Raja* stories as books (*wedha*) containing ancient wisdom.

Only one of the puppeteers I interviewed actually owned a handwritten manuscript of a Pustaka Raja Purwa text, and he had acquired it in 1982. Some puppeteers said the work was written in poetic form (*macapat*), although Ranggawarsita's texts were in prose. It appeared to me and my Javanese colleagues from the Academy that some puppeteers were embarrassed to admit that they had never seen a volume of the work, although they often believed that the stories they performed were recounted in these texts.

The story of the puppeteer who had a copy of a Pustaka Raja Purwa manuscript in 1982 is an interesting example. He acquired the handwritten text and brought it to his teacher, a famous Solonese puppeteer. The teacher was educated and poor, and, because the young puppeteer could not read the text, the two decided that the older teacher could transliterate the text into Roman script and try to make some money by selling it to

29. Interview with Pak Gandasugeng, 21 January 1984, as excerpted in Feinstein et al., *Lakon Carangan*, 1:439.

other puppeteers and, as it turned out, interested foreign researchers. Many of the younger puppeteers today have difficulty reading Javanese script or cannot read it at all. The work was completed and puppeteers as well as students and teachers from the Academy were eager to see the texts. All was fine until a young woman who worked in the Solonese palace, the daughter of another famous puppeteer, maintained that this was not the *Pustaka Raja Purwa* of Ranggawarsita because in this version the stories had already been arranged according to the structure of the shadow puppet plays (*sampun dipun lampahaken*). The *Pustaka Raja Purwa* of Ranggawarsita, as noted above, tells the stories in prose, with one story running into the next. The so-called spurious Pustaka Raja Purwa was identified as a regional Pustaka Raja Purwa text (called a Ngasinan text, referring to the home of the author/copyist),[30] and some of its prestige was diminished, although it still served its purpose adequately. This incident again indicated that hardly any of the puppeteers actually knew very much about the form or structure of Ranggawarsita's texts.

Puppeteers, since the early part of the century, who wanted to improve their command of the tradition might beg, borrow, or, in one case, even steal a volume of the Pustaka Raja. The texts could give them new ideas for creating stories—new characters to work with and new ogre kingdoms to conquer. The text enriched the shadow theatre tradition but did not limit it in any way. Pustaka Raja Purwa texts could not be used as scripts because they only gave the outlines of the stories; the texts could only increase a puppeteer's knowledge of the tradition. Each puppeteer continued to tell the stories as he or she had heard them.

The puppeteers used the texts in creative ways. Sometimes episodes from the earlier part of the Mahabharata cycle would have the Pandhawa heroes and their allies inserted into them. Thus Kresna, Arjuna, or Bima would enact the stories which were actually associated with the early lives of Abiyasa, Bisma, or Samtanu, characters who the audiences feel are ancient and unfamiliar. Occasionally an ogre figure from an earlier part in the story cycle would be linked with a familiar hero, but the use of a

---

30. See N. Florida, *Javanese Literature*, vol. 1, p. 221, for a description of a text, dated 1928, by Cermasuwarna, of Jongga Beji, copied by Cermadiyasa of Ngasinan (ᴋs 400) which contains prose summaries of 105 *wayang lakon*. The text was copied at the behest of Pangeran Hadiwidjaja, of the Kraton Solo, who was also a leading figure at the Museum Radya Pustaka.

Storytellers, Categories, Tales

Pustaka Raja Purwa ogre would enhance the puppeteer's rendering of the story. Then again, the clown characters, who appear in every shadow play performance, might be introduced into the action of the earlier parts of the story cycle (where they are felt to be slightly anachronistic as they are most often associated with the Pandhawa heroes). Written texts became fluid in the hands of the puppeteers, partly because they existed more as an abstract ideal than as a tangible reality, and partly because the puppeteers used the texts in original ways. The puppeteers did not read the texts in a linear fashion. If they had an opportunity, they referred to a text to see how a story was told there and possibly to incorporate parts of that telling into their own interpretation of the story.

The Javanese puppeteers distinguish between the Pustaka Raja Purwa, which recounts all of the cycles of *wayang* stories, and the Mahabharata, which they also acknowledge to be a source of their tradition. But it is difficult to determine exactly what they mean by Mahabharata. Mahabharata stories were transmitted from India to Java in the early centuries of this millennium, but only eight of the eighteen books of the Sanskrit Mahabharata exist in Java—the *parwa* texts mentioned above—and these are essentially unintelligible today to all Javanese except scholars of Old Javanese. Although one could speculate that the missing volumes once existed, most shadow play stories seem to be based on episodes from the extant volumes and those stories retold in the ancient *kakawin* poetry. The modern renderings of the Old Javanese *kakawin* written in the late eighteenth and the nineteenth centuries were also fragmentary. Written versions of the Bratayuda exist in modern Javanese, but these texts recount only the stories which lead directly into the great battle between the Pandhawa and Korawa, starting with Kresna's futile visit to the court of Ngastina to try and negotiate a peaceful settlement for the war.

More elaborate, or more Indian, Mahabharata texts do exist in Java today, but their route to Java has been rather circuitous. A puppeteer connected with the Mangkunagaran court in Solo (Ki Darsamartana) maintained that the text used at the court was written by R. M. Partowiroyo in the early twentieth century. Partowiroyo is said to have translated an Engish text, presumably brought to Java by a Dutch scholar, and presumably a translation of a Sanskrit text made by an English scholar.[31] The

31. Pigeaud, *Literature of Java*, vol. 1, p. 240, records the request of the Solonese ruler Pakubuwana VII for a Javanese translation of an English summary of the Valmiki

*Figure 2. Advertisement for
a Flash Gordon story in a
Mahabharata Kawedhar
text from the late 1930's.*

Partowiroyo Mahabharata follows the format of Janamejaya's snake sacrifice, like many Indian tellings, with the recitation of the story of the Pandhawa and Korawa by Vaisampayana. This frame of the Mahabharata is not very popular or well known in Java, and rarely enters into the shadow theatre performance tradition. A second inscription of the Mahabharata was produced in Java in the 1920s and 1930s by Resi Wahana,[32] probably based on the work of Partowiroyo. This telling, called the *Mahabharata Kawedhar*, is heavily influenced by mystical beliefs and Resi Wahana was known to have been an avid Theosophist.[33]

Ramayana from C. F. Winter in the mid-nineteenth century. Winter's *Javaansche Zamenspraken*, 3d ed. (Amsterdam: Muller, 1882), summarized Carey and Marshman's English translation of the Valmiki Ramayana (1846–47 edition). See Perlman, "Theosophy in Java and the Re-Indicization of the Wayang Kulit," p. 20 n. 34.

32. R. M. Soetanta Hardjawahana, *Mahabharata Kawedhar* (Solo: n.p., 1936–40?).

33. R. M. Soetanta Hardjawahana's *Mahabharata Kawedhar* was published monthly ("medal saben tanggal 1 woelan walandi," appears every first day of the Dutch month) in Roman script and was available for purchase. The texts contained advertisements for other publications and for European items that were popular in the hybrid Javanese-Dutch cultural world of the 1930s. In several issues of the Hardjawahana *Mahabharata Kawedhar* that I have seen from 1938, the advertisements in the text include one for Flash Gordon stories—"battles that are always horrifying"—as well as ads for hair stylists and a list of books available for purchase in either Roman-script Malay or Javanese-script Javanese. The differences between these two lists is striking. For example, the Malay list includes books about vegetarian cooking, medical advice, dream interpretation, learning Japanese, the women's movement, yoga, Islamic mysticism, Javanese *babad* texts, stenography, batik "recipes," and a few enticing titles like "Secrets in the [Bed]room," "Napoleon and Islam," "The Secret of Polygamy," and others. The Javanese list, on the

Storytellers, Categories, Tales

These two tellings of the Mahabharata are known among many contemporary puppeteers literate in Javanese or Roman script, although the
stories from these texts are more foreign than the Pustaka Raja Purwa
stories. Editions of these texts, in particular the Hardjawahana texts, were
published serially and supposedly distributed to puppeteers by the Mangkunagaran court in the late 1930s. The main story that I encountered
during my years in Java that could be traced to the Mahabharata texts was
the *Wiratha Parwa*, the story of the Pandhawas' thirteenth year in exile,
when they had to come out of hiding in the forest to live incognito for one
year at the court of Wiratha.[34] A published text by the Solonese puppeteer
Ki Naryacarito is very close to Indian renderings of this story,[35] with each
of the Pandhawa brothers and Drupadi taking the appropriate disguises
and not revealing their true identities until after the battle with their
treacherous cousins, the Korawa. A *parwa* (prose) text of this story does
exist in Old Javanese and dates back to A.D. 996.[36]

The Pustaka Raja Purwa and the Mahabharata texts are considered to
be the main trunks of the shadow puppet theatre tradition from which the
branch stories sprout. In the words of one puppeteer:

What is called the main trunk of the tradition is the Pustaka Raja and the Mahabharata, these are the trunks. But the Mahabharata contains religious teachings while
the Pustaka Raja contains kingly teachings.[37]

Because *wayang purwa* plays usually contain mystical rather than sectarian
religious teachings, this shows how the puppeteers connect the Mahabharata to the Theosophical version of Hardjawahana. Another puppeteer
commented on the Javanese use of the Mahabharata:

---

other hand, includes a mix of Javanist and Islamic mystical texts, quite a few *babad*,
prophecy texts, a biography of Ranggawarsita and several of his literary works, and
texts of Mahabharata stories.

34. Perlman, in "Theosophy in Java and the Re-Indicization of the Wayang Kulit,"
has identified *Sesaji Raja Suya* and *Pandhawa Matirtha* as two other stories that come out of
this renewed interest in Indian Mahabharata stories. All three were apparently commissioned by Mangkunagara VII from R. Ng. Wignjasutarno, who was the favorite *dhalang*
of the Mangkunagaran court in the 1930s.

35. Cf. C. V. Narasimhan, *The Mahabharata* (New York: Columbia University Press,
1965); Naryacarito, *Wirata Parwa* (Surakarta: Akademi Seni Karawitan Indonesia, n.d.).

36. Zoetmulder, *Kalangwan*, pp. 71–74, 95.

37. Ki Gandamaktal, interview, 5 January 1984.

Apparently, what is used as the source [of the tradition] is the Mahabharata but then it has been reworked by the Javanese, in the Javanese way, and connected to the needs of the traditional [*tradisionil*] culture.[38]

Written versions of these Mahabharata texts have come to have specified roles among communities of Solonese puppeteers and are believed to be the sources of the majority of the shadow play stories, even if many of the puppeteers have never seen these texts and even if the stories they perform are not in them. Puppeteers can see the performances of other puppeteers who use material from the texts and can assimilate information from these texts in secondary ways. These texts also connect to the two major divisions of shadow play stories, the trunk stories (*lakon baku*, *lakon pakem*) and the branch stories (*lakon carangan*), but this relationship is a complicated one. The Dutch scholar Pigeaud, who spent almost twenty years in Java in the 1920s and 1930s, commented perceptively on the intricate relationship between Indian and Javanese stories as well as the one between trunk and branch stories.

The lakon, whose stories one does not find in India, form the largest part of the group named lakon sempalan and tjarangan, a group whose number exceeds that of the "original" lakon. In this group, in fact, one finds the stories that are considered the most ethnologically significant, such as counterparts of the Pandji stories or older tales. Also included here are the lakon that with some certainty can be said to have been recently created, and to this group of lakon sempalan and lakon tjarangan belong the plays which in Java are at present the most known and loved and the most often performed, as for example Srikandhi magoeroe manah, Srikandhi learns to shoot a bow. If one speaks about what the Javanese now know as the wajang, then this group should certainly not be neglected. The term Hindoe-Javanese creation is certainly not applicable to it.[39]

While one might expect that trunk stories would be most closely associated with written texts, and branch stories would circulate mainly in the oral tradition, evidence points to a close relationship between written versions and branch stories and the extensive circulation of trunk stories through the workings of the oral tradition.

38. Ki Darsamartana, interview, 27 February 1984.
39. Pigeaud, *Javaansche Volksvertoningen*, pp. 367–68.

Storytellers, Categories, Tales

Trunk and Branch Stories in Javanese Shadow Theatre

Javanese puppeteers divide the *wayang purwa* stories into trunk and branch stories, although the boundary between the two types of stories is hazy. Puppeteers often disagree over the classification of stories as trunk or branch, but, in general, trunk stories are those stories which lead up to and recount the events of the Bratayuda War. Trunk stories also include those stories which recount the births, marriages, and deaths of the main heroes and heroines of the Mahabharata and Ramayana stories. The *Serat Sastramiruda*, the nineteenth-century Solonese court text considered to have established certain conventions for shadow theatre performances, gives one of the earliest Javanese explanations for the differences between trunk and branch stories.[40] First of all, this text calls the trunk stories *lakon jejer* or "standing" stories, stories that are basic to the tradition, like the first audience-hall scene of every shadow puppet play, which is also called the *jejer*. The text also mentions the word *pakem*, or plot outline, another word often associated with the trunk stories—those stories that have a fixed outline. The *Sastramiruda* says:

As for the standing [*jejer*] stories which can be considered to be *pakem* [having a fixed outline], the stories follow one another, one by one, [each] to be performed for one night. The next night the play will be a continuation of the story, flowing on like the court chronicles [*babad*].

The *Sastramiruda* continues with a description of *lakon carang kadhapur*, "derived branch stories," and *lakon carangan* or "branch stories."

The derived branch stories are like standing stories but then lead into branch stories which still follow the main story. This is called a derived branch story, which means the story has been derived [from a standing story]. But the regular branch stories are cut off from the standing stories, because there is no continuation.

The image of a flow of stories appears here. The branch stories are different from trunk stories because they lead away from the Bratayuda War, while a derived branch story still carries on the flow of stories toward the Great War.

40. K.P.H. Kusumadilaga, *Serat Sastramiruda*, pp. 164–65.

I suspect that the separation between trunk and branch stories might be a nineteenth-century Javanese answer to the Dutch question of why Javanese stories differed from their supposed Indian "originals." The concepts of trunk and branch make the most sense in a thought-world that sees the Mahabharata stories from the point of view of a written textual tradition or an "authentic" one. The British scholars who studied Mahabharata and Ramayana stories in India also distinguished between trunk and branch stories, relegating the latter to appendices in the critical editions of these story cycles produced under the encouragement of European and British-educated Indian scholars. Taking the Serat Kandha texts as examples of Javanese literary mentalities in the eighteenth century, one finds a textual tradition in which divisions between Islamic, "Hindu-Buddhist," and Javanese thought-worlds do not really exist. To use a more Islamic metaphor, all the stories are waves in an ocean of stories that absorbs and carries the stories along through the centuries. It takes an outsider looking at the tradition to decide that part of it is foreign; such a thought would not occur to those who create and transmit the stories themselves. As the research below suggests, the puppeteers do see a need to match certain types of stories with certain occasions—births, deaths, marriages—thus making some stories more important than others, and they have come to accept the divisions between trunk and branch stories, probably a product of interlacing Javanese and Dutch mentalities as well.

The *lakon* Wahyu Pancadharma (The Boon of the Five Obligations), as performed by Ki Naryacarito in the spring of 1984, serves as an example of a "derived branch story." *Wahyu* (boon) stories are quintessential branch stories wherein the Pandhawa and Korawa cousins compete to receive a boon from the gods, usually in the form of mystical knowledge or magical weapons. Ki Naryacarito, a respected older puppeteer, took the germ of this boon story, which he had seen performed by elder family members, and inserted this germ in a significant place in the Mahabharata cycle—after the episode of the fire in the lacquer house (Bale Sigala-gala)—when the Korawa believe they have killed the five Pandhawa brothers and their mother, Kunthi. Ki Naryacarito, who teaches at the Academy, described what he considered to be important about his rendering of this story, when asked if the significant part of the story was who received the boon.

Yes, that's one thing. The second thing that is important is the clarity of the issue. Thus the research is important—besides the receiving of the boon, what is the narrative like? What I consider significant in connection with the research is that the narrative of the story is clear . . . how is the narrative presented—that is important. In my telling, I have mixed things up and used the ogre Supala and his father, who are directly from the *Pustaka Raja Purwa*. What connects [the parts of] the story is that the ogre Supala was adopted by Palasara. Outside the *Pustaka Raja* this story does not exist. But the narrative of the story is clear.[41]

For Ki Naryacarito, the important point is how the puppeteer links the problem of a particular story to the ocean of stories that flow in and around the Pandhawa and Korawa characters. In the story mentioned above, the problem for Naryacarito is brought out in a debate between the celibate Bisma, great uncle to both the Pandhawa and Korawa, and King Drestarata, the blind father of the Korawa. Bisma, assuming that the Pandhawa were killed in a fire, informs Drestarata that his sons have killed their cousins, the Pandhawa, and reminds the King how he had neglected his duty by failing to give the kingdom back to the Pandhawa. Naryacarita then uses the ogre Supala in the story to further integrate the early history of the ancestors of the Pandhawa with the main characters in his story.

Ki Naryacarito's story, which eventually tells how Yudhistira, the eldest Pandhawa brother, receives the mystical knowledge of kingship from the gods, supports the flow of stories toward the Great War. The plot line of the story, the competition for mystical knowledge, carries the story away from the Great War, but by receiving this mystical knowledge, Yudhistira will be better able to rule the kingdom. The story is well connected to the culminating action of the Mahabharata and is also connected to Ranggawarsita's *Pustaka Raja Purwa*. The late puppeteer Ki Catur Tulus, who was with me at another puppeteer's performance of the same story, explained why the second puppeteer inserted this branch story in a different place in the cycle of Mahabharata stories. Pak Tulus maintained that what was important was who received the boon—in this case, Yudhistira—and that it did not matter where the story was placed in the cycle.[42]

Another puppeteer isolated a different aspect of trunk stories. Sri Kamto connected the concept of trunk story with a person or a regional area rather than a text or even an idea of textual continuity. He explained that

41. Interview, 3 June 1984. The language of this quotation is Indonesian rather than Javanese, and there is a difference in presentation between those who speak in Javanese and those who speak in Indonesian.

42. Field notes, 31 March 1984.

Yudhistira and his wife
Drupadi.

what comes to be considered *pakem* (fixed oral text) is what many puppeteers imitate and perform. He said that stories become codified, but that they are written in the heart rather than in a book. Then he associated these *"pakem"* or fixed stories with a particular village area, or even with a particular family. He said that puppeteers from one village would not dare to use another village's *"pakem,"* because they have their own ideas for rendering fixed stories. This definition of *"pakem"* turns the relationship between trunk and branch stories around.

The seed of the *pakem* is actually from the branch story—branch stories that are taken from the main texts. . . . Thus trunk stories take their inspiration from branch stories because of the ability of the puppeteer [to create stories]—many people imitate [this version] because it has already been accepted, but only those from my circle, only those from around here.[43]

Sri Kamto is associating a puppeteer's ability to create branch stories, one mark of a skillful puppeteer, with the *performance style* of a particular village area. The creativity of the individual puppeteers contributes to the development of a regional style, which is reflected in the performance of trunk as well as branch stories. Sri Kamto stressed repeatedly that the

43. Ki Sri Kamto, interview, 28 November 1983.

important thing about *pakem* stories was that the *pakem* of one area were different from the *pakem* of another area. Thus the concept of *pakem* as "fixed text" has a very local meaning. *Pakem* are something that a village area possesses; something that gives its artistic traditions prestige and weight.[44]

Delving further into the relationship between trunk and branch stories, there is a process in which stable branch stories are then imitated by other puppeteers. One example is the famous branch story Kilat Buwana, examined briefly in chapter 1, which tells of a mysterious priest who comes to the court of Ngastina with a way to resolve the conflict between the Pandhawa and Korawa over the rights to the kingdom. In order to resolve the conflict, the Pandhawa must kill either their trusted adviser Kresna or their trusted clown-servant Semar (in reality the older brother of Batara Guru) or both. The priest, named Kilat Buwana, is really Batara Guru (Siwa), and one of the highlights of the story is a skillful debate between Kresna and Kilat Buwana.

Puppeteers cite the *lakon* Kilat Buwana as a blueprint for many other branch stories. One puppeteer calls Kilat Buwana the trunk story for other plays that build upon this theme.[45] In creating a branch story, the puppeteer takes a story that already exists and changes it around a bit; s/he may change the name of the play and perhaps the names of the foreign kingdoms or ogres. Maybe the new story starts in a different court than in the one s/he is remembering. S/he spices the story in his or her own way, and it becomes "his" or "her" branch story. According to Ki Kandha Sanyata:

Imitation! It's just a different name and it's arranged differently. For example, I created the story Kresna Cupu. This is only a borrowing from Kilat Buwana that's being told again. . . . What I mean by copying from an original here is that the arrangement is changed. Thus actually, although we say we create a story, there are

---

44. Brandon commented insightfully on the significance of the *carangan* stories: "It is not surprising that the true essence of wajang lies in the invented tjarangan plays. The very special world of wajang, centering on the glorious and adventurous period of Amarta, was created in them. And from them the 'classic' form of wajang play, with its conventionalized structure and highly systematized techniques of performance, gradually evolved." *On Thrones of Gold*, p. 14.

45. Ki Soetikna, interview, 5 January 1984.

rules [*waton*]. It isn't that I branch off [diverge from] the rules, not at all, it's that we use the rules, that's what we do.[46]

Nyi Kenyacarito, who had been a popular court puppeteer in her youth, described in chapter 2 a similar process for the creation of trunk stories. She spoke of *lakon karangan*, composed plots, or *lakon bangunan*, built-up plots.[47] The *lakon* that she mentioned were considered to be trunk stories, but she said they were fixed up by the puppeteers. The weak parts were taken out and new parts were added. She believed that this was the way that the puppeteers created all of their stories. Another very successful puppeteer spoke of the old ways, but he suggested there really was no such thing as a trunk story.

What comes from the imagination (*imaginasi*), that is called *carangan*. Thus, according to the old ways, according to my own criteria, all the plays are *carangan*. Thus, whatever uses the first scene, the second scene, and so forth, this is already *carangan*. Because here it is clear that you already have something that has been seasoned according to the tastes and opinions of the performer.[48]

This ties in with an attitude expressed by two of the most educated puppeteers. One of these puppeteers was familiar with the Dutch scholarship on the shadow theatre,[49] and the other had read much of the Javanese literature on the shadow theatre.[50] These two puppeteers said that there was no such thing as a *pakem* or trunk story—all the plays were *carangan* or branch stories. According to Ki Naryacarito:

In my opinion, all stories that are performed by puppeteers who draw the stories from the source of the *pakem*, all these are actually branch stories. This is because they are not the same as the contents of the *pakem*. Because it is not possible that the *pakem* can be performed precisely, without being rearranged or changed. Because the *pakem* is only the basic story. . . .[51]

Ki Naryacarito's use of the word *pakem* here suggests the sense of *pakem* as

---

46. Interview, 14 November 1984.
47. Nyi Kenyacarita, interview, 13 November 1983.
48. Ki Mujaka Jaka Raharja, interview, 2 January 1984.
49. R. Soetrisno, "Thek Kliwering Lampahan Carangan" (Sarasehan Dalang 1984, Akademi Seni Karawitan Indonesia, Solo), p. 1.
50. Ki Naryacarito, interview, 6 March 1984.
51. This quotation was also translated from Indonesian rather than Javanese.

both written text and stable oral text, which is how the Pustaka Raja Purwa stories exist for most puppeteers. Naryacarito and Soetrisno felt all the stories to be *carangan* because they were familiar with European or American performance ideas and written playscripts. They thus realized how far their tradition was from the notion of a memorized text. They were making the leap that Goody and Watt described where literate members of a culture see their oral traditions in written form, and begin to recognize contradictions within their knowledge of the tradition.[52] To disentangle oral from written or Javanese from Indian components of this performance tradition seems increasingly unproductive and futile.

Indian and Javanese Tellings of Mahabharata Stories

An example of the intricate permutations between Indian tellings of the Mahabharata and Javanese ones can be illustrated by the different treatment of the role of the sage Vyasa, supposed author of the Sanskrit Mahabharata. Even though, as Doniger explains for the Indian traditions,[53] the part of the Sanskrit text that tells the story of the sage Vyasa dictating the text to the elephant-headed son of Shiva has been relegated to an appendix in the Critical Edition, Vyasa's role as both teller and actor in the story is an important one in India.[54] In addition to his role as author, Vyasa also serves as a critical link in the lineage of the Bharata family. When the sons of Shantanu failed to produce male heirs and their older brother Bhisma could not procreate because of his great vow of celibacy, Bhisma's half-brother Vyasa[55] was called in from his forest hermitage to

52. J. Goody and I. Watt, "The Consequences of Literacy," in *Literacy in Traditional Societies*, ed. J. Goody (New York: Cambridge University Press, 1968).

53. Doniger, "Fluid and Fixed Texts in India," pp. 33–34.

54. The sage Valmiki, supposed author of the Sanskrit Ramayana, has a similar paradoxical quality. When Sita is banished by Rama from Ayodhya, she goes to stay at the hermitage of Valmiki, where the sage teaches Rama's sons to sing the tales of the father they have never met.

55. In the Sanskrit text, Bhisma and Vyasa are not exactly half-brothers. Bhisma's mother Ganga, after killing her seven other sons by him, leaves Shantanu to raise Bhisma alone. Shantanu later falls in love with Satyavati, a fisher king's daughter, who will only marry him if Bhisma gives up his rights to the kingdom, which Bhisma does by taking his oath of celibacy. But, before she married Shantanu, Satyavati had once been impregnated by an old sage named Parasara (Jav. Palasara) who also took away her

impregnate the widowed wives of Vichitraveerya. The sage came straight from the forest with unkempt hair, wearing only the clothes of a hermit—not exactly a pleasing sight to the women of the palace. The first wife could not bear to look at him and kept her eyes tightly closed. Thus was Dhritarashtra born, a blind man. The second wife blanched when she saw the sage—thus was Pandu born, an albino. When the queens were called to go to him again, they sent their maidservant. She gave herself willingly to the sage, producing Vidura, of noble heart but, in some tellings, lame.

In Javanese shadow tales, the sage Vyasa, known as Abiyasa in Java, appears in almost every play. His Indian role as narrator of the story does not seem to be known. Rather he is seen as the grandfather of the Pandhawa, and he lives in his forest hermitage. At the beginning of the second act, *pathet sanga*, which usually takes place these days at about one o'clock in the morning, the setting often moves to the forest hermitage of Abiyasa. Soon the hero of the story, Arjuna, or one of his sons, will appear at the hermitage to ask for advice from their grandfather or great-grandfather. This moment in the play serves several purposes: it seems to juxtapose palace and forest, kingdom and hermitage, and age and youth, and eventually turns into the comic interlude where the clown-servants Semar and his sons take over and trade songs with the attractive female singers who adorn every performance.

In Javanese texts and performances of Mahabharata tales, Resi Vyasa rules the Bharata kingdom for a time under the name of Kresnadipayana (or King Abiyasa), before surrendering the kingdom to his albino son Pandu.[56] Then Resi Vyasa becomes the forest sage that he remains in Indian tellings of the story before he is called to impregnate the widowed royal queens. In Sanskrit texts, Vyasa goes back to the forest after siring his sons, leaving his half-brother Bhisma to rule the kingdom until the sons come of age, but Vyasa reappears after the devastating Bharatayuddha War. He is the one who will tell the story of the war to Arjuna's grandson and great-grandsons. By having Abiyasa appear in each *wayang* performance, the Javanese in their own way preserve the central role that Vyasa

---

unpleasant fishy smell and blessed her with a fragrant aroma. The result of the union of Satyavati and Parasara was the son named Vyasa.

56. See Ward Keeler's *Javanese Shadow Puppets* (New York and Singapore: Oxford University Press, 1992), pp. 5–37, for a description of a recent performance of the story of King Abiyasa's surrendering of his kingdom to his second son Pandu.

Storytellers, Categories, Tales

plays in the Indian stories. Although not always seen as the author or teller of the stories, his presence has become central to the reenactment of almost every story. In many Javanese tellings of these stories, Arjuna's grandson, who rules the kingdom after the war, is called Parikesit-Dipayana, blending the roles that Vyasa and Parikesit play in the Indian stories.

Another way in which the Javanese preserve Indian ideas in Java concerns the *bhakti* or devotional tellings of the stories of Rama and Krishna. In India, it is believed propitious to hear or mention the names of Rama and Krishna. While this idea was known in the ancient Old Javanese Mahabharata and Ramayana stories, it seems to have disappeared along with the ability to read these texts. On the other hand, all Javanese who enjoy watching shadow plays believe that it is auspicious to attend these events. Shadow plays were given at the *kraton* in Solo on Wednesday and Saturday nights,[57] and often on the nights that the Sunan was not in the palace, in the belief that the shadow play would protect the court. In the villages, people who sponsor shadow plays believe that the performance will bring safety to their house and possibly their lives or the lives of those for whom the performance is commemorating a life-cycle ritual.

This discussion leads to a reconsideration of what the concept of trunk story might mean to the performing artists of Java. I have related how the notion of trunk stories suggested but did not overlap with the notion of a written text. Javanese words connected with trunk stories all suggest an image of a stable rather than a written text, although the word *pakem* can refer to these trunk stories, to written scenarios, or to the main outlines of the stories which flow through the tradition. In addition to the term *pakem*, other words used to refer to the trunk stories are *baku* or *pokok*, both with the meaning of main part, *deleg*, or trunk, and *jejer*, which by itself means standing upright. The *pakem* record, in both oral and written forms, what we might call the core images of particular stories.[58] In turn, some puppeteers describe *pakem* stories as those stories that recount the births, marriages, and deaths of the major *wayang purwa* characters—the main turning points in a person's life. It is here that the relation of trunk to

57. Florida, *Javanese Literature*, p. 22.

58. In the scholarly terminology generated to explain the workings of oral traditions, the Javanese word *pakem* seems similar to the concept of core images used to describe oral text production in African tales. See Vansina, *Oral Tradition as History*, p. 43, and H. Scheub, *The Xhosa Ntsomi* (Oxford: Oxford University Press, 1975), pp. 90–100.

branch stories as well as that of Indian to Javanese versions becomes significant. For Javanese puppeteers, the stories closest to Java and Javanese cultural values are those considered to be trunk stories, despite how far they may diverge from the main story line of Indian tellings of Mahabharata tales.

This was the case in a story I saw performed in Java in 1984, which sprang directly from the Indian *Adi Parva*, the first book of the Sanskrit Mahabharata. This story describes the burning of the Khandava forest, and the *lakon* is called Babad Wana Khendawa in Java. While the story that I saw followed the Indian version of the story exactly, most of the Javanese puppeteers called this a branch story.[59] They said that the Javanese trunk story describing the burning of the Khandava forest was the *lakon* Babad Wanamarta. The Javanese trunk story Babad Wanamarta concerns ogre characters searching for release from their ignoble births. Babad Wanamarta has all the markings of a branch story, but it has been placed in the sequence of trunk stories because it describes the preparation of the forest for the building of the kingdom of Ngamarta (Indraprastha) while simultaneously reinforcing Javanese cultural beliefs about the purification of ogres.

The overwhelming concern in the Javanese *wayang* stories with the exorcism of ogre characters springs from magical and mystical beliefs that pervade the shadow theatre tradition. More than any ability to read court texts, puppeteers in Javanese villages were, and often still are, respected for their ability to manipulate the unseen forces of the world. Puppeteers often performed as shamans and healers, and even today many of the older puppeteers I knew would be visited frequently by people asking for magical healing charms or ethical instruction. The puppeteers acquired their powers through ascetic practices called *laku*, a word with various meanings from "walk" to "behavior" to a concept of success. In the context of Javanese mysticism, *laku* indicates a certain spiritual exercise that tests the body for the evolution of the spirit. Most *dhalang* that I knew

59. Perlman (oral communication, February 1992) has confirmed my findings about the *lakon* Babad Wana Khendawa. Perlman discussed the origins of this *lakon* with Ki Suripto, a dance master and *dhalang* connected with the Mangkunagaran court in Solo. Suripto told Perlman that the *lakon* Babad Wana Khendawa had been created (*dikelirke*) decades ago by the Mangkunagaran puppeteer almarhum R. Ng. Wignyasutarno after the famous *dhalang* had read Hardjawahana's Theosophist rendering of the Mahabharata.

in Java had been given various *laku* in their youth by their fathers or other teachers. These *laku* might entail eating only white rice (*mutih*) for forty days or sitting in cold mountain streams (*kungkum*) at night while repeating various mantras. One puppeteer told me his father had locked him in a room for three days, a *laku* known as *ngebleng*,[60] but he had begged to come out after a day and a half (to the great disappointment of his father). Many *laku* involve staying up all night, and one can see the benefit of such an exercise for an aspiring young puppeteer, who will be expected to enact all-night performances. Oral tradition in Solo has it that the famous Solonese puppeteer Anom Suroto regularly meditates in graveyards to augment his powers.

Because of the charisma and power that the puppeteers gain through these ascetic practices, people believe that it is beneficial to attend shadow puppet performances. The texture of the *gamelan* music is believed to keep harmful spirits away, and staying up late into the night is a sign of spiritual strength in Java. There is also a genre of shadow play stories that are used specifically for exorcistic purposes. Arising from long-lived parts of the oral tradition that are strongly connected with spirit belief and black magic, these stories support the exorcism of ogre characters in many of the shadow play performances. In fact, many of the stories that are considered to be *pakem* stories by the puppeteers introduce ogre characters who are looking to be exorcised, *pangruwating diyu* in Javanese.[61] The concept of *pangruwating diyu* is also connected to the power of the *sastrajendra*, the mystical teaching that was discussed in chapter 1. The *sastrajendra*, which might have conveyed an Islamic sufi interpretation of the oneness of humanity and Allah to those Javanese receptive to this secret teaching, was understood by many village Javanese as another magical charm with which to exorcise demons, both in the shadow play stories and, perhaps, in real life.[62] Seen in this light, the *sastrajendra* resonates with connections

60. Cf. Keeler, *Javanese Shadow Plays*, p. 42.

61. An emphasis on the exorcism of ogre characters is prevalent in India also. In the medieval *bhakti* or devotional *Ramcaritmanas* of Tulsidas, Ravana is happy to be killed by Rama because it will exorcise his demonic spirit.

62. See Florida, *Javanese Literature*, pp. 317–18, for a listing of *sastraharjendra* (The Book of Sublime Writing) texts in the collection of the Kraton Surakarta. These texts were inscribed in the early twentieth century. Florida maintains that they are Javano-Islamic texts representing a radical-union mystical tradition. In line with my arguments in chapter 1, I suggest that twentieth-century interpretations of *sastrajendra* have become

to the Old Javanese texts,[63] Islamic Sufi literature, and Javanese exorcistic beliefs. These connections and the emphasis in the *Pustaka Raja Purwa* on the exorcism of ogres support the idea that Ranggawarsita collected the shadow play stories that were performed in the villages at that time and included them in his famous text. But the *sastrajendra* is also the base upon which Theosophical speculation builds its argument for the deep, mystical resonances of the *wayang* tradition. Theosophical beliefs look back to the earliest Dewaruci texts and to the blending of Shaivite, Buddhist and Islamic mystical teachings. Thus any attempt to unravel the mystical strands of shadow theatre beliefs is overdetermined from the beginning.

The stream of village people who come to *dhalang* for advice, healing potions, and astrological information shows that many puppeteers are still respected for their supernatural abilities. The power of village *dhalang* was and is thus not specifically connected with religion; rather it was the abstract accumulation of power described by Anderson[64] that rested on the ability of the practitioner to accrue power through mystical exercises. I would emphasize this belief in the power of the *dhalang* in any attempt to decipher the "meaning"[65] of the tradition. There are so many ways in which the *wayang* tradition has meaning—in mystical, aesthetic, political, exorcistic, and comic terms—and I have argued in this book that this meaning changed over time. In days gone by, Javanese audiences appreciated the *wayang* tradition for reasons associated with village rituals and life-cycle rites, but the emphasis on pleasing audiences, the aesthetic dimension, should not be underestimated. Mantras have been recited by *dhalang* from ancient times to the present to insure the rapt attention of

---

less Islamic than in earlier periods. Florida notes that the texts usually recount "Hindu" gods talking about Javano-Islamic mysticism; the texts associate the *sastrajendra* with metaphysical speculations about the Javanese alphabet, as I learned from Javanese mystics in the 1980s.

63. See Supomo's essay on cacography, "Sastra Djendra: 'Ngelmu' yang timbul karena kakografi," pp. 177–86.

64. Anderson, "The Idea of Power in Javanese Culture."

65. For interesting speculations on the meaning of the *wayang* tradition in the Javanese past, see Geertz, *Religion of Java*; Anderson, *Mythology and the Tolerance of the Javanese*; Paul Stange, "Mystical Symbolism in Javanese Wayang Mythology"; and Keeler, *Javanese Shadow Plays*. Like Keeler, I prefer to let Javanese scholars and mystics explain the meaning of the tradition and to focus my work on other aspects of the tradition.

audiences.[66] Even Raffles in the early nineteenth century commented on the attentiveness of Javanese *wayang* audiences, showing that performers have always used a variety of means to captivate their audiences.

Javanese Mentalities and *Dhalang* Schools

In the previous chapter, I discussed several major events in the history of the *wayang* theatre that took place in the 1910s and 1920s, when the court schools were opened. At that time, several conferences of puppeteers were held under court patronage and certain of the *wayang* traditions were standardized and refined. By 1923, the position of the *pesindhen* (female singer) was fixed as inferior to that of the puppeteer, and the mood songs (*suluk*) were supposedly given lyrics from the new nineteenth-century Javanese poetic works, while *pathet* (mode) and other musical traditions were standardized. After these conferences, expanded *pakem* were written, exhibiting the same standardization that the conference leaders were hoping for in the performance tradition. But, in the villages, these new conventions penetrated slowly and were modified by the tastes of village audiences and the skills of the puppeteer. The Dutch scholar Kats published his great tome on the Javanese shadow theatre, *Het Javaansche Tooneel*, in the same year that a conference was held in Solo to "upgrade" the tradition. Scholars have long assumed that Kats was documenting the tradition as it had existed for decades, but the evidence presented here suggests that Kats may have been documenting the new conventions that were being accepted as the official court style at that time.

Although scholars have given the shadow theatre tradition an ancient history, it is far from clear how performance practice changed over the centuries. Pigeaud warned many years ago against the dangers of seeing certain elements of artistic traditions as very old and pointed to problems in the idea that any art form could have been so faithfully transmitted from the past. He added:

Rather one comes to the conclusion that much has assumed its present-day refined form in relatively late times, perhaps only in the 18th century, under the influence

66. Zoetmulder, *Kalangwan*.

of the kratons of the Principalities, probably including the well-developed combination of the lakon and the musical diversity. That is also conceivable from the form of the puppets.[67]

New standards and conventions developed in the early decades of the twentieth century may have displaced older aesthetic preferences in *wayang* performances, but these changes did not happen overnight, and they are still happening today. Criteria for judging court performance practice began shifting away from the mastery of occult power toward a mastery of mystical exegesis, older poetic forms, musical complexity, and skillful puppet manipulation. These changes were originally favored by certain court elites on several levels. I argued in the previous chapter that, in the first quarter of the twentieth century, court elites,[68] mainly from the minor courts of Solo and Yogya, and their Dutch colleagues joined together using the patronizing rhetoric of the Ethical period and the mystical vocabulary of Theosophy to suggest that new aesthetic criteria could improve the tradition. On the other hand, the courts had long feared the occult power of the rural *dhalang* and those other supposedly subversive religious figures who inhabited the Javanese countryside, the Islamic *kyai*.[69] The Javanese rulers had usually summoned the village puppeteers to perform at the courts to show off their skills while monitoring the puppeteers' power, and older stories tell of Javanese kings who kept powerful, and often strange, people and objects near them to augment their power.[70] Certainly

67. Pigeaud, *Javaanse Volksvertoningen*, p. 75.

68. My use of the term *elite* in this and in the preceding chapter distinguishes the high-born, educated, and Dutch-influenced Central Javanese nobility from the modernizing Javanese intelligentsia described by Heather Sutherland, "Pudjangga Baru: Aspects of Indonesian Intellectual Life in the 1930s." The people who made up the intelligentsias were often lower officials who turned away from Javanese culture to European culture and learning, sometimes to offset their humble birth and sometimes because they believed that European modernity was the path to power.

69. For a discussion of the Javanese *kyai* in the 1950s, see C. Geertz, "The Javanese Kijaji: The Changing Role of a Cultural Broker," *Comparative Studies in Society and History* 2, no. 2 (1959–60): 228–49. For *kyai* in Javanese history, see Sartono Kartodirdjo, *The Peasants' Revolt of Banten in 1888: Its Conditions, Course, and Sequel: A Case Study of Social Movements in Indonesia* ('s Gravenhage: Martinus Nijhoff, 1966), pp. 154–75, and G.W.J. Drewes, *Drie Javaansche Goeroe's. Hun Leven, Onderricht en Messiasprediking* (Leiden: Drukkerij A. Vros, 1925).

70. For discussions of the relationships between rulers and *dhalang* in the Javanese past see Moertono, *State and Statecraft in Old Java*, p. 66; Pigeaud, *Javaanse Volksver-*

one sign of the acquisition of power in older times had been the ability to require the attendance of rural notables at the court.[71]

This is another example of the shifting and interlacing of Javanese and Dutch mentalities that reconstituted the ways in which Javanese elites conceived of power. In his celebrated article, Anderson has drawn attention to the intersecting constructions of Javanese and Euroamerican ideas of power.[72] The changing position of the *wayang* theatre and the *dhalang* in Java at the turn of the century is a good example of this shift. If power was believed to radiate out from a center according to the efforts that the practitioner had devoted to ascetic exercises, the Dutch scholarly concern with texts and accuracy, and their own displays of power through the command of modern technology, contested the belief that power could be acquired through such mystical practices as meditating in graveyards, fasting, or going without sleep.

In the 1920s and 1930s, some Dutch-educated Javanese intellectuals shifted emphasis away from forms of power that had meaning for many Javanese throughout the nineteenth century, and they began to emphasize skills and attitudes that could be acquired through European-language education as they embraced a world where power was believed to be unlimited.[73] During the late colonial period, certain Javanese admired and imitated Dutch ways. Chapter 3 explained how Mangkunagara VII brought together Dutch scholars and Javanese scholars and elites under the influences of Theosophical beliefs that stressed universal humanitarian values.[74] As noted above, performances of human and puppet plays held at the court of Mangkunagara VII were esoteric mystical events. Mangkunagara VII's interest in the *wayang* theatre, or the use of the *wayang* for his own political ambitions, led him to collect and publish several volumes of *wayang* stories, which were disseminated to village puppeteers. I argued above that the publication in Dutch and English of this prince's philosophical speculations on the *wayang* theatre[75] led many European and American

toningen, p. 58; Keeler, *Javanese Shadow Plays*, pp. 166–67; G. Mudjanto, *The Concept of Power in Javanese Culture* (Yogyakarta: Gadjah Mada University Press, 1986), p. 103.

71. Cf. Florida, *Writing the Past*.

72. Anderson, "The Idea of Power in Javanese Culture."

73. Cf. Pemberton, *On the Subject of "Java."*

74. See also Sutherland, "Pudjangga Baru," pp. 121–22 n. 47.

75. Mangkunagara VII, "Over de wajang-koelit"; Holt translation, *On the Wayang Kulit*.

scholars to assume that the mystical side of the *wayang* tradition was more important than it actually may have been. In the same way that rowdy village *wayang* traditions were sometimes refined in the palaces, the complex of occult and shamanistic practices long associated with the *wayang* theatre were blended into a Theosophical mysticism.[76]

By the 1930s in Solo, some village *dhalang* began to believe that attending the court schools would increase their popularity. Since those called court *dhalang* were often ritual specialists more skilled at reciting magical formulas and airing (*ngisis*) the puppets than in performance technique, famous puppeteers from the countryside had to be brought in to perform at the courts and to attend the new palace schools. Some *dhalang* who went to the court schools and learned the new techniques were patronized by the courts, and they were influenced by the hybrid Javanese-Dutch values which predominated at the courts. The attitudes that the *dhalang* learned at the court schools included a respect for written texts, a conception of personal power based on education as well as mystical prowess, and, possibly, a reinforcement of their belief that the skills of the *dhalang* had to be inherited rather than learned. One could not learn to be a *dhalang* at a court school; rather one had to be a *dhalang* even to think of entering the schools. When *dhalang* who had studied at the courts returned to the countryside, they brought their new values and techniques with them;[77] through the performance tradition some of these new ideas spread. The *dhalang*, as always, were responsible for changing their own traditions because they were the ones who accepted and spread the new attitudes and techniques. It was a change in the mentality of the performers that was

76. There have been recent debates in the scholarly world over the relationship between scholarship on Java and Javanese mysticism. See Paul Stange, "Deconstructions of Javanese 'Tradition' as Disempowerment," *Prisma* 50 (September 1990): 89–110. Stange criticizes several scholars who work on Javanese culture for devaluing the particular Javanese relationship to the spirit world. Yet Stange seems to posit the very essentialism in Javanese *wayang* that this book argues against. Certainly mysticism is an "overdetermined" element in Javanese culture. By this I mean that mysticism existed in Java before Indian influence, was enriched by a variety of Indian and Islamic mystical practices, and has incorporated new forms and beliefs up until the present day. To say that for a certain period in the 1920s and 1930s Javanese elites gained cultural capital vis-à-vis the Dutch for their understanding of mystical practices in no way undermines the importance of all kinds of spiritual practices in Javanese culture and history.

77. Often the *dhalang* found that the things they had learned at the court schools did not make them more popular in the villages. They did gain a certain mystique, however, from having spent time at the courts.

important, and this is still true today. This can be illustrated by the general Dutch scholarly disdain for branch stories even though the so-called branch stories have remained the most popular stories in the repertoire.

Branch Stories and *Wayang* Repertoires

Although I have shown how difficult it is to fix the meaning of trunk and branch within the community of puppeteers, the discourse about branch stories within the shadow puppet repertoire as a whole remains controversial. Looking at Javanese history over the past century, it appears that different types of stories have been popular in different periods. In the 1930s, mystical branch stories pleased the patrons of the *wayang* theatre as did political branch stories in the turbulent 1960s. Today in Java, *wahyu* or boon stories—quintessential branch stories—are believed to be the most popular, perhaps because people believe that they may bring relief from the pressures of contemporary life. Scholars in recent decades have felt that branch stories were on the rise, pushing the older trunk stories into the background of the repertoire.[78] I suggest that branch stories have always been the most popular *wayang* stories, but they were discounted while the tradition was under the patronage of Dutch-educated elites and Dutch scholars, who believed that the branch stories were the corrupted part of a pure classical tradition hailing from India.

The Dutch scholar Hazeu noted with a touch of nostalgia the popularity of branch stories and the scarcity of trunk stories in the early twentieth century.

Nowadays the old *lakon jejer* are performed less and less. People find them not "*rame*" [lively] enough, and in performing them have too little opportunity to insert new scenes, different dances, etc. That is why at present in the grand *wayang* performances in the kraton, etc. almost all the time *lakon carangan* are performed. Only if, for example, on an anniversary, the king (especially the Sultan of Jogja) has a *lakon* performed in an intimate setting, then a suitable *lakon jejer* is sometimes chosen for that. One can see from this that as time goes by the drama for the Javanese becomes more and more purely secular, and the more original religious character is lost.[79]

78. Cf. Keeler, *Javanese Shadow Plays*, pp. 194–95.
79. This quotation was a handwritten note in the copy of Hazeu's dissertation of

But Hazeu could not have known if the old *lakon jejer* whose loss he mourned had ever been popular in Central Java. The lists of *lakon* in the palace libraries[80] show that a wide array of stories have been popular since the late eighteenth century, most of them so-called branch stories, *if* one accepts the debatable idea that branch stories were those furthest from Indian tellings of the Mahabharata stories.

Branch stories have always been considered politically subversive as they are the easiest stories in which to insert messages extraneous to the plot, but a good *dhalang* can get his or her point across even in the most innocent and well-known trunk story. Comments about the high visibility of branch stories may be in part a reaction to court promotion of certain types of stories that were introduced to village puppeteers under the influence of the court schools. In the early 1980s, when I first arrived in Solo, there seemed to be a rising interest in trunk stories and in Pustaka Raja Purwa texts until we began the Lakon Carangan project. After we had chosen the stories of Wahyu Panca Dharma and Kilat Buwana to be the two main stories for emphasis in the work of the project, I noted that these stories in a variety of tellings were frequently performed, seemingly in response to our interest in them. Similar situations probably occurred in the nineteenth century when several Dutch scholars showed interest in the stories of Palasara and Abiyasa.

The branch stories are certainly the most dynamic part of the *wayang* repertoire and show off the great creativity of the puppeteers. This was noted by several Dutch commentators in the nineteenth and twentieth centuries but from different points of view. Hazeu, writing in the period of rising appreciation for ethnological studies of Javanese culture that was to culminate in the Ethical period, commented approvingly on the Javanese ability to produce branch stories.[81]

1897, now owned by the University of Michigan, that was filled with notes for a possible revised edition. While Hazeu wrote the dissertation before he had ever been to Java, the handwritten notes seem to have been based on his two decades of experience in Java in the early twentieth century. The note is written on the blank page facing page 136. (This particular edition of the dissertation has a blank page facing every page of text.)

80. Florida, *Javanese Literature*, pp. 217–25.

81. But compare Perlman's citation of Hinloopen Labberton's disgust ("Theosophy in Java," p. 18) with this attitude of appreciation for the branch stories. Hinloopen Labberton was writing from the point of view of a Theosophist who saw the *wayang* as an opportunity for ethical and mystical uplift, as noted in chapter 3.

Storytellers, Categories, Tales

New lakon keep appearing, especially at the Kraton Solo, as we learned from the writings of Pangeran Adipati Arja Mangkoenegara IV. . . . This is understandable and shall continue as long as the total of the now officially recognized tradition is not adapted for performance, and even after that people will still be able to invent more *lakon carangan*. For the court dhalangs who are experienced in dramatic technique, as described above, it is enough to give them the main points, the frame of the story, and in a short time the story can be dramatically adapted and performed, following the familiar technical instructions.[82]

The Dutch *wayang* aficionado te Mechelen, only twenty years earlier, made a similar observation, but he attributed the creativity to a Bupati who thought up simple plot outlines rather than to the puppeteers who performed for eight or nine hours.

I even know that Raden Mas Djojodhiningrat, the Boepati Keparak Kiwo of the [Kraton] Soerakarta, thanks to whose fertile imagination many new lakon have been created, could only compose them by communicating the subject orally in brief outline to his dhalang, who a few days later had to perform the piece for him.[83]

Te Mechelen described a fascinating division of labor in the creation of a tale, but his words could have been turned around to highlight the creativity of the *dhalang* rather than the inability of the Bupati to compose according to te Mechelen's ideas of composition. This dismissal of Javanese creativity in the nineteenth century and the celebration of Javanese creativity in the twentieth are consistent themes in Dutch scholarship on Java and illustrate the discursive shift that I have traced in chapters 2 and 3. Te Mechelen, however, took issue with the mid-nineteenth-century dismissal of the *macapat* poetry that retold the *wayang* tales, even bringing his complaints to the Bataviaasch Genootschap. He did not understand why, in C. F. Winter's *Javaansche Zamenspraken*, used to teach Javanese to future Dutch civil servants in the 1830s and 1840s, the *macapat* retellings of *wayang* stories were not given more credit. He tried to unravel an answer to his question given by his Javanese informant, whom he believed to be very knowledgeable about *wayang* lore.

In answer to my question why, in the enumeration of the products of authentic

---

82. G.A.J. Hazeu, *Bijdrage tot de Kennis*, pp. 122–24.
83. Te Mechelen, "Een en ander over de wajang," pp. 82–83.

Javanese literature in the here-mentioned *Zamenspraken*, no attention was paid to the present-day rewritings of the Old Kawi works, which have wajang stories as their subject and have been summed up under the general name of *lakon*, [my informant] must have concluded this from the word *nganggit* [interlace] used by the writer [Winter] that, indeed, in spoken use resembles *ngarang*, but still the meaning implies *something drawn from one's own creativity*, in distinction from *editing*.[84]

Te Mechelen, albeit in an abstruse way, was trying to understand why Winter ignored *wayang tales* sung in *macapat* poetry. He finally concluded that this poetry was excluded from the categories of Javanese literature because the word used to indicate its creation was *nganggit*, which means to interlace and refers to the way many Javanese describe the creation of literature and drama.[85] The idea conveyed by the term *nganggit* is the weaving together of ideas, phrases, episodes, or words to create something new and distinct. But te Mechelen assumed that in the 1830s and 1840s, the Dutch in Solo dismissed modern Javanese poetic writings because they saw them as degenerate copies rather than as creative literature. Part of the difficulty that some nineteenth-century scholars faced stemmed from their misunderstandings about the interweaving of oral and written styles of composition and transmission. In Javanese literary traditions, both orally performed and written-out plays are called *lakon*, fixed oral and written texts are called *pakem*, sung oral and written poetry is called *macapat*, and oral and written stories are *crita*. For Javanese authors and performers, creativity arises out of the act of interlacing old and new whether in written text or in oral performance.[86]

Dutch philological ideas enhanced the status of written materials for the Javanese, as the Indian concern with writing had done hundreds of years earlier. Although Dutch influences made an increasing number of

84. Ibid., p. 75. Te Mechelen left several Javanese words and phrases in Javanese script in this quotation.

85. Florida, in *Javanese Literature*, p. 24, has an especially lucid discussion of the Javanese distinctions between "one who writes" and "one who composes." The words *nganggit* and *ngarang* are also used to refer to the way a puppeteer composes a shadow play. Puppeteers, in particular, discuss the quality of a performer's *anggitan* or *sanggit* to describe the way a puppeteer develops his or her plot.

86. This may also help to explain why European and American scholars are often frustrated when they ask Javanese to copy or transliterate texts and they discover that their "copyists" take liberties with the texts and fail to render the exact texts that the foreign scholar demands or expects.

books available to Javanese readers and authors, these texts fitted into the literary traditions of the shadow theatre in established ways. As noted in the last chapter, it is often European-language education, or educational systems modeled on European ideas, rather than the presence of written texts, that changed and continues to change the mentalities of puppeteers. There is no indication that familiarity with written texts improved a puppeteer's performance in any significant way. According to an instructor at the Academy in Solo:

A lot of reading by a puppeteer certainly increases the richness of his talent for stringing language together, for arranging words, but this richness in arranging does not necessarily bring life to his performances if the words are not well arranged or if the language is too thick with alliteration. Too much poetry sometimes produces a feeling like having eaten too much food.[87]

What was more important was the ability of puppeteers to respond to particular situations in spontaneous and appropriate ways. The late Ki Gandamaktal said that a puppeteer should be able to evaluate the abilities and tastes of a particular area or group so that s/he could harmonize his or her performance with those conditions.[88]

This resonates with the view of branch stories as vehicles for incorporating new material into the tradition. If the branch stories admit politics and other contemporary matters into the stories, the puppeteer then bends this material to the tastes of his or her audience. One puppeteer cited this phenomenon in a disapproving way.

Branch stories are only those stories which puppeteers use for their own benefit. They can use the stories to enhance their own image or the image of a political party, if we are speaking of the era of the political parties. They can also use the branch stories to show off contemporary events but it will be only their followers who are satisfied.[89]

Older puppeteers may also be critical of newer branch stories that are not connected to the *pakem* in conventional ways. Perhaps reacting to techniques that were stressed in the schools, another puppeteer argued that in

87. B. Murtiyasa, "Lampahan Carangan Satleraman," Sarasehan Dalang 1984, Akademi Seni Karawitan Indonesia, Solo, p. 4.
88. Interview, 5 January 1984.
89. Ki Sri Kamto, interview, 28 November 1983.

the past a good puppeteer would try to hide the fact that he or she was creating a branch story. Ki Naryacarito compared his rendering of a branch story with a popular branch story created by the famous puppeteer Ki Anom Suroto.

Puppeteers who are already experienced create branch stories which don't seem like branch stories because they are closely related to the trunk stories. For example, I placed Wahyu Dharma right after Bale Sigala-gala (The Fire in the Lacquer House) so that the story still flows but Semar Mbangun Kahyangan (Semar Builds Up Heaven), where does that story come from? How can heaven be destroyed; heaven is an object of worship; in whose imagination can it be destroyed?

Although Anom Suroto's branch stories might lack the connections that older *dhalang* feel are necessary to tie a particular tale to a story cycle, they are the most popular plays in Solo today, have been recorded on commercial cassettes, and are widely imitated by other puppeteers.

The phenomena that I have been describing show that it is not easy to separate oral and written features of the Javanese shadow theatre tradition. "Oral" and branch story do not fit neatly on one end of the continuum with "written" and trunk story on the other. Since stories that highlight ogre characters are often considered to be trunk stories by Javanese puppeteers, these are the stories that are written down in an attempt to preserve the dynamism of the tradition in written forms. In some cases, a written text itself may document the passage of a branch into a trunk story because the story is recorded in writing. Moreover, the written texts associated with the shadow theatre often disseminate their ideas in oral ways. This oral dissemination of material from the written texts is described by Nyi Kenyacarita, who spoke of her grandfather attending an upgrading session with B.K.P. Kusumadilaga, author of the *Serat Sastramiruda*. She said these upgradings were held once a year during the Javanese month Sura, when the palace teachers would explain to the puppeteers the nature of the important characters and interpretations of the stories popular in the courts. Although Kusumadilaga was a well-known author of *wayang* texts, when I asked Nyi Kenyacarita if they used books at these upgrading sessions, she scoffed at me with the attitude of older puppeteers who wonder what books have to do with being a good performer.[90]

90. Cf. Poensen, "De Wajang," pp. 205–6.

Storytellers, Categories, Tales

Written texts record oral features of the tradition, and oral performances draw on the written texts. The relations between these elements have been diverse and flexible, showing that written and oral texts mingled harmoniously in the performance traditions of the Javanese villages. Scholarly literature, however, has often interpreted these relations according to the intellectual priorities of particular periods and schools of thought. Different features of the performance tradition become important in relation to the status given to written, printed, and oral materials within Dutch and Javanese intellectual and political worlds. These tensions between trunk and branch stories, Javanese and Indian stories, and oral and written ones still exist today, keeping the tradition alive and innovative.

Social and Political Effects of the Court Schools

The so-called court tradition that I have been discussing in this chapter and the preceding one had an active life of roughly forty years (1923–65).[91] It is this refined tradition that many European and American scholars of this century have considered to be "authentic," the tradition by which scholars have marked their ideas of degeneration and decline. That the court tradition struck deep roots in Javanese villages can be seen from a comparison of the performance styles of contemporary puppeteers; almost all of the *dhalang* in Solo and the surrounding villages that I encountered in the early 1980s were able—if it was required—to perform more or less according to the strictures laid out by the court schools. When *wayang* competitions are held in Central Java today, the judges are generally teachers from the old court schools, indicating that the court tradition still holds an important position in the aesthetic world of Central Java. But since the power of the courts has faded, especially in Solo, the patrons and teachers of the old court tradition are disappearing. The puppeteers who have risen to fame and popularity in Solo in recent years are becoming more and more courageous in their willingness to depart from the standards of the court tradition.

Although this tradition is still taught in poorly attended court schools

91. Although in chapter 2 I describe nineteenth-century court efforts to refine *wayang* traditions, I date the prominence or hegemony of what I am calling the court style from the founding of the first Solonese school for puppeteers in 1923.

and in the high school of performing arts (SMKI) and at the Academy in Solo, other styles compete for the attention of Javanese audiences. The Academy in Solo was opened by the government in 1964 and represents the transfer of artistic authority from the palaces to the postcolonial Indonesian school. It is interesting to note that the school, called ASKI or the academy of musical arts in that period, was even located within the walls of the *Kraton*, thus drawing on the waning authority of the palace even as it began seriously to undermine its traditions. These matters will be discussed in depth in the next chapter.

By the 1920s the Boedi Oetomo, the first Javanese political party founded in 1908, had given up its attempt to unify nationalist sentiment around Javanese traditions and tried to appeal to Indies rather than Javanese audiences. The plan to steep Javanese young people in the Javanese performing arts remained alive in the Taman Siswa (Garden of Learning) schools of Soewardi Soerjaningrat. Only by forging a lasting link with the re-constructed traditions of Javanese culture did Soewardi believe that young people would know how best to use European knowledge and technology. In the political realm, the Indonesian nationalist movement remained split between secular and stricter Islamic factions, a split that remains significant in Indonesia today.

The political policy first advocated by Snouck Hurgronje at the turn of the century—the support of *adat* as a bulwark against the rise of militant Islam—can be seen to have had an unexpected cultural legacy in the massacres of the 1960s, when hundreds of thousands of Javanese peasants, supposedly nurtured by the *wayang* tradition, were slaughtered by their more devout Islamic neighbors. The shadow theatre in that period served as a propaganda vehicle for many of the political parties, including the land reform programs of the Indonesian Communist Party (PKI); these programs served to threaten both economically and culturally the more Islamic elements of village society. Dutch cultural and political efforts to carve out an area of Javanese culture that could remain separate from Islam may in fact have exacerbated the schism between Javano-Islamic and more orthodox styles of Islamic identification. But the upgraded shadow theatre tradition of the late colonial period failed in its role as the purveyor of a conservative moral order promoting the ideas of Dutch Ethici and Dutch-educated Javanese elites, since, as chapter 5 discusses, hundreds of thousands of Javanese peasants were attracted by PKI ideas wrapped in *wayang* clothing, showing the uncertainty of trying to manipulate cultural symbols. Those puppeteers who identified themselves with the PKI and its arts organization LEKRA suffered brutal retaliation at the hands of the Indonesian army and government as well as from groups of village youths. Some puppeteers whom I met in the 1980s were still not allowed to perform because of their political allegiances in the 1960s, and some had spent time in jail. Because the puppeteers today realize that they must be very chary of mixing in local or national politics, they make fun of the older refined traditions of *wayang* performance, an act of resistance that seems irrelevant to the government and that goes unnoticed by most educated Javanese.

This chapter has described an array of accepted beliefs about the shadow theatre tradition in the words of the puppeteers who perform and transmit the stories. In the next chapter, I turn from the stories to their settings in particular performance environments. In order to avoid reifying a "normative" performance style, I move around the edges of contemporary *wayang* performance traditions, giving examples of older exorcist performances as well as newer performance styles sponsored by popular urban and rural *dhalang* as well as innovations coming out of the Academy in Solo.

5 Revolutionary Rhetoric and Postcolonial

Performance Domains

. . . the *wajang* states in an emotionalist vocabulary the same formulation of what perhaps is the basic dilemma of Indian religious thought as it is presented in the Mahabharata—how is action possible, given compassion?[1]—Clifford Geertz

Here for centuries there has been no intellectual, no cultural life, no progress any more. There are the much-praised Eastern art forms—but what else are these than the rudiments of a feudal culture, which for us, the people of the twentieth century, are impossible to fall back on. The *wajang*, all the simple symbolism and mysticism—which is parallel to the allegory and medieval wisdom in Europe, what can they offer us intellectually and culturally? Almost nothing.[2]—S. Sjahrir

The opening quotes above, the first by the noted American anthropologist Clifford Geertz and the second by the Dutch-educated nationalist Sjahrir, capture the Euroamerican celebration and Indonesian dismissal of the *wayang* theatre as a signifying feature of postcolonial Indonesian life. Sjahrir, of course, was not Javanese, but neither was he the first to dismiss the *wayang* or to see it as useful only within the failed future of a Javanese rather than an Indies nation. Tjipto had gone beyond Javanese nationalism by the second decade of the twentieth century, although he, too, at times situated himself both within and outside what Pramoedya called "the major lines of thought in the *wayang*." But if the *wayang* was indeed useless for the realization of Indonesian independence, if it was useless for the "evolution" of postcolonial Indonesia into a modern nation, why did it appear as the central feature of Javanese life to American and European anthropologists, political scientists, and other foreigners who went to Indonesia during the Soekarno years?

My discussion in chapters 3 and 4 of the "uplifting" of the shadow

1. Geertz, *Religion of Java*, p. 272.
2. S. Sjahrir, *Indonesische Overpeinzingen* (Amsterdam: De Bezige Bij, 1945), pp. 60–61, which he published under the pseudonym of Sjahrazad. The translation is by C.L.M. Penders, as quoted in his *The Life and Times of Sukarno* (London: Sidgwick and Jackson, 1974), p. 29. For the Indonesian translation of Sjahrir's journals, see *Renungan Indonesia* (Djakarta: Pustaka Rakjat N. V., 1951).

Rhetoric and Performance Domains

theatre tradition in the early decades of the twentieth century, resulting in the creation of puppeteering schools in the 1920s and 1930s, helps to explain why Geertz and others saw the *wayang* as the essence of Javanese, and even of Indonesian, national consciousness.[3] Theosophical influences in the Indies had convinced a small number of the Dutch-educated Javanese elite, especially those with aspirations for position in the postcolonial state, that the *wayang* was a useful element of Javanese life that could be used to convince Europeans and Americans of the contemporary elegance and classical heights of Javanese performance traditions, and thus of Java itself.[4] The conflations of *wayang* with Java and Java with Indonesia are ones that continue to be used by orientalist scholars and Indonesian business and tourist promotion schemes—not to mention the political ruling elite in Jakarta.[5] Especially with the rise of Islamic fundamentalism and the representation of the perceived threat of Islam in European and American media, the exotic sounds of *gamelan* music and the delicately carved *wayang* puppets are appealing and nonthreatening signs of postcolonial Indonesia, which contains the largest Islamic population of any nation in the world. The counterpart to this image of Java is the equally alluring one of Bali, where Balinese Hinduism is the dominant religion.

When Geertz discovered through his extensive field research in Pare in the early 1950s that the Javanese philosophy of life was a restatement of the ethos of the Indian Bhagavad Gita, he showed the success of the Javanist nationalist and Dutch scholarly efforts of the preceding decades to remake the earthy village shadow theatre tradition, described as decadent

3. The schools may also have helped to revive the Bratayuda mystique among audiences made up of poorer *abangan* peasants, for whom traditional millennialism had become linked to the idea of an Islamic Holy War.

4. For an idea of just how small the number of Dutch-educated Indies students was, the *Encyclopedie van Nederlandsch-Indie* of 1921 shows that out of a population of 48,304,620, only seventy-eight went on to secondary schools. In the eleven years between 1917 and 1927, only about seven Indies students a year passed the final exams. See B. Dahm, *Sukarno and the Struggle for Indonesian Independence*, pp. 29–30.

5. Aware of the Javanese cultural domination of Indonesian politics, McVey noted: "This cultural weight grew heavier under Sukarno's Guided Democracy (and would increase still more under Suharto's New Order), when the Indonesian political vocabulary became infused with Javanese images and words" in "The Wayang Controversy in Indonesian Communism," p. 27. See also Anderson's brilliant articles on Javanese language and Indonesian politics, "The Language of Indonesian Politics," and "*Sembah-Sumpah*: The Politics of Language and Javanese Culture," both reprinted in Anderson, *Language and Power*.

and degenerate by several nineteenth-century Dutch scholars, into a refined, elite art.[6] Geertz, a member of the MIT-Harvard team of anthropologists sent to study various aspects of Javanese life in the early 1950s,
described religious practices and myths—some of which were refurbished
variants of older traditions—set in place by the apparatuses of the colonial
government and the efforts of those Javanese allied with it.[7] In the most
important myth, Islam was something foreign to Java, a shallow overlay
on a deeply ingrained Hindu-Buddhist Javanese past.[8]

Geertz and his followers portrayed Javanese Islam as incomplete, im-
pure, a shallow layer under which the less-threatening "animist" and
Hindu beliefs slumbered, ever ready to break through into view. Islam was
a religion of the desert, not appropriate for the luxuriant tropics, where
unveiled and visibly active women seemed to mock the dangers and
mysteries of the female body implied in Islamic thought. But Geertz
received his ideas from the scholars who preceded him.[9] Although he
certainly broke new ground with his studies of Javanese religion and

6. Even in the 1913 study, *Neerlands Indië, land en volk, geschiedenis en bestuur, bedrijf en
samenleving* (Amsterdam: Elsevier, 1913), put together under the direction of the retired
colonial administrator H. Colijn, the discussion of the shadow theatre lamented the
"fearful mangling" of the Old Javanese poetry sung by the puppeteers, and the authors
concluded: "In the true sense of the words, the Javanese theatre is really a 'folktheatre,'
and we can only regret that no influence for the elevation of the folk can come out of it"
(pp. 157–62).

7. This argument was also made by the Dutch-educated Sumatran nationalist leader
and postcolonial statesman Dr. Abu Hanifah: "The Dutch studies about the *wajang* and
the mystics of Java were very thorough indeed and this knowledge was put to good use
in their colonial administration. The Dutch encouraged the *wajang* performances and
they spread the belief that Ardjuna, the mighty warrior-prince of the Mahabharata, was
reincarnated. Slyly they implied that the Dutch governor could be compared to a kind of
'Ardjuna', and because of that, it could be expected that the government loved the
people very much" in *Tales of a Revolution*, p. 22.

8. As Geertz expressed it: "The otherness, awfulness, and majesty of God, the
intense moralism, the rigorous concern with doctrine, and the intolerant exclusivism
which are so much a part of Islam are very foreign to the traditional outlook of the
Javanese" in *Religion of Java*, p. 160. Other members of the research team included
Hildred Geertz, Robert Jay, Alice Dewey, Donald Fagg, and Edward Ryan; they arrived
in Java in the early 1950s with a team of scholars from Harvard sponsored by a grant
from the Ford Foundation.

9. Jane Atkinson, Professor of Anthropology at Lewis and Clark College, has pointed
out to me that Geertz was also commenting upon some reigning anthropological para-
digms of mid-century American anthropology: functionalist notions of the totality of
village life and synchronic approaches to "patterns of culture."

Rhetoric and Performance Domains

agricultural life, he observed Javanese village life in the 1950s through the outlines of Dutch colonial scholarship, in which Indies Islam and its potential as a rallying point for anticolonial uprisings were threatening images.[10]

Coming to Java from Holland, Geertz formulated the *"aliran"* model in which great vertical cleavages, tied together internally by ideological coherence, divided Javanese society, and all societal organizations were affiliated with one of several main ideological clusters.[11] Such organizations included women's associations, youth groups, labor, sports, charities, and so forth, all subsumed into "religiopolitical ideologies." These ideological cleavages were aligned in Geertz's scheme with a threefold division of Javanese society into *abangan* (so-called Hindu-animist peasants), *priyayi* (a secular, syncretic, or occasionally modernist Islamic, white-collar class), and *santri* (a variety of Islamic class and religious groupings), even though his own detailed discussions—in addition to those of his critics—belie the naiveté of these divisions.[12] In a clear refusal of simplistic class critiques, Geertz mixed religious, class, and political identifications because, at that moment in Javanese society, these elements were indeed intertwined.

Proceeding from these perceived societal divisions, Geertz chose to group the shadow theatre in what he called the *priyayi* refined-arts complex, although he cautioned:

The traits I shall discuss under *prijaji* are not confined to them. The *gamelan* orchestra and the *wajang* shadow-play, for example, could hardly be said to be

10. See the interview with Geertz in the *Bulletin of Indonesian Economic Studies* 24, no. 3 (December 1988): 31–49, where he explains how he read all the Dutch scholarship he could find and went to Holland for three months before going to Java. He notes that he read Boeke, Scheltema, and Van der Kolff, and in Holland he met Wertheim, who introduced him to the work of Van Leur, Schrieke, and Burger.

11. C. Geertz, *The Social History of an Indonesian Town* (Cambridge: M.I.T. Press, 1965), pp. 125–30, and *Religion of Java*. In McVey's introduction to the translation of Soekarno's famous speech on nationalism, Islam, and Marxism, she compared the *aliran* thesis with the Dutch *verzuiling*, another vertical organization of society along ideological-religious, rather than class, lines. See *Nationalism, Islam and Marxism*, trans. Karel H. Warouw and Peter D. Weldon, introduction by R. McVey (Ithaca: Cornell Modern Indonesian Project, 1969).

12. Geertz, *The Social History of an Indonesian Town*, pp. 131–52. Koentjaraningrat, in "Review of *The Religion of Java* by Clifford Geertz," *Madjalah Ilmu-ilmu Sastra Indonesia* 1, no. 2 (September 1963): 188–91, noted the confusion of class and religious distinctions in Geertz's work. Ricklefs, in "Six Centuries of Islamization in Java," pp. 118–21, modified the *kolot/moderen* (old-fashioned/modern) axis embedded within Geertz's religious and social distinctions in *Religion of Java*.

absent from peasant life; but they are included in this context because their cultivation, the elucidation of their religio-philosophical meaning, and their most elaborate variations are found in a *prijaji* context. . . .[13]

By placing the colonial constructions of the shadow theatre at the center of his analysis, Geertz's scholarship picked up where the Dutch had left off and set the shadow theatre up as a foundational element of Javanese culture for several more decades. Geertz's paradigm-setting work helped to bring colonial orientalist discourses that marginalized Indonesian Islam into the postcolonial period. Inheriting Dutch attitudes toward Islam, the scholarship about Java in the 1950s and 1960s continued to see Islam as a shallow overlay on the "culture" of Central Java. Shadow theatre became the essential ritual that both authorized and epitomized postcolonial Java for foreign scholars and other students and admirers of Javanese traditions.

Soekarno and Shadow Theatre Discourses

Although Geertz's work was important for representing the *wayang* in some European and especially American scholarship, no one was more pivotal in making the shadow theatre the center of postcolonial Indonesian life than Indonesia's charismatic first president Soekarno. Raised on a diet of Theosophy and *wayang*,[14] Soekarno came to see the solution to most

13. Geertz, *Religion of Java*, p. 234. Geertz noted that *wayang* was part of both an "*abangan* ritualistic-polytheistic-magical religious pattern" and the "*prijaji* mystical-pantheistic-speculative religious pattern" in ibid., p. 268. He added that the former was decreasing more rapidly than the latter. In this chapter, I suggest the reverse: it has been the village *wayang* traditions that have always been most important, and this continues to the present day. After his return to Indonesia in the mid-1980s, Geertz changed his mind about *wayang* and other Javanese arts. See "'Popular Art' and the Javanese Tradition."

14. For Soekarno and Theosophy, see Hanifah, *Tales of a Revolution*, p. 16; Penders, *Life and Times of Sukarno*, p. 206 n. 10; and Cindy Adams, *Sukarno: An Autobiography As Told to Cindy Adams* (New York: Bobbs-Merrill, 1965), pp. 23–24. All the studies that refer to Soekarno and *wayang* theatre are too numerous to mention. Bernard Dahm's respected biography of Soekarno, *Sukarno and the Struggle for Indonesian Independence*, consistently places Soekarno within a mythologizing *wayang* world, but this is a bit unfortunate since it appears that Dahm's understanding of the *wayang* is quite shallow. Dahm, on pp. 23–28, follows Indian ideas and occasionally an Old Javanese telling of a

problems facing the nationalists as well as the postcolonial Dutch-educated leaders in a synthesis of religion, ideology, and nationalism that was symbolized most eloquently and powerfully in the human incarnation of Soekarno himself.[15] As a great synthesizer, he also identified himself quite closely with the shadow theatre performance tradition as well as the Ramayana and Mahabharata stories. Soekarno believed that he was the spokesman for the Indonesian nation. His epitaph reads: "Here lies Bung Karno, mouthpiece of the Indonesian people." All the titles that he regularly used evoke for some the different names that puppeteers recite to introduce famous *wayang* heroes: Presiden Republik Indonesia, Panglima Tertinggi Angkatan Bersendjata (Commander in Chief of the Armed Forces), Perdana Menteri Pemerintah (Government Prime Minister), Penjambung Lidah Rakjat Indonesia (Mouthpiece of the Indonesian People), Pemimpin Besar Revolusi (Great Leader of the Revolution).[16]

Soekarno can be seen as a paradigmatic Javanese monarch fitting into earlier patterns of Javanese political authority. As Koch described him many times in his popular novel *The Year of Living Dangerously*, Soekarno in his white helicopter was like Wisnu in his magic car swooping down from the heavens.[17] Soekarno, in public, always looked impeccable. He lived in

---

Pandhawa and Korawa story in which the Korawa are brought back to life after the Bratayuda War—a story I have only encountered in Zoetmulder's *Kalangwan*, although it was translated into Dutch by J. L. Swellengrebel in 1936. From this, Dahm assumes a kind of harmonious dynamic between Pandhawa and Korawa that was not familiar to any Javanese puppeteers or *wayang* aficionados whom I knew. In his autobiography as told to Cindy Adams (pp. 101–2), Soekarno also tells of his love for the *wayang* theatre. His speeches often refer to Mahabharata characters or contain phrases from the *dhalang*'s narration. The most interesting fictional study of Soekarno and shadow theatre in English is C. J. Koch's *The Year of Living Dangerously* (New York: St. Martin's Press, 1978); the novel is much more useful for historical purposes than the film of the same name. The book is modeled on a *wayang* play, being divided into the three major parts of most *wayang purwa* performances. Scholars who carried out research in Indonesia in the 1950s and 1960s have told me how Soekarno would regularly hold *wayang* performances in his palace in Jakarta. In his speeches and in his autobiography, he claims to have performed as a *dhalang*. I have not come across any references to his skills as a shadow play performer.

15. As the American columnist who was chosen to write Soekarno's autobiography, Adams noted (p. 1): "The simplest way to describe Sukarno is to say that he is a great lover. He loves his country, he loves his people, he loves women, he loves art, and, best of all, he loves himself."

16. Soekarno, *Tahun "Vivere Periculoso"* (Jakarta: B. P. Prapantja, 1964), pp. 43–44.

17. J. D. Legge, *Sukarno: A Political Biography* (New York: Praeger Publishers, 1972),

several palaces. Reminiscent of his beloved *wayang* hero Arjuna, he had many mistresses but, in accordance with Islamic law, he restricted himself to four wives at any one time. He spoke many languages and hobnobbed with other *dewa-dewi* (gods). Like King Yudhistira, eldest of the five Pandhawa heroes, who brought all the neighboring kings to his kingdom in the Theosophy-inspired *wayang lakon* Sesaji Raja Suya, he was leader of the 1955 Bandung Conference of Asian and African nations. He told Americans to go to hell with their foreign aid. He was a prince and one of the people (*rakyat*) at the same time. In many of his speeches, Soekarno was able to speak to the Javanese audiences using the metacommunicative codes of the shadow theatre, but the associations among Java, *wayang*, and the new state of Indonesia were clear.

Soekarno's ability to inspire and arouse audiences with his speeches was a talent he learned from his mentor and one-time father-in-law—the early nationalist leader Tjokroaminoto—practiced in the 1920s and then honed in the 1940s in radio broadcasts, when he worked with the Japanese during World War II. Scholars argue that he identified himself with either Arjuna, Bima, or Gathotkaca—all major heroes from the Mahabharata—but less often with his own namesake, the Pandhawa hero Karna, abandoned by his mother at birth because he was born out of wedlock, who then chooses to fight against his own brothers on the side of the Korawa in the Bratayuda war. The Sumatran statesman Abu Hanifah described Soekarno's speeches and their effects vividly.[18]

I have heard Soekarno many times in the past suddenly thundering during a

---

p. 308, states: "His [Soekarno's] charismatic authority owed . . . much to his ability to project himself to the Javanese in traditional terms. To the appeal of his Jacobin radicalism was added something of the aura which had surrounded the old Javanese rulers."

18. The following quotes from Hanifah are all originally written in English. In *Sukarno*, p. 105, Dahm argues that Soekarno presented himself as Bima in his first speeches in 1928 and 1929. In *Tales of a Revolution*, pp. 22–23, Hanifah remembers Arjuna and Gathotkaca as the characters Soekarno identified with most often. In his noncommital introduction to the fanciful book *Perang Tipu Daya antara Bung Karno dengan Tokoh Tokoh Komunis* (The Deceitful War between Bung Karno and the Communists) by H. Ahmad Muhsin, the respected Muslim leader Abdurrahman Wahid notes the power of myth and leaves it up to the reader to judge the historical accuracy of Muhsin's contention that Soekarno, like his famous namesake Adipati Karno, made the ultimate sacrifice and was forced to become a traitor to save his honor and the honor of his family name.

Rhetoric and Performance Domains

*The Pandhawa hero
Bima.*

speech to the masses that they must consider him their leader, also their Ardjuna, and that they should believe that he was the incarnation of Ardjuna who would protect his people and would make them happy in a new and better world. . . .

At such moments I realised that because of the centuries-old influence of the *wajang* on them, these people indeed believed in Soekarno as their Savior. From the devotion in their faces you could see he was their king.

And Hanifah also described how Soekarno was able to turn his weakness for women to his advantage through his identification with Arjuna.[19]

He compared himself very often to Ardjuna, the hero from the Mahabharata, the supreme fighter, the ladies man, the enchanter, the king. So even his affairs with women should be seen in the light of his mystical beliefs.

19. Hanifah, *Tales of a Revolution*, p. 18.

Hanifah explained what he saw as Soekarno's faults and excesses by attributing them to the "old-fashioned" Javanese who raised him and allowed him to spend his childhood immersed in the mythical world of the *wayang*, "where kings and queens were almost real." He also saw Soekarno, like himself and many other Dutch-educated Javanese, as caught between the mystical, mysterious East and the cold, rational West, something they could never overcome.[20]

Soekarno's real brilliance lay in his ability to combine elements of the Javanese past with the Indonesian future to present his audiences with new ways of envisioning their identities in the postcolonial world. Widely read in several European languages, but concerned to present himself as a man of the people, he could make fun of his European education and show it off at the same time. In speaking to a group of teachers in Java in the early 1940s, he argued:[21]

Why is it that many among us are insulted by the younger generation with the epithets "*cultuurmaniak*," "Boroboedoer-*aanbidder* [worshipper]," "*tijang Djawi*" [refined Javanese] and other phrases even more ridiculous? Is it not because they themselves really long for the older history, in the way of *dooden-cultus* [death cults] and *dooden-aanbidding* [death-worshipping] that I spoke of earlier, long for the days of old and the beautiful young girl who has already died. I urge you teachers, do not follow these cults of the dead. Rather than crying over the corpse of the beautiful young girl, it is better to admire a live Gatotkatja!

What Soekarno is saying here, of course, is that the teachers should forget the past and admire him, the Gathotkaca of the modern age. But even as he makes fun of the fruits of Dutch scholarship, he cannot help but use the very terminology he criticizes.

No longer a naive student, after spending most of the 1930s in Dutch prisons or in exile, Soekarno was a seasoned—perhaps even a suspicious—politician when he became a world-recognized leader in the 1950s, and his main goal became to hold on to power at any cost. As he perceived

20. Ibid., p. 6.

21. This is the last speech in the collection of Soekarno's speeches called *DiBawah Bendera Revolusi*, vol. 7 (Jakarta: Panitya Penerbit DiBawah Bendera Revolusi, 1964). It is titled "To be a Teacher in a Time of Development" and is presented in the book in Soekarno's own handwriting. It does not say where or when the speech was given, but since they are arranged in chronological order, it was probably given in the 1940s to a Central Javanese audience.

Rhetoric and Performance Domains

it at the time, one useful way to endear himself to the densely populated masses of the Javanese heartland was to build upon the mythologies of the *wayang* theatre, representing himself and his political programs in the idioms of the shadow theatre tales.

In fact, I related how in Jakarta I even performed as a *dhalang*, describing how Ki Dhalang has told the story of the ideals of the Indonesian people in the past . . . well, from the time of Sunan Kalidjaga, ladies and gentlemen. Yes, people say that *wayang kulit* was created by Sunan Kalidjaga but actually this is not true. *Wayang kulit*, in fact, was here before the Hindus came. Just read Brandes. Brandes said that *wayang kulit* was authentically Indonesian. There were already *lakon* which were then enriched by the Ramayana and Mahabharata, but before the Ramayana and Mahabharata entered Indonesia, we already had *wayang kulit*. It has been clearly proven by Brandes. When I performed the *wayang* in Jakarta, I explained that socialism has informed the ideals of the Indonesian people for hundreds of years.[22]

Soekarno then introduced several sentences in Javanese from the opening narration of the *dhalang* which told of the harmony and prosperity of the land: domestic animals went out and came home by themselves, trading went on night and day, and all the roads were safe to travel. This harmony and prosperity was what he equated with socialism, a socialism that the "Indonesian" people had known for hundreds of years.[23] He made these ideas more explicit at another speech given at Gajah Mada a year and a half later.

As I have said in speeches in Jakarta about Indonesian socialism, don't think that this is my invention, the invention of Bung Karno or Pak Leimena, no. They are the words of the *dalang*, I said in Jakarta, the words of the *dalang* that were written in the *pakem*-books from hundreds of years ago; what they describe is already social-

---

22. This speech, titled "Milikilah Dedication of Life" or "Possess Dedication of Life" was presented at the Sitihinggil in front of students from Gajah Mada University on 1 April 1961 in Yogyakarta and is collected in *Warislah Api Sumpah Pemuda: Kumpulan Pidato Bung Karno di hadapan pemuda 1961–64* (Jakarta: C V Haji Masagung, 1988), p. 50.

23. Soekarno frequently used the same phrases from the *dhalang*'s *janturan* (opening narration) in his speeches to Javanese audiences and argued that this was what he meant by socialism. See his speech to another gathering of students in Bandung in January 1961 reprinted in *Warislah Api Sumpah Pemuda*, pp. 1–18, especially pages 14–15. Since most Sundanese people speak Sundanese rather than Javanese, Soekarno was careful to translate the Javanese phrases more explicitly than he did in Central Java.

ism, maybe an old-fashioned socialism that's not yet modern. But those ideas are the same as socialism.[24]

Soekarno's discourse on *wayang* was rooted in the ideas of Dutch philology and European Marxism. But Soekarno's Marxism, like his approach to "Democracy," had been emptied of its European meanings and refilled with ideas that were uniquely Indonesian.[25] Soekarno called his version of Marxism "Marhaenism," and it referred to the poverty-stricken Javanese peasant or Marhaen, who owned his or her own tiny bit of land and a few tools. In his struggle to Indonesianize European concepts, Soekarno did not hesitate to authorize his concepts with European pedigrees, and, as noted above, he used the work of the Dutch scholar Brandes to back up his claim that the *wayang* was indigenous to Java.[26] Except for the few Gajah Mada students who might have been introduced to the Dutch scholarship on *wayang* in their classes, most of his audience probably found this claim strange since they would not have expected the *wayang* to come from anywhere *but* Java. When he was speaking in Yogyakarta, he felt free to use Javanese, to use actual quotes from the *wayang*, confident that his audience would understand him.[27]

24. Soekarno, *Warislah Api*, p. 127.

25. In his critique of "Western" Democracy, Soekarno began to argue in 1956 for a concept of "Guided Democracy" that did not include the tyranny of a majority made up of 50 percent plus one. Guided Democracy (*Demokrasi Terpimpin*), which would allow room for consensus and mutual help (*gotong royong*), became the official state policy in 1957, although the policy continued to evolve over the next two years. See Daniel S. Lev, *The Transition to Guided Democracy: Indonesian Politics, 1957–59* (Ithaca: Cornell University Modern Indonesia Project, 1966).

26. In her excellent analysis of the Communist discourse on *wayang* theatrical traditions in the 1950s and 1960s, McVey comments on the Communist leader Sakirman's use of Dutch sources to defend the *wayang* tradition against those who argued that it was not indigenous to Java: "Critics of *wayang* had found a vulnerable point in its foreign ancestry and demanded that the old *lakon* be rejected as alien imports. To ward off this campaign, Sakirman supplied erudite references to Dutch authorities on the autochthonous origins of the *wayang*; Dutch scholars might be reactionary imperialists, but they could be thought neutral on the matter of *wayang*'s ancestry." See "The Wayang Controversy in Indonesian Communism," p. 30.

27. When Soekarno spoke in areas outside Central and East Java, he was careful to use words and themes that would resonate for more Islamic audiences. Although he is associated so clearly with *wayang* imagery, he made many speeches about Islam. See some of his collected speeches in *DiBawah Bendera Revolusi*, vol. 1, especially "Nationalisme, Islamisme dan Marxisme," "Surat-surat Islam dari Endeh," "Tidak pertjaja bahwa Mirza Gulam Ahmad adalah Nabi," "Me'mudah'-kan pengertian Islam," "Apa

Rhetoric and Performance Domains

In a delicate concession to Islam, he noted the widespread belief that the *wayang* had been introduced to Java by Sunan Kalijaga, one of the nine saints believed to have brought Islam to Java, but then, out of the thought-world of Dutch rather than Javanese mentalities, he chose to authenticate the *wayang* with Dutch scholarship rather than harmonize it with Islam. He continued to combine his ideas of nationalism and his broad interpretation of Islam and to equate them with his particular brand of Communism, a message he had been preaching in various ways for forty years.[28] Since he compared himself with the shadow theatre heroes, and the *dhalang* who manipulated them, the blurring of *wayang* and Communism became more pronounced and necessary as the army and the Communist Party were locked in their deadly power struggle in the 1960s. Soekarno needed the *rakyat*, the people, to help balance the growing strength of the army, and the identification of *wayang* and Communism became more and more urgent and more and more dangerous for a peasantry who were slowly starving as their hero and patron tried to hold on to the reins of power. The stories of an inevitable war between brothers were certainly apt metaphors for the rising tensions of Javanese life in the 1960s.

Communist Discourse and Shadow Theatre

Ruth McVey has described the ways in which the discourse of *wayang* became a theoretical problem for the cultural and doctrinal policies of the Communist Party in the 1950s and 1960s.[29] Because of its feudal associations—associations that had been strengthened and enhanced in the pre-Independence years by the intertwining of the *wayang* with colonial rule and the celebration of the *wayang* by colonial elites—the shadow theatre posed problems for the cultural organizations connected with the Indonesian Communist Party or PKI (Partai Komunis Indonesia). The Institute of

---

sebab Turki memisah agama dari negara," "Islam sontolojo," and "Bloedtransfusie dan sebagian kaum Ulama." Of course, these speeches did not necessarily interpret Islam in ways that all Indonesian Muslims would approve of, but they did indicate Soekarno's wide-ranging knowledge of Islamic issues and communities around the world.

28. See Karel H. Warouw and Peter D. Weldon's translation of Soekarno's famous speech: *Nationalism, Islam and Marxism* (1969).

29. McVey, "The Wayang Controversy in Indonesian Communism."

People's Culture, known by its acronym LEKRA, felt an ambivalence toward shadow theatre that it did not feel toward those arts that were less closely associated with the Javanese courts. Until the late 1950s, LEKRA solved this problem by ignoring the shadow theatre and devoting attention to what were considered popular rather than high arts.[30] The Conference on Revolutionary Art and Literature turned its attention in 1964 to dance forms and passed a resolution arguing for banning what were considered to be frivolous, erotic, or formalist features. The Conference also condemned stories that stressed individualism, *sikap individu*, rather than those that incorporated mass struggle.[31]

One of the contradictions facing the cultural wing of the Communist Party was how to develop a popular or mass art that still maintained high artistic and aesthetic standards. One of the more innovative suggestions in the party newspaper called for a refined worker puppet, somewhat of a contradiction in terms. As McVey cogently comments:

They [the refined worker puppets] raised him [common man] to the mythical plane, made him part of official rather than experienced reality, the common man as his leaders would like to have him—a portrayal as removed from social reality as the delicate mantis-figure of Arjuna. The *halus* [refined] worker-puppet was thus a hybrid, combining the assumptions of socialist realism with the representational techniques of the *wayang purwa*.[32]

Despite the contradictions faced by higher-echelon members of the Communist Party, shadow theatre performances did serve to promulgate messages of the competing political parties in the 1950s and 1960s. Because of the brutal mass killings of 1965–66 and the remaining stigmas associated with Communism in Indonesia, this is an area of study that has been avoided by both foreign and Javanese researchers of the shadow theatre tradition. People say that many *dhalang* were killed in the purges following the fall of the Old Order government, but statistics are impossi-

30. Ibid., p. 28.

31. Quoted in ibid., p. 47 n. 48, from the Communist newspaper *Harian Rakjat*, 27 September 1964. For the best study of LEKRA and its influence on Indonesian artistic development during the Soekarno years, see Keith Foulcher's *Social Commitment in Literature and the Arts: The Indonesian "Institute of People's Culture" 1950–1965* (Clayton, Victoria: Centre of Southeast Asian Studies, Monash University, 1986).

32. McVey, "The Wayang Controversy in Indonesian Communism," p. 37.

Rhetoric and Performance Domains

ble to find, and informants remain silent. Even in the 1980s and 1990s, *dhalang* who were suspected of any involvement with the Communist Party twenty-five years ago were still not allowed to perform. I have heard that performances of the period used various Mahabharata stories and figures to represent the variety of ideological positions, but this is an area of research that remains frustratingly opaque.

Foreign scholars who visited Java both before and after the bloody killings of the mid-1960s suggest that the army and the Communists were represented by politicians and puppeteers as Korawa and Pandhawa, the warring cousins of the Bratayuda stories. One essay by the Indonesian scholar G. J. Resink remains significant in arguing for the importance of the Mahabharata stories in somehow justifying, enabling, or explaining the killings.[33] Resink assembles his argument mostly from the work of other European and American scholars as well as his own experiences in his mother's village of Karangasem, between Solo and Yogya. He remembers a performance of the Bratayuda from his youth where the men got so worked up in the frenzy of the enactment of the war that the women had to flee the performance area.[34] He also mentions a staging of the Bratayuda in the late 1950s, when an earthquake coincided with the terrifying death of Arjuna's son Abimanyu. But even Resink states that his argument is only a hypothesis: "and a hypothesis it will remain, since any likely witnesses for or against are bound to remain as silent as the proverbial grave from sheer shame or fear. . . ."

In Resink's argument, the Communists—mostly *abangan* (red) Javanese—are represented as the Korawa, the side associated with the left side of the *dhalang*, and the traditionalist Muslims affiliated with the political party Nahadatul Ulama are represented as the heroic Pandhawa. In 1994, I asked Pipit Rochiyat, one of the very few Javanese who has described the atrocities of 1965–66 and the role he played in them, whether Bratayuda stories were circulating during that period. He replied as follows:

33. Resink, "From the Old Mahabharata—to the New Ramayana—Order," pp. 214–35. See especially pp. 214–23.

34. I once witnessed a very special type of exorcist performance in Klaten, outside of Solo, which condensed about eight episodes from the Bratayuda War into a single night's performance. This village and its *dhalang*, however, were known for their humor rather than their violence, and I and the rest of the audience eerily chuckled through the performance that began just after the death of Abimanyu and ended with the death of Duryodana.

Simpingan tengen, *the puppets of the right, are always arrayed to the right side of the puppeteer.*

Referring to the chaos of '65–'66, my parents had some maidservants who believed that the Bharatayuda had truly begun—only there was no gamelan. And it was clear that the Communists were the Kurawa, and we non-Communists were the Pandawa. They told me, and I was still a kid, that the behavior of the Kurawa was exactly like that of the Communists: they grabbed things, they were coarse, they didn't know the rules, etc. (demonstrations, demands, uproar, boycotts, etc.). This was pretty much the public perception among the people in the villages around the Sugar Factory of Ngadirejo, fourteen kilometers south of Kediri (East Java). You may know that at that time we Pandawa were continually harassed by the Communist Kurawa. They liked to grab land, just like the Kurawa took the land of the Pandawa. Thus it was fitting or "normal" to kill the Kurawa, even to slaughter them in brutal ways (remember the story of Sangkuni's mouth being ripped apart, Duryudana alias Suyudana's head being smashed or Dursasana's throat being slashed and his blood gulped down a wide-open mouth and then pissed out until it was all gone, just like Johnny Walker).

In a similar vein, a number of European, Australian, and American scholars and reporters have noted that Bratayuda imagery was common both before and during the chaos and slaughter that accompanied the fall of the

Simpingan kiwo, *the puppets of the left, are always arrayed to the left side of the puppeteer.*

Soekarno government. Most interesting, in this respect, is Ruth McVey's presentation of the testimony of Sudisman, one of the five leaders of the Communist Party, who felt the Communist leaders were the Pandhawa.[35] Thus the stories were open for interpretation, serving as allegories for the brutalities and politics of the time. Other scholars mention that Soekarno's Foreign Minister Dr. Soebandrio was associated, in the early years of the New Order government, with the *wayang* character Durna, a sly and two-faced mentor to both factions in the Mahabharata stories.[36]

All the examples cited above show that during the Guided Democracy period, Javanese as well as non-Javanese observers were making associations between the shadow theatre and the political world reflected through it. But these connections were encouraged by Soekarno for his own political ends. Although Soekarno filled postcolonial Indonesia with *wayang*

35. See, for example, Resink, "From the Old Mahabharata"; Anderson, *Language and Power,* p. 7; McVey, "The Wayang Controversy"; Legge, *Sukarno,* pp. 398–99; Cribb, *The Indonesian Killings,* pp. 34–35; B. May, *The Indonesian Tragedy* (London: Routledge and Kegan Paul, 1978), pp. 48–49, 124; and H. Ahmad Muhsin, *Perang Tipu Daya.*

36. See Resink, "From the Old Mahabharata," p. 222, and Anderson, *Language and Power,* p. 149 n. 11.

imagery, this Javanist infusion was to have unpredictable results. Through his strengthening of the links among a complex *abangan* peasantry, *wayang*, and Communism, Soekarno encouraged the process begun under the Dutch—and furthered through the work of Javanese nationalists—in which a certain segment of Java's population was estranged from Islam. In her article on the Taman Siswa schools of Soewardi and Soetatmo, McVey noted the Javanist nationalist attempt to fuse a newly refurbished Javanese "tradition" with European ideas of innovative schooling.[37] This hybrid reconstruction of Javanese and Dutch mentalities and sensibilities created and nurtured those spaces in Javanese society where *wayang* was celebrated as the essence of Java and Islam was marginalized. By distancing certain villagers from identifying with Islam, social transformation through a Marxism associated with modernist ideas became ideologically acceptable. Soekarno constantly reinforced ideas that connected the images of the *dhalang* with a socialist worldview, and the land reform promises of the government left a land-hungry, war-weary, and starving peasantry receptive to Marxist rhetoric that promised land, food, and clothing in abundance—just what the *dhalang*'s narrations described and Soekarno's speeches constantly repeated.[38]

As noted above, *dhalang* were used in the 1960s to promote the messages of the various political parties—but most commonly Soekarno's PNI (Partai Nasional Indonesia) and the Communist PKI. Although the puppeteers, as entertainers who desired to please their audiences, had always slanted their stories in particular directions, this process became more pronounced and exceedingly dangerous by the mid-1960s. The associations between the words and ideas of the *wayang* with Soekarno's socialist program, and Soekarno's increasing support of the Communists as the strength of the Army grew in the 1960s, implicated certain groups of *dhalang* in the brutal turn against the Communists initiated by General Soeharto in October of 1965.

37. R. McVey, "Taman Siswa and the Indonesian National Awakening," p. 140.

38. Sartono Kartodirdjo argued that millennial traditions envisaged a world in which oppressive taxes would disappear, the land would be divided equally, and material needs would be satisfied. He used the typical Javanese phrase to refer to this utopian vision—*murah sandang pangan*—food and clothing cheap to buy—a phrase often used by shadow puppeteers. See "Agrarian Radicalism, In Java: Its Setting and Development," in *Culture and Politics in Indonesia*, ed. Claire Holt (Ithaca: Cornell University Press, 1972), p. 94.

The level of Communist complicity in the abortive coup of 30 September 1965 is still a debated point.[39] Whether or not the Communists were involved, the mythology of the New Order has made them the perpetrators. While evidence points to middle-level army discontents, and certainly it was army men who carried out the killing of the six generals and one adjutant on the night of September 30, the Communists were quickly implicated in the killings as rumors and lies were woven into the official story.[40] The Pemuda Rakyat and Gerwani—Communist-associated male and female youth groups—which had been involved in paramilitary training near the Halim air force base, the site of the well from which the bodies of the generals were exhumed, were wrongly accused of helping to kill the generals. After these murders of seven army men, over a period of several months from late October 1965 through January of 1966, gangs of Islamic and nationalist youth—including Catholic youth groups—aided and abetted by the Indonesian army, slaughtered hundreds of thousands of Javanese peasants and others who, for the most part, were believed to be politically associated with the PKI. Although the most brutal killings took place in Java, Bali, and northern Sumatra—often across ethnic, religious, ideological and class lines—there was little question in Central and East Java of ethnic cleavages; Javanese were killing Javanese. Often villagers turned against their neighbors, and sometimes family members turned against each other.

The Soekarno years were a second disjunctive period of political promise and disorder in the history of twentieth-century Indonesia. During those years the shadow theatre was swept up into Soekarno's increasingly fiery and insistent messages to continue and complete the revolution that had begun in 1945, in contrast to the colonial concern for *rust en orde* and the postcolonial New Order repression in the name of *ketertiban* or law and order. Because *wayang* performances have always been lively and sugges-

39. Crouch, *The Army and Politics in Indonesia*, pp. 97–134.

40. Robert Cribb, "Problems in the Historiography of the Killings in Indonesia"; Crouch, *The Army and Politics in Indonesia*; Resink, "From the Old Mahabharata." This story was documented in the film made by one of Indonesia's most prominent film directors, Arifin C. Noer. Called *Pengkhianatan G.30.S/PKI*, the September 30th PKI Treason, and passed off by the New Order government as a semidocumentary (Buku Petunjuk 1984), the film effectively constructs the Communists as enemies of the state as well as subhuman killers. The film is shown every year on television and all Indonesians are encouraged to watch it. It is a frightening example of New Order propaganda.

tive, far from being a conservative preserver of colonial hierarchies, the *wayang* served new purposes and constituencies during the Soekarno years, constituencies that disappeared in the violent fall of the Old Order government.

It is within this disjunctive moment in Indonesian politics that the work of scholars like Ben Anderson and Ruth McVey must be placed.[41] Brilliant observers of the *wayang* tradition and its complex expression of Indonesian politics, both scholars shattered naive speculations that held the *wayang* apart from the political rhetoric that surrounded it, and they disrupted its "naturalness" as an essential feature of Javanese life. But *wayang* was, in many ways, less substantial and more persistent than the work of these scholars suggests. As I have argued throughout this book, the *wayang* theatre was not an unchanging feature of Javanese life. As a theatrical medium with the potential to absorb and reinterpret political allegories, *wayang* has served the purposes of various governments, not least that of the New Order.

By implicating so many Indonesians in the killings of 1965–66, the New Order government has ensured that no one will want to identify killer and victim, for to do so would require vengeance and such vengeance would destroy the state. In the preceding chapters, I have woven together mythical and historical narratives to look at colonial and postcolonial discourses that governed ways of talking about the *wayang* theatre in Java. I have proposed the beginning of a new mythical cycle in the late eighteenth century; this is when the Dutch were incorporated into Javanese mythology as the only ones who could prevent Javanese fratricide. The New Order regime of Soeharto and the Army has now taken over the Dutch myth; they have become the ones who can prevent Javanese fratricide and they need only point to the internecine strife in the Javanese countryside in 1965–66 to illustrate their point. They were the ones who called an end to the killings; what they have no need or wish to emphasize is their role in setting the killings in motion.

One way to end the cycle of violence is to diffuse or displace the myths. Perhaps this can explain, in part, the expanding identification since the

41. I refer in particular to Anderson's *Mythology and Tolerance* and "The Idea of Power" and to McVey's "The Wayang Controversy." I thank Dan Lev for helping me to think through this complex intermingling of politics, *wayang*, and power in scholarship on the Soekarno years.

1980s of the New Order government with Islam. In the immediate post-1965 period, the government attempted to keep the dual threats of Communism and Islamic extremism alive as a way of rationalizing the powerful role of the army in New Order Indonesia. More recently, President Soeharto has made increasing concessions to Islam to strengthen his role vis-à-vis the army: Islam is allowed increasing visibility—the profusion of mosques and the Islamic clothing that rising numbers of Indonesian women choose to wear are most noticeable—in exchange for a low political profile, as Islamic leaders are now engaged in mutual concession-swapping with the state.

In addition to its accommodations with Islam, the New Order government has also encouraged the revival of regional arts. The New Order government of President Soeharto sees the manipulation of regional cultures as vital elements of political control. Being Central Javanese, however, Soeharto is careful to cast his message to the puppeteers and other performers in oblique ways. Speaking to the *dhalang* in 1978 at one of the Wayang Weeks [Pekan Wayang] that have been held every five years or so since the early years of the New Order rise to power, Soeharto explained his ideas about the role of the puppeteers and their duties to the state.

Certainly it would not be appropriate for us to change the artistic role of the *dhalang* into that of a mouthpiece for development, for if we did *wayang*'s artistic coherence would be destroyed. This would harm all of us, harm the artistic culture which we should develop. But I believe you *dhalang* understand what needs to be done. The development message can be conveyed while preserving the artistic level and coherence of the *wayang*.[42]

By his stress on using the *wayang* theatre for the uplift of the masses, President Soeharto has returned to the cultural rhetoric of colonial dis-

42. This quotation is from the President's Address at a Meeting with *dhalang* for the Wayang Week of 27 July 1978, Soeharto, *Sambutan Presiden Kepada Pertemuan dengan para dalang dalam Rangka Pekan Wayang pada tanggal 27 Juli 1978 di Jakarta* (Jakarta: Departemen Penerangan Republik Indonesia, 1978), p. 7, quoted in McVey, "The Wayang Controversy," p. 49 n. 59. Clara van Groenendael, *The dalang behind the wayang*, has explored the ways in which the New Order government has attempted to use the shadow theatre for purposes of political propaganda. At the time of her research in the late 1970s, as in the past, the results of efforts to use the *wayang* for political control or ethical uplift were often unpredictable.

courses. In 1995, the president again appealed to the *dhalang* to deliver his message of development—both spiritual and economic—to their audiences. On 21 January, there was a meeting of Pepadi (Persatuan Pedalangan Indonesia, or Indonesian Shadow Theatre Association), and forty *dhalang* were called to the Istana Merdeka (Freedom Palace) in Jakarta to hear a speech by the President. In his speech, Soeharto referred to the problems and successes of his New Order government. He lectured the *dhalang* about poverty and economic development, the problems of the conglomerates that dominate the Indonesian economy, and, most importantly, about Javanese mysticism. According to the famous *dhalang* Ki Anom Suroto: "Pak Harto is really amazing in his ability to deliver this knowledge in very unpretentious language."[43] Suroto's use of the word *ilmu* or knowledge can refer to both scientific and mystical knowledge, and this conflation is very evident in the President's speech. It is obvious that President Soeharto continues to see the *wayang* theatre as a significant feature of Javanese life.

Previous chapters have looked at how foreign observers saw the shadow theatre tradition in the nineteenth and twentieth centuries. To assess the ways in which shadow theatre performances continue to appeal to Javanese audiences, I turn now to look at several different environments in which the *wayang* was flourishing in the early 1980s and 1990.

Contemporary Performance Environments

Contemporary Javanese shadow theatre puppeteers continue to manipulate the Ramayana and Mahabharata stories that have mingled in the shadow theatre tradition for centuries. One can, however, find both older and newer styles of shadow play performance in Java today. In the older domains, Javanese village aesthetics seem dominant—coincidence, embellishment, and the subversion of linearity continue to generate meaning. The dense texture of *wayang* performances that is built up through a layering of music, song, poetry, genealogy, mysticism, shadows, puppets, performers, and patrons ties contemporary audiences to the various re-

43. "Pesan-pesan Pak Harto pada Ki Dalang," *Kompas*, Monday, 23 January 1995. For detailed information about Soekarto's mystical inclinations, see Pemberton, "On the Subject of Java," pp. 304–10.

ligious and literary periods of Java's past. Older performance styles are pleasing both because they are *ramai* or lively[44] and because they are predictable: the puppets, music, and stories are familiar, and everyone who attends the performance knows his or her proper place in the audience as the audience knows the proper place of all the puppets in the *wayang* hierarchy. The rest of this chapter investigates the clash of old and new authorities, and old and new aesthetics, in contemporary *wayang* performance domains.

In many shadow theatre performances that I observed in the 1980s, texture, embellishment, and "density of context" marked the dramatic concerns of the Javanese puppeteer. In the aesthetic world of the shadow theatre, mood development is achieved through embellishment and the building of texture—the interplay of music, recitation, tapping, and the clashing of metal plates, not to mention the activity of the puppets on the screen and the story line, which often seems extraneous to the performance. In a nine-hour performance that ends at the beginning or begins at the ending, and whose plot often seems to go nowhere, the sheer texture of the performance, moving in toward the puppeteer and out toward the audience, seems to motivate its action. Any linearity, even in the simple sense of genealogy, which the Indian stories brought to Java, has been mediated by Javanese concerns with texture and density of context. These motifs can be explored in three contemporary performance domains of the Javanese shadow puppet theatre: *ruwatan*, or exorcistic performances; *Rebo Legi* (Wednesday Legi) performances, which take place monthly in the home of a famous Solonese puppeteer; and *padat*, or condensed performances, which have been created at the Academy in Solo.

Exorcistic Performances

Ruwatan, or exorcistic performances, have been part of the shadow puppet repertoire since at least the seventeenth century.[45] Today in Central Java, there is generally one story used, Murwakala or The Birth of Kala. In this story, the gods descend to the earth to perform in a *wayang* play in order to

44. Becker, "Text-Building."
45. Brandon, *On Thrones of Gold,*" p. 5.

halt the murderous assault of the ogre-god Kala (son of the high god Siwa) who symbolically pursues the child or adult being exorcised. The represented victim then hides in one of the instruments being used in the performance within the *ruwatan* performance and, as the puppeteer reads the powerful *mantra* or spell, Kala is appeased, the victim is exorcised, and order returns for a time to the world.

One performance that I attended in April of 1984, in a village outside the city of Solo, was a Sadranan, a special type of *ruwatan* that combines an offering made at the graves of the ancestors with a *ruwatan* shadow play—a common practice in contemporary Java. I heard about this performance accidentally when a friend stopped by and asked if I would like to drive with him to the performance on my motorbike. *Ruwatan* performances usually take place in the daytime, beginning around ten o'clock in the morning and ending around four o'clock in the afternoon. Since it is a daytime performance, the invited audience generally sits behind the puppeteer watching the puppets on the screen rather than inside the house watching the shadows, as is common in other performances. Only older male puppeteers from puppeteering families stretching back many generations, whose fathers have already died, are supposed to be strong enough to handle the magical forces which surface in *ruwatan* performances.

It is when the gods descend to the earth to take part in the *wayang* performance in the Murwakala play that the *ruwatan* becomes texturally rich and dense. The gods must disguise themselves and take on the forms of other characters, *malihan* in Javanese. Wisnu, a high god, becomes the puppeteer but takes on the form of Arjuna, the noble warrior; Brama, another god, becomes the *gender* player and takes the form of Arjuna's wife Sumbadra; and Narada, a funny, misshapen god, takes the form of Semar, clown-servant to the hero Arjuna and older brother of the high god Siwa, and becomes the *pengendang* or drummer. In this way, two *wayang* performances intersect—the one that is being held and the play within the performance.

Because the performance was an offering to the ancestors as well as an attempt to address the problems of the family holding the ritual, the ancestors appeared in the story. Coincidentally, this particular family happened to be a family of puppeteers and musicians. After the ancestors had been on the screen for a while, fiercely pursued by Kala, the present

The high god Siwa, or Guru (left), facing the misshapen messenger god Narada.

living family members, who were holding the performance, appeared as puppets on the screen.

Then a few twists were added to the ceremony. The puppeteer performing the play, the father of the famous Solonese *dhalang* Anom Suroto, was related to the family holding the performance and so was familiar with the characters on the screen. By coincidence, I happened to know the woman who was holding the performance and who was being represented by a puppet on the screen. I had no idea when I came to the performance that she was the one who had organized it, but I had once bought some puppets from her. She was pleased to have Americans at her performance, especially one whom she knew—it raised her status in the eyes of the neighbors—and she came over and sat down next to me. As I was sitting next to her and she was also being represented by a puppet on the screen, I felt as though I, too, had been drawn into the performance and soon might be face-to-face with the terrifying Kala himself.

On the screen, the living family members met their ancestors, and they asked for permission to hold the ceremony that was currently being held. This was enacted in a very humorous way revolving around the Javanese concept of *pangling*. *Pangling* means to fail to recognize someone you know. When one meets good friends in Java they often say *"Kok, pangling aku,"* one implicit meaning being "I didn't recognize you because you looked better (or worse) than I remembered." To apply this concept to one's ancestors, who have been dead for generations, is at once funny and familiar. The living relations confronted and threatened Kala. One of the living relatives happened to be a musician in the performance, and he was struggling to play his instrument while watching his own antics on the screen and accompanying, on his instrument, the movements of the puppet representing him. As he was being portrayed by the puppeteer in a very buffoonish manner, this all caused much hilarity. A Yudhistira puppet appeared next, depicting a member of the living family whose daughter could not get along with her husband. This group met the first group, and the puppeteer enacted a clever bit of family therapy. They all decided to hold the ceremony that was being held, and they then met the puppeteer, who was a *malihan* (disguise) for the high god Wisnu.

I think that I have described enough to indicate the nature of this event and the density of texture that is so meaningful in Javanese *wayang*. All the puppets in a *ruwatan* performance are disconnected from their usual roles—all the associations are displaced. Any linearity of plot development has been tempered as the meanings of the performance multiply and resonate in unpredictable ways. *Ruwatan* performances are the most Javanese of shadow play performances in their disconnection from the action of the Mahabharata stories. The stress on *malihan*, one puppet disguised as another, is another common phenomenon in many performances. Ogre characters or gods disguised as heroes motivate the action of many *lakon* and further subvert the linearity of plot development.

This *ruwatan* performance reached out and drew the audience in, and reached out further, as the puppeteer was the father of Anom Suroto, a national figure, who was present at the performance and became the butt of many of his father's jokes. The performance reached back across time to the world of the gods and the ancestors, and brought them face-to-face with members of the audience. The ancient connections between aesthetics and shamanism are emphasized in *ruwatan* performances, as it is the ascetic power of the shadow puppeteer expressed through his art that enables him to heal the psychic imbalances that prompt families to hold exorcist performances. The authority in these performances belongs to the puppeteer, who displays the cultivation of his own inner strength despite the use of "Hindu-Javanese" gods. The gods are displaced and disconnected from their usual roles in the performance. In a sense, their power is tapped and tamed. The *ruwatan* performance represents the way in which the Javanese have tapped the power of foreign authorities and then used these powers for their own purposes.

The interaction of text and performance is also unique in *ruwatan* plays. While formerly the use of written texts in all *wayang* performances was frowned upon, the reading of a particular written text containing the sacred *mantra* recited at the end of the *ruwatan* performance is, in fact, prescribed. Usually puppeteers wrote the sacred *mantra*, which they had received from their father or teacher, on pieces of paper, which they then brought to the performance. The reading of the *mantra* was believed to activate their power. The recording of these sacred *mantras* in printed form may be due to the influence of the Solonese literatus R. Tanaya, who in the 1930s published a version of the Murwakala text—a sign of fear, perhaps, that the sacred text might be lost if it was not written down.[46] Since only older male *dhalang* who are respected for their command of mystical knowledge are allowed, or are brave enough, to perform *ruwatan* plays, it is the power of the *dhalang* as well as the power of the text which is important in these plays. The puppeteer may be strong enough to handle the sacred *mantras*, or the power of the *mantras* could harm him. In the Murwakala story, the *mantras* which must be recited to ward off the rapacious Kala are supposedly written on Kala's body. Although even the victim could technically read the *mantras* and thus send Kala away, it is Wisnu pretending to be a *dhalang* who must recite the *mantras* out loud in order to release their power.

In older styles of *wayang* performances, the power of the puppeteer controls the power of the written or oral texts. Although the importance of shadow theatre plays may be diminishing for the modernizing elites who have moved to Jakarta from the villages of Central Java, *ruwatan* performances are surprisingly popular in contemporary Java. Several *dhalang* whom I knew in Solo were invited to Jakarta to perform *ruwatan* plays for high government figures as well as family members who had moved to the big city. Perhaps this phenomenon is linked to the popularity of *wahyu*

---

46. See R. Tanaya, *Cariyos Padhalangan Lampahan Dhalang Kandhabuwana Murwakala* (Kediri: Tan Khoen Swie, 1954).

(boon) branch stories, mentioned in chapter 5; contemporary Javanese villagers and elites still seek divine intervention to help them accommodate to the problems of their modernizing world or to help them forget the horrors of the 1960s.

Rebo Legi Performances

Rebo Legi performances are held every thirty-five days (the intersection of the five- and seven-day Javanese weeks) to celebrate the Javanese birthday of the Solonese puppeteer Ki Anom Suroto. Suroto invites puppeteers from all over Java to perform in his home for payment or exchange.[47] It is mostly other puppeteers and *wayang* enthusiasts who are invited to these performances, and many students from the fine arts academies, as well as the stray foreign tourist, also attend.

These performances differ from other *wayang* performances, as they gather a number of puppeteers from different areas in one place. In older times, puppeteers were wary of performing outside their own villages because of the possibility of running into black magic, which their *mantra*s and other charms might not be strong enough to counter. Since so many well-known puppeteers attend these events, performers are often thrust into a position of wanting to amuse their friends and make fun of their host through friendly but pointed humor. Thus a style of flashy puppet movements, suggestive humor, and the breaking of conventions has become dominant in these performances.

Other customs are displaced in the *Rebo Legi* performances. To begin with, there are often no shadows.[48] Since the main emphasis is on the

47. Puppeteers often exchange performances for their family or friends. It is a good idea to exchange with Anom Suroto, as his performances are now said to run up to two thousand dollars per night.

48. When I was in Java between 1982 and 1984, the positioning of the screen against the wall at these performances rarely enabled the audience to see the shadows. When there were shadows, they were often seen only by the crowds outside, the opposite of village performances, where the invited guests see the shadows and the uninvited onlookers see the puppeteer. Recently, Suroto has redesigned the performance area to permit audiences to see the shadows. It is interesting that at radio-station performances, held once a month in Solo in a European-style theatre, audiences were denied access to the puppeteer rather than to the shadows in the mid 1980s. In 1990, the audience was able to watch the puppeteer rather than the shadows.

puppeteer and since there is no ritual ceremony other than Suroto's Java-nese birthday connected with the event, a certain foreshortening of the tradition takes place, both in the texture of the unseen dimensions of the performance—the ritual and mystical side—and in the texture of physical possibilities. In the mid-1980s one could only sit in back of the puppeteer, as the screen was most commonly placed against a wall. At performances like this, the audience is displaced, and invited and uninvited guests share the same space. At many village *wayang* performances, the invited guests sit watching the shadows inside or near the home of the host of the performance, while uninvited people from the neighborhood gather in back of the puppeteer and musicians to watch the performances.[49]

Many other conventions are broken during these performances. There is often interaction between the audience and the puppeteer, and on occasion the puppeteer will turn around and say something to the host or to a heckler. Many modern and English words have worked their way into a tradition that in the past frowned upon the entry of Indonesian into inappropriate parts of the plays. The puppet movements are very innova-tive, and often puppets are thrown off the screen or onto the screen in unconventional and abrupt ways. Fights take place between characters who would never fight in more conventional performances, and the jokes often begin in the first audience hall scene, a place where humor was usually banned.

On one particular night, the young puppeteer whom I most often followed was scheduled to perform at Anom Suroto's *Rebo Legi.* He had been studying with a serious older puppeteer, who was attempting to impart the refined older practices of the tradition to him. My young friend was considered one of the better up-and-coming puppeteers and was also a good friend of Anom Suroto, the host of the *Rebo Legi* performances. The story that he was preparing was a trunk story considered to be important among the main stories of the Mahabharata.

I went to the performance and stayed until quite late (three o'clock in the morning). My friend was performing conventionally for a while. His audience hall scene was very dignified, and he can be a very moving puppeteer when he is serious. But after a while the environment began to

49. This practice seems to be changing in the Java of the 1990s. There seems to be a greater emphasis on the puppeteer these days, and, especially in city performances, the invited guests are often placed in back of the puppeteer.

get the better of him and he began to respond to the crowd. He often turned and looked at the audience and replied to his hecklers with quick humor. Then, by the middle of the performance, all restraint was thrown to the wind and he enacted a lewd clown scene, using a very phallic looking weapon puppet for a clown battle. To the insistent beat of the strong-style *gamelan* pieces that accompany battle scenes, the weapon became the clown's giant penis battering opponents with well-positioned jabs. Needless to say, the crowd loved him, but his older teacher did not talk to him for days. The point here, I believe, is not merely prudishness—village performances have a history of coarse humor. His teacher was disappointed because the younger puppeteer had lost his composure and dignity and pandered to the whims of the crowd. This episode clearly illustrates the clash between the refined *wayang* tradition of the Solonese courts and the village tradition. In the accepted code of behavior for village *wayang* performances, the puppeteer is supposed to cater to the tastes of the audience. But in the "court" tradition, *wayang* was supposed to be refined and elegant, not earthy and coarse. The younger puppeteer's mentor had been raised by a Dutch woman whom his father—a well-known puppeteer—had married; the older puppeteer shared the vision of *wayang* that he believed would have been acceptable in the Solonese courts.

Rebo Legi performances, while not typical performance events, are certainly significant performance events in the world of Solonese *wayang*. Innovative styles from one area of Central Java are seen at these performances and then carried away to other areas of Java. Students from the fine arts academies see a side of the tradition they do not often encounter in their formal schooling. Some puppeteers stay away from *Rebo Legi* performances, as they dislike the association of the host with Golkar, the ruling political vehicle in Indonesia.

In the flattening or foreshortening of the *wayang* tradition in the *Rebo Legi* performances, refined aesthetic patterns are being supplanted, and cultivated texture is giving way to flatter styles of generating meaning. By emphasizing the play of humor and fancy puppet movements, the mystical side of the tradition is being displaced and channeled into more predictable grooves. Noble characters who once wielded authority and power are now ridiculed, and the clown characters, representative of the Javanese folk, assume larger and more important roles. Javanese people today

Rhetoric and Performance Domains

are as likely to watch American or Hong Kong Chinese movies and TV programs as they are to watch *wayang* performances. On the government TV station, human personifications of the clowns from the *wayang kulit* are used to promote government programs of health care and village cleanliness. The hierarchy and etiquette of the Javanese courts are now more a source of humor and mockery than a model for correct behavior. Thus the *Rebo Legi* performances reflect the changing tastes of Javanese society as European and American styles and beliefs become more prominent in Javanese life. *Rebo Legi* performances are dynamic and the audiences love them. It is through the innovations seen at these performances that one knows that the *wayang* tradition is still alive and vital, and the interactions between the puppeteers, the host, the audience, and instructors from the fine arts academies may lend new types of texture to these performance events.

The changes evident in *Rebo Legi* performances are changes within the oral tradition. While some of the puppeteers who perform use unobtrusive notes or written materials, these performances are still primarily oral. New techniques or styles are still *seen* and *heard*; when I once asked a famous older puppeteer how she learned the tradition she responded, "With my eyes and ears." There are changes in puppet movements, changes in the characters who fight with one another, and humor has free reign, but the order of scenes, the stories, the use of music, and the performance length are all intact.

The *Rebo Legi* puppeteers are innovating from a position of total mastery over the tradition. If they break the rules, it is because they know the rules so well. The rules that the puppeteers are breaking at these performances are the rules that were enforced upon the village *dhalang* in the 1920s and 1930s by the Dutch-influenced court elites. Thus some puppeteers believe they are defying the once great power of the Solonese courts when they handle the puppets in new and irreverent ways. These performances are modernist in that they appeal to modernizing audiences and they incorporate contemporary problems into the performances. Little about these performances is particularly European or American, except for the occasional use of a gun puppet rather than an arrow. Occasionally performers from the Academy will be invited to perform. The Academy puppeteers will try out the new styles being generated there, but the hall will empty out before midnight and the usual hilarity will not prevail. *Rebo*

Legi puppeteers wield increasing power over the tradition, and yet, at these performances, one feels a subtle struggle between the unseen authority at the performance—the Jakarta government—and the visible authority of the individual puppeteers. The aftermath of the turbulent sixties lingers at these performances, and the lines drawn at that time still seem to have meaning. The puppeteers are careful to direct their humor in innocuous ways so as not to upset the government authorities, who also attend the performances on occasion. When these same *dhalang* perform in the villages, the crowds they draw are impressive. One night in Sragen, a town outside the city of Solo, there may have been close to a thousand people surrounding the home of a famous *dhalang*, who had asked one of these popular innovating *dhalang* to perform. These *Rebo Legi* puppeteers ensure that the *wayang* tradition continues to have meaning for contemporary audiences.

Padat Performances

The third and last contemporary performance style to be discussed is the wayang *padat* or "compressed" *wayang*, developing in the milieu of the Academy in Solo.[50] One cannot speak of *wayang padat* without evoking the spirit of "Gendon" Humardhani, the late director of the Solo Academy and brother of a now deceased general in the Jakarta government. While *wayang* performances of less than nine hours have been around for a long time, and any puppeteer is able to shorten a performance as the needs of the occasion demand, Humardhani and the well-known author Sri Mulyono, who were students together at Gadjah Mada, are credited with visualizing the metaphor of the shadow puppet theatre as an empty bucket with a thin layer of water on the bottom. They believed that the size of the bucket needed to be in proportion to its contents and said that the

---

50. There is a distinction made at the Academy between *wayang padat* and *wayang ringkas*. *Wayang ringkas* (shortened *wayang*) may be performed in three or four hours, but the basic structure and content of the performance remains very similar to the regular performance format. In *padat* performances, rules are broken, stories are changed, puppet movements are innovative, and the musical accompaniment can be very radical. At the Academy, first- and second-year students study traditional performance styles; in the third year they study *wayang ringkas*, taught by an older puppeteer; in their final two years they study *wayang padat*, taught by the younger and more innovative instructors.

Rhetoric and Performance Domains

The old-style blencong, *or oil lamp, whose light made the shadows flicker and dance, is rarely used in Central Java today.*

essence (*isi*) of *wayang* needed to be separated out and worked over (*digarap lagi*) to produce a style of performance more in keeping with the times. Although trained as a medical doctor, Humardhani had spent several years in Europe and paid a few visits to America, where he encountered new performing arts and performance styles.

One possible influence on the development of the *wayang padat*—although I am sure that Academy intellectuals do not realize it—is the vision of the *wayang* theatre promoted by the arts organization LEKRA (Institute of People's Culture, mentioned at the beginning of this chapter) in the 1950s and 1960s. The technical changes desired by the LEKRA theorists included the shortening of the *wayang* night, the use of an electric lightbulb rather than the flickering oil lamp (which distorted the shadows), the use of a stage without a screen, the use of more than one puppeteer (which could then represent the masses), and the abandoning of the dress requirement for puppeteer and musicians.[51] More general changes promoted by LEKRA included making the *wayang* more accessible to other cultural groups within Indonesia, reforming the interpretation so it could fulfill the

51. McVey, "The Wayang Controversy," pp. 30–31.

needs of the revolution and of development, creating new *lakon* to enhance political messages, and expanding the role of the clowns. Although some of this agenda—the use of an electric light bulb and the expansion of the role of the clowns—has come into general use in many contemporary *wayang* performances, the creators of *wayang padat* seem to have brought to life a particular part of this agenda. The new Academy use of more than one puppeteer and the abandonment of the dress code for *padat* performances have received sharp criticism from more traditional puppeteers. The *padat* plays developed at the Academy also seek to promulgate new ideas and values that often conflict with the interpretations of puppeteers of earlier generations.

Differences that set the Academy *padat* players apart from the LEKRA agenda include the Academy use of only the most conventional trunk stories for development into *padat* plays. These were the stories most often recognized as feudal by the promoters of socialist realism, but the Academy interpretations also reject the feudal values by upsetting the traditional hierarchical placement of the puppets on the screen (*tanceban*). The Academy performances have also curtailed rather than expanded the role of the clowns, in contrast to common practice in most of Java today. The Academy, of course, rejects any association with LEKRA and the Communist movement of the 1950s and 1960s. As an organization associated with and supported by the New Order, the Academy staunchly promotes the values and programs of the New Order among students and faculty, and these values permeate the padat plays as well.

Padat performances involve the use of written playscripts, which are either memorized or read in performances, and generally run between an hour and an hour and a half (and I did see one once that was twelve minutes long). Although *padat* performances may have the same author and performer, often one person writes the script, another performs the script, a third person organizes the musical accompaniment (a crucial part of any *wayang* performance), and a fourth person directs the whole show.

If the audience was displaced in *Rebo Legi* performances, the audience is effaced in *padat* performances. There are no audiences for *wayang padat* in Java outside the fine arts academies and the activities they generate.[52]

52. Bambang Murtiyasa, an instructor at the Academy, commented: "At Sasanamulya [the place where the Academy was then located] we often have performances for various reasons—to honor guests, receptions, exam presentations, competitions, fes-

Rhetoric and Performance Domains

Padat performances are often created to be performed in Europe when Academy groups go on annual tours, and all the students in the puppeteering section of the Academy are required to write and perform a *wayang padat* in their final semester. *Padat* performances are also brought to the annual festivals in which the various fine arts academies sponsored by the Indonesian government participate.

The stories most often chosen for *wayang padat* are the Bratayuda stories, the stories recounting the great war of the Mahabharata. These are the stories most avoided in conventional *wayang* performances, as they are felt to be too "heavy" to handle—catastrophes tend to happen in the wake of these performances, or so is the belief.[53] Bratayuda stories are also the most linear of all the stories associated with the shadow theatre. I believe that these stories are chosen to lend weight to the performances, a weight that cannot be achieved in any other way. The concept of weight is highly valued in *wayang* performances, and the Javanese word used, *bobot*, resonates with the American slang word "heavy."

As mentioned above, Humardhani, one of the creators of *wayang padat*, had been to Europe and was familiar with American performance styles, too. He read English fluently and was familiar with European dramatic criticism and aesthetic theory. Humardhani disapproved of humor in *padat* performances, and generally the clown scenes in these performances are brief and scarce. What *wayang padat* lacks in the way of humor it more than makes up for in the way of volume. The musical accompaniment for *padat*

---

tivals, experimental performances, etc.—the audience overflows and yet it is limited to our own closed circle or to a specific group." "Kegelisahan kehidupan seni yang menggelisahkan," p. 2.

53. Two stories in particular are told of this belief that performing the stories of the Bratayuda will lead to catastrophe. Mantle Hood, speaking of the staging of these *lakon* in 1957 and 1958 in the Sasana Inggil, the north side of the open field to the south of the *kraton*, says there was a serious earthquake in the course of the performance when the death of Abimanyu, Arjuna's son, was staged. See "The Enduring Tradition: Music and Theater in Java and Bali," in *Indonesia*, ed. R. T. McVey (New Haven: Southeast Asia Studies, Yale University, 1963). McVey tells of the LEKRA-sponsored performances in Yogya in 1964, when the sponsors purposefully did not burn incense or take any of the customary ritual precautions. See "The Wayang Controversy," p. 49 n. 63. The performances were held on five consecutive nights for five hours each (*Harian Rakjat Minggu*, 9 February 1964). One could speculate on the results of this flaunting of the spirit world. As noted above, Pipit Rochiyat said that during the time of the mass killings in 1965–66, many people saw the killings in the allegorical terms of the Bratayuda stories.

plays is loud, fast, and dramatic. The mood-setting songs of village performances are shorter and more romantic (in certain court styles this was
not considered appropriate for *wayang* performances), and the strictures
against abrupt mood changes seem to have been abandoned for *wayang*
padat.

Other interesting innovations in *padat* performances include changing
the story line to admit contemporary values into the tradition. Thus, in the
playscript *Srikandhi Maguru Manah* (Srikandhi Learns Archery),[54] Srikandhi, the second wife of the refined hero Arjuna, is actually the one who
kills Jangkungmardea, rather than Arjuna, as in older tellings. The renowned puppet-maker Bambang Suwarno even created a new puppet for
this performance—a woman character who wears pants. Humardhani
also asked his students to have the characters take responsibility for their
own actions—no longer are the gods allowed to become incarnate in
humans and be the cause of their ignoble actions.

An example of the innovations which can arise in *padat* performances is
illustrated by the playscript *Karna Tinandhing*, which was written by various members of the puppeteering section of the Academy in the spring of
1983 for the IKI (Institute of Indonesian Arts) Festival, which was held in
Solo at that time. Humardhani was still alive then, and his intense energy
and spirit filled the *wayang* and dance performances. The students were
encouraged to innovate. Rehearsals were frequent and frantic. Compositions were criticized by the other students and instructors, and changes
were made. The whole process was exciting and exhilarating, as though
Humardhani was forcing creativity out of his students.

The story of Karna Tinandhing (Karna Meets his Match) is one of the
most famous stories of the Mahabharata cycle. It is a Bratayuda story and
tells of the battle between the half-brothers Karna and Arjuna, so equally
matched that it is hard to tell the difference between them. The puppeteering section of the Academy was allowed twenty minutes for its performance. The gimmick of their interpretation was to use a very large screen
so as to permit the different puppets each to be handled by separate
students who would also say their own lines. The lamp was moved
further back from the screen, which allowed the shadows to be greatly
enlarged. And the shadows were all that was offered to the audience,

54. B. Suwarno, *Srikandi Maguru Manah* (Surakarta: Sub Bagian Proyek ASKI, 1980).

Rhetoric and Performance Domains

Arjuna and his half-brother Karna.

although the activity backstage was rough and lively—all these people running around with puppets in their hands.

The effects produced in the performance fell somewhere between shadow puppetry and cinema (an image suggested to me by Roger Vetter), and there were special combinations of horses and chariots and riders used for the battle scenes which were very impressive. There were also creative effects achieved in the final battle between Karna and Arjuna by having three representations of the battle going on at the same time—one large image and then two smaller images of the fight, thus six puppets used in all. The music for the performance was innovative, suggesting the dignity and sobriety of Gregorian chant, with no female singers. The first audience-hall scene also broke conventions as the characters just floated around, displaced from their usual hierarchical positions on the screen. Several *gunungan*, or "tree of life" puppets as they are sometimes called, were used dramatically to create shadows and spaces and to fill the large screen. Lastly, the script was written in Indonesian so as to be understandable to the students from the fine arts academies in Bali and Sumatra.

The performance was well received by the audience of students and faculty from the various government-sponsored fine arts academies, as well as by the members of the educated and artistic elites of Solo, who

Scene from the innovative Sandosa performance of Karna Tinandhing.

were also in attendance. It was a successful example of the content (*isi*) of a conventional story being reworked (*digarap lagi*) and presented in a fitting container. And for all the Javanese who saw it, it was still a part of the *wayang* tradition. The basic realities of a *wayang* performance—screen, shadows, and Mahabharata characters—were all there, although the language, the music, the conventional puppet movements, the time depth, and the puppeteer were all displaced. The audience was offered no texture—they were denied access to the activities behind the screen and could no longer rely on the predictability of performance format, which allows any one performance to be suggestive of all the performances of the past. The plot of the story was totally linear, ending in the death of a major Mahabharata hero—the plot actually went somewhere. The mood of the performance was serious from beginning to end, and I and others felt moved at the end of the performance; I knew a great hero had fallen.

The Academy performance of *Karna Tinandhing* was one of the best *padat* performances that I encountered between 1982–84 in Java. Students and instructors at the academy are not yet satisfied with their efforts to refine the *padat* style. *Padat* plays, in general, have been released from the constraints of the structure of the tradition as well as from the content of the conventional stories. If one of the rules of a conventional *wayang* says

Arjuna (left) and Karna in the Sandosa performance of Karna Tinandhing.

that all *wayang* stories must begin and end in a court, *wayang padat* no longer feels the need to abide by this rule. The puppet arrangements on the screen (*tanceban*) also have been the targets of innovation, and puppets do things that make the older puppeteers cringe. According to Alan Feinstein,[55] in a *padat* performance of 1984 a young Academy puppeteer had substituted the puppet of a different character altogether to represent a well-known character in his story. "Who is speaking" in *wayang padat* performances no longer has the weight of tradition and consensus; rather it arises from the creativity, or naiveté, of the author or the performer.

The Story of Rahwana's Birth at the Fine Arts Academy

To return to the story of the birth of Rahwana discussed in chapter 1, it is useful to compare a *padat* text of the story with a more conventional text. One of these texts of the shadow play titled Alap-alapan Sukesi was written by an older village puppeteer in the *ringkas* style,[56] and the other

---

55. Personal communication, 25 December 1984.
56. Ki Naryacarito, *Alap-alapan Sukesi* (Surakarta: Sub Bagian Proyek ASKI, 1980).

was written by the latter's nephew in the newer *padat* style.[57] *Ringkas*, or shortened performances, usually reduce the nine-hour performance format to two or three hours, while the *padat*, or condensed performances, as noted above, generally run from one and a half hours to as little as twelve minutes.

The *ringkas* style has a long history. In the past, as today in the villages, there was usually a shadow play performance in the afternoon before an evening performance. This afternoon performance was sometimes performed by younger puppeteers and often lasted only four or five hours. Older puppeteers also remember periods in this century when Dutch curfews meant that evening shadow play performances had to end by midnight, resulting in three- or four-hour performances. *Ringkas* performances can thus be classical, deviating little from the standard form in terms of structure, music, puppet movements, characterization, and story content. Almost any puppeteer who performs regularly can enact a *ringkas* performance with little or no preparation.

Padat performances are innovative, and most of the rules adhered to in conventional performances can be broken. Two skilled puppeteers from the Academy, sons of well-known puppeteers, argued that *padat* is a better form than *ringkas*, which must follow the conventional rules, and thus does not leave much room for creativity.[58] *Padat* performances want to do away with what are nowadays felt to be unnecessary parts of the tradition—for example, excessive repetition in dialogue, puppet movements, number of scenes, or musical accompaniment. Formulaic phrases, embellishments, and subplots that are not connected to the main story are all marked for deletion.[59]

I had the opportunity to follow the rehearsals for the *padat* performance of Alap-alapan Sukesi, which the Academy students were preparing for a showing on national TV. They were to be allowed thirty minutes for the performance, which meant cutting down the already abbreviated script. The script that was chosen to be performed was the text of Soemanto, head of the puppeteering section of the Academy and nephew of Ki Naryacarito. As is typical of *padat* performances, one young puppeteer,

57. Soemanto, *Alap-alapan Sukeksi* (Surakarta: Sub Bagian Proyek ASKI, 1980).
58. Fieldnotes, 30 January 1983.
59. B. Murtiyasa, "Tinjuan lakon Alap-alapan Sukeksi dalam pakeliran padat susunan Soemanto," p. 9.

known for his beautiful singing voice, was chosen to be the puppeteer; another puppeteer, known for his skillful puppet movements, was chosen to direct the performance. This diffusion of authority, common to many European or American dramatic performances, is very new in the shadow puppet tradition.

For my argument, the compositions of Soemanto and Naryacarito become significant. How do these texts differ, both from each other and from the earlier versions of the story? One obvious major difference in the *padat* text is the displacement of the mystical teaching, the *sastrajendra*, with which this story has long been associated. There is no room in Soemanto's text for the puppeteer to fill in his own mystical teaching; in fact, whose mystical belief would be incorporated—the author's, the director's, or the performer's? Another classical theme—absent from both modern interpretations—is the mention of Rahwana's birth. In the oldest tellings of this story in old Javanese poetry and prose, the point of the story was to retell the history of this significant Ramayana character. Today's interpretations are cut off from the spiraling continuity of the story cycles. The important elements in the *padat* text are the personal conflicts and character development of the main characters—what LEKRA theorists and New Order upgrading courses would call *sikap individu*, that undesirable individualism imported from the "West." Naryacarito, however, still paints the shadow theatre world in the fatalistically determined beliefs of earlier periods.

One of the most significant features of Soemanto's text is that it breaks with the older interpretation of the story where the gods intercede to punish Wisrawa for revealing his mystical knowledge inappropriately. Explaining actions by the intervention of the gods is frowned upon in the texts produced at the Academy. In Soemanto's text the gods do not appear, and Sukesi and Wisrawa must bear the responsibility for their own actions. In Naryacarito's more conventional text, Sukesi and Wisrawa are inappropriately attracted to one another because they have been entered by the god Siwa and his demonic wife Durga, and the action of the story is explained, in the end, as a test of the gods.

Sukesi is portrayed as a strong and assertive woman in Soemanto's text. She speaks for herself, rather than through her father, or because she has been entered by the demoniacal Durga. A comparison from each text of her words to Wisrawa after the mystical teaching has been revealed is insightful, on the level of both style and content. In Naryacarito's text, Sukesi responds to Wisrawa's plan to take her back to Lokapala to marry his son with the following words:

O respected one, revered one, it has always been my intention that whoever could explain the mystical teaching *sastrajendra*, he would be the one I would serve until the earth stopped moving. When the sun can be separated from its heat, or water separated from its coldness, still Sukesi will not be separated from her intention. If forced to marry your son king Dhanaraja [Dhanapati], my wish is just to die.

In Soemanto's text Sukesi responds:

O respected one, for you to force your will would be like casting [me] into a ravine of disrepute. Sukesi would be the most shameful of god's creatures if [she] deviated from her intention. Since you were the one who gave the explanation, it is you whom I must serve. If you do not agree, then it is best that you just kill me.[60]

There is a directness and conciseness in the second text that is not apparent in the older text. The language in the first passage is more formulaic than the language of the second text. The example shows how Soemanto used Naryacarito's text in the production of his own text while creating a very different effect. The passage in both texts shows how far Sukesi has come from the speechless maiden of the Old Javanese texts who was only doing her father's bidding when she came to Wisrawa to ask for children. The passage in Soemanto's text is significant because Sukesi no longer has the excuse of speaking through the goddess Durga. She is responsible for her own actions and speech.

What are the new themes in Soemanto's text? Unavoidably the notion of romantic love appears, that falling under the sway of passions that allow people to forget their proper duty. Since Soemanto no longer can use the gods to explain his character's actions, he has Sukesi and Wisrawa fall in love. There is no romance in Naryacarito's text, while Soemanto's text is full of the *rasa pernes* (the romantic sentiment) which some puppeteers suggest was inappropriate in the court tradition of *wayang* plays in former times.[61] The music acompanying the performance of Soemanto's text also supports this romantic mood.

60. Soemanto, *Alap-Alapan Sukesi*, p. 25.
61. The rise of the *rasa pernes*, the romantic mood, in contemporary *gamelan* reper-toires and shadow puppet plays poses problems for scholars who study these artistic

Rhetoric and Performance Domains

In Soemanto's text, psychological explanations are needed to interpret the actions of the characters. Wisrawa suffers, but from a contemporary sense of guilt. The characters pursue their destinies, almost as in a Greek tragedy. Dhanapati chooses Sukesi himself and there is no conventional talk of pestilence in the kingdom as a sign that the king needs to get married. Sukesi chooses Wisrawa in a contemporary assertive way. Wisrawa is the one character portrayed in passive terms. In Naryacarito's text, Wisrawa comes to his son's kingdom because he has seen in his meditations that the kingdom is in trouble. In Soemanto's text, Wisrawa is called to the kingdom by his son because the son wishes to get married. Wisrawa gives the mystical teaching in Soemanto's text because he is asked by Sumali, and he has sex with Sukesi because she is pretty and she cries and she wants him. Then Wisrawa offers to let his son kill him because he guiltily knows he has done wrong. Murtiyasa, a colleague of Soemanto, comments on this.

In short, Wisrawa falls in love because of Sukesi's beauty and her tears after she receives the mystical teaching. Wisrawa responds because of Sukesi's sentimental pleading, which weakens the characterization of Wisrawa as a revered holy man and a former god-like king.[62]

Soemanto's text asserts the duty of a son toward his father at a time when family values are being questioned in Indonesian society. What the Indonesian government fears in the "Western" attitude of individualism, sikap individu,[63] appears in the actions of the characters in Soemanto's play.

---

forms. Philip Yampolsky, an ethnomusicologist who studied Solonese music for many years, suggested in 1984 that this phenomenon was a new element in Javanese gamelan music, inappropriate in the classical repertoire. Whether or not the pernes mood really was discouraged for gamelan and wayang repertoires connected with the Solonese courts, I believe it has always been an important element in village performances. A recent article titled "Seks Wayang Kulit" in Kompas Minggu (1 May 1994), the Sunday edition of the major newspaper for certain groups of educated Indonesians, noted the heavy use of sexual allusions in Solonese and Yogyanese wayang performances. Many of the examples mentioned in the article reminded me of jokes and allusions common to many wayang performances I had watched in the early 1980s. From the comments of the Dutch scholars noted in chapter 2, I assume this is a very old practice.

62. Murtiyasa, "Tinjuan lakon Alap-alapan Sukeksi dalam pakeliran padat susunan Soemanto," p. 58.

63. Sikap individu, or with an individualistic attitude, is how the Indonesian government describes the way "Westerners" relate to one another. I have heard from my

Perhaps Wisrawa's portrayal as a very weak and passive person is suggestive of the way the younger generation today perceives the older generation. Certainly the students at the Academy make fun of the older conventional teachers in a manner they would not dare to use with the younger
and more powerful instructors. Although Dhanapati is considered wrong
to take up arms against his father, he does so in the heat of passion, and
then gains control of himself on his own—he no longer needs the gods to
wake him up. Dhanapati is not rewarded at the end of Soemanto's story
with beautiful celestial nymphs; he is obviously looking for a "meaningful
relationship."

The examples above show how the new *padat* style contests the flexibility of the oral tradition. Soemanto's text does away with many features
of the oral performance style. Formulaic passages, repetitions for mne-
monic purposes, didactic speeches, and emphasis on the rules of court
etiquette are replaced by a concise, poetic style that may draw on the
tradition of *macapat* poetry[64] as well as on more conventional texts produced by older puppeteers such as Naryacarito. Soemanto's text is written
to be memorized and rehearsed—two procedures inimical to spontaneous
oral production. Soemanto changes stylistic features of the tradition as
well as thematic ones. His composition style represents a general consensus of opinion at the Academy, held by the young instructors nurtured
by the late Humardhani, who was familiar with Euroamerican artistic
traditions and artistic criticism. Murtiyasa says:

Indonesian friends that during the *penataran* or upgradings, when government workers
are retrained in the ideals of Pancasila, the fivefold ethical path promulgated by the
Indonesian government, "Westerners" are criticized for their individualistic attitude,
which is felt to be incompatible with the Indonesian ideals of community effort and
togetherness.

64. This is a hard point to document. Soemanto is known at the Academy for his
command of poetic language, and he teaches a course which shows the students how to
write aesthetically pleasing shadow play texts. His texts are poetic in a way that differs
from the oral practices of the classical shadow theatre plays, and other instructors at the
Academy cautiously agree on this point. Soemanto is said to be well read, and this
would indicate familiarity with the *macapat* texts connected with the shadow theatre
tradition—the works of the famous court *pujangga* Yasadipura I and II, Ranggawarsita,
and Sindusastra. For studies of *macapat* poetry see Ben Arps, *Tembang in Two Traditions:
Performance and Interpretation of Javanese Literature* (London: School of Oriental and African Studies, 1992); Martin Hatch, "Lagu, Laras, Layang: Rethinking Melody in Javanese
Music" (Ph.D. diss., Cornell University, 1980); and Margaret Kartomi, *Macapat Songs in
Central and West Java* (Canberra: Australian National University Press, 1973).

Rhetoric and Performance Domains

Soemanto's interpretation actually results from criticism within the context of public conferences and symposiums on *padat* performances held at the Academy, and from private discussions on plot development held in the puppeteering department of the Academy.[65]

Murtiyasa also admits that the young faculty at STSI are becoming aware that the creation of new interpretations of conventional stories poses a difficult problem that is not easy to face. He says: "Clearly this challenges us all."[66]

The new themes in Soemanto's text, individualism and romantic love, are pressing issues in contemporary society that do not even surface in Naryacarito's text, written only a few years earlier. Naryacarito's text is a transitional text that highlights the ephemerality of older concerns in present-day society.

As author types, Naryacarito and Soemanto are also exemplary. Naryacarito represents the older village puppeteer who wielded mystical power in his youth. He functioned in his village as a healer/artist and, for various reasons, was alternately respected and criticized in these different roles. Today Naryacarito is paid very little to teach two courses at the Academy. His son, who holds the coveted *sarjana lengkap*, roughly equivalent to a master's degree, is paid a reasonable salary as a *pegawai negeri* (government worker) at the Academy, but rarely performs as a puppeteer. Soemanto, a cousin of Naryacarito from this illustrious family of puppeteers, is head of the puppeteering section of the Academy, but is never called upon to perform as a shadow puppeteer. Soemanto earns a reasonable salary, which is guaranteed for life, and commands a good deal of respect both for contemporary and older forms of knowledge. He is considered to be a diviner in his village, and is petitioned to ascertain the correct dates for marriages and other ritual events.

Soemanto's *padat* text indicates an intentional shift from oral performance and oral transmission to a literary and dramatic style dependent on written texts. Written texts are easier to standardize and easier to control. In Soemanto's text, sex, knowledge, and power are seen in more individualistic terms than in the past. Individuals, rather than the gods or their

65. Murtiyasa, "Tinjuan lakon Alap-alapan Sukeksi dalam pakeliran padat susunan Soemanto," p.32.
66. Ibid., p. 61.

parents, can control their own destinies. It is significant that this attitude of individualism should arise at a time when the Indonesian government's control over sex, knowledge, and power is more pervasive than at any time in the past. Today in Indonesia, the government has launched an intense and successful birth control program which has drawn the puppeteers into supporting its message.[67] The government has greater control over the shadow puppet tradition than ever before, through monitoring what stories are performed, channeling the tradition into the government sponsored fine arts academies, and having the academies take an increasing role in the development of the tradition outside the academies. *Wayang* competitions (*lomba*) are frequently sponsored by city and village government organizations, and judges for these events are inevitably drawn from the fine arts academies. The government also oversees the stories that are chosen for the monthly performances that are broadcast on the national radio station.

In contemporary Java there is a proliferation of authors in a tradition that previously worked with anonymous authors or authors who merely retold and reinterpreted conventional stories. Academy puppeteers today are starting to think about copyright laws, and I attended a panel at a shadow puppeteering conference held at the Academy in 1983 that was devoted to such problems. Questions of copyright led into questions more fundamental to the contemporary practice of the shadow puppet tradition. The late Ki Mujaka Jaka Raharjo, a famous puppeteer who attended the panel, asked: "What are the limits of change in [shadow puppet] performances?" ("Sampai dimana perobahan-perobahan dalam penyajian?")[68] There was discussion of whether puppeteers were offended when others used their stories. The problem of using other puppeteers' *naskah*, written texts, is a complicated one. In earlier times, if a puppeteer borrowed another puppeteer's story, s/he had to rework and reinterpret the story in order to make it his or her own. Now puppeteers can memorize and deliver someone else's text, often with little understanding of the issues that the text helps to explicate. Puppeteers can be asked to deliver texts with which they do not agree.

Today at the Academy, students who have not yet mastered the basics

67. See Clara van Groenendael, *The dalang behind the wayang*, pp. 179–80, 182–83, 186–87.
68. Field notes, 28 February 1983.

of the tradition are taught new styles. Those students are losing touch with the oral texts of the tradition that have been handed down for generations. In the past, puppeteers could choose one oral text from their remembered repertoire to use in many different situations. By the freezing of the oral texts at the Academy and the limiting of stylistic possibilities, students learn fewer ways of doing things. They become dependent on their texts. By using different people to write, perform, and direct *padat* plays, the power of the puppeteer is diffused. In the Academy, written texts are becoming more important than the puppeteers who perform them. The individual puppeteer's voice cannot be heard in *padat* performances—his voice blends into the Academy's voice.[69] The ever-present authority in Academy performances is the Indonesian government, and certain foreign attitudes and ways of thinking make the government's voice stronger.

Despite the increasing opportunity for aspiring puppeteers to learn the tradition in an academic environment, a majority of the graduates of the academies are not successful puppeteers, and the successful puppeteers for the most part are not graduates of the academies. Anom Suroto and Manteb Soedarsono, the two most popular Solonese puppeteers since the death of Nartosabdho, are not graduates of any academy, although they are claimed as honorary teachers by the Academy in Solo today. Of the aspiring puppeteers at STSI, several are quite successful in the villages, although their success at performing came before they began to attend the Academy. In fact, there seems to be an increasing tension within the Academy between those who are successful teachers, or directors of the new *padat* plays, or whose skill at scholarly analysis brings them prestige within the Academy. One of the more successful instructors and performers at the Academy in the mid-1980s, especially in *padat* styles, told

69. When I was observing the courses in the puppeteering section of the Academy in the early 1980s, there were no women studying to be puppeteers. In 1990, I was told that there were one or two women in the puppeteering section, but I never saw them perform as puppeteers. There are several famous women *dhalang* who perform in and around Solo and Jogja. The most famous, perhaps, is Suharni Sabdawati, who was a follower of the late Nartosabdho. Interestingly, although married with husband and children, Suharni Sabdawati wears pants like a man and smokes cigarettes in public—two things rarely done by women of her age and position. She speaks a very rough style of Javanese. When people ask about her husband, she laughs and says he's at home with the kids.

me in 1990 that he felt quite frustrated at the Academy and he was increasingly going outside the Academy to perform. His aspirations seem to be changing from a desire for success within the Academy to a desire for success as a popular *dhalang* catering to the tastes of mass audiences rather than Academy intelligentsias.

The relations between the Academy and the popular domains are growing more complex. Styles pass from the Academy into the popular domain with increasing frequency. An example of this is illustrated by the dramatic rise to prominence of Manteb Soedarsono. When I was in Java from 1982 to 1984, Manteb was a rising young star. He was popular in Solo and the surrounding villages because of his skillful and unconventional *sabetan* or puppet movements. He fitted well into the group of puppeteers in the *Rebo Legi* domain, who emphasized flashy puppet movements and bawdy humor in their performances. He was also one of the few puppeteers outside the Academy who was willing to try his hand at performing a *wayang padat* in those days. Although not well educated, he was smart enough to be able to recognize and use innovative material.

When I returned to Java in 1990, Manteb's popularity in Java seemed to be surpassing that of Anom Suroto. He performed continually—all over Java—and was said to command several million rupiah per performance. I believe that some of the reasons for his rise to fame illustrate the subtle connections between innovative changes in the tradition worked out at the Academy and what is accepted by audiences in the popular domains outside the Academy.

In line with other *Rebo Legi* puppeteers, Manteb's innovations were more likely to be modernist than European or American. He was particularly adept at incorporating modern technology into his performances. He is now known for using a halogen lamp rather than an ordinary electric lightbulb, because the former produces brighter light and sharper shadows.[70] Along with the halogen light, Manteb uses colored light in his performances by placing colored paper over the lamp. This is a technique that Manteb has borrowed from the Academy, where it was used in Sandosa *padat* performances. In fact, because of all the innovative lighting,

70. The use of the halogen lamp has its dangers also. It seems to lose its power momentarily on occasion, although I never saw it go out altogether.

Manteb now needs and uses a lighting specialist, who controls the lighting under Manteb's direction when Manteb performs.

Moving from lighting to musical innovation, Manteb regularly includes trumpets, a snare drum and cymbal set, and a triangle-like instrument to accompany performances. The trumpets are used for special effect, and several are sounded together at appropriate moments in the performance. The drums have been used by other modernizing puppeteers for several years and are not unique to Manteb. The triangle—reminiscent in sound of the triangle that is often the first instrument one plays in kinder-garten—is taken from *gandrung* Banyuwangi and is used to punctuate the puppet movements. The first time I heard it I could not tell where it was coming from; only later did I learn that the puppeteer sitting in back of Manteb and helping him—a common practice—was highlighting Man-teb's puppet movements with this instrument. Manteb uses a Banyumas-style *gara-gara*, the scene that opens *pathet sanga*, the second part of the *wayang* night, beginning around one o'clock in the morning. This is a technique that was popularized by Nartosabdho; it is also an assimilation of a Yogyanese style into Solonese-style performances. Finally, Manteb has Bu Waljinah, a famous *keroncong* singer, regularly join his group of six or seven *pesindhen* or female singers. Manteb has humorous conversations with Bu Waljinah through the puppets while he performs, and she an-swers the questions posed by the puppets; this differs from the bawdy humor and slurs that puppeteers usually direct toward the female singers which the singers must endure silently. Audience members even send up slips of papers with song requests for Bu Waljinah to sing, a practice associated with Sundanese performance styles where the *pesindhen* have become as important as the puppeteers in performances.

It is in the area of *sabetan* or puppet movements, however, that Manteb really excels. He uses at least a half-dozen *gunungan* or tree-of-life puppets when he performs, and these have been procured from the best Javanese and European puppet-makers. At one performance in Solo in August of 1990, at the *pagelaran*, the *pendapa* or performance hall north of the Kraton, he used one innovative *gunungan* that had been made by Bambang Su-warno from STSI and one that had been made by a Frenchman who had studied the art of shadow theatre for many years. The practice of using many *gunungan* in performance is another technique that Manteb has borrowed from Academy *padat* performances. He has taken the practice a step further, and in his *perang kembang* or flower battle scenes, he is said to use as many as seven *Cakil*, the particular ogre who fights with a refined knight in the middle of every performance.[71] Manteb also modifies the course of the performance because of his particular skills. Since his specialty is puppet movements, he expands the *jaranan*, a scene in which the various animals from the *wayang* chest can be brought out and made to prance and cavort according to the skills of the puppeteer. Some puppeteers make this scene very brief, but Manteb can make it last for an hour or more, to the great delight of his audience. Because of the expansion of this scene, Manteb eliminates the Limbukan or female clown scene, a specialty for certain other puppeteers.

Although some evidence of Manteb's reliance on innovative techniques from the Academy is evident from the descriptions above, it is his use of Academy puppeteers as paid advisers that shows the increasing connections between the Academy and the *Rebo Legi* puppeteers. He has the best musician from the puppeteering section of the Academy to arrange his music; he has the puppeteer who is best known for innovative puppet movements to help direct his performances; and he continually gets ideas from talking to the scholars and performers from the Academy. In addition, rumor at the Academy has it that Manteb has older puppeteers who write out *lakon* for him, complete with dialogues and humorous exchanges. Occasionally when Manteb performs, he will put on his glasses so that he can read from some papers in his lap. Since he is no longer just a village *dhalang*, another puppeteer told me that he feels that he has to upgrade his performances to cater to the tastes of the generals in Jakarta who continually call him there to perform.

Because of his fame and success, he has now organized a *wetonan* or birthday celebration of his own, comparable to the *Rebo Legi* of Anom Suroto. Manteb's *wetonan* is *Selasa Legi* (Tuesday Legi), and like Suroto, he invites *dhalang* from all over Java to perform at his house. The atmosphere at Manteb's *wetonan* differs from the rowdy mood at Anom Suroto's. Manteb's celebration is more serious; but he videotapes all the performers—as does Suroto—and also speaks of his duty to preserve the older

71. The noted scholar and author Umar Kayam told me (October 1990) that Manteb watches Kung Fu performances on television to gather ideas for his puppet movements.

Rhetoric and Performance Domains

A gunungan, *or* kayon, *sometimes known as the tree-of-life puppet, is used to mark changes of scene and special effects in all* wayang *performances.*

styles by inviting older performers. As noted above, the devaluation of the shadows seems to be taking place at Manteb's *wetonan* also. It is almost impossible to sit and watch the shadows at Manteb's house, as the area is only wide enough for one or two sleeping children. Although there is a large area in the back of the screen where people can sit and talk at low Javanese tables, there are room dividers set up which block one's vision of the shadows. To remedy this, and perhaps as another indication of current tastes, there is a video image of the puppeteer available on the shadow side for those who wish to watch the performer.

For all his adoption of new technology and new techniques, Manteb himself maintains that he is not changing the tradition in any way. When I talked to Manteb in July of 1990, he told me that Nartosabdho had excelled in *sanggit* (plot development), Anom Suroto excelled in *suluk* (singing), and he had seen the need for someone who excelled in *sabet* (puppet movement). He assured me that the trumpets and the drums were to keep the interest of the *anak muda*, young people, and that the tradition was *masih utuh*, still complete or intact. Rumors say that Manteb undertakes mystical exercises to enhance his powers; then again, such rumors abound about many Javanese public figures.

Whenever he performs these days, Manteb attracts huge crowds, running into the high hundreds in the areas around Solo and into the thousands in Jakarta. Through his performances, other aspiring young puppeteers gain new ideas for their own performances. It is the influence of the Academy as popularized and channeled through Manteb that shows the ways in which Academy ideas enter the popular domains. So far, the popularity of Manteb has spread entirely through the performance tradition. It was only in the late 1980s that Manteb was asked to make recordings for the recording industry. He is said to have made three such recordings, which were not yet available in the cassette shops in Solo when I left Java in August of 1990. It is in these recordings, which are made in Manteb's own recording studio in his village outside Solo, that Manteb is most likely to read the *lakon* that have been written out for him by other puppeteers. Since Manteb is a puppeteer whose fame is based on puppet movements, his major skills become invisible in recordings and are unlikely to please the recording industries in the way that Anom Suroto's beautiful voice does.

While Manteb uses modern technology in his art, one can also note many older ideas of Javanese accumulations of power in the way that he has risen to fame. He is careful to gather talented people and new technologies about him, which he then can control as he controls the puppets. As puppeteers in the past were said to control the unseen forces of the universe, Manteb continues in that tradition by manipulating light and sound in spectacular ways—the new unseen forces of the universe. He continues to practice Javanese mysticism, and he carefully takes the advice of older spiritual teachers. Manteb takes the same ideas and technology that remain esoteric in the hands of Academy puppeteers, and he makes them accessible to wide audiences. In the words of Umar Kayam, Manteb along with Anom Suroto and the late Nartosabdho are "*dhalang* entrepreneurs" or super *dhalang*. They are producers who produce themselves as public spectacles for the masses. Certainly this public display fits in with Javanese ideas of Power noted by Anderson years ago. While Academy puppeteers draw minuscule audiences, the *dhalang* entrepreneurs have been able to absorb and rechannel Academy ideas for Javanese audiences.

Creation of mood through embellishment, the intertwining of the mystical and the aesthetic experience, and sheer density of context—all seem to be giving way to European and American ways of thinking at the Academy. One-and-a-half- to two-hour play formats, linear plots, directors, scripts, and rehearsals have all been derived from European and American performance styles. These are felt to be modern and more in tune with the contemporary changes in Javanese lifestyles.

The fascination that foreign scholars experience when they encounter Javanese ways of putting the world together might be compared to the fascination with which Javanese performers are currently embracing European and American ways of thinking. For a Javanese growing up with musical gong cycles, intersecting calendrical cycles, and circular *wayang* plots, the myth of starting from A and actually arriving at B in a direct manner must be as seductive as understanding the many layers of a Javanese shadow play is for the foreign scholar.

The three performance styles discussed in this chapter—and the ways that the boundaries among them shift and change—are representative of the variety of performances that exist in Java today. Colonial, modern, and postmodern *wayang* authorities intertwine, and the lines between them grow increasingly difficult to decipher. Students from the Academy bring new ideas to the villages which are incorporated into village performances. *Rebo Legi* puppeteers mingle with puppeteers from the Academy and are invited to the Academy to take part in the series of conferences and workshops which form part of the Academy student's curriculum. The Academy uses respected older puppeteers to teach the first few years of courses to aspiring puppeteers, and the innovating puppeteers at the Academy are often the sons of famous village puppeteers. The existence of this activity argues for the continued popularity of the tradition and its rich and complex legacy for succeeding generations. The world of the shadow theatre in the villages surrounding the city of Solo is in flux, reflecting and recording the changes in contemporary Javanese life. The concluding chapter looks at how the stories are breaking free from their frames and appearing in new forms, and how these changes support or modify theory and praxis.

6 Fiction, Images,

and Allegories

Thinking this afternoon of our recent talk about that historical work, I decided that its major flaw, as history, is just what seems to be its greatest virtue, namely that it is clear and forceful. This is cruelly deceptive (and attractive—even now, with a great deal of contrary evidence, I still find myself thinking first of all in terms of that pie, then by an effort correcting myself. In a way, my whole education about the Revolution has been a process of freeing myself, one by one, from the pictures given of the events of the period, and this is especially hard because of the clarity and consistency of [those] pictures).

I carried the idea further to the thought that the only possible attitude of a proper historian to his work is one of sorrow, in a sense more like *sajang* [compassion]. He must know at all times that he cannot know more than a little of what he wants to know, that his picture must always be flawed. This is more than simply remarking that he can only know a fraction of a percent of the facts of the matter; the crux of the matter, as [Carl L.] Becker says, lies within the historian, and no historian can fully or properly recreate in his own vision what has passed. The sorrow lies just there, that while he wants to know the past, what he comes to know through his studies is himself—though this, indeed, if he is aware of it, refines this awareness, is a precious thing, as valuable as the past-as-it-was-lived which he is searching for.

From this the [older] type of book of remote. Whatever its factual, provable failings may be its chief feature lies in the whole attitude with which it is written, the unexamined assumption that what was being discovered, described was the real past and not the writer's image of it.[1]—John R. W. Smail

This book's analysis of the *wayang* tradition has differed from several earlier studies that focused on the *wayang* as a court tradition. The scholars who have seen the *wayang* as an elite tradition were usually taking the early twentieth century as a starting point for assessing the develop-

1. From the field notes of John R. W. Smail, 5 September 1960, recently donated by John and Laura Smail to the archives of the Suzzallo Library of the University of Washington.

ment of the tradition. By accepting the work of the Dutch scholar Kats[2]— who described the tradition that Javanese princes and Dutch scholars were creating in the 1920s—as a seminal starting point for the study of the *wayang* tradition, Solonese shadow theatre in recent years may seem to have fallen from the classical heights it had reached in the early twentieth century. But looking at the Javanese shadow theatre over the longer span of its history, the Dutch-influenced period assumes its proper proportions and can be seen as a wave in the tradition's history rather than as "the" classical period in the tradition's development. Some scholars have seen the declining refinement of the performance tradition over the past few decades as a degeneration, but this book has argued that the current move away from refined court styles marks a resurgence of lively village forms that have always appealed to Javanese audiences.[3]

The puppeteers who perform at *Rebo Legi* performances cater to current and fashionable tastes. They want audiences and laughter. Many of the puppeteers had their encounter with politics in the 1960s. Those who survived do not discuss politics anymore. Yet the Academy performers refuse an aesthetic move that caters to popular tastes. They want to set rigorous artistic standards for the shadow theatre. While the court elites in the 1920s and 1930s wanted to educate and raise the vulgar tastes of the "little people" (*wong cilik*), the Academy teachers and performers do not seem so concerned with what goes on outside its walls. In the words of Bambang Murtiyasa, one Academy teacher:

The aesthetic worth of shadow theatre includes concepts of dignity, excitement, enchantment, significance, attentiveness, wit, eloquence, and so forth [*regu, greget, sem, nges, renggep, cucut, tutuk dan sebagainya*]. Aesthetic concepts of the shadow theatre like these are now usually forgotten by a good number of *dhalang*. What

---

2. Kats, *Het Javaansche Tooneel I.*

3. Although he does not address the question of folk and elite traditions, Becker, in "Text-Building," creates new aesthetic and epistemological contexts for understanding the way Javanese audiences enjoy shadow theatre performances. Becker suggests that analyses of the enjoyment Javanese derive from *wayang* performances may appear meaningless within European aesthetic frames. Adopting Becker's methodological approach, Keeler, in *Javanese Shadow Plays*, avoids the search for "meaning" in the Javanese shadow theatre. If earlier scholars were overly concerned with elite interpretations of the tradition, Keeler's study balances that preoccupation by presenting a view of the tradition as it appears to the Javanese villagers who have nurtured it.

appears most often these days are concepts that stress liveliness above all, humor, action, and things like that, until they fail to offer things that are meaningful for our spiritual life. This has occurred to satisfy the taste of the audience, which is really very shallow.[4]

Murtiyasa's remarks reflect a continuation of Dutch colonial evaluations of Javanese literary and performance traditions. The Dutch descriptions of the *wayang* in the nineteenth century show that performances have long been lively, funny, and lewd rather than edifying. Ideas of *merusak pakem* or breaking the rules that were constituted in the nineteenth-century courts are still being debated by intellectuals both at the Solonese Academy and in publications to which they contribute. In one recent publication, the Javanese scholar Singgih Wibisono spoke about breaking the rules (melanggar pakem) contained in the *wayang pakem*.

One encouraging development is that the *dalang* of today are no longer afraid to be singled out for *"merusak pakem pedalangan"* or *"nyebal pakem,"* the ignoring of conventions. The freedom to invent stories is more likely to enrich *pedalangan* literature as long as these inventions make the *lakon* more meaningful as literature, are able to raise problems that invite thought and reflection from the viewers, are able to elevate the comprehension of the viewers during the performances, and can fulfill the aesthetic expectations of the viewers beyond what has already been offered.[5]

Wibisono also mentions that the once-new technique of *banjaran* (lined up in rows) stories, where puppeteers tell the life history of one particular Ramayana or Mahabharata character in a single night, is now becoming a convention rather than an invention. The stories of the characters Bisma, Karna, and Durna were first told by the late Ki Nartosabdho in the 1970s; a *banjaran* story has even been told about a female character, *Dewi Sinta* of

4. Bambang Murtiyasa, "Sebuah Tinjauan tentang Pakem dan Masalah-Masalahnya," p. 11.

5. Singgih Wibisono, "Konvensi dan Invensi Dalam Sastra Pedalangan," *Gatra* 16 (1987): 7–9. Murtiyasa, in "Sebuah Tinjauan tentang Pakem dan Masalah-Masalahnya," argues that the concept of *"melanggar pakem"* is basically false and usually taught by those who are not *dhalang* themselves. Yet in the previous quote, Murtiyasa, who teaches at the Academy, showed that he thinks the tastes of audiences outside the Academy are shallow and that *dhalang* must conform to those tastes if they want to be popular.

Fictions, Images, and Allegories

the Ramayana, by Ki Timbul Hadiprayitno of Yogyakarta. For a time also in the 1980s, stories from the life of the Mahabharata hero Bima were performed every month in a series by Ki Manteb Sudarsono. Perhaps once again, linear ideas of historical flow are intersecting with these Javanese tales. By continual movements in and out of the thought-world of the *wayang*, by recognizing the persistent displacement of stories and meanings, I see Mahabharata and Ramayana tales as potential sites of struggle in the postcolonial politics of the Indonesian state.

This book has questioned the categories of "myth" and "history," suggesting that both are constructed discourses interacting within the world of power relations. As John Smail noted almost thirty-five years ago in the long quote that opened this chapter, historians do not write "real" pasts, but only their images of them. These images must necessarily be made up of fragments from the arbitrary categories of story, myth, and history. And yet, if contesting long-lived Javanese myths of fratricidal war could help to undermine the ability of postcolonial governments to coerce people into carrying out state violence, then iconoclastic stories must be composed that tell the old tales in new ways. Such stories are appearing in novels, comic books, and television programming. This chapter begins by assessing the effects of commodification in the domain of shadow theatre performances and then looks at how the stories have moved into cassettes, comic books, and into modern fiction.

Commodification and Javanese Tales

Wayang performances have become commodified since the 1970s in the sense that there are public performances that people can pay to see. Every Saturday night the government radio station (RRI) stages a performance in either Solo, Yogyakarta, Semarang, or Jakarta. The performance is free to those who have access to radios, but interested spectators can watch the performance for a modest fee. If the puppeteer is a popular one, the hall will fill up for a good part of the performance. Many of the puppeteers who perform at the radio station use written notations to insure that their performances will exhibit the expected style. They are aware that the medium of radio concentrates attention on their voice rather than their puppet movements. Sweeney notes that in Malaysia, performances are regularly held for paying audiences.[6] The radio-station performances were the only example of performances held for paying audiences that I came across during my stay in Java (1982–84). When I returned in 1990, I heard that performances for pay were being held in Jakarta, particularly performances by Ki Manteb. Rich patrons would be asked to contribute twenty thousand rupiah to pay for the costs of the hall and the *dhalang*.

The commodification of the *wayang* tradition can diminish the "aura" of performances,[7] but only if the observer's historical vision is limited to the court tradition so valued by European scholars and Javanese elites in the 1920s and 1930s. Exhibition value could only replace cult value, and *wayang* performances move from ritual to entertainment,[8] in a thought-world that ignores the stress on pleasing audiences that seems to have been an important part of the tradition for as long as it has been known.[9] If technology and entertainment value are conditioning the performances of the puppeteers, they seem little more than a continuation of a stress on voice production, puppet manipulation, and humor. While *wayang* performances are still held to commemorate life-cycle rites and rituals, and puppeteers still practice various forms of asceticism to empower their art, innovative puppeteers are consistently drawing their material from ever-expanding written, televised, and foreign sources. The older puppeteers with connections to the court traditions of the early twentieth century, whom Javanese, European, and American scholars and aficionados often see as more "authentic," are not valued in the public domain because contemporary audiences do not find their performances entertaining or exciting; they are rarely commissioned to perform.

Perhaps in response to President Soeharto's continuing interest in the *dhalang* cited in the preceding chapter, I encountered a professed respect for regional Javanese arts when I was in Java in 1990. One of the puppeteers told me that Harmoko, the Indonesian Minister of Information, had recently come to Solo to encourage the preservation of Javanese as well as

---

6. A. Sweeney, "Literacy and the Epic in the Malay World."

7. Benjamin, "The Work of Art in the Age of Mechanical Reproduction," in *Illuminations*, pp. 217–52.

8. V. Turner, *From Ritual to Theatre* (New York City: Performing Arts Journal Publications, 1982).

9. Sears, "Rethinking Indian Influence in Javanese Shadow Theatre Traditions."

Fictions, Images, and Allegories

other regional performance traditions. Every *desa* or village is supposed to have its own *gamelan*, even if it is iron rather than bronze. Associations of novice musicians that used to be known as women's groups are now formed by men from various professions who want to familiarize themselves with Javanese musical styles. Another puppeteer related that groups of young people in the villages will occasionally combine funds to commission a shadow play performance that does not mark the passing of a major life-cycle ritual—this, too, was unknown ten years ago. In Solo, several sponsors have formed the organization known as Punakawan, one of many new organizations loosely promoted by the government to keep "traditional arts" alive. Punakawan holds a *wayang* performance once a month in the city of Solo and produces a monthly newspaper. Businesses, too, are jumping on the cultural bandwagon: The newspaper *Jawa Pos* sponsored eight *wayang* performances in Central and East Java in the summer of 1990. The newspaper hired Manteb for all the performances and supposedly paid him three million rupiah per performance.[10] Like Anom Suroto today, Manteb is a politically safe *dhalang*. His humor and innovative puppet movements do not dwell on embarrassing social problems; through Manteb and other innovative puppeteers the government can encourage and support the spectacle of Javanese culture while turning peasant communities into modernizing consumers.

The proliferation of cassette recordings of *wayang* performances is another site of the increasing commodification of the tradition. Central Javanese *wayang* performances have been available since the 1970s as a set of eight or nine cassettes that can be used at weddings and celebrations in place of a real performance. Very little research has focused on the effects of the production of cassettes on the tradition. This commodification has been proceeding in a controlled way because of the monopoly that Anom Suroto and the late Nartosabdho had over the recording of Solonese-style *wayang* performances. When I left Java in 1984, Anom Suroto was the only Solonese puppeteer making cassette recordings. Some of the reasons for this were financial and some were political: Suroto could afford his own recording studio, and cassette recording companies knew that his recordings would sell. As noted above, Suroto is also considered politically safe;

10. The minimum daily wage in Central Java has recently been raised from 2,000 to 2,700 Rupiah per day, but that does not mean that Javanese employers comply with these rules.

he actively supports the Golkar line. In the month preceding the parliamentary elections that were held in Indonesia in early 1987, Suroto was the only puppeteer who was allowed to perform in the city of Solo.[11]

I have remarked that Manteb has now begun to produce recordings as well. The late appearance of cassette recordings of Manteb's performances shows that Manteb's rise to fame had nothing to do with the recording industry.[12] The latter, showing its conservative tendencies, waited until Manteb's fame was secure so that they were sure that his recordings would sell. Since cassette audiences cannot see his flashy puppet movements, it is also possible that Manteb's conscious enhancement of his verbal skills through his study and use of written materials has made him more acceptable to the industry.

The conservative tendencies of the recording industry mean that the people who buy Solonese *wayang* cassettes have greater choice among stories than among performers. This fits into the pattern of control that the Indonesian government has over radio and television programming as well, although satellite technology and the addition of new, private television stations are rapidly overtaking the government's surveillance techniques. This control may have unpredictable results: Suroto's and Nartosabdho's voices have been amplified by cassette technology, and the lack of competing voices will inspire either conformity or resistance to what may come to be considered normative configurations of the tradition.[13]

The government also uses *wayang* characters to support its messages on television. In the 1970s the government attempted to coopt the puppeteers into working with them to promote government policy with mixed results;[14] returning to the style of the 1960s, the government can again use the *wayang* characters directly. It is always the clowns who are marked to deliver seemingly innocuous government directives. Clown characters from the *wayang orang* plays, usually Semar and his sons, will tell jokes and laugh as they encourage villagers to support birth control, inoculation programs, and village cleanliness. Reminiscent of Javanese and Dutch

---

11. Personal communication from Kent Devereaux, spring 1988.

12. This point was brought to my attention by Philip Yampolsky, who has written several unpublished essays on the cassette recording industry in Indonesia.

13. In Yogyakarta, there are at least four or five puppeteers who record in Yogyanese style.

14. Clara van Groenendael, *The dalang behind the wayang*, pp. 133–51.

colonial ideas from the early twentieth century, the Indonesian government is using the *wayang* tradition for *opvoeding*, to raise the tastes and practices of the Javanese folk. Important recent events in the circulation of Ramayana and Mahabharata stories have been the television airings of Indian videotapes of both story cycles. I have heard that these programs, given Indonesian subtitles, have been immensely popular in Java. Endo Suanda told me that puppeteers in Cirebon, where he has been carrying out doctoral research, refuse to be disturbed during these television broadcasts.[15] Some puppeteers also consider the Indian stories to exhibit that sense of "authenticity" that Dutch scholars attributed to Indian tellings of the stories. Indonesian women friends who live in Jakarta have reported that the Indian television Ramayana has reinforced oppressive New Order government constructions of the self-sacrificing wife through the portrayal of Sita in these programs.

In the comic-book retellings of the stories and the new fiction discussed below, Javanese and Indonesian authors are continually moving in and out of a thought-world in which the *wayang* assumes a central place. Several American scholars have commented upon the novels of Yudhistira Ardi Noegraha.[16] Yudhistira's novels have been received with ambivalence by the Indonesian government because they make fun of the characters of the *wayang* world, showing the ways in which the New Order is invested in preserving the *wayang* as an artifact to serve its purposes. Plans to turn one of Yudhistira's *wayang* novels into a film were halted by the government because he was unwilling to change all the *wayang* names of his characters as the censors demanded. For these reasons, the medium of the film is as yet unexplored as a new site of experimentation for *wayang* performances. Because film producers can edit and splice materials, this could be an area of great creativity for innovative shadow puppeteers. The ability of shadow puppeteers and other artists to use the forces of industrial commodification for their own purposes may be closely related to the "protection" or surveillance which the tradition receives from the government. Were the recording industry to pursue unlimited recording and marketing of performers on cassettes, and were the government to allow

15. Personal commuication, 16 June 1994.

16. See Savitri Scherer, "Yudhistira Ardi Noegraha: Social Attitudes in the Works of a Popular Writer," *Indonesia* 30 (October 1980): 31–52, and Benedict Anderson, "*Sembah-Sumpah*: The Politics of Language and Javanese Culture," pp. 194–240.

proliferation of newer styles of radio and television programming of performances and the free publication of literature that ridicules or criticizes the stories and the characters, the future of the tradition might look very different.

R. A. Kosasih and the *Wayang* Comics

An important vehicle today for the transmission of Mahabharata and Ramayana stories are the comic-book tellings, *cergam* (*cerita gambar* or picture tales) as they are called. R. A. Kosasih is the best-known and most successful of the Indonesian artists who create comic books of the Mahabharata and Ramayana stories.[17] According to Leila Chudori, quite a number of Indonesian intellectuals read and collect the Kosasih Ramayana and Mahabharata comics—for themselves as well as for their children. In her article, Chudori quotes from well-known figures like Umar Kayam, Marsilam Simanjuntak, Agus Dermawan T., Sita Aripurnama, Haryono Guritno, and several others. Guritno, who is head of the *wayang* museum in Jakarta, passed on to Chudori his thoughts about the history of the *wayang* repertoire.

In the past, *wayang* stories were documented in a serious way. The stories, which were standardized (*dibakukan*) by Ronggowarsito, were collected in the library of Paku Buwana IV.

Now, from the nineteenth century until today, the *wayang*s [*perwayangan*] have been going "downhill" [because] they didn't have to be serious. Kosasih is unique among those who have succeeded in popularizing *wayang*, in his own way, in the shape of comics.[18]

17. This discussion of Kosasih is drawn from the excellent article published by Leila Chudori, "R. A. Kosasih: Di Tengah Pandawa dan Kurawa," *Tempo*, 21 December 1991, pp. 41–67. *Tempo* was the premier weekly news magazine published in Indonesia until it was banned in June of 1994. It was edited by the respected critic and author Goenawan Mohamad. On Indonesian comic books, see M. Bonneff, *Les bandes dessinées indonesiennes; une mythologie en image* (Paris: Puyraimond, 1976).

18. This is quoted in Chudori, "R. A. Kosasih," p. 43. The first part of the quote is Chudori's summary of Guritno's ideas; the second part is an actual quotation of his words.

Fictions, Images, and Allegories

Guritno is, of course, passing along the received colonial discourse of decadence in the development of the *wayang* tradition.

Another piece of received and recorded wisdom about the Kosasih comics is that they present Indian versions of the stories rather than Javanese, Sundanese, or Balinese ones. Kosasih has said he does this intentionally to prevent "regionalism." He even includes small frames on his story-picture pages, with messages appearing as if on ancient parchment, to make his intentions clear to his readers.

As a nation that is civilized, obviously we must also value the cultures of other ethnic groups. For example, the *wayang* stories (*wayang purwa* [*sic*]), have their source in the *Mahabharata*, the civilization of *Ancient India*, and because of that the storyline is a little different, because the *Mahabharata* has already been swallowed up by the people of *Indonesia* as their own culture and has been changed over hundreds of centuries even more to harmonize with the life and customs of *Indonesia* . . . [*sic*].[19]

Kosasih will occasionally interrupt his story-pictures to explain the difference between the Indian interpretations he is introducing and the stories as they are known by Javanese or Sundanese audiences. He even inserts the geographical place-names of ancient India into his stories, rather than localizing the stories in Java, as Javanese authors and performers have always done.

Another interesting set of stories introduced by Kosasih concerns the life and times of Sri Kresna, incarnation of Wisnu, and adviser and friend to the Pandhawa heroes. It is possible that Kosasih picked up the idea of introducing so-called life histories of particular characters from the late puppeteer Ki Nartosabdho, since the Kresna series is dated, as far as I can tell, from 1983, after Nartosabdho had introduced the Banjaran technique in the late 1970s. The stories of Sri Kresna included in the Kosasih series of four volumes exhibits Kosasih's usual method of combining elements from both Indian and Javanese tellings of the stories. For example, the stories of Kresna's youth—so beloved in parts of India—do not seem to

19. R. A. Kosasih, "Pandawa Diperdaya 1," *Seri Mahabharata*, vol. 12, *Antara Baju Tamsir dan Senjata Konta* (Jabar: Langlangbuwana, 1977), p. 22. In this quote it seems a little unclear if Kosasih wants to respect the other cultures of Indonesia or to value that of India.

have been particularly popular or well-known in Java in older times. These stories are mostly taken from the Bhagavata Purana of medieval India, when Krishna in Indian mythology was making the transition from an epic hero to an elevated deity within the Indian *bhakti*, or devotional, tradition. Some of the stories Kosasih chooses to tell concern the baby Krishna's naughtiness in his youth. Other popular stories of the young Krishna from India recount his role as the flute-playing cowherd who was able to make love to a thousand *gopi*, or maidens who tended the cows, and who was able to satisfy each maiden by using the love-making techniques of each one's fantasies. Kosasih has chosen to ignore these stories, perhaps because of their erotic overtones.

In the three-volume collectionof Ramayana comics, called *Rama Sinta* or *Ramayana*, that were given to me by novelist and playwright Putu Wijaya in 1988—with the subtle message that if I wanted to understand the contemporary state of the *wayang* stories, I should be reading these—I noted many divergences from all the Indian, Javanese, and Balinese tellings of the Ramayana stories that I know.[20]

The most startling example concerns the fight between Rahwana and his brother Wibisana, two of the characters whose births were discussed in chapter 1, over Rahwana's abduction of Rama's wife Sita. This story has been touted as an important political allegory in Java because of the message it gives about family loyalty. In the Indian Sanskrit text of Valmiki, the Old Javanese Ramayana, and almost all Ramayanas I have ever seen or heard, Wibisana stands up to Rahwana in the court of Langka and tells him that his actions are dishonorable and he should return Sita to Rama immediately. Rahwana's older brother Kumbakarno also tells Rahwana that his actions are despicable, but then he says, you are my brother right or wrong and I will support you. Rahwana gets furious at Wibisana and kicks him in the face. Wibisana endures this insult with great humility and then tells Rahwana he can no longer abide by his actions; Wibisana then leaves to join the forces of righteousness on the side of Rama. In

20. I lived in India for several years and completed an M.A. degree in Indian history in 1977. My M.A. thesis was a study of the devotional Ramayana of the North Indian saint Tulsidas—the *Ramcaritmanas*. For excellent studies of this very important work, see Philip Lutgendorf's article, "Words Made Flesh: The Banaras *Ramlila* as Epic Commentary," *Boundaries of the Text*, ed. Flueckiger and Sears, and his 1992 book *The Life of a Text: Performing the Ramcaritmanas of Tulsidas* (Berkeley: University of California Press, 1991).

Fictions, Images, and Allegories

Indonesian political discourse, people are judged by whether they side with the actions of Kumbakarno, putting family loyalty over moral conviction, or whether they follow the model of Wibisana, pursuing virtue at the expense of family. Anderson suggested in 1965 that Kumbakarno was the much more admired hero.[21]

Kosasih, however, deals with this episode in a unique way. Rather than simply have Rahwana kick Wibisana in the face, Kosasih has Rahwana *kill* Wibisana and then has his body thrown into the woods. By happenstance, on his trip home from Langka where he went to bring Rama's ring to Sita and to find out if she was still alive (and pure), Hanuman comes across the body of Wibisana. He brings the body to Rama who orders that Hanuman find the magic Wijayakusuma flower and restore Wibisana to life. Thus, when Wibisana is revived, he is already with Rama. He commits no ignoble action since Rahwana did not only kick him in the face but went so far as to kill him. Thus, in this interpretation, no one can fault Wibisana for siding with Rama. I have asked Indian scholars who study Indian Ramayana traditions if this telling is known in India. So far, no one from India or any of the areas of Indonesia where Ramayana stories are told has ever heard of this interpretation. I cite this example to show that Kosasih, like all tellers of Mahabharata and Ramayana tales, tells them in his own way. He may follow Indian tellings of the story when it is convenient to do so, but he also weaves in local tellings and, most importantly, totally new creations.

One important intervention made by Kosasih, in my opinion, is his decision to separate Ramayana and Mahabharata stories from what he calls *Wayang Purwa* stories. Because of his desire to rely on Indian rather than Indonesian regional tellings of the stories, Kosasih has made significant judgments about what to call the different story cycles that he has presented in his comic books over the past thirty years. His comic books have been so successful that he has continually expanded his repertoire. What he clearly sees as Mahabharata stories are included under the category *Seri Mahabharata* or Mahabharata Series. This series is made up of nineteen books, all but one of which is a two-volume set, thirty-seven

21. Anderson, *Mythology and the Tolerance of the Javanese.* One wonders whether the increasing frustration and digust in Indonesia today with the excessive spread of enormous wealth to President Soeharto's children and family is forcing a rethinking of these ideas about family loyalties.

volumes in all.[22] Kosasih has divided up the rest of the stories into a whole range of new linear categories: *Wayang Purwa*, *Leluhur Hastina* (Hastina Ancestors), *Mahabharata*, *Bharata Yudha*, *Pandawa Seda* (The Death of the Pandhawa), *Parikesit*, and then tales of individual characters and stories. In his own words, he explains this decision.

Wayang purwa tales form a *wayang* narrative created by our ancient poets, especially on the island of Java, who also took the Mahabharata as their primary source. Nevertheless many changes in the personalities of the characters were adapted to that period of religious change from Hinduism to Islam so that the many tensions that arose from the various beliefs that still existed in those days could be accepted by a broad sector of society. Because a middle path was taken, new characters appeared like Semar, Togog, Batara Narada, Sanghyang Otipati (Adi Guru) and many characters whose personalities were adapted to the teachings of Islam.[23]

Kosasih makes the same connections between what he calls *wayang* stories and Islam that I made in chapter 2. In contrast to his category of Mahabharata, something he sees as intrinsically Indian, *wayang* stories come into being with the entry of Islam to Java. Even more important, the stories that Kosasih retells in his *Wayang Purwa* series are the same stories retold in the *Paramayoga* of Ranggawarsita and Yogyanese Purwakanda texts, the books of that revered category of Javanese *adiluhung* (high culture) literature kept in palace libraries. Thus the texts that many Javanese consider too sacred to read, the "essence" of their traditions, are now being reintroduced into the villages from which they came through Kosasih's work.[24]

22. It is interesting to note Kosasih's choice of spellings. He prefers Bharatayuddha, the Indian spelling, over the more common Javanese Bratayuda. He uses the more Indian names Hastina and Indraprasta rather than the Javanese Ngastina and Ngamarta for the kingdoms of the Korawa and Pandhawa, respectively. Kosasih's usage is generally a mix of Javanese and Indian forms; in the 1920s and 1930s, following Dutch practice, many Javanese intellectuals chose Sanskrit spellings, complete with diacritics, over local Javanese ones. If one peruses the articles in the Javanese nationalist periodical *Wederopbouw*, discussed in chapter 3, one will find many examples of these Indian Sanskritic spellings.

23. R. A. Kosasih, *Wayang Purwa*, vol. A. (Bandung: Erlina, 1983), p. 1.

24. On the *adiluhung* literature, see N. Florida, "Reading the Unread in Traditional Javanese Literature." For a discussion of Javanese literature by a Javanese Catholic priest who is a noted fiction writer and essayist, see Y. B. Mangunwijaya's essay "Linaksanan: Mitologi Sebagai Legitimasi oleh Para Dewa" (Mythology as a Legitimation of the Gods),

Fictions, Images, and Allegories

Although chapter 3 argued that the Mahabharata and Ramayana were failed narratives of the nation in the late colonial and pre-independence period, Kosasih's works may yet bring these Javanese, Sundanese, and Balinese tales to wider Indonesian audiences as they continue to be retold in Indonesian novels, romances, and comic books. The transition of Mahabharata and Ramayana stories from the banana-log stages of shadow plays and the pages of palace manuscripts into colorful cartoons is one that both comments on and reconceptualizes the transmission of tales. The flatness of comic images or, at times, the reduction to black and white of what could be more colorful drawings, is not a great leap from the flatness of leather puppets or the chiaroscuro of shadows. And the distance from puppets to humans seems no greater than that between cartoon images and humans. In fact, the evolution of the present day *wayang* comic books is a fascinating one. When Kosasih, the inventor of Mahabharata and Ramayana comic-book characters, first began to draw cartoon characters, he was most inspired by American superheroes like Superman and Flash Gordon. But these were the early years of the new nation, and its charismatic leader Soekarno was beginning to adopt his anti-West and anti-imperialist stance. According to Kosasih, Soekarno did not like the "Western" influence of the superheroes at a time when the young nation was struggling to find its own unique identity. So Kosasih came up with the brilliant idea of recasting the beloved heroes and heroines of the shadow theatre as cartoons. He also decided to dress these heroes in the clothing of the *wayang orang* (human *wayang*) theatre that was flourishing at that time, especially in Solo, Semarang, Yogyakarta, and Jakarta.

So Kresna and Arjuna, Semar and his sons, and Sumbadra and Srikandhi strut across the pages of the comic books in theatrical costume, set against a background of imagery that draws its inspiration from ancient Java, ancient India, and the Javanese countryside. Once again, this does not seem particularly new, since the *wayang orang* actors have been doing this commercially for decades against hand-painted backdrops of court and country scenes.

Several things, however, do seem new about the comic-book medium.

---

in *Sastra dan Religiositas* (Jakarta: Sinar Harapan, 1982). He discusses the *Paramayoga* of Ranggawarsita and the Purwakanda (pp. 18–19).

The ambiguity of the comic books begins with their location somewhere between drama and narrative. Although it is tempting to situate comic books within narrative genres, the way that the narrative must be told through the mouths of individual characters more clearly resembles dramatic literature. Lutgendorf has noted that the extravagant *Ramlila* dramas of northern India may have begun more as pantomimes than as dramas.[25] Even today, he notes that performances are often stopped for a moment to present *jhanki* (glimpses) of the gods in frozen tableaux. Comic-book frames have much in common with this idea of frozen tableaux and thus seem a logical receptacle for Ramayana and Mahabharata stories as they move from enacted dramas to printed pages.

Along these same lines, much more than romances or novels, comic books are meant for private reading, since readers want to dwell on the pictures as well as on the words of the story. One does not need to be completely literate to enjoy the comic books. In this sense, comic books encourage the practice of private reading much more than film or television, which lead would-be readers away from printed pages. Comic books stress private reading even more than newspapers or "dollar dreadfuls" because people want to look at the pictures and are not content to sit and listen to the stories being read to them. Comic books also encompass the old familiar stories in one of the many moods or modes of modernity. To read a comic book is to feel a part of the modern nation that makes the production of these books possible. But this aura of the modern is couched in the comfortable surroundings of the familiar. The whole gang is still here, so to speak. What is missing is only the joke-telling and allegory-creating puppeteer, who used to be necessary to bring these storyrealms into being. Like Islam, which made temples, churches, and priests unnecessary to reach the divine, comic books do away with visible mediators between the individual and the story-world.

Perhaps most significantly, on both a visual and cognitive level, comic book characters have more sensual bodies than the leather puppets. And these bodies, for the most part, appear with very European features. In most of the comic books that I have seen, the characters appear very white, except for those who are painted in darker hues to show their lower evolution or crude ways. This is not very different from images of beauti-

25. Lutgendorf, "Words Made Flesh," p. 86.

Fictions, Images, and Allegories

ful young Eurasian bodies that appear regularly in most other modern media in Indonesia today. Film stars and models who are of Eurasian birth seem to be the preferred choice of casting directors and magazine editors.

Much of the sensuality at a shadow play performance takes place off the screen. There is an abundance of sights, sounds, and smells to mesmerize the senses: clove cigarettes, incense, snacks, toys, wide-eyed children, little stalls lit with oil lamps, hustle and bustle among the expectant crowds outside the performance of a well-known puppeteer, gambling tables set up for those who see the gathering as a chance to pick up some quick cash,[26] eager orderliness among the invited guests, pop music blaring out to the crowds through old and poorly working loudspeakers, the first hushed sounds of the *gamelan* signaling that the performance will soon begin.[27] Sensuality within the performance is also not lacking. A good puppeteer will season his or her performance with suggestive jokes that often make fun of members of the audience or members of the *gamelan* orchestra. S/he may create a love scene which mimics a present or past love affair of someone at the performance. For those who are intimately familiar with the stories and the characters, certain heroes and heroines can be portrayed with great sensitivity to their thwarted passions. A favorite theme is the Korawa King's wife Banowati's infamous passion for the Pandhawa arch-rival Arjuna. *Dhalang* with a penchant for humor might make the female clowns the subject of good-natured raunchy jokes. And a trait that seems to be gaining popularity in Solo is the playful banter between *dhalang* and *pesindhen* that is characteristic of Sundanese *wayang*.

26. In his article on the *wayang*, discussed in chapter 3, Tjipto comments somewhat disapprovingly on the gambling that goes on at *wayang* performances: "Chinese card games are laid ready on the mats because even as in Western society, all too often the masterworks of, for example, an Ibsen are not understood and would only cause tedium among the spectators, so also in Javanese society people appear who do not understand the significance of a *wajang* story and will kill time by playing cards." "De Wajang," p. 531.

27. For the invited guests and the performers, the round of food offerings that will punctuate the night begins soon after arrival: a whole meal—which means rice—is served to the performers before the performance begins; snacks and tea appear for performers and guests soon after the performance begins; another rice meal is served around midnight, after which most of the invited guests will leave; coffee and more snacks appear about two or three in the morning—beer or hard liquor is offered to the *gamelan* players at some performances; and lastly, when the performance is over, a final rice meal is served to all the performers.

Shadows of Empire

Although teasing the *pesindhen* is certainly not new to Solonese *wayang*, the skill and bravery of *pesindhen* who respond publicly to such teasing may signal some female resistance to the patriarchal authority of the *dhalang*.

These types of sensuality, however, do not surface in comic-book retellings of the stories. In fact, a striking feature of the comic books is their impersonality. There is no way to use the finely drawn cartoon characters to suggest personal village or urban love affairs in Java today.[28] But by drawing the ancient heroes and heroines in the style of American superheroes, they exude a sensuality that is associated with the bodies of Europeans and Americans, bodies that are free to engage in "free sex" in an imagined modernity that is both part of contemporary Indonesian society and condemned by it. A striking example of this new sensuality is given in the comic-book retelling of the story *Sembadra Larung* by Yoen Yoewono.[29] This well-known story, composed in a famous *macapat* telling by the court poet Sindusastra in the mid-nineteenth century, tells of the burning infatuation of Burisrawa, the half-ogre brother-in-law of the Korawa king, for Arjuna's beautiful wife Sembadra, who is also the sister of Kresna. In Yoen Yoewono's drawings, suggestive, sensual images of Sembadra appear, even though the image is connected with Sembadra's virtuous nephew Gatotkaca, who is innocently hiding his aunt in his headdress to transport her to safety. Nevertheless, readers become the voyeurs of sensual imaginings in a way that leather puppets, *macapat* poetry, or modern romances do not encourage. Given the image of a possibly naked Sembadra—and it is hard to imagine nudity for all but the

28. Sita Aripurnama, former head of the women's organization Kalyanamitra, remembers the effect of the comic-book drawings on her own imagination when she was younger, even though she had known the shadow theatre forms for many years: "Because I often danced the roles of Lesmana in the Ramayana or Raden Inu Kertapati in the Panji Semirang, what I imagined were the drawings of Kosasih." Quoted in Chudori, "R. A. Kosasih," p. 43.

29. Yoen Yoewono, *Sumbadra Larung* (Cergam) (Jakarta: Yayasan Nawangi & P. T. Inaltu, 1976). Yoen Yoewono won a competition, sponsored by the Institute for the Cultivation of Indonesian Wayang (Yayasan Pembinaan Pewayangan Indonesia) in 1976. They called the competition a "*sayembara*," a term in the past used to refer to the competition for a bride among male combatants. The field of the competition is called "*cergam*" *wayang*, a kind of Indonesian acronym for *cerita gambar wayang* or "*wayang* picture stories." I am not sure why the term *comic book* is avoided, unless it is because comics are still seen as "Western" imports that may harm Indonesian moral sensibilities.

Fictions, Images, and Allegories

In a comic book telling of Sembadra Larung, *the* wayang *hero Gatotkaca uses his magical powers to hide his Aunt Sembadra, wife of Arjuna, in his headdress.*

most ogre-like *wayang* puppets—readers can add new frames in their own minds.

By focusing on the bodies of the cartoon characters, an evolutionary story appears on the pages of these comic books. Kosasih was Dutch-educated in the prewar period, and he learned the Dutch scholarly interpretations of Javanese and Indonesian pasts. Particularly in his Ramayana comics, there are the Indic temples of Java's past being built by monkeys who look all too much like the simple Mongoloid peoples whom the ancient Aryans were supposed to have enriched with their noble blood. Not only the monkeys, but also minor characters, who will be killed by the heroes, appear to be several steps lower on the evolutionary ladder than the noble princely warriors, who the Theosophists said still carried the blood of the ancient Indo-Aryans.

Thinking more deeply about the move from puppet to comic-book character, there is another domain in which this shift takes on significance. In the world of shadow play performance, each character is restricted to a certain type and number of bodily movements. An *alus* or refined character like Arjuna cannot stand with his hands on his hips or take great strides

Scenes depicting evolutionary thought, from the comic book Rama Sinta, *or the Ramayana, as drawn by the famous comic book artist R. A. Kosasih.*

across the stage.[30] Women characters, for the most part, are even more restrained. Their arms can only rise so high, their steps are dainty, they move slowly and gracefuly. All these movements contain a treasury of information about what Pierre Bourdieu calls bodily hexis or the body movements associated with different classes of people. Bourdieu is known for his studies of habitus, bodily hexis, and even, simply, taste, which in combinations can determine what he has called cultural capital—those actions that accrue wealth or most often prestige to those who know how to manipulate them. According to Bourdieu, signs of class position are encoded in the way people walk, the way they talk, and the amusements they choose, whether they are aware of this or not: "Bodily hexis is political mythology realized, *em-bodied*, turned into a permanent disposi-

---

30. Of course, one way to innovate or amuse audiences is to have characters violate these rules. The great pleasure of Yudhistira Ardi Noegraha's novels derives from the fact that his characters do transgress these unwritten rules.

Fictions, Images, and Allegories

Scene showing the movement of comic book figures from R. A. Kosasih's Rama Sinta.

tion, a durable way of standing, speaking, walking, and thereby of feeling and thinking."[31]

For many class-conscious Javanese, there are ways of walking that are associated with refinement just as there are ways of walking and talking associated with lack of refinement—*mambu desa,* or to reek of the village, is one way that Javanese express this idea. This is, of course, true for all societies. These ways of walking and talking—Bourdieu's bodily hexis— are deeply encoded in the characterizations and body movements of the *wayang* world.[32] When characters move from puppet image to comic book, there is a certain release from all the bodily movements that have been associated with that character for decades and probably centuries. The amount of movement allowed comic-book characters represents a true liberation from the class positions encoded in the shadow theatre and in

31. P. Bourdieu, *Language and Symbolic Power* (Cambridge: Harvard University Press, 1991), pp. 69–70.

32. For discussions of these character movements, see Brandon, *On Thrones of Gold*, and Sears, "Rethinking Indian Influence."

the *wayang orang*, performances with human actors, which have been structured to follow the puppet movements very carefully.[33]

From bodily hexis, Bourdieu also makes the move to *mentalités*, the way people think and feel. If *wayang* characters have served to represent Javanese to themselves for centuries, and this process has constantly been in flux, another dramatic shift in thinking and feeling is taking place as the Mahabharata and Ramayana characters are released from the elaborate and restrictive codes set in place by the hybrid intellectual exchanges of the colonial period. As the Mahabharata and Ramayana stories move into comics, novels, television programs, and romances, the celebration of *wayang* stories by European and American scholars as the "essence" of the "Agama Jawa" or the Javanese religion—one example of colonial and postcolonial attempts to distance Javanese elites and peasants from Islam—becomes both ambiguous and, perhaps, a relic of a colonial past.

Negotiating Knowledges

To enter the *mentalités* of Indonesian intellectuals who are negotiating the mythical boundaries that delineate Mahabharata and Ramayana tales, two recent portrayals of the revered Mahabharata hero Bhisma, great-uncle to both Pandhawa and Korawa and one of the more fair-minded of the older generation of the Bharata clan, are pertinent. The first reflection on Bhisma comes from Goenawan Mohamad, noted Indonesian (Javanese) author and editor of the widely read and respected Indonesian weekly *Tempo*, which was banned by the government in June 1994. Goenawan's depiction of Bhisma's death has a very Indian flavor to it; in addition, he often chooses Indian spellings of the names of the characters. To me this indicates that Goenawan has read and in some sense accepted Indian tellings of the stories as having that elusive quality of "authenticity." His writings capture a particular sense of high tragedy and despair that the Mahabharata evokes among many Indian followers of the stories.

For several months in early 1987, Goenawan included his musings on different Mahabharata and Ramayana characters in his acclaimed column,

---

33. See Lindsay, "Klasik Kitsch or Contemporary," and P. Choy, "Texts through Time: The Golek Dance of Java," in *Aesthetic Tradition and Cultural Transmission in Java and Bali*, ed. S. Morgan and L. J. Sears.

Fictions, Images, and Allegories

known as "Catatan Pinggir" or "Sidelines," in his magazine *Tempo.* One of the columns described the death of Bhisma on the battlefield of Kurusetra. After Arjuna and Srikandhi have shot their arrows into the body of Bhisma, bringing him to the precipice of death, Arjuna lays down his weapons and kisses Bhisma's feet. Bhisma moans Arjuna's name and then tells him how he refused to marry the princess Amba in his youth after he had taken his vow of celibacy, expressing his regret and responsibility for her accidental death and his acceptance of his demise by her hand through her incarnation in the form of Srikandhi. In his last words, Goenawan has Bhisma tell Arjuna:

It is true that we must discharge our obligations: the warrior only develops through duty. I have done my duty—even in this war among brothers, this great disaster. We have worked with great ambition, my grandson. But I kept asking myself at the same time, what could it be that happened to us in this sacrifice and sadness and evil. . . .

Arjuna bent down. The sun finally set, and Bhisma passed away facing the eleven hills of Kurusetra, and the Pandawa warrior who had killed his own grandfather knew: in that twilight he, too, felt that doubt.[34]

In contrast, Balinese writer and director Putu Wijaya's short story about Bisma [*sic*] starts on a note of reverence and then proceeds into a postmodern world where borders collapse and knowledge is open to unending negotiations.

Bisma arose from the earth, air, and water that had consumed his body for thousands of years, since the time of destruction known as the Bharatayuda War. His massive figure, bent with age, was majestic, pierced by a thousand arrows. Framed with long white hair and beard, his wrinkled face shone, radiant and clear. This ascetic, who had made so enormous a sacrifice, suddenly appeared in Senen Market.[35]

After noting that if he had thought about it more clearly, he might have

34. Goenawan Mohamad's *Catatan Pinggir 3* (1987; Jakarta: Pustaka Utama Grafiti, 1991), pp. 232–34.

35. Putu Wijaya, *BOMB: Indonesian Short Stories*, ed. Ellen Rafferty and Laurie J. Sears (Madison: University of Wisconsin Center for Southeast Asian Studies, 1988), pp. 212–13. This translation was done collaboratively by Ellen Rafferty and me. I have made several small changes in the translation since it was published in 1988.

decided to marry Dewi Amba rather than sacrifice his rights to the throne, or at least he might have sought some good therapy, Bisma wanted to show the crowds in the Market that, although celibate, he was still a real man.

Saying that, Bisma pulled the arrows from his body. He took off his headdress and costume. He stood there on the steps stark naked. "Look!" he said, "I haven't been castrated. I have all the necessary parts and they work just fine. Watch if you don't believe me."

Then he opened a plastic bag which he had been carrying. He took out a pair of jeans, a T-shirt, a pair of Reebok shoes, and a can of spray deodorant. He put these clothes on nonchalantly, seeming at ease with contemporary fashions. Then he put on a pair of sunglasses, lit a cigarette that smelled like a joint, picked up a guitar, and sang a protest song à la Bob Dylan.[36]

Putu Wijaya plays with the ancient myths and fables by humanizing, confusing, and distorting the tales. Sometimes his changes seem playful and innocent; other innovations show that Wijaya has thought deeply about the implications of the ancient stories and how they are used to manipulate popular opinions or to mask the disturbing contradictions of life in Indonesia today. Wijaya's stories blend Balinese, Javanese, and even Indian tellings of Mahabharata tales in postmodern ways. Whether Wijaya's retellings will reverberate in the future remains to be seen. They do, however, mark the intersection of multiple and contradictory historical and mythical trajectories. I offer here my translation of a few pages from Wijaya's novel *Perang*—a biting comment on contemporary Indonesian society told as a fictional representation of the world of the Javanese shadow theatre.[37]

The novel situates the clown-servants of the Javanese shadow theatre, Semar and his three sons Petruk, Gareng, and Bagong, as contemporary villagers living in their *desa* (village) of Karang Tumaritis. Wijaya revels in equipping these well-known and well-loved characters from the past with the latest technological accoutrements. Intersecting plot lines run through the novel, blurring the edges between myth and fantasy in innovative and humorous ways. At the moment in which I interrupt the story, the Pan-

36. Putu Wijaya, *BOMB: Indonesian Short Stories*, pp. 218–19.
37. Putu Wijaya, *Perang* (Jakarta: Pustaka Utama Grafiti, 1990), pp. 211–22.

dhawa and Korawa warring cousins are having a party on the border of their two kingdoms of Ngamarta and Ngastina—also located in the contemporary Javanese countryside—to celebrate the resolution of problems that had arisen because Ngamarta suffered an earthquake and Ngastina, under the guise of trying to help, had sent in troops, which were then lured into fighting, as everyone (mis)interpreted the intentions of the crafty Korawa adviser Sengkuni. Now the scene has switched to the kingdom of Batara[38] Kresna, adviser to the Pandhawa and incarnation of the high god Wisnu; Kresna has been hard at work rearranging the past and future on his computer. He is being monitored from the heavens by the messenger god Batara Narada, who peeks out of the skies with a telescope or, when necessary, resorts to using a [cellular?] phone. Exhausted from his efforts to predict when the Bratayuda War will erupt, Kresna has finally fallen asleep in his office.

A mouse jumped down from behind the roof. He was trying to land on top of the bookcase, but missed and fell on the table, right on the "keyboard."[39] He quickly jumped to his feet and began sniffing around. The letters on the keyboard smelled of fish sauce.[40] Clearly Kresna often forgot to wash his hands before going to work.

The mouse moved from one letter to the next. He licked and sniffed, nibbling a bit and pressing here and there. The computer screen lit up and began to work. The mouse was frightened, but when things still seemed safe he continued licking and sniffing. Satisfied at last, he jumped off and left.

But in a little while the mouse reappeared, and this time he wasn't alone. His wife and children tagged along. The little animals scurried onto the keyboard and turned the screen on again. Several documents disappeared, then were expanded and combined. Sometimes things were going so fast that the computer shrieked to be given the commands more slowly.

Kresna was disturbed by the sounds. So he got up. Like lightning the mice threw themselves onto the floor, seeking a safe hiding place under the dresser. Kresna rubbed his eyes and yawned. He gulped down a bit of stale coffee that was still on the table. Then he left his office looking for a quieter place to go back to sleep.

38. *Batara* is an honorific for a deity in the language of Javanese literature and performance traditions.
39. The English word is used in Wijaya's text.
40. An important condiment in Javanese cooking.

As soon as he closed the door, the mice resumed their attack. Now it wasn't just one family. The neighbors came along, too. They ransacked the keyboard. They didn't just lick and sniff, they frolicked on the keyboard. The computer went on again—erasing, lengthening, shortening documents. The computer shrieked repeatedly because the mice were hitting the keys so quickly. But Kresna didn't reappear. The animals became more daring.

Batara Narada[41] heard the computer's cries. Surprised, he wondered why Kresna was working so late. He reached anxiously for the phone and tried to get in touch with Kresna.

"Hello, hello, what's happening that's making you work so late?"

"Oh, it's just my assistants. Nothing to worry about."

"But such an uproar."

"I know."

"Is there some new development?"

"Maybe."

"Wait, what do you mean? It's not going to upset our plans? I hope you're going to deal with it."

Narada shook his head. He was sure that half the brain of this incarnation of Wisnu was still dreaming.

"What?"

There was no answer.

"Hello, hello. What's happening?"

"What?"

"What's going on that's causing all this noise in the middle of the night?"

"It's nothing."

"Are you sure?"

"I've thought of everything. Everything's under control."

· ·

The sky that morning was really red. Everyone was shocked. It was as if the earth were wrapped in a glowing dome. The clouds were like drops and clots of blood [spurting] from a person being slaughtered. Little children were crying and didn't want to look up, and the elderly began to make nasty predictions.

On the Amarta-Astina[42] border, the festivities were interrupted. Everyone

41. Messenger of the Hindu pantheon. In the Javanese shadow theatre, Narada is portrayed humorously, as a cross between a god and a clown-servant. In the novel, Narada and the other gods reside in heaven, where they can peer through the clouds to observe what is happening on the human earth below.

42. Amarta-Astina is another way of writing Ngamarta-Ngastina.

looked at the sky suspiciously. They kept asking questions and looking for an-
swers. But nobody around could come up with any news about what had occurred.

Bagong, Petruk, and Gareng looked for [their father] Semar, but he was nowhere in sight. Yudistira[43] gathered his brothers together and got ready in case
something happened. The Korawa did the same. They huddled together, glancing
at the sky while waiting for a word from Suyudana.[44] Suyudana himself was
engrossed in a private meeting with Dorna and Sengkuni.

Kresna had woken up and was already in his office. He studied the computer
screen to check and see what the mice had done in the night. Several documents
were totally ruined. But some new documents had appeared unexpectedly. After
sorting, separating, assembling, and fixing what the mice had done the night
before, Kresna finally came up with something. He was amazed. He was as-
tonished.

At that moment Semar abruptly appeared.

"What's going on here?" asked Semar angrily.

Kresna was surprised.

"Huh?"

Semar shook his head.

"Take a look outside. The sky has gone all funny!"

Kresna opened the window and peered outside. He, too, was shocked to see
how red the sky was. Then he hurried outside to make sure, followed by a
mumbling and grumbling Semar. It was clear. The whole arc of the sky was red.
The color bounced off everything that was around. Even Semar's body was red.
The trees, grass, buildings, the palace, all appeared to be painted red. The world
had suddenly become a big red ball.

"Baginda Yudistira sent me to find out, what does all this mean, my good sir?"

Kresna thought about it.

"Has the Bratayuda begun?"

Kresna still didn't answer. He was busy turning the evidence around in his
mind. Finally he motioned for Semar to follow him inside. Then he sat down at the
computer and went back to work.

"Why has the Bratayuda come so early?" asked Semar accusingly. "It's too
soon."

Kresna examined the computer intently.

43. Yudhistira is the eldest of the Pandhawa brothers and king of Ngamarta.
44. Suyudana, or Duryodana, is the eldest Korawa brother and king of Ngastina.
Dorna and Sengkuni are his major advisers.

"Maybe the Bratayuda doesn't have to occur."

Semar was amazed. He drew near and examined the computer. There were all kinds of codes and formulas on it that he didn't understand. To Semar it all looked like a drawing of a horse.

"It looks like a horse."

"What?"

"Now like ants."

Kresna pressed on the keyboard. Now three figures appeared on the screen.[45]

"Look."

"Who's that?"

"Look carefully."

Semar looked closely. Suddenly he screamed.

"Why it's those little frogs, leave them for a minute and now they're here!"

. . . .

"So they'll be part of the fight when the Bratayuda erupts?"

Kresna smiled.

"The Bratayuda is not going to erupt."

"Why not?"

"Because each person has already fought the war in his/her own mind. You can see the blood. The earth has already received the sacrifice that it wanted. We don't need to fight if there's no longer any reason."

Semar was shocked.

"You mean there won't be a war? Don't put me on."

"It's not necessary, but if you want it, okay. Do you?"

Semar looked at Kresna, feeling discouraged.

"Don't play around with an old man."

Kresna laughed.

"Try to look at the facts. Try to come up with a different interpretation—why did the sky suddenly turn red if it wasn't trying to fulfill the demands that the earth requires. So why do we need a war if the sacrifice has already been performed. Huh?"

Semar shook his head.

"The Bratayuda does not just have value as a sacrifice, but as history. This history will become frozen in human memory in the future as a reminder so that

45. The three figures are Petruk, Gareng, and Bagong, Semar's sons.

there will never again have to be a war between brothers. I think that's the important thing. If this fratricidal war doesn't come off now, the consequences will be worse later."

Kresna nodded.

"Well, if that's the case, don't keep saying that those who want this war are only the kings, but even someone like you; it's precisely people like you who wish for this war."

"Not wish for."

"Then what?"

"See the purpose."

"That's wanting it."

Semar was quiet.

"Isn't that wanting it?"

"That's true, too."

"So it's the same?"

Semar kept quiet. Kresna then turned off the computer.

"Okay, tell Yudistira I'll be there as soon as I bathe and have some breakfast. I'll come quickly. Just wait patiently. Tell him that the Bratayuda isn't going to erupt. The sky has taken on this red glow as a sign of the earth's blood sacrifice. There's no need for more blood to flow. We'll start making peace, not war. The world of the future will have peace, not fratricidal war." Semar appeared doubtful.

"Why are you hesitant?"

Then Semar sat down again to think.

"It would feel better to fight than to repress those feelings like this."

Kresna looked at Semar.

"What do you mean?"

"Yes, I've been examining my own feelings. Peace is good. We all like peace, of course. But how can we have peace if in our hearts we want to fight. Eventually things will appear peaceful but in our hearts we'll feel defeated."

"Then?"

"Yes, then I've been thinking, if it's true that our hearts won't be peaceful, what will the peace be for? Ultimately, it will be a lie."

"So?"

"Yes, so I've concluded, isn't it better just to fight, if indeed from the beginning we wanted to fight, rather than holding it all in like this. Maybe the war won't be as bad as we thought. Maybe it won't be good for each individual, for the family, because some will die and we'll be sad. But really there are already too many people who do too much wailing. But if we remember history, that's important, too. This affair has a lot of meaning. It's like. . . ."

"Like what?"

"I'm afraid to say it."

"Just say it, no one's listening, and you're already thinking it."

"But this isn't my opinion, it's just a passing thought."

"If that's so then just say it."

"But I'm afraid."

"Why?"

"Because it's a dangerous thought to utter."

Kresna smiled.

"I understand. Pak Semar now wants to say that, in fact, this war is a large-scale selection of civilization, of humanity, that will give birth to a new stage of history, that will put the cart-wheel in motion, change the moral center and values, and also give birth to new hope that may be better but could also be worse. Because war is an enactment of a battle maneuver, a conflict, a dispute that has already congealed into enmity and has reached a dead end. Because war is a last road of absolution that is both revered and creates heroes on either side? Because war is a role that exists in a drama along with us that not only takes shape as the result of people's actions but also stands alone and has power outside human authority. Why else, Pak Semar?"

Semar was lost in thought.

"If you search, there are so many reasons. But are they valid?"

Kresna smiled.

"So it's best to fight?"

"Isn't it? So that everything will be complete. Hasn't it been planned for so long?"

Semar himself was startled by those words. Kresna laughed. Suddenly Semar remembered what Petruk had once said. He looked at Kresna keenly.

"What?"

"My child Petruk once said something. Now I've suddenly remembered it. I think it should be considered."

"What did he say?"

Semar kept thinking about it.

"Don't be coy, just say it."

Semar blinked his eyes.

Fictions, Images, and Allegories

The puppets Karna and Semar.

"I didn't pay attention to it then. Now it's come to mind. He said that our enemy wasn't the Korawa and it wasn't ourselves. Our enemy was The Noble One. Sri Kresna."

Kresna nodded.

. . . .

Semar didn't answer. All of a sudden the computer started ringing loudly. Kresna quickly went over to it. He stared intently at what was happening on the screen. Then he quickly went to work. Suddenly white lines appeared on the screen.

Kresna stopped abruptly. After a time he finally turned around.

"Damn, the Bratayuda will erupt in a little while."

But Semar had already left. All you could hear was his grumbling carried along from far away. Kresna went outside and called and called.

"Kakang[46] Semarrrrrrr! Tell them to be careful, the Bratayuda will erupt soon!"

This episode is one among many in Wijaya's book that show his ability to rewrite the shadow tales in humorous, dark, and disturbing ways. Wijaya is playing here with one of the basic characterizations of the shadow theatre tradition: the god-incarnate Kresna as main adviser and

46. Honorific for older male intimates.

friend to the Pandhawa and their loyal clown-servants. Semar and Kresna have always served to lead the Pandhawa to the moment when they will defeat their ignoble cousins in the Bratayuda War. Anderson offered his interpretation of Javanese characterizations of this most most complex of Mahabharata heroes thirty years ago.

> By far the most intellectually brilliant of the Pendawa faction, it is Kresna who makes their final victory possible. On the other hand, he is a conscienceless liar and an unscrupulous schemer who never hesitates to break the rules when he feels it necessary. Though a *satrya* [warrior-king], he repeatedly ignores the lesser values of the *satrya* class. Only the duty to carry out the will of the gods and his own destiny claim his allegiance. . . . In the long struggle between Kurawa and Pendawa, both sides use treachery and cunning. Only Kresna, however, wins approval since his ultimate aims accord with the will of the gods to destroy the Kurawa and since he himself is of divine origin, these factors make his actions appropriate.[47]

But Wijaya is questioning Kresna's intentions in arguing for the necessity of war, especially a war between brothers. Even more startling, Wijaya is questioning Kresna's age-old exemption from the *satriya* code because of his divine origins. If the will of the gods calls for devastating human sacrifice, maybe it is the gods who must be disregarded or discarded. Wijaya is imagining a future—is telling a Mahabharata tale that spills over and blurs the boundaries between myth and history—that envisions a history in which the Bratayuda War might not have to happen. Wijaya is placing his retelling of this story outside those powerful thought-lines of the *wayang* tradition that Pramoedya identified. Rather than being constituted as a subject of the *wayang*, Wijaya has subjected the *wayang* to his own fertile imagination.

Afterthoughts: Allegory, Myth, and History

She who knows she cannot speak of them without speaking of herself, of history without involving her story, also knows that she cannot make a gesture without activating the to-and-fro movement of life.[48]—Trinh T. Minh-ha

47. Anderson, *Mythology and the Tolerance of the Javanese*, p. 14.
48. Trinh T. Minh-ha, *When the Moon Waxes Red: Representation, Gender and Cultural Politics* (New York: Routledge, 1991), p. 76.

Fictions, Images, and Allegories

My analysis of Javanese Ramayana and Mahabharata stories has initiated an intellectual journey: by representing the possibilities that exist within the technologies of Javanese performance traditions, I have taken my readers for a turn upon the stage. Often at shadow play performances I attended in Java, the puppeteer might choose to comment on my presence at the life-cycle ritual—for most performances are celebrations of births, deaths, weddings, and other liminal moments that remind people of their mortality. And almost always the puppeteers did not just comment on the fact that a foreigner was there trying to understand a Javanese dramatic genre. The puppeteers also took the opportunity to praise this effort at cross-cultural understanding, to chide the Javanese for not taking a greater interest in their own performance traditions, and to express a bit of surprise that the most powerful country in the world would send people to Java to learn its language and arts. At that moment, the academic institutions that enabled my research entered the world of the performance just as those performances have here entered the world of academia.

Puta Wijaya came to the University of Wisconsin on a Fulbright grant in 1985 when I was writing up the results of my research. As he was devouring American culture, he found it humorous and quaint that I and other Americans were so touched by our experiences in Indonesia that we spent hours playing and listening to *gamelan* and other Indonesian musics, smoked Indonesian clove cigarettes, cooked Indonesian foods, and often disdained the kaleidoscope of American culture that surrounded us. Wijaya read the shadow-play story collections of the Javanese documentation project that I conceived and headed in Solo from 1983–84; the resulting research had been written down and published under the auspices of the Solonese Academy and the Ford Foundation.[49] Being a Balinese who had lived in both Yogyakarta and Jakarta for many years, and who had spent time in Japan and America, his knowledge of the Javanese shadow theatre was enriched by Balinese performances of the stories that he had seen in his youth, Indicized tellings he had read in Jakarta comic books, and Javanese renderings he had seen through the performances of both human and puppet theatres in Central and West Java.

Putu Wijaya wrote a novel about the Javanese shadow theatre while he was living in Madison, Wisconsin, and some of the inspiration for that book was gleaned from research carried out by foreigners in his own

49. See Feinstein et al., ed., *Lakon Carangan*, vols. 1–3.

country. In turn, I have examined how Wijaya has reshaped these ancient stories and characters into his works of contemporary fiction. As I have read Wijaya's novels, I have also been gently coerced to take part in several presentations of his performance art. When in Jakarta in 1990, my daughter and I went with Wijaya and his wife to watch imported Japanese dramas as well as Javanese Mahabharata plays; in midwest America we went to movies and garage sales.[50] I cite these incidents to show the intricate interweavings of Indonesian and American cultural worlds and how these worlds enter into and out of academic environments. Who is the participant and who the observer? Who is observing whom and for what purpose? If I have constituted Wijaya as a subject in this study of the thickly layered mythologies that make up the world of Javanese narrative traditions, he has created me as the subject and object of the tales he tells, as audience and performer of the plays he directs. These observations illustrate one of the main themes of this work: the interweaving of mythologies and histories in the changing stories that Javanese performers and writers, and non-Javanese scholars, tell about the past.

In several chapters of this work I have proposed the beginning of a new mythical cycle in the late eighteenth century; this is when the Dutch began to appear in Javanese histories and mythologies as the only ones who could prevent Javanese fratricide. But the price of putting off the fratricidal Bratayuda War was a division of the Javanese realm and eventually a division between Occident and Orient, a division between colonialism and culture, and Islam and *adat*. The New Order regime of Soeharto and the Indonesian Army have taken over the Dutch myths of empire; they have become the ones who can prevent Javanese fratricide and they need only point to the internecine strife in the Javanese countryside in 1965–66 to illustrate their point. By imagining a telling of Mahabharata stories in which the Bratayuda War does not have to take place or by imagining a telling of Ramayana stories in which Rahwana kills Wibisana, Indonesian authors may be marking the beginning of new mythical cycles in the constellation of Javanese tales.

This book has argued that Javanese Mahabharata and Ramayana traditions, specifically as they have converged with and been represented in the *wayang purwa* performed in the villages surrounding the Central Java-

---

50. Wijaya used to be the drama reviewer for *Tempo* before it was banned.

Fictions, Images, and Allegories

nese court city of Solo, rather than ever-changing collections of mythical stories, should be seen as allegorical commentaries on life and literature as well as strategies for living. Perhaps the suggestion that *wayang* tales are allegories rather than myths is just another move in a postcolonial imperialist mode of description—the description that Aijaz Ahmad argued was part of the machinery of colonial rule.

To see Javanese Ramayana and Mahabharata tales as allegories argues that they are a language of politics and a praxis of history. The tales encode and interpret events, situating those events in the lives of both tellers and hearers of the stories. I have argued that these tellers and hearers of the stories have formed textual communities, communities whose members include those who pass on the stories in village performances and in scholarly texts. These and other sites of inscription have interacted over the centuries, producing, during the period of colonial domination, performance styles that appealed to hybrid audiences of Dutch scholars and Javanese elites as well as the uninvited guests of each shadow theatre event, the villagers or subaltern city dwellers who are usually the most attentive listeners to the allegorical commentary of the shadow puppeteers.

The main focus of this book has been the intersection of Ramayana and Mahabharata tales with a storytelling mechanism that requires puppets, puppeteers, musicians, singers, and a banana-log stage. This intersection that found expression in Javanese *wayang* theatre reveals few signs of losing its appeal to urban and rural audiences, who are among the poorest members of the consumer society of postcolonial Indonesia. But other audiences require new vehicles for their Ramayana and Mahabharata tales. These new vehicles may mark disruptions and displacements of form and content in *wayang* tales as allegories, as Scholem has observed:

Indeed the allegory arises, as it were, from the gap which at this point opens between the form and its meaning. The two are no longer indissolubly welded together; the meaning is no longer restricted to that particular form, nor the form any longer to that particular meaningful content. What appears in the allegory, in short, is the infinity of meaning which attaches to every representation.[51]

This book has argued that Javanese Mahabharata and Ramayana stories as allegories were for a time intricately interlaced with shadow theatre

51. Gershom Scholem as quoted in Susan Buck-Morss, *The Dialectics of Seeing*, p. 236.

apparatuses and poetic texts. But today in Java, as the boundaries between region and postcolonial state continue to blur, these stories are filling and opening up new Indonesian contexts in novels, romances, comics, and electronic representations. The form, shadow theatre, and its content, the Ramayana and Mahabharata stories, are no longer, and they never were, indissolubly welded together. Scholem's idealist association of form and meaning has fractured in the postmodern world. Scholem's friend Walter Benjamin may have come closer to describing this transformation.

The allegoricist reaches now here, now there, into the chaotic depths that his knowledge places at his disposal, grabs an item out, holds it next to another, and sees whether they fit; that meaning to this image, or this image to that meaning. The result never lets itself be predicted; for there is no natural mediation between the two.[52]

In Benjamin's view, form and meaning are always arbitrary, never predictable. Form and meaning still interact, but new meanings are continually woven into all "traditions," and new forms generate unpredictable stories for new audiences. If one set of "meanings" of Javanese *wayang* traditions is located in the stories, and these stories are allegories whose meanings can never be fixed, are always unpredictable, then *wayang* can no longer be seen as a meaning-full essence of "Java." *Wayang* tales and the shadow theatre performances that convey them are always already empty, waiting to be filled again and again by the voices of new storytellers.

The feminist Marxist critic Gayatri Spivak has questioned whether the subaltern can ever speak. In her focus on what she calls the subaltern third-world woman, she has even been hesitant to give the status of "subject" to this figure.[53] Spivak presents the third-world woman as a subject-effect, a blur, shuttling back and forth between or among her sites of oppression. Yet Indonesian writer Leila Chudori, questioning Sita's role as the ever dutiful and faithful wife, imagines a Ramayana in which Sita

---

52. Quoted in ibid., p. 241.

53. See Gayatri Spivak, "Can the Subaltern Speak?" in *Marxism and the Interpretation of Culture*, ed. Cary Nelson and Lawrence Grossberg (Urbana: University of Illinois Press, 1988), for her discussion of subaltern subjects, and L. Sears, "Fragile Identities: Deconstructing Women and Indonesia," in *Fantasizing the Feminine in Indonesia* (Durham: Duke University Press, 1995), for a different look at subaltern postcolonial subjects.

Fictions, Images, and Allegories

doubts Rama's fidelity to *her* during the long years of their separation.[54] I certainly am aware of the pitfalls of assuming that Javanese or Indonesian subaltern subjects have some measure of agency in a postcolonial society that absorbs, reconfigures, and spits out for consumption everything that falls in its path. This book, however, has suggested that the subaltern is always speaking. The problem and challenge for postcolonial intellectuals—whether they have inherited the subject position of colonizers or that of the colonized—is how to listen when the subaltern speaks. By listening for the voices of these speakers, one may catch the traces or even glimpse the faces of the storytellers who cling to the stories.

54. Chudori read "The Purification of Sita" in Seattle in June 1991 at the Social Science Research Council and American Council of Learned Societies workshop titled "Perspectives on Gender in Indonesia."

Selected Glossary

abangan - Lit., red. Term for those Javanese who follow Javano-Islamic practices.

Abiyasa (Skt, Vyasa) - Grandfather of the Pandhawa and Korawa in Javanese tellings of Mahabharata stories.

ada-ada - Type of *suluk* used in shadow play performances to build excitement.

adat - Customary law.

adiluhung - Term used today to refer to what is believed to be high or "traditional" Javanese culture.

Alap-alapan Sukesi - Shadow play story of Rahwana's birth.

alus - Refined.

Ardjoeno - Dutch spelling of shadow play character Arjuna.

Arjuna (Skt and modern Indonesian) - Middle brother of the five Pandhawa brothers, major shadow play character; refined hero of Mahabharata cycle. Also known as Janaka.

Arjunawijaya - Poems in Old Javanese and modern Javanese of the Arjunasasrabahu story.

ASKI - Akademi Seni Karawitan Indonesia—older name for the Academy of Javanese Performing Arts in Solo. See STSI.

babad - Lit., to clear the forest. Javanese term for chronicle or historical text.

baku - Main part; stable shadow play story.

bangsa - Family, group, or nation.

Batara Guru - Another name for the god Siwa.

Bima (Skt, Bhima) - Second eldest of the five Pandhawa brothers; major shadow play character. Also known as Werkadara.

blencong - Oil lamp or electric light-bulb used to illuminate the shadows on the white cotton screen in a shadow play performance.

bobot - Weighty; important.

Bratayuda (Skt, Bharatayuddha) - The Great War between the Pandhawa and Korawa over the rights to the kingdom of Ngastina.

bupati - Regent. Highest Javanese official in Java except for the Sunan, the Sultan, the Mangkunagaran, and the Paku Alaman.

Cakil - Small ogre character, who fights with a refined hero in most shadow puppet plays or human plays using *wayang* stories.

cultuurstelsel - The system of forced cultivation imposed on Javanese farmers from 1830 until about 1870 to make the colonies profitable for the Dutch.

carangan - Branch; shadow play story often considered to lead away from the main story line of Javanese tellings of Mahabharata and Ramayana stories.

deleg - Trunk; stable shadow play story.

desa - Rural areas of Java.

Dewaruci - Shadow play *lakon* about Bima's search for mystical knowledge; the miniature god, in Bima's own image, who reveals the mystical knowledge to Bima.

dhalang - Javanese puppeteer or dance master.

Drupadi (Skt, Draupadi) - Wife of Yudhistira, eldest of the five Pandhawa brothers in Javanese Mahabharata stories.

gamelan - Javanese bronze gong ensemble that accompanies shadow play performances.

gender - Metallophone musical instrument that is essential in most *gamelan* ensembles; most important instrument in contemporary *gamelan* ensembles that accompany *wayang* performances.

gendhing - Orchestral compositions performed by the Javanese *gamelan* ensemble.

Guru - Batara Guru, Javanese name for the Indian god Siwa; also a Javanese word for teacher.

hadith or *hadits* (Ar., *hadith*) - Oral traditions about the life of the Prophet with genealogies leading back to the days when the Prophet was alive or to the period right after his death.

haji - Title reserved for those Muslims who have made the pilgrimage to Mecca.

inlander - Dutch word for Indies native.

jarwa dhosok - Javanese folk etymolo-

gies that are essential to all *wayang* plays.

janturan - Opening formulaic passages of shadow play stories in rhythmic prose describing the glories of the kingdom where the action is going to take place.

jejer - Standing; can refer to audience-hall scenes in *wayang* performances and can be used to describe the more stable *wayang lakon*.

Jogjakarta (also Jogja, Yogya, Yogyakarta) - Famous court city in Central Java.

Kaikesi - Sanskrit name for Sukesi in the Old Javanese *Arjunawijaya*.

kakawin (Skt, *kavya*) - Poetry in Old Javanese, dating back to the ninth century C.E., drawing its themes from Ramayana and Mahabharata tales.

Kala - Demon son of Barata Guru who figures prominently in *ruwatan* performances of the Murwakala story.

Karna - Older brother of the five Pandhawa heroes, born from the union of Dewi Kunti and the Sun God Surya before Dewi Kunti was married. He is abandoned by his mother and, as a young man, becomes a loyal supporter of the Korawa. He is destined to fight his half-brother Arjuna in the Bratayuda War.

kasar - Coarse or rough.

kavya - Sanskrit court poetry dating back to at least the fourth century C.E.

kavi (Skt) - Poet.

Kawi, *kawi* - Old Javanese language;

Selected Glossary

poet in ancient Java. Archaic literary Javanese.

kawi jarwa - Poetic language used in the late eighteenth- and early nineteenth-century reworkings of Old Javanese poetry.

kawi miring - Slanting *kawi*; modern Javanese poetry in *sekar ageng* meters, which were renderings of the Old Javanese poetry.

kebathinan - Javanese mysticism.

ki or *kyai* - Term used to refer to respected Islamic teachers or shadow puppeteers.

kidung - Old and Middle Javanese poetic texts written in indigenous rather than Sanskritic meters.

Kilat Buwana - Famous branch story about a mysterious priest who comes to Ngastina with a plan to resolve the conflict between the Pandhawa and the Korawa and cancel the Bratayuda War.

Korawa - The ninety-nine sons and one daughter of King Destarata; cousins and archrivals of the Pandhawa.

krama - Polite or high register of modern Javanese language.

kraton (or Kraton as part of proper name) - Palace or residence of the *ratu*, king or queen.

Kresna (Skt, Krishna) - King of Dwarawati; friend and adviser of the Pandhawa heroes in Mahabharata tales.

Kumbakarno - Brother of Rahwana; largest Javanese shadow puppet.

kyai or *ki* - Term used to refer to respected Islamic teachers or shadow puppeteers.

lakon - Story arranged for dramatic

purposes according to certain conventions; plot.

laku - Ascetic exercise undertaken to gain special powers.

Lokapala - Kingdom of Wisrawa, Dhanapati, and Arjunasasrabahu, who finally defeats the demon Rahwana.

lapan - A period of thirty-five days in Javanese calendrical systems by which Javanese reckon their Javanese "birthdays."

macapat - Modern Javanese sung poetry in indigenous metres.

Mahabharata - A pan-Asian cycle of stories dating back to ca. 400 B.C.E. which tells of the events leading up to and including the Bratayuda War between the five Pandhawa brothers and their cousins, the ninety-nine Korawa, over the rights to the kingdom of Ngastina. The stories are known in countless oral and written tellings throughout South and Southeast Asia.

malihan (from the Jav. verb *alih*, to change) - Generally used to refer to a character in a Javanese shadow play who is disguised as someone else. At the end of the play, the character's original identity is revealed. Often an ogre character can be a *malihan* for one of the gods, and vice versa.

mantra - Recitation of holy words or syllables for mystical purposes.

mukmin (Ar.) - A devout follower of Islam.

Murwakala - Birth of Kala; story used in *ruwatan* performances.

Ngalengka - Kingdom of Sumali and Sukesi; kingdom of Rahwana.

Ngamarta (also Amarta; Skt, Indra-prastha) - Kingdom of Yudhistira; eldest of the Pandhawa brothers.

Ngastina (also Astina; Skt, Hastina-pura) - Kingdom of Kurupati (Duryudana); eldest of the ninety-nine Korawa brothers.

ngelmu (Ar., *'ilm*) - Knowledge or se-cret teachings.

nges - Significant; interesting.

ngoko - Low or familiar register of modern Javanese language.

ni or *nyai* - Wife of a *kyai*; term for older respected rural women; mis-tress, usually of a Dutchman.

opvoeding - Dutch word for upbring-ing or education.

padat - Lit., condensed; style of shadow play performance devel-oped at the Academy in Solo.

pakem - (1) The core images of a shadow play story; (2) plot out-line or play scenario; (3) the per-formance style of a puppeteer or a village area.

panakawan - The misshapen clown-servants of Javanese dramatic genres.

Pancasila - The Five Principles that undergird the Constitution of the Indonesian state.

Pandhawa - The five sons of Pandu who are the heroes of the Maha-bharata stories.

pangling - To meet people one knows and not recognize them.

pangreh praja - Dutch-controlled Java-nese administrative corps during the colonial period.

pangruwating diyu - The exorcism of ogre characters.

parwa - Late tenth-century prose texts of Mahabharata stories in Old Javanese, interspersed with San-skrit *sloka*.

pasemon - Allusion; type of shadow play where events in the story mirror events in everyday life or court intrigues.

pasisir - The north coast areas of Java.

pathet - Musical mode, three of which are used in *wayang* performances.

pathetan - Type of *suluk* or song used in shadow puppet plays.

pesindhen - Female singer in the *game-lan* ensemble that accompanies shadow play performances.

pesantren or *pondhok* - Rural Islamic schools.

pokok - Essential; main.

prampogan - Marching army shadow play puppet.

priyayi - Javanese bureaucratic class who often worked with the Dutch in colonial times; white-collar class in postcolonial Java.

pujangga - Javanese court poet or per-son of letters, occasionally be-lieved to have prophetic powers.

purana - Collections of Sanskrit tales that followed the Ramayana and Mahabharata or expanded the stories.

pusaka - Heirloom, usually in the form of a weapon, believed to have magical or sacred powers; occasionally a text, a *gamelan*, or a set of *wayang* puppets.

pusing (Ind.) - Dizzy; headache.

Pustaka Raja Purwa - Book of Kings, written by Ranggawarsita in the mid-nineteenth century, telling a

Selected Glossary

history of Java from Nabi Adam to the historical Javanese kings. Many inscriptions of Pustaka Raja Purwa texts exist in libraries and private collections in Java.

putihan (or *poetihan*) - Term for those Javanese who adhere to strict Islamic practices.

Ramayana - A pan-Asian story cycle, dating from ca. 200 B.C.E., about the noble prince Rama whose wife Sita is stolen by the demon king Rahwana. The stories are known in countless oral and written tellings throughout South and Southeast Asia.

raksasa - Ogres or demons in Javanese dramatic genres.

rame - Lively, noisy, bustling—and thus, to Javanese, enjoyable.

Ranggawarsita, R. Ng. - Nineteenth-century court poet—grandson of Yasadipura II—and author of the *Pustaka Raja Purwa*, or Book of Kings, among many other writings. He is also revered as a prophet of the *zaman edan* (era of madness).

rasa - Mood or sentiment created by the interplay of character, poetry, and music in Javanese theatrical traditions; taste or feeling.

Rahwana (Skt, Ravana) - Demon son of Wisrawa and Sukesi; heroic villain of the Arjunasasrabahu and the Ramayana story cycles.

rebab - Three-stringed Javanese musical instrument.

Rebo Legi - Wednesday *Legi*; a day in the Javanese month; the Javanese "birthday" of the famous puppeteer Ki Anom Suroto.

ringgit - Krama or high Javanese word for *wayang*.

ringkas - Traditional shortened style of *wayang* play preserving plot and musical structure.

ruwatan - Exorcistic shadow play performances.

sangkala - Chronograms used for dating Javanese texts and *wayang* puppets.

Sanskrit - Indian literary language used frequently for religious, poetic, and dramatic texts. Language of ancient inscriptions in South and Southeast Asia.

santri - One who strictly follows Islamic teachings. In earlier times the term indicated a student or seeker of Islamic mystical knowledge.

sastrajendra - Esoteric mystical teaching.

sastrajendrayuningrat - Sastrajendra; esoteric mystical teaching.

sekar ageng - Large or high poetic metres that preserved the metres of the Old Javanese prosody.

Semar - Clown servant to Pandhawa heroes; in reality the god Ismaya, older brother of Batara Guru (Siwa).

semu - Tinged with or colored by. The word also connotes something hidden or concealed.

sendhon - Type of *suluk* or song used in shadow play performances; lyrical emotional verses.

Serat Cabolek - Eighteenth-century *macapat* text attributed to Yasadipura I.

Serat Kandha - Books of Tales dating from the *pasisir* period (ca. six-

teenth and seventeenth centuries), in both *macapat* and prose
versions.

Serat Lokapala - *Macapat* text of the Arjunasasrabahu story, written by
the court poet Sindusastra in the
mid-nineteenth century.

Serat Sastramiruda - Late nineteenth-
century text written by B.K.P.
Kusumadilaga which set standards for court and village dramatic performances.

shariat (Ar., *shari'a*) - Outward rules
for the practice of Islamic law and
behavior.

Siwa (Skt, Shiva) - One of the highest gods in Javanese mythology;
also said to be the younger
brother of Semar in *wayang* lore.

śloka - Two lines of Sanskrit poetry of
sixteen syllables each, which is
the metre of the Sanskrit Mahabharata and Ramayana texts.

SMKI - Sekolah Menengah Konser-
vatori Indonesia—the high school
of the performing arts in Solo.

Solo - Famous court city in Central
Java—also known as Surakarta.

Soeharto - Indonesian general and
second and present president of
the Indonesian state.

Soekarno - Nationalist leader during
the colonial period and independent Indonesia's first president.

STSI -Sekolah Tinggi Seni Indonesia—present name for the Academy of Javanese Performing Arts
in Solo, formerly called the Akademi Seni Karawitan Indonesia.

Sufi - One who practices unorthodox
mystical traditions of Islam.

Sufism - Unorthodox mystical tradition of Islam.

Sukesi (Skt, Kaikesi) - Daughter of
the *raksasa* king Sumali of Ngalengka, from the Arjunasasrabahu
cycle of stories.

suluk - Lyrical songs sung by the
puppeteer to establish mood in
shadow play performances. Also
a genre of Islamic mystical
poems, usually in *macapat* verse.

Sunan or Susuhunan - Title for the
rulers of Solo, as opposed to the
use of *Sultan* in Yogya. Originally
used for Islamic saints; the literal
meaning is "respected one."

Sumali - *Raksasa* king of Ngalengka
and father of Sukesi in Arjunasasrabahu stories.

Sumbadra (Skt, Subhadra) - Refined
wife of Arjuna in Javanese literature and drama.

Surakarta - Famous court city in Central Java—also known as Solo.

Surpanaka - Demon sister of Rahwana, Kumbakarna, and Wibisana. Child of Wisrawa and
Sukesi.

Mpu Tantular - Fourteenth-century
Javanese author of the Arjunawijaya *kakawin*.

tariqat - Paths or schools of Sufi or
esoteric Islamic teachings.

tayuban or *taledhekan* - A rowdy dance
party featuring young male or female dancers for hire that was
popular for centuries in many
parts of Java.

tinandhing - To be matched (in battle).

ulama (plural of Ar., *'alim*) - Those
learned in Islamic religion.

urip - Alive.

Uttara Kandha - The last book of the

Selected Glossary

Sanskrit Ramayana, which scholars believe to be a later addition to the work.

Valmiki - Mythical author of the Sanskrit Ramayana.

voc - Verenigde Oost-Indische Compagnie or United East Indies Company. Dutch trading company in the Indies from 1602 to 1799.

Vyasa (Sanskrit for Abiyasa) - Grandfather of the Pandava (Pandhawa and Kaurava (Korawa).

wadhah - Vessel.

wahyu (Ar., *wahy'*) - Boon, sometimes in the form of radiant light, from the gods that usually conveys mystical knowledge or temporal power.

wanda - Different shadow puppet representations of the same character in different moods or different stages of life.

wali - The nine mythological saints, known for their spiritual and mystical powers, who supposedly brought Islam to Java.

waton - Convention.

wayang - Lit., shadow. Javanese marker of dramatic genres.

wayang kulit - Leather shadow; shadow puppet theatre.

wayang orang - Indonesian language term for commercial Javanese theatrical tradition modeled after the shadow puppet theatre but using human actors.

wayang purwa - Shadow play repertoire that uses stories based on Ramayana and Mahabharata stories as well as indigenous exorcistic plays.

wayang wong - Javanese theatrical tradition nurtured in the courts of Solo and Yogya modeled after the shadow puppet theatre but using human actors.

Wederopbouw - Lit., reconstruction. The name of a Javanese nationalist periodical.

Wibisana (Skt, Vibishana) - Noble brother of the demons Rahwana, Kumbakarna, and Surpanaka; child of Wisrawa and Sukesi.

wiji - Seed.

Wisnu (Skt, Vishnu) - One of the major gods in the *wayang purwa* stories.

Wisrawa (Skt, Vishravas) - Father of Dhanapati, king of Lokapala, who marries Sukesi in the Arjunasasrabahu cycle of stories.

wong cilik - Lit., little people; the Javanese folk.

Yasadipura I - Eighteenth-century court poet known for his modern Javanese poetic works.

Yasadipura II - Nineteenth-century court poet known for his modern Javanese poetic works; son of Yasadipura I.

Yogyakarta (also Yogya, Jogja, Jogjakarta) - Famous court city in Central Java.

Yudhistira (Skt, Yudhisthira) - Eldest of the Pandhawa brothers and king of Ngamarta in *Mahabharata* tales.

Selected Bibliography

Abu Hanifah. *Tales of a Revolution*. Sydney: Angus & Robertson, 1972.

Adams, C. *Sukarno: An Autobiography As Told to Cindy Adams*. New York: Bobbs-Merrill, 1965.

———. *My Friend the Dictator*. New York: Bobbs-Merrill, 1967.

Adamson, W. L. *Hegemony and Revolution: A Study of Antonio Gramsci's Political and Cultural Theory*. Berkeley: University of California Press, 1980.

Adas, M. "The Great War and the Decline of the Civilizing Mission." In *Autonomous Histories, Particular Truths: Essays in Honor of John R. W. Smail*, ed. Laurie J. Sears, pp. 101–21.

Adorno, T. W. *Philosophy of Modern Music*. Trans. A. G. Mitchell and W. V. Blomster. New York and London, 1973.

———. *Prisms*. Trans. Samuel and Shierry Weber. 1967. Cambridge: MIT Press, 1981.

Adorno, T. W., and Max Horkheimer. *The Dialectic of Enlightenment*. New York: Continuum Publishing Company, 1972.

Adorno, T. W., W. Benjamin, E. Bloch, B. Brecht, G. Lukacs. *Aesthetics and Politics*. 1977. London: Verso, 1980.

Ahmad, Aijaz. "Jameson's Rhetoric of Otherness and the 'National Allegory.'" *Social Text* 17 (Fall 1987).

———. *In Theory: Classes, Literatures, Nations*. London: Verso, 1992.

H. Ahmad Muhsin. *Perang Tipu Daya antara Bung Karno dengan Tokoh-Tokoh Komunis*. Jakarta: Golden Terayon Press, 1989.

Althusser, L. "Ideology and Ideological State Apparatuses." In *Lenin and Philosophy*, trans. Ben Brewster. New York: Monthly Review Press, 1971.

Ambary, H. M. "Epigraphical Data from 17th–19th Century Muslim Graves in East Java." In *Cultural Contact and Textual Interpretation*, ed. C. D. Grijns and S. O. Robson. Dordrecht: Foris Publications, 1986.

Anderson, B.R.O'G. *Mythology and the Tolerance of the Javanese*. Ithaca: Cornell Modern Indonesia Project, 1965.

———. "The Last Picture Show: Wayang Beber." In *Proceedings of the Conference on Modern Indonesian Literature*, ed. J. Taylor. Madison: University of Wisconsin Center for Southeast Asian Studies, 1974.

———. "The Idea of Power in Javanese Culture" [1972]. In *Language and Power: Exploring Political Cultures in Indonesia*. Ithaca: Cornell University Press, 1990.

———. "The Languages of Indonesian Politics" [1966]. In *Language and Power: Exploring Political Cultures in Indonesia*. Ithaca: Cornell University Press, 1990.

———. "*Sembah-Sumpah*: The Politics of Language and Javanese Culture" [1984]. In *Language and Power: Exploring Political Cultures in Indonesia*. Ithaca: Cornell University Press, 1990.

————. *Imagined Communities*. Rev. ed. London: Verso, 1991.

Appadurai, A., F. Korom, and M. Mills, eds. *Gender, Genre, and Power in South Asian Expressive Traditions*. Philadelphia: University of Pennsylvania Press, 1991.

Arps, B. "Volkstradities en instituties in het middenjavaanse wayangtheater." In *Theater op Java*, ed. C. P. Eskamp. Zutphen: de Walberg Pers, 1985.

————. "Sekar Ageng: Over Antieke Javaanse Versvormen." Unpublished master's thesis, Leiden University, 1986.

————. *Tembang in Two Traditions: Performance and Interpretation of Javanese Literature*. London: School of Oriental and African Studies, 1992.

————, ed. *Performance in Java and Bali: Studies of Narrative, Theatre, Music, and Dance*. London: University of London School of Oriental and African Studies, 1993.

Austin, J. L. *How to Do Things with Words*. New York: Oxford University Press, 1962.

Babcock, B. A. "The Story in the Story: Metanarration in Folk Narrative." In *Verbal Art as Performance*, by Richard Bauman. 1977.

Bakhtin, M. M. *The Dialogic Imagination*. Trans. C. Emerson and M. Holquist. Ed. M. Holquist. Austin: University of Texas Press, 1981.

Balfas, M. *Dr. Tjipto Mangoenkoesoemo: Demokrat sedjati*. 1952. Jakarta: Penerbit Djambatan, 1957.

Barthes, R. "From Work to Text." In *Textual Strategies: Perspectives in Post-Structuralist Criticism*, ed. J. V. Harari. Ithaca: Cornell University Press, 1979.

Barzun, J. *Classic, Romantic and Modern*. 1961. Chicago: University of Chicago Press, 1975.

Bauman, R. *Verbal Art as Performance*. Prospect Heights, Illinois: Waveland Press, 1977.

————. *Story, Performance, and Event: Contextual Studies of Oral Narrative*. Cambridge: Cambridge University Press, 1986.

Bauman, R., and C. L. Briggs. "Poetics and Performance as Critical Perspectives on Language and Social Life." *Annual Reviews of Anthropology* 19 (1990): 59–88.

Bauman, R., and J. Sherzer, eds. *Explorations in the Ethnography of Speaking*. New York: Cambridge University Press, 1974.

Becker, A. L. "Text-Building, Epistemology, and Aesthetics in Javanese Shadow Theatre." In *The Imagination of Reality*, ed. A. L. Becker and A. A. Yengoyan. Norwood, N.J.: Ablex, 1979.

————, ed. *Writing on the Tongue*. Michigan Papers on South and Southeast Asia, no. 33. Ann Arbor: University of Michigan Center for South and Southeast Asian Studies, 1989.

Becker, J. *Gamelan Stories: Tantrism, Islam, and Aesthetics in Central Java*. Arizona State University Monographs in Southeast Asian Studies. Phoenix, 1993.

Behrend, T. E. "The Serat Jatiswara: Structure and Change in a Javanese Poem, 1600–1930." Ph.D. diss., Australian National University, 1987.

Benda, H. *The Crescent and the Rising Sun*. The Hague: W. van Hoeve, 1958.

Benjamin, W. *Illuminations*. New York: Schocken, 1969.

————. *Reflections*. New York: Schocken, 1986.

Selected Bibliography

Bennett, T. *Outside Literature*. London: Routledge, 1990.

Berg, C. C. "Javaansche Geschiedschrijving." In *Geschiedenis van Nederlandsch Indie*, part 2, ed. F. W. Stapel. Amsterdam, 1938.

———. "The Javanese Picture of the Past." In *An Introduction to Indonesian Historiography*, ed. Soedjatmoko. Ithaca: Cornell University Press, 1965.

Besant, A. *The Masters*. Adyar, Madras: Theosophical Publishing House, 1912.

Bhabha, Homi. "Signs Taken for Wonders: Questions of Ambivalence and Authority under a Tree outside Delhi, May 1817." In *"Race," Writing, and Difference*, ed. Henry Louis Gates, Jr. Chicago: University of Chicago Press, 1985.

———. "Remembering Fanon: Self, Psyche, and the Colonial Condition." In *Remaking History*, ed. Barbara Kruger and Phil Mariani. Seattle: Bay Press, 1989.

———, ed. *Nation and Narration*. New York: Routledge, 1991.

Blackburn, S. H. "Epic Transmission and Adaptation: A Folk Ramayana in South India." In *Boundaries of the Text*, ed. J. B. Flueckiger and L. J. Sears. 1991.

Blackburn, S. H., et al., eds. *Oral Epics in India*. Berkeley: University of California Press, 1989.

Blavatsky, H. *An Abridgement of the Secret Doctrine*. London: Theosophical Publishing House, 1966.

Bonneff, M. "Ki Ageng Suryomentaraman, Javanese Prince and Philosopher (1892–1962)." *Indonesia* 57 (1994): 49–70. Originally published in *Archipel* 16 (1978): 175–203.

Bosch, F.D.K. "The Problem of the Hindu Colonisation of Indonesia" [1946]. In *Selected Studies in Indonesian Archaeology*. KITLV Translation Series, 3. The Hague: M. Nijhoff, 1961.

Bourdieu, P. *Language and Symbolic Power*. Cambridge: Harvard University Press, 1991.

Brandes, J.L.A. "Een Jayapattra of Acte van een Rechterlijke Uitspraak van Çaka 849." *Tijdschrift Voor Indische Taal-, Land- en Volkenkunde* uitgegeven door het Bataviaasch Genootschap voor Kunsten en Wetenschappen 32 (1889): 123–24.

———. "Pararaton (Ken Arok) Tweede druk bewerkt door N. J. Krom." *Verhandelingen van het Bataviaasch Genootschap van Kunsten en Wetenschappen* 62 (1920): 112–16.

———, ed. and trans. *Pararaton (Ken Arok) of het boek der koningen van Tumapel en van Majapahit*. 2d ed. Ed. N. J. Krom. *Verhandelingen van het Bataviaaasch Genootschap van Kunsten en Wetenschappen* 62 (1920).

Brandon, J. R. *On Thrones of Gold*. Cambridge: Harvard University Press, 1970.

Brantlinger, P. *Crusoe's Footprints: Cultural Studies in Britain and America*. New York: Routledge, 1990.

Braudel, F. "Histoire et sciences sociales: La longue durée." *Annales E.S.C.* 13 (1958): 725–53.

Bruner, E. M. "Introduction: The Opening Up of Anthropology." In *Text, Play, and Story: The Construction and Reconstruction of Self and Society*, ed. E. M. Bruner. Washington, D.C.: The American Ethnological Society, 1984.

Buck-Morss, S. *The Dialectics of Seeing: Walter Benjamin and the Arcades Project.* Cambridge: MIT Press, 1989.

Buitenen, J.A.B. van. *Two Plays of Ancient India.* New York: Columbia University Press, 1968.

———. *The Mahabharata.* 3 vols. Chicago: University of Chicago Press, 1973–78.

Carey, P.B.R. *The Cultural Ecology of Early Nineteenth Century Java.* Occasional Paper, no. 24. Singapore: Institute of Southeast Asian Studies, 1974.

———. "The Role of *Wayang* in the Dipanagara War." *Prisma* 7 (1977): 15–27.

———. *The Archive of Yogyakarta.* Vol. 1. London: Oxford University Press for the British Academy, 1980.

———. "Aspects of Javanese History in the Nineteenth Century." In *The Development of Indonesian Society,* ed. Harry Aveling. New York: St. Martin's Press, 1980.

Casparis, J. G. de. *Prasasti Indonesia II: Selected Inscriptions from the 7th to the 9th Century A.D.* Bandung: Dinas Purbakala Republik Indonesia, 1956.

Castles, L. "Notes on the Islamic School at Gontor." *Indonesia* 1 (April 1966): 30–45.

Certeau, M. de. *Heterologies: Discourse on the Other.* Minneapolis: University of Minnesota Press, 1986.

Chakrabarty, Dipesh. "Postcoloniality and the Artifice of History: Who Speaks for 'Indian' Pasts?" *Representations* 37 (Winter 1992): 1–26.

Chandra, Lokesh, ed. *The Art and Culture of South-East Asia.* New Delhi: International Academy of Indian Culture and Aditya Prakashan, 1991.

Chatterjee, Partha. *Nationalist Thought and the Colonial World: A Derivative Discourse.* London: Zed Books, 1986.

———. *The Nation and Its Fragments: Colonial and Postcolonial Histories.* Princeton: Princeton University Press, 1993.

Choy, P. "Texts through Time: The Golek Dance of Java." In *Aesthetic Tradition and Cultural Transmission in Java and Bali,* ed. S. Morgan and L. J. Sears. Wisconsin Monographs on Southeast Asia, no. 2. Madison: University of Wisconsin Center for Southeast Asian Studies, 1984.

Chudori, L. "R. A. Kosasih: Di Tengah Pandawa dan Kurawa." *Tempo,* 21 December 1991, pp. 41–67.

Clara van Groenendael, V. M. *The dalang behind the wayang.* Dordrecht: Foris Publications, 1985.

———. *Wayang Theatre in Indonesia: An Annotated Bibliography.* Dordrecht: Foris Publications, 1987.

Clifford, J. *The Predicament of Culture: Twentieth Century Ethnography, Literature, and Art.* Cambridge: Harvard University Press, 1988.

Clifford, J., and G. E. Marcus, eds. *Writing Culture: The Poetics and Politics of Ethnography.* Berkeley: University of California Press, 1986.

Coedes, G. *The Indianized States of Southeast Asia.* 1948. Honolulu: The East-West Center Press, 1968.

Cohen Stuart, A. B. *Serat Bratajoeda djarwa sekar macapat.* Batavia, 1856.

Selected Bibliography

————. "Brata-Joeda, Indisch Javaansche heldendicht." *Verhandelingen van het Ko-ninklijk Bataviaasch Genootschap voor Kunsten en Wetenschappen* 27 en 28 (1860).

————. *Serat Bratajoeda djarwa sekar macapat.* 2d ed. Semarang: n.p., 1877.

Cole, M., and S. Scribner. *Culture and Thought.* New York: Wiley, 1974.

————. *The Psychology of Literacy.* Cambridge: Harvard University Press, 1981.

Colijn, H. *Neerlands Indië, land en volk, geschiedenis en bestuur, bedrif en samenleving.* Amsterdam: Elsevier, 1913.

Coomaraswamy, A. "Notes on the Javanese Theatre." *Rupam* 7 (n.d.): 5.

Cote, J., trans. *Letters from Kartini: An Indonesian Feminist, 1900–1904.* Clayton, Victoria: Monash Asia Institute, 1992.

Crawfurd, J. *History of the Indian Archipelago.* 3 vols. Edinburgh: Archibald Consta-ble, 1820.

Cribb, R. "Problems in the Historiography of the Killings in Indonesia." In *The Indonesian Killings 1965–1966,* ed. Robert Cribb. Clayton, Victoria: Centre of Southeast Asian Studies, Monash University, 1990.

Crouch, H. *The Army and Politics in Indonesia.* Rev. ed. Ithaca: Cornell University Press, 1988.

Dahm, B. *Sukarno and the Struggle for Indonesian Independence.* Trans. Mary F. Somers Heidhues. 1966. Ithaca: Cornell University Press, 1969.

Damais, L. C. "Études d'épigraphie indonesienne, III Liste des principales inscrip-tions datées de l'Indonesie." *Bulletin de l'École Française d'Extrême Orient* 46 (1952): 11.

Day, J. A. "*Babad Kandha, Babad Kraton* and Variation in Modern Javanese Litera-ture." *Bijdragen tot de Taal-, Land- en Volkenkunde* 134 (1978): 433–50.

————. "Meanings of Change in the Poetry of Nineteenth-century Java." Ph.D. diss., Cornell University, 1981.

————. "Islam and Literature in South-East Asia: Some Pre-modern, Mainly Ja-vanese Perspectives." In *Islam in South-East Asia,* ed. M. B. Hooker. Leiden: E. J. Brill, 1983.

Derrida, J. *Of Grammatology.* Trans. with an introd. by G. C. Spivak. Baltimore: Johns Hopkins University Press, 1974.

————. *Writing and Difference.* Trans. with an introd. by Alan Bass. Chicago: Uni-versity of Chicago Press, 1978.

————. "The Supplement of Copula: Philosophy *Before* Linguistics." In *Textual Strategies: Perspectives in Post-Structuralist Criticism,* ed. Josue Harari. Ithaca: Cornell University Press, 1979.

Dewantara, Ki Hadjar. *Dari Kebangungan Nasional sampai Proklamasi Kemerdekaan: Kenang-kenangan Ki Hadjar Dewantara.* Djakarta: N. V. Pustaka Penerbit "En-dang," 1952.

De Wit, A. *Java: Facts and Fancies.* 1912. Singapore: Oxford University Press, 1987.

Dirks, N. "Introduction." In *Colonialism and Culture,* ed. Nicholas Dirks. Ann Arbor: University of Michigan Press, 1992.

Djajadiningrat-Nieuwenhuis, M. "Noto Soeroto: His Ideas and the Late Colonial Intellectual Climate." *Indonesia* 55 (1993): 41–72.

Doniger, W. [O'Flaherty]. "Fluid and Fixed Texts in India." In *Boundaries of the Text*, ed. J. B. Flueckiger and L. J. Sears. 1991.

Drewes, G.W.J. *Drie Javaansche Goeroe's: Hun Leven, Onderricht en Messiasprediking.* Leiden: Drukkerij A. Vros, 1925.

———. "The Struggle between Javanism and Islam as Illustrated by the Serat Dermagandhul." *Bijdragen tot de Taal-, Land- en Volkenkunde* 122 (1966): 310–65.

———. "Ranggawarsita, the Pustaka Raja Madya and the Wayang Madya." *Oriens Extremus* 21 (1974): 199–215.

———. "Snouck Hurgronje en de Islamwetenschap" [1957]. In *Honderd Jaar Studie van Indonesie 1850–1950: Levensbeschrijvingen van Twaalf Nederlandse Onderzoekers*, ed. Koninklijk Instituut voor Taal-, Land- en Volkenkunde. Den Haag: Smits, 1976.

———, ed. and trans. *The Admonitions of Seh Bari: A Sixteenth Century Javanese Muslim Text, Attributed to the Saint of Bonang.* The Hague: M. Nijhoff, 1969.

———, ed. and trans. *An Early Javanese Code of Muslim Ethics.* The Hague: M. Nijhoff, 1978.

Eisenstein, E. *The Printing Press as an Agent of Change: Communications and Cultural Transformation in Early-Modern Europe.* 2 vols. New York: Cambridge University Press, 1979.

Ellen, R. F. "Social Theory, Ethnography and the Understanding of Practical Islam in South-East Asia." In *Islam in South-East Asia.* Leiden: E. J. Brill, 1983.

Errington, J. J. *Language and Social Change in Java.* Ohio Monographs in International Studies, Southeast Asian Series, no. 65. Athens, Ohio: University of Ohio Press, 1985.

Errington, S. "Some Comments on Style in the Meanings of the Past." *Journal of Asian Studies* 38, no. 2 (1979): 231–44.

Fabian, J. *Time and the Other: How Anthropology Makes Its Object.* New York: Columbia University Press, 1983.

———. "Keep Listening: Ethnography and Reading." In *The Ethnography of Reading*, ed. J. Boyarin. Berkeley: University of California Press, 1993.

Fasseur, C. "The French Scare: Taco Roorda and the Origins of Javanese Studies in the Netherlands." In *Looking in Odd Mirrors: The Java Sea*, ed. V. J. Houben et al. Leiden: Semaian, 1992.

———. *The Politics of Colonial Exploitation: Java, the Dutch and the Cultivation System.* Ithaca: Southeast Asia Publications, 1992.

———. *De Indologen: Ambtenaren voor de Oost 1825–1950.* Amsterdam: Uitgeverig Bert Bakker, 1993.

Febvre, L., and H.-J. Martin. *The Coming of the Book: The Impact of Printing, 1450–1800.* 1958. London: New Left Books, 1976.

Feierman, S. *The Shambaa Kingdom.* Madison: University of Wisconsin Press, 1974.

Feinstein, A., et al., eds. *Lakon Carangan*. Vols. 1–3. Surakarta: Akademi Seni Karawitan Indonesia, 1986.

Finnegan, R. "What Is Oral Literature Anyway? Comments in the Light of Some African and Other Comparative Material." In *Oral Literature and the Formula*, ed. B. Stolz and R. Shannon. Ann Arbor: University of Michigan Press, 1976.

———. *Oral Poetry: Its Nature, Significance, and Social Context*. Cambridge: Cambridge University Press, 1977.

Florida, N. "Reading the Unread in Traditional Javanese Literature." *Indonesia* 44 (October 1987): 1–15.

———. "Writing the Past, Inscribing the Future: Exile and Prophecy in an Historical Text of Nineteenth-Century Java, Volumes I and II." Ph.D. diss., Cornell University, 1990.

———. "Crossing Kraton Walls: On Santri Aspects of the Literary Culture of a Premodern Javanese Court." Paper presented at the 1991 Annual Meeting of the Association for Asian Studies, 1991.

———. *Javanese Literature in Surakarta Manuscripts*. Vol. 1. Ithaca: Cornell Southeast Asia Program Press, 1993.

———. *Writing the Past, Inscribing the Future: History as Prophecy in Colonial Java*. Durham: Duke University Press, 1995.

Flueckiger, J. B. "Literacy and the Changing Concept of Text: Women's Ramayana *Mandali* in Central India." In *Boundaries of the Text*, ed. J. B. Flueckiger and L. J. Sears. 1991.

Fleuckiger, J. B., and L. J. Sears, eds. *Boundaries of the Text: Epic Performances in South and Southeast Asia*. Michigan Papers on South and Southeast Asia. Ann Arbor: University of Michigan Center for South and Southeast Asian Studies, 1991.

Foucault, M. *The Archaeology of Knowledge*. New York: Pantheon, 1972.

———. "What is an Author?" In *Textual Strategies: Perspectives in Post-Structuralist Criticism*, ed. J. V. Harari. Ithaca: Cornell University Press, 1979.

———. "Nietzsche, Genealogy, History." In *The Foucault Reader*, ed. Paul Rabinow. New York: Pantheon Books, 1984.

———. *The History of Sexuality*. Vol. 1, *An Introduction*. 1978. New York: Vintage, 1990.

Foulcher, K. *Social Commitment in Literature and the Arts: The Indonesian "Institute of People's Culture" 1950–1965*. Clayton, Victoria: Centre of Southeast Asian Studies, Monash University, 1986.

Fox, J. J. "'Standing' in TIme and Place: The Structure of Rotinese Historical Narratives." In *Perceptions of the Past in Southeast Asia*. Singapore: Heinemann Educational Books (Asia) Ltd., 1979.

Freedle, R., ed. *Discourse Production and Comprehension*. Norwood, N.J.: Ablex, 1977.

———, ed. *New Directions in Discourse Processing*. Norwood, N.J.: Ablex, 1979.

Geertz, C. "The Javanese Kijaji: The Changing Role of a Culture Broker." *Comparative Studies in Society and History* 2, no. 2 (1959–60): 228–49.

――――. *The Religion of Java*. Chicago: University of Chicago Press, 1960.

――――. *The Social History of an Indonesian Town*. Cambridge: M.I.T. Press, 1965.

――――. *Islam Observed*. Chicago: University of Chicago Press, 1968.

――――. *The Interpretation of Cultures: Selected Essays*. New York: Basic Books, 1973.

――――. "Blurred Genres: The Refiguration of Social Thought." *American Scholar*, Spring 1980, pp. 165–79.

――――. " 'Popular Art' and the Javanese Tradition." *Indonesia* 50 (October 1990): 77–94.

Geertz, H. *The Javanese Family*. Glencoe, Ill.: The Free Press, 1961.

――――. "Comment." *Journal of Asian Studies* 24, no. 2 (1965): 294–97.

Gendron, B. "Theodor Adorno Meets the Cadillacs." In *Studies in Entertainment*, ed. T. Modleski. Bloomington: Indiana University Press, 1986.

Genovese, E. D. *Roll, Jordan, Roll: The World the Slaves Made*. New York: Vintage, 1972.

Goenawan Mohamad. *Catatan Pinggir 3*. 1987. Jakarta: Pustaka Utama Grafiti, 1991.

Goffman, E. *Frame Analysis*. New York: Harper and Row, 1974.

Goldman, R. "India's Great War." *Journal of Asian Studies* 35, no. 3 (1976): 466.

Goody, J. *The Domestication of the Savage Mind*. Cambridge: Cambridge University Press, 1977.

――――. *The Interface between the Written and the Oral*. Cambridge: Cambridge University Press, 1987.

Goody, J., and I. Watt. "The Consequences of Literacy." In *Literacy in Traditional Societies*, ed. J. Goody. New York: Cambridge University Press, 1968.

Graaf, H. J. de. *De Vijf Gezantschapsreizen van Rijklof van Goens naar het Hof van Mataram 1648–1654*. 's Gravenhage: M. Nijhoff, 1956.

Graaf, H. J. de, and Th. G. Th. Pigeaud. *Chinese Muslims in Java in the 15th and 16th Centuries*. Monash Papers on Southeast Asia, no. 12. Melbourne: Monash University, 1986.

Gramsci, A. *Selections from the Prison Notebooks*. New York: International Publishers, 1971.

Guha, R., and G. Spivak, eds. *Selected Subaltern Studies*. New York: Oxford University Press, 1988.

Habermas, J. *Philosophical-Political Profiles*. 1983. Cambridge: MIT Press, 1990.

Hall, S. "Encoding/Decoding." In *Culture, Media, Language*, ed. Stuart Hall et al. London: Hutchinson, 1980.

Harari, J. V. *Textual Strategies: Perspectives in Post-Structuralist Criticism*. Ithaca: Cornell University Press, 1979.

Harding, S. "The Ramayana Shadow-play in India." *Asia* 25, no. 4 (1935): 234–35.

Hardjowirogo, R. *Sedjarah wajang purwa*. Djakarta: Balai Pustaka, 1968.

Hatch, M. "Lagu, Laras, Layang: Rethinking Melody in Javanese Music." Ph.D. diss., Cornell University, 1980.

Havelock, E. A. *Origins of Western Literacy*. Toronto: Ontario Institute for Studies in Education, 1976.

———. "The Ancient Art of Oral Poetry." *Philosophy and Rhetoric* 12 (1979): 187–202.

———. *The Muse Learns to Write: Reflections on Orality and Literacy from Antiquity to the Present.* New Haven: Yale University Press, 1986.

Hazeu, G.A.J. *Bijdrage tot de Kennis van het Javaansche Tooneel.* Leiden: E. J. Brill, 1897.

———. "De Lakon Arimba." *Bijdragen tot de Taal-, Land- en Volkenkunde* 49 (1898): 333–88.

———. "Het Oud-Javaansche Adiparwa en zijn Sanskṛt-origineel." *Tijdschrift van het Koninklijk Bataviaasch Genootschap van Kunsten en Wetenschappen* 44 (1901): 289–357.

———. *Oud en nieuw uit de Javaansche letterkunde.* Leiden: E. J. Brill, 1921.

Heath, S. B. "Protean Shapes in Literacy Events: Ever-shifting Oral and Literate Traditions." In *Spoken and Written Language*, ed. D. Tannen. Norwood, N.J.: Ablex, 1982.

Heath, S. B., and G. Skirrow. "An Interview with Raymond Williams." In *Studies in Entertainment*, ed. T. Modleski. Bloomington: University of Indiana Press, 1986.

Hefner, R. W. *Hindu Javanese.* Princeton: Princeton University Press, 1985.

———. *The Political Economy of Mountain Java.* Berkeley: University of California Press, 1990.

Heider, K. *Indonesian Cinema: National Culture on Screen.* Honolulu: University of Hawaii, 1991.

Henige, D. *The Chronology of Oral Tradition: Quest for a Chimera.* Oxford: Oxford University Press, 1974.

———. *Oral Historiography.* London: Longman, 1982.

Herrnstein Smith, B. *On the Margins of Discourse: The Relation of Language to Literature.* Chicago: University of Chicago Press, 1978.

———. "Narrative Versions, Narrative Theories." In *On Narrative*, ed. W.J.T. Mitchell. 1981.

Hexter, J. H. *On Historians.* Cambridge: Harvard University Press, 1979.

HIll, A. H., ed. "Hikayat Raja-Raja Pasai," *Journal of the Malay Branch of the Royal Asiatic Society* 33, 2 (1960).

Hinloopen Labberton, C. van. *The Wajang or Shadow Play as Given in Java.* N.p., 1912?.

———. "De Wajang of het Schadwenspel." *Wederopbouw* 4, nos. 8–9 (1921): 121–45.

Hinzler, H.I.R. *Bima Swarga in Balinese Wayang.* Verhandelingen van het Koninklijk Instituut voor Taal-, Land- en Volkenkunde 90. The Hague: M. Nijhoff, 1981.

Hobsbawm, E., and T. Ranger, eds. *The Invention of Tradition.* Cambridge: Cambridge University Press, 1983.

Hodgson, M. *The Venture of Islam: Conscience and History in a World Civilization.* 3 vols. Chicago: University of Chicago Press, 1974.

Holt, C. *Art in Indonesia: Continuities and Change.* Ithaca: Cornell University Press, 1967.

———, ed. *Culture and Politics in Indonesia.* Ithaca: Cornell University Press, 1972.

Hood, M. "The Enduring Tradition: Music and Theater in Java and Bali." In *Indonesia*, ed. R. T. McVey. New Haven: Southeast Asia Studies, Yale University, 1963.

Hooker, M. B., ed. *Islam in Southeast Asia*. Leiden: E. J. Brill, 1983.

Hooykaas, C. "Javaansche uitgaven van Volkslectuur (Bale Poestaka)." *Djawa* 12 (1932): 93–115.

———. "The Old-Javanese Ramayana: An Exemplary Kakawin as to Form and Content." *Verhandelingen der Koninklijk Nederlandse Akademi van Wetenschappen* 65, Afd. Letterkunde. Nieuwe Reeks, 1958.

———. "Kama and Kala: Materials for the Study of Shadow Theatre in Bali." *Verhandelingen der Koninklijke Akademie van Wetenschappen*, Deel 79. Afd. Letterkunde. Nieuwe Reeks, 1973.

Houben, V.J.H., H.M.J. Maier, and W. van der Molen, eds. *Looking in Odd Mirrors: The Java Sea*. Rijksuniversiteit Vakgroep Talen en Culturen van Zuidoost-Azie en Oceanie, Semaian 5. Leiden: Rijksuniversiteit te Leiden, 1992.

Hoult, P. *A Dictionary of Theosophical Terms*. London: Theosophical Publishing House, 1910.

Hughes, J. *The End of Sukarno*. London: Angus and Robertson, 1967.

Humardhani, S. D. *Kumpulan Kertas tentang Kesenian*. Solo: Akademi Seni Karawitan Indonesia, 1983.

Humme, H. C. *Abiâsâ: Een Javaansch Tooneelstuk, (Wajang)*. 's Gravenhage: M. Nijhoff, 1878.

Hymes, D. "Introduction: Toward Ethnographies of Communication." In *The Ethnography of Communication*, ed. D. Hymes and J. J. Gumperz. Washington, D.C.: American Anthropological Association, 1964.

———. *Foundations in Sociolinguistics: An Ethnographic Approach*. Philadelphia: University of Pennsylvania Press, 1974.

———. "Ways of Speaking." In *Explorations in the Ethnography of Speaking*, ed. R. Bauman and J. Sherzer. Cambridge: Cambridge University Press, 1974.

Jameson, F. "Modernism and Imperialism." In T. Eagleton, F. Jameson, and E. Said, *Nationalism, Colonialism, and Literature*. Minneapolis: University of Minnesota Press, 1990.

Jay, M. *The Dialectical Imagination: A History of the Frankfurt School and the Institute of Social Research, 1923–1950*. Boston: Little, Brown and Company, 1973.

———. *Adorno*. Cambridge: Harvard University Press, 1984.

Jay, R. R. *Religion and Politics in Rural Central Java*. Yale University Southeast Asia Studies, Cultural Report Series Number 12. New Haven, 1963.

———. *Javanese Villagers: Social Relations in Rural Modjokuto*. Cambridge: MIT Press, 1969.

Johns, A. H. "Muslim Mystics and Historical Writing." In *Historians of Southeast Asia*, ed. D.G.E. Hall. London: Oxford, 1961.

———. "Sufism as a Category in Indonesian Literature and History." *Journal of Southeast Asian History* 2, no. 2 (1961).

Selected Bibliography

———. "The Role of Structural Anthropology and Myth in Javanese Historiography." *Journal of Asian Studies* 24, no. 1 (1964): 91–99.

———. "From Buddhism to Islam: An Interpretation of the Javanese Literature of the Transition." *Comparative Studies in Society and History* 9, no. 1 (1966–67): 40–50.

———. *Cultural Options and the Role of Tradition: A Collection of Essays on Modern Indonesian and Malaysian Literature.* Canberra: Faculty of Asian Studies in association with the Australian National University Press, 1979.

Josselin de Jong, P. E. de. "Reply to Professor Geertz." *Journal of Asian Studies* 24, no. 2 (1965): 297–98.

———. *Structural Anthropology in the Netherlands: A Reader.* The Hague: M. Nijhoff, 1977.

"Journal of an Excursion to the Native Provinces on Java in the Year 1828, during the War with Dipo Negoro." *Journal of the Indian Archipelago and Eastern Asia* 7 (1853): 1–19, 138–57, 225–46, and 358–78; 8 (1854): 80–174.

Juynboll, H. H. "Drie boeken van het Oud-Javaansche Mahabharata in Kawi-tekst en Nederlandsche vertaling, vergeleken met den Sanskrit-tekst." Ph.d. diss., Leiden, 1893.

———. "De verhouding van het Oudjavaansche Udyogaparwa tot zijn Sanskṛt-origineel." *Bijdragen tot de Taal-, Land- en Volkenkunde* 69 (1914): 219–96.

Karni, Rahadi S., ed. *The Devious Dalang: Sukarno and the So-called Untung-putsch, Eye-witness Report by Bambang S. Widjanarko.* The Hague: Interdoc Publishing House, 1974.

Kartomi, M. *Matjapat Songs in Central and West Java.* Canberra: Australian National University Press, 1973.

Kats, J. *Het Javaansche Tooneel I, De Wajang Poerwa.* Vol. 1. Weltevreden: Commissie voor de Volkslectuur, 1923.

Keeler, W. *Javanese Shadow Plays, Javanese Selves.* Princeton: Princeton University Press, 1987.

———. "Sharp Rays: Javanese Responses to a Solar Eclipse." *Indonesia* 46 (1988): 91–101.

———. "On Javanese Interpretation: A Scene from a Wayang." In *Writing on the Tongue*, ed. A. L. Becker. 1989.

———. *Javanese Shadow Puppets.* New York and Singapore: Oxford University Press, 1992.

Kern, H. "Bijdrage ter verklaring van eenige uitdrukkingen in de wayang-verhalen Palasara en Paṇḍu." *Bijdragen tot de Taal-, Land- en Volkenkunde* 16 (1869): 1–23.

———. "Eene Indische Sage in Javaansch Gewaad." *Verhandelingen der Koninklijke Akademie van Wetenschappen, afdeeling Letterkunde* 9 (1876): 1–32 and 1–14.

———. "Het Javaansche wajangstuk Irawan Rabi." *Mededeelingen der Koninklijke Akademie van Wetenschappen, afdeeling Letterkunde*, 2d series, 9 (1880): 125–32.

———. "Taco Roorda" [1928]. In *Honderd Jaar Studie van Indonesie 1850–1950: Levens-*

beschrijvingen van Twaalf Nederlandse Onderzoekers, ed. Koninklijk Instituut voor Taal-, Land- en Volkenkunde. Den Haag: Smits, 1976.

Koch, C. J. *The Year of Living Dangerously.* New York: Penguin, 1983.

———. *Crossing the Gap: A Novelist's Essays.* London: Chatto & Windus, 1987.

Koentjaraningrat. "Review of *The Religion of Java* by Clifford Geertz." *Madjalah Ilmu-ilmu Sastra Indonesia* 1/2 (September 1963).

Kosasih, R. A. *Rama Sinta (Ramayana).* Vols. A–C. Bandung: Erlina, 1975.

———. *Seri Mahabharata.* Vols. 1–19. Bandung: Erlina, 1975.

———. *Bharata Yudha: Bhagavatgita, Lanjutan Mahabharata.* Bandung: Benalines, 1977.

———. "Pandawa Diperdaya 1." *Seri Mahabharata 12: Antara Baju Tamsir & Senjata Konta.* Jabar: Langlangbuwana, 1977.

———. *Pandawa Seda.* Vols. A–B. Bandung: Benalines, 1978.

———. *Parikesit.* Bandung: Benalines, 1979.

———. *Batara Kresna.* Vols. A–D. Bandung: n.p., 1983?.

———. *Wayang Purwa.* Vols. A–D. Bandung: Erlina, 1983.

———. *Luluhur Hastina: Ceritera Sebelum Mahabharata.* Vols. A–C. Bandung: Erlina, n.d.

Kraemer, H. "Het Instituut voor de Javaansche taal te Soerakarta." *Djawa* 12, no. 6 (1932): 261–75.

Krom, N. J. *Hindoe-Javaansche Geschiedenis.* 2d ed. 's Gravenhage: M. Nijhoff, 1931.

Kumar, A. "Javanese Court Society and Politics in the Late Eighteenth Century: The Record of a Lady Soldier, Parts I, II." *Indonesia* 29, 30 (1980): 1–46, 67–111.

———. "The 'Suryengalagan Affair' of 1883 and Its Successors: Born Leaders in Changed Times." *Bijdragen tot de Taal-, Land- en Volkenkunde* 138, nos. 2/3 (1982): 251–84.

———. "On Variation in Babads." *Bijdragen tot de Taal-, Land- en Volkenkunde* 140 (1984): 223–47.

———. *The Diary of a Javanese Muslim: Religion, Politics, and the Pesantren, 1883–1886.* Canberra: Australian National University, 1985.

Kunst, J. *Music in Java* [1949]. 3d ed. Vols. 1–2. Ed. E. L. Heins. The Hague: M. Nijhoff, 1973.

Kusumadilaga, K.P.H. *Serat Sastramiruda.* Jakarta: Proyek Penerbitan Buku Sastra Indonesia Dan Daerah, Departemen Pendidikan & Kebudayaan, 1981.

Lakoff, R. T. "Some of My Favorite Writers are Literate: The Mingling of Oral and Literate Strategies in Written Communication." In *Spoken and Written Language: Exploring Orality and Literacy,* ed. D. Tannen. Norwood: Ablex Publishing Corporation, 1982.

Lampahan baku kaliyan carangan (n.a.). *Padhalangan* 3, no. 3 (15 March 1937): 49–51.

Larson, G. D. *Prelude to Revolution: Palaces and Politics in Surakarta, 1912–1942.* Dordrecht: Foris Publications, 1987.

Selected Bibliography

Leach, E. "Word of Mouth: A review of *The Interface between the Written and the Oral* by Jack Goody." *London Review of Books* 10, no. 5 (3 March 1988): 22.

Legge, J. D. *Sukarno: A Political Biography.* New York: Praeger Publishers, 1972.

Leitch, V. B. *Deconstructive Criticism.* New York: Columbia University Press, 1983.

Lev, D. S. The Transition to Guided Democracy: Indonesian Politics 1957–1959. Ithaca: Cornell Modern Indonesia Project Monograph Series, 1966.

———. "Colonial Law and the Genesis of the Indonesian State." *Indonesia* 40 (October 1985): 57–74.

Levi, S. *Sanskrit Texts from Bali.* Gaekward Oriental Series, 67. Baroda, 1933.

Lévi-Strauss, C. *La Pensée Sauvage.* Paris: Plon, 1962.

Lewis, B. "The Question of Orientalism." *New York Review of Books,* 24 June 1982.

Lindsay, J. "Klasik Kitsch or Contemporary: A Study of the Javanese Performing Arts." Ph.D. diss., University of Sydney, 1985.

Lord, A. *The Singer of Tales.* Cambridge: Harvard University Press, 1960.

Lutgendorf, P. "Words Made Flesh: The Banaras *Ramlila* as Epic Commentary." In *Boundaries of the Text,* ed. J. B. Flueckiger and L. J. Sears. 1991.

———. *The Life of a Text: Performing the Ramcaritmanas of Tulsidas.* Berkeley: University of California Press, 1991.

Lutyens, M. *Krishnamurti: The Years of Awakening.* New York: Farrar, Straus & Giroux, 1975.

MacDonald, B. "Kawi and Kawi Miring: Old Javanese Literature in Eighteenth Century Java." 2 vols. Ph.D. diss., Australian National University, 1985.

The Mahabharata. 19 vols. Critical Edition. Ed. V. S. Sukthankar et al. Poona, India: B.O.R.I. 1933–59.

Maier, H.J.M., and A. Teeuw, eds. *Honderd jaar studie van Indonesië, 1850–1950:* Ithaca: Cornell Southeast Asia Publications, 1988.

Maier, H.J.M., and A. Teeuw, eds. *Honderd jaar studie van Indonesie, 1850–1950: Levensbeschrijvingen van twaalf Nederlandse onderzoekers.* Den Haag: B. V. Drukkerij en Uitgeverij Smits, 1976.

Mangkunagara VII, K.G.P.A.A. "Over de wajang-koelit (poerwa) in het algemeen en over de daarin voorkomende symbolische en mystieke elementen." In *Djåwå* 13 (1933): 79–97.

———. *On the Wayang Kulit (Purwa) and Its Symbolic and Mystical Elements.* Trans. Claire Holt. Data Paper, no. 27. Ithaca: Cornell University Southeast Asia Program, 1957.

———. *Serat Padhalangan Ringgit Purwa.* 1930–32. Jogjakarta: U. P. Indonesia, 1965.

Mangunwijaya, Y. B. "Linaksanan: Mitologi Sebagai Legitimasi oleh Para Dewa." In *Sastra dan Religiositas.* Jakarta: Sinar Harapan, 1982.

———. *Sastra dan Religiositas.* Jakarta: Sinar Harapan, 1982.

———. "Pengakuan Seorang Amatir." In *Mengapa dan Bagaimana Saya Mengarang,* ed. Pamusuk Eneste. Jakarta: Gunung Agung, 1986.

Marcus, G., and M. Fischer. *Anthropology as Cultural Critique.* Chicago: University of Chicago Press, 1986.

Marx, K, and F. Engels. *The German Ideology.* Ed. C. J. Arthur. 1947. New York: International Publishers, 1970.

———. *The Marx-Engels Reader* [1972]. 2d ed. Ed. Robert C. Tucker. New York: W. W. Norton & Co., Inc., 1978.

May, B. *The Indonesian Tragedy.* London: Routledge and Kegan Paul, 1978.

McLuhan, M. *The Gutenberg Galaxy: The Making of Typographic Man.* Toronto: University of Toronto Press, 1962.

McNeill, W. H. *Mythistory and Other Essays.* Chicago: University of Chicago Press, 1986.

McVey, R. "Taman Siswa and the Indonesian National Awakening." *Indonesia* 4 (October 1967): 128–49.

———. "Faith as an Outsider: Islam in Indonesian Politics." In *Islam in the Political Process*, ed. James P. Piscatori. Cambridge: Cambridge University Press, 1983.

———. "The Wayang Controversy in Indonesian Communism." In *Context, Meaning, and Power in Southeast Asia*, ed. M. Hobart and R. Taylor. Ithaca: Cornell Southeast Asia Publications, 1986.

Mechelen, Ch. te. "Drie-en-twintig schetsen van wajang-stukken (Lakon's) gebruikelijk bij de vertooningen der Wajang-Poerwå op Java." *Verhandelingen van het Koninklijk Bataviaasch Genootschap voor Kunsten en Wetenschappen* 40 (1879): 1–437.

———. "Een en ander over de Wajang." *Tijdschrift voor Indische Taal-, Land- en Volkenkunde uitgegeven door het Bataviaasch Genootschap voor Kunsten en Wetenschappen*, jaargang 25, 1879.

———. "Drie teksten van tooneelstukken uit de wayang poerwå." *Verhandelingen van het Koninklijk Bataviaasch Genootschap voor Kunsten en Wetenschappen* 43 (1882): 1–494.

Meinhard, H. "The Javanese Wayang and Its Indian Prototype." *Man* 94 (1939): 109–11.

Miller, B. S., ed. *The Theatre of Memory: The Plays of Kalidasa.* New York: Columbia University Press, 1984.

Miller, J. C., ed. *The African Past Speaks.* Hamden, Conn.: Archon Books, 1980.

Mitchell, W.J.T., ed. *On Narrative.* Chicago: University of Chicago Press, 1980. The articles in this volume originally appeared in *Critical Inquiry* 7, no. 1 (Autumn 1980) and 7, no. 4 (Summer 1981).

Modleski, T., ed. *Studies in Entertainment.* Bloomington: University of Indiana Press, 1986.

Moertono, S. *State and Statecraft in Old Java: A Study of the Later Mataram Period, 16th to 19th Century.* 1968. Ithaca: Cornell Modern Indonesia Project, 1981.

Mortimer, R. *Indonesian Communism under Sukarno: Ideology and Politics, 1959–1965.* Ithaca: Cornell University Press, 1974.

———. "Traditional Modes and Communist Movements: Change and Protest in Indonesia." In *Peasant Rebellion and Communist Revolution in Asia*, ed. John Wilson Lewis. Stanford: Stanford University Press, 1974.

Selected Bibliography

Mudjanto, G. *The Concept of Power in Javanese Culture.* Yogyakarta: Gadjah Mada University Press, 1986.

Mulyanto, R. I., et al. *Biografi Pujangga Ranggawarsita.* Jakarta: Departemen Pendidikan dan Kebudayaan, 1990.

Mulyono, I. S. *Asal-usul, Filsafat dan Masa Depannya.* Jakarta: Gunung Agung, 1975.

———. *Tripama, Watak Satria dan Sastra Jendra.* Jakarta: Gunung Agung, 1978.

Murtiyasa, B. *Tinjuan lakon Alap-alapan Sukeksi dalam pakeliran padat susunan Soemanto.* Surakarta: Akademi Seni Karawitan Indonesia, 1981.

———. "Kegelisahan Kehidupan Seni yang Menggelisahkan." Unpublished manuscript presented at the Diskusi Teater, PKJT, Sasanamulya, 10 April 1984.

———. "Lampahan Carangan Satleraman." Sarasehan Dalang 1984, Akademi Seni Karawitan Indonesia, Solo.

———. "Sebuah Tinjauan tentang Pakem dan Masalah-Masalahnya." *Gatra* 19, no. 1 (1989): 7–11.

Nagazumi, A. *The Dawn of Indonesian Nationalism: The Early Years of the Budi Utomo.* Tokyo: Institute of Developing Economies, 1972.

Narasimhan, C. V. *The Mahabharata.* New York: Columbia University Press, 1965.

Naryacarito. *Alap-alapan Sukesi.* Surakarta: Akademi Seni Karawitan Indonesia, 1980.

———. *Wirata Parwa.* Surakarta: Akademi Seni Karawitan Indonesia, n.d.

Noer, D. *Administration of Islam in Indonesia.* Cornell Modern Indonesia Project Monograph Series. Ithaca, 1978.

Nojowirongko M. Ng. [Ki Atmotjendono]. *Serat Tuntunan Padhalangan* I, II. Ngajogjakarta: Tjabang Bagian Bahasa, 1948.

———. *Serat tuntunan pedhalangan caking pakeliran lampahan Irawan Rabi,* Jilid 1/2, 3/4. Surakarta: Akademi Seni Karawitan Indonesia, 1976 (stenciled copy of 1960 edition).

O'Flaherty, W. See Doniger, W. [O'Flaherty].

Olthof, W. L., ed. *Poenika serat Babad Tanah Djawi wiwit saking Nabi Adam doemoegi ing tahoen 1647.* 's Gravenhage: M. Nijhoff, 1941.

Ong, W. J. *Rhetoric, Romance, and Technology.* Ithaca: Cornell University Press, 1971.

———. *Interfaces of the Word.* Ithaca: Cornell University Press, 1977.

———. *Orality and Literacy: The Technologizing of the Word.* New York: Methuen, 1982.

Ongkokham. "The Residency of Madiun: Pryayi and Peasant in the Nineteenth Century." Ph.D. diss., Yale University, 1975.

Orr, K. "Schooling and Village Politics in Central Java in the time of turbulence." In *The Indonesian Killings 1965–1966,* ed. Robert Cribb. Clayton, Victoria: Centre of Southeast Asian Studies, Monash University, 1990.

Padmapuspita, J. *Serat Kandhaning Ringgit Purwa,* Jilid 2. Jakarta: Penerbit Djambatan dan KITLV, 1985.

Padmosusastro. *Serat Pustaka Radja Purwa.* Vols. 6–8. Ngajogjakarta: N. P. Voeren H. Boening, 1906.

Pakem Ringgit Purwa (n.a.). Late nineteenth century. Uncatalogued ms. D-49, SMP/ Radyapustaka #250C, Surakarta, pp. 129–131.

Partini: Recollections of a Mangkunagaran Princess. As told to Roswitha Pamoentjak Singgih. Jakarta: PT Djambatan, 1986.

Pemberton, J. *On the Subject of "Java."* Ithaca: Cornell University Press, 1994.

Penders, Chr. L. M. *The Life and Times of Sukarno.* London: Sidgwick and Jackson, 1974.

Penders, Chr. L. M., ed. and trans. *Indonesia: Selected Documents on Colonialism and Nationalism, 1830–1942.* St. Lucia, Queensland: University of Queensland Press, 1977.

Perlman, M. "Theosophy in Java and the Re-Indicization of the Wayang Kulit." Unpublished paper, 1993.

Pigeaud, Th. *Javaanse Volksvertoningen.* The Hague: M. Nijhoff, 1938.

———. *Java in the Fourteenth Century.* Vols. 1–4. The Hague: M. Nijhoff, 1960–63.

———. *Literature of Java.* Vol. 1. The Hague: M. Nijhoff, 1967.

———. *The Literature of Java.* Vol. 2. The Hague: M. Nijhoff, 1968.

Poensen, C. "De Wayang." *Mededeelingen van wege het Nederlandsche Zendeling-genootschap* 16 (1872): 59–115, 204–22, 233–80, and 17 (1873): 138–64.

Poerbatjaraka, R. Ng. "Arjuna-Wiwaha, tekst en vertaling." *Bijdragen tot de Taal-, Land- en Volkenkunde* 82 (1926): 181–305.

———. *Kapustakan Djawi.* Djakarta: Penerbit Djambatan, 1952.

Poerwadarminta. *Baoesastra Djawa.* Batavia: J. B. Wolters, 1937.

Poerwoto Prawirohardjo. "Kesoesasteraan Indonesia Djawa." *Poedjangga Baroe* 1, nos. 6, 7–12 (1933–34).

Polanyi, L. "Literary Complexity in Everyday Storytelling." In *Spoken and Written Language,* ed. D. Tannen. Norwood, N.J.: Ablex, 1982.

Prakash, G. "Writing Post-Orientalist Histories of the Third World: Indian Historiography Is Good to Think." In *Colonialism and Culture,* ed. N. Dirks. Ann Arbor: University of Michigan Press, 1992.

Pramoedya Ananta Toer. *Rumah Kaca.* Kuala Lumpur: Wira Karya, 1990.

———. "Ma'af, Atas Nama Pengalaman." *Kabar Seberang* 23 (1992): 1–9.

Press, G. A. *The Development of the Idea of History in Antiquity.* Kingston and Montreal: McGill-Queen's University Press, 1982.

Quinn, G. "The Case of the Invisible Literature: Power, Scholarship, and Contemporary Javanese Writing." *Indonesia* 35 (April 1983): 1–36.

———. *The Novel in Javanese.* Leiden: KITLV Press, 1992.

Raffles, T. S. *The History of Java* [1817]. 2d ed. 2 vols. London: John Murray, 1830.

Ramanujan, A. K. "Three Hundred Ramayanas: Five Examples and Three Thoughts on Translation." In *Many Ramayanas: The Diversity of a Narrative Tradition in South Asia,* ed. Paula Richman. Berkeley: University of California Press, 1991.

Ras, J. J. "The Panji Romance and W. H. Rassers' Analysis of its Theme." *Bijdragen tot de Taal-, Land- en Volkenkunde* 129 (1973): 411–56.

Selected Bibliography

———. "The Historical Development of the Javanese Shadow Theatre." *Review of Indonesian and Malaysian Studies* 10 (1976): 50–76.

———. *De schending van Soebadra: Javaans schimmenspel.* Amsterdam: Meulenhoff, 1976.

———. "The Babad Tanah Jawi and Its Reliability." In *Cultural Contact and Textual Interpretation,* ed. C. D. Grijns and S. O. Robson. Dordrecht: Foris Publications, 1986.

Rassers, W. H. *Pandji, the Culture Hero.* 1931. The Hague: M. Nijhoff, 1959.

"Rasverschil onder Inlanders." *De Indische Gids* (1912): 123–25.

Reid, A. "The Nationalist Quest for an Indonesian Past." In *Perceptions of the Past in Southeast Asia,* ed. A. Reid and D. Marr. 1979.

———. *Southeast Asia in the Age of Commerce: The Lands below the Winds.* New Haven: Yale University Press, 1988.

———. "Islamization and Christianization in Southeast Asia: The Critical Phase, 1550–1650." In *Southeast Asia in the Early Modern Era.* Ithaca: Cornell University Press, 1993.

———, ed. *On the Making of an Islamic Political Discourse in Southeast Asia.* Clayton, Victoria: Monash University Centre of Southeast Asian Studies, 1993.

Reid, A., and D. Marr, eds. *Perceptions of the Past in Southeast Asia.* Singapore: Heinemann Educational Books (Asia) Ltd., 1979.

Resink, G. J. "From the Old Mahabharata—to the New Ramayana—Order." *Bijdragen tot de Taal-, Land- en Volkenkunde* 131, nos. 2/3 (1975): 214–35.

Ricklefs, M. C. *Jogjakarta under Sultan Mangkubumi 1749–1792.* London: Oxford University Press, 1974.

———. *Modern Javanese Historical Tradition.* London: University of London, School of Oriental and African Studies, 1978.

———. "Six Centuries of Islamization in Java." In *Conversion to Islam,* ed. Nehemia Levtzion. New York: Holmes & Meier Publishers, Inc., 1979.

———. "Unity and Disunity in Javanese Political and Religious Thought of the Eighteenth Century." In *Looking in Odd Mirrors: The Java Sea,* ed. V.J.H. Houben, H.M.J. Maier, and W. van der Molen. 1992.

———. *A History of Modern Indonesia since c. 1300.* 1981. Rev. ed., Stanford: Stanford University Press, 1993.

———. *War, Culture and Economy in Java 1677–1726: Asian and European Imperialism in the Early Kartasura Period.* Sydney: Asian Studies Association of Australia in association with Allen and Unwin, 1993.

———, ed. *Islam in the Indonesian Social Context.* Clayton, Victoria: Monash University Centre of Southeast Asian Studies, 1991.

Ricoeur, P. "The Model of the Text: Meaningful Action Considered as Text." In *Interpretive Social Science: A Reader,* ed. P. Rabinow and W. M. Sullivan. Berkeley: University of California Press, 1979.

Robison, R. "Culture, Politics, and Economy in the Political History of the New

Order." In *Interpreting Indonesian Politics: Thirteen Contributions to the Debate*, ed.
B. Anderson and Audrey Kahin. Ithaca: Southeast Asia Program Press, 1982.

Robson, S. O. *Wangbang Wideya: A Javanese Panji Romance*. The Hague: M. Nijhoff,
1971.

Rochijat, Pipit. "Am I PKI or Non-PKI?" *Indonesia* 40 (1985): 37–56.

Roorda, T. "De lotgevallen van Raden Pandji, volgens de Javaansch wajangver-
halen," *Bijdragen tot de Taal-, Land- en Volkenkunde* 11 (1864): 1–65.

———. *De wajang–verhalen van Pålå-Sårå, Paṇḍoe en Raden Pandji, in het Javaansch,
Met aanteekeningen*. 's Gravenhage: M. Nijhoff, 1869.

Rosaldo, R. "Doing Oral History." *Social Analysis* 4 (1980): 89–99.

Rush, J. R. *Opium to Java: Revenue Farming and Chinese Enterprise in Colonial Indonesia,
1860–1910*. Ithaca: Cornell University Press, 1990.

Sahlins, M. *Islands of History*. Chicago: University of Chicago Press, 1985.

Said, E. W. *Orientalism*. New York: Vintage, 1979.

———. *The World, the Text, and the Critic*. Cambridge: Harvard University Press,
1983.

———. "Intellectuals in the Post-colonial World." *Salmagundi* 70–71 (Spring-
Summer 1986).

Sajid, R. M. *Bauwarna Kawruh Wajang*. Surakarta. "Widya Duta," 1971.

Sarkar, H. B. *Corpus of the Inscriptions of Java, up to 928 A.D.* 2 vols. Calcutta: Firma
K. L. Mukhopadhyay, 1971–72.

Sartono, Kartodirdjo. *The Peasant's Revolt of Banten in 1888: Its Conditions, Course, and
Sequel: A Case Study of Social Movements in Indonesia*. 's Gravenhage: Martinus
Nijhoff, 1966.

———. "Agrarian Radicalism in Java: Its Setting and Development." In *Culture and
Politics in Indonesia*, ed. Claire Holt. Ithaca: Cornell University Press, 1972.

Schechner, R. *Between Theater and Anthropology*. Philadelphia: University of Pennsylvania Press, 1985.

Scherer, S. P. "Harmony and Dissonance: Early Nationalist Thought in Java."
Master's thesis, Cornell University, 1975.

———. "Yudhistira Ardi Noegraha: Social Attitudes in the Works of a Popular
Writer." *Indonesia* 30 (October 1980): 31–52.

Scheub, H. *The Xhosa Ntsomi*. Oxford: Oxford University Press, 1975.

Scollon, R., and Scollon S.B.K. "Cooking It Up and Boiling It Down: Abstracts in
Athabaskan Children's Story Retellings." In *Coherence in Spoken and Written
Discourse*, ed. D. Tannen. Norwood, N.J.: Ablex, 1984.

Scott, A. C. *Theatre in Asia*. New York: Macmillan Publishing Company, 1972.

Scribner, S. "Modes of Thinking and Ways of Speaking: Culture and Logic Recon-
sidered." In *New Directions in Discourse Processing*, ed. R. O. Freedle. Norwood,
N.J.: Ablex, 1979.

Sears, L. J. "Epic Voyages: The Transmission of the *Ramayana* and *Mahabharata* from
India to Java." In *Aesthetic Tradition and Cultural Transition in Java and Bali*, ed.

Selected Bibliography

S. Morgan and L. J. Sears. Madison: University of Wisconsin Center for Southeast Asian Studies, 1984.

——. "The Contingency of Autonomous History." In *Autonomous Histories, Particular Truths: Essays in Honor of John R. W. Smail*, ed. L. J. Sears. 1993.

——. "Rethinking Indian Influence in Javanese Shadow Theatre Traditions." *Comparative Drama* 18 (Spring 1994).

——, ed. *Autonomous Histories, Particular Truths: Essays in Honor of John R. W. Smail*. Madison: University of Wisconsin Center for Southeast Asian Studies, 1993.

——, ed. *Fantasizing the Feminine in Indonesia*. Durham: Duke University Press, 1995.

Sears, L. J. and J. B. Flueckiger. "Introduction." In *Boundaries of the Text: Epic Performances in South and Southeast Asia*, ed. J. B. Flueckiger and L. J. Sears. 1991.

Seltmann, F. "Schattenspiel in Mysore und Andhra Prades." *Bijdragen tot de Taal-, Land- en Volkenkunde* 127 (1971).

——. "Schattenspiel in Kerala." *Bijdragen tot de Taal-, Land- en Volkenkunde* 128 (1972).

"Sena Wangi." *Pathokan Pedhalangan Gagrag Banyumas*. Jakarta: Balai Pustaka, 1983.

Serrurier, L. *De Wajang Poerwa: Eene ethnologische studie*. Leiden: E. J. Brill, 1896.

Shastri, H. P. *The Ramayana of Valmiki*. Vol. 3. London: Shanti Sadan, 1959.

Shiraishi, T. "The Dispute between Tjipto Mangoenkoesoemo and Soetatmo Soeriokoesoemo: *Pandita* vs. *Satria*." *Indonesia* 32 (1981): 93–108.

——. *An Age in Motion: Popular Radicalism in Java, 1912–1926*. Ithaca: Cornell University Press, 1990.

Simuh. *Mistik Islam Kejawen*. Jakarta: Penerbit Universitas Indonesia, 1988.

Sindusastra, R. Ng. *Serat Lokapala*. Vol. 1. 2d ed. Batavia: Bale Pustaka, 1936.

Siswoharsojo. *Wahyu Purbasejati*. Ngayogyakarta: Gondolayu Kulon, 1966.

Sjahrazad [S. Sjahrir]. *Indonesische Overpeinzingen*. Amsterdam: De Bezige Bij, 1945.

Smail, J.R.W. "On the Possibility of an Autonomous History of Modern Southeast Asia." *Journal of Southeast Asian History* (July 1961): 72–102.

Smail, L. L. "John Smail: Reflections on an Academic Life." In *Autonomous Histories, Particular Truths*, ed. L. J. Sears. 1993.

Snouck Hurgronje, C. *Oeuvres Choisies de C. Snouck Hurgronje* par G.-H. Bousquet et J. Schacht. Leiden: E. J. Brill, 1957.

Soebardi, S. "The Book of Cabolek." Ph.D. diss., Australian National University, 1967.

——. "Santri-religious Elements as Reflected in the Book of Tjentini." *BKI* 127, no. 3 (1971): 331–49.

——. *The Book of Cabolek*. The Hague: M. Nijhoff, 1975.

Soedarsono. *Living Traditional Theaters in Indonesia*. Yogyakarta: Akademi Seni Tari Indonesia, 1974.

Soeharda Sastrasoewignja. "Hal Wajang Poerwa dan Djalan-djalan oentoek Memperbaharoeinja." *Poedjangga Baroe* 2, nos. 1–4 (July, August, September, October 1934).

Soekarno. *Marhaen and Proletarian*. Trans. Claire Holt. Ithaca: Cornell Modern Indonesia Project, 1960.

———. *Toward Freedom and the Dignity of Man: A Collection of Five Speeches by President Sukarno of the Republic of Indonesia*. Jakarta: Department of Foreign Affairs, 1961.

———. *Tahun "Vivere Pericoloso."* Jakarta: B. P. Prapantja, 1964.

———. *DiBawah Bendera Revolusi*. Jakarta: Panitya Penerbit DiBawah Bendera Revolusi, 1964.

———. *Nationalism, Islam, and Marxism*. Trans. Karel H. Warouw and Peter D. Weldon. Introduction by R. McVey. Ithaca: Cornell Modern Indonesian Project, 1969.

———. *Warislah Api Sumpah Pemuda: Kumpulan Pidato Bung Karno di hadapan pemuda 1961–64*. Jakarta: C V Haji Masagung, 1988.

Soemanto. *Alap-alapan Sukeksi*. Surakarta: Akademi Seni Karawitan Indonesia, 1980.

R. M. Soetanta Hardjawahana. *Mahabharata Kawedar*. Solo: n.p., 1936–40?

Soetatmo Soeriokoesoemo. "Gewijd aan mijn Kameraden in 'Insulinde'." *Wederopbouw* 1, no. 1 (1918): 7–9.

———. "Het Javaansche Vraagstuk." *Wederopbouw* 1, no. 1 (1918): 4–7.

———. "Theosofie en Javaansch Nationalisme." *Wederopbouw* 3, nos. 4–7 (1920): 73–77.

———. "Geschiedenis van Java: Gelicht uit het prea-advies van R.M.S. Soeriokoesoemo." *Wederopbouw* 5, nos. 1–5 (1922): 51–56.

———. "De Twijfel van Djanaka." *Wederopbouw* 5, nos. 1–5 (1922): 26–32.

———. "Het Heilige Schrift in beeld. De Wajang." *Wederopbouw* 6, nos. 1–3 (1923): 30–39.

Soetopo? [Sutapa]. "De behoefte aan intellectueele dalangs in verband met de ontwikkeling van het wajangspel." *Djawa* 1 (1921): 129, Appendix B.

Soetrisno, R. "Thek Kliwering Lampahan Carangan." Sarasehan Dalang 1984, Akademi Seni Karawitan Indonesia, Solo.

———. "Dunia Wayang Kulit." Unpublished typescript, n.d.

Spivak, G. C. "Can the Subaltern Speak?" In *Marxism and the Interpretation of Culture*, ed. Cary Nelson and Lawrence Grossberg. Urbana: University of Illinois Press, 1988.

———. "Subaltern Studies: Deconstructing Historiography." In *Selected Subaltern Studies*, ed. Ranajit Guha and Gayatri Chakravorty Spivak. New York: Oxford University Press, 1988.

———. *The Post-Colonial Critic: Interviews, Strategies, Dialogues*. Ed. Sarah Harasym. New York: Routledge, 1990.

Spurr, D. *The Rhetoric of Empire*. Durham: Duke University Press, 1993.

Stange, P. "Mystical Symbolism in Javanese Wayang Mythology." *The South East Asian Review* 1, no. 2 (1977): 109–22.

Selected Bibliography

———. "The Logic of Rasa in Java." *Indonesia* 38 (October 1984): 113–34.

———. "Deconstructions of Javanese 'Tradition' as Disempowerment." *Prisma* 50 (September 1990): 89–110.

———. "Inner Dimensions of the Indonesian Revolution." In *Autonomous Histories, Particular Truths: Essays in Honor of John R. W. Smail*, ed. L. J. Sears. 1993.

Steenbrink, K. A. *Dutch Colonialism and Indonesian Islam: Contacts and Conflicts, 1596–1950*. Amsterdam: Editions Rodopi B.V., 1993.

Steinberg, D. J., et al. *In Search of Southeast Asia*. New York: Praeger, 1971.

Stock, B. *The Implications of Literacy: Written Language and Models of Interpretation in the Eleventh and Twelfth Centuries*. Princeton: Princeton University Press, 1983.

———. *Listening for the Text: On the Uses of the Past*. Baltimore: Johns Hopkins, 1990.

Stocking, G. W., Jr. *Victorian Anthropology*. New York: Free Press, 1987.

Sulastin Sutrisno et al., eds. *Bahasa, Sastra, Budaya*. Yogyakarta: Gadjah Mada University Press, 1985.

Sullivan, B. M. *Kṛṣṇa Dvaipayana Vyasa and the Mahabharata: A New Interpretation*. Leiden: E. J. Brill, 1990.

Sumahatmaka. *Ringkasan Centini*. Jakarta: PN Balai Pustaka, 1981.

Sumarsam. "Historical Contexts and Theories of Javanese Music." Ph.D. diss., Cornell University, 1992.

———. *Gamelan: Cultural Interaction and Musical Development in Central Java*. Chicago: University of Chicago Press, 1995.

Sunardi, D. M. *Arjuna Sasrabahu*. Jakarta: Balai Pustaka, 1982.

Supomo, S. "Sastra Djendra: 'Ngelmu' yang timbul karena kakografi." *Majalah Ilmu-Ilmu Sastra Indonesia* 2 (1964): 177–86.

———. *Arjunawijaya: A Kakawin of Mpu Tantular*. 2 vols. The Hague: M. Nijhoff, 1977.

———. "The Image of Majapahit in Later Javanese and Indonesian Writing." In *Perceptions of the Past in Southeast Asia*, ed. Anthony Reid and David Marr. 1979.

———. "Kama di dalam Kakawin." In *Bahasa, Sastra, Budaya*, ed. Sulastin Sutrisno et al. Yogyakarta: Gadjah Mada University Press, 1985.

Surjomihardjo, Abdurrachman. "National Education in a Colonial Society." In *Dynamics of Indonesian History*, ed. Haryati Soebadio and Carine A. du Marchie Sarvaas. Amsterdam: North Holland Publishing Company, 1978.

Sutarsa, S. *Sekar Jatikusuma*. Solo: Toko Buku K.S., 1976.

Sutherland, H. "Pudjangga Baru: Aspects of Indonesian Intellectual Life in the 1930s." *Indonesia* 6 (October 1968): 106–29.

———. *The Making of a Bureaucratic Elite: The Colonial Transformation of the Javanese Priyayi*. Singapore: Heinemann Educational Books (Asia) Ltd., 1979.

Sutton, R. A. "Change and Ambiguity: Gamelan Style and Regional Identity in Jogjakarta." In *Aesthetic Tradition and Cultural Transmission in Java and Bali*, ed. S. Morgan and L. J. Sears. Wisconsin Monographs on Southeast Asia, no. 2. Madison: University of Wisconsin Southeast Asia Program, 1984.

Suwarno, B. *Srikandi Maguru Manah.* Surakarta: Akademi Seni Karawitan Indonesia, 1980.

Sweeney, A. "Professional Malay Storytelling: Some Questions of Style and Presentation." *Journal of the Malaysian Branch, Royal Asiatic Society* 46, no. 2 (1973): 1–53.

———. *Authors and Audiences in Traditional Malay Literature.* Berkeley: Center for South and Southeast Asian Studies, 1980.

———. *A Full Hearing: Orality and Literacy in the Malay World.* Berkeley: University of California Press, 1987.

———. "Literacy and the Epic in the Malay World." In *The Boundaries of the Text*, ed. J. B. Flueckiger and L. J. Sears. 1991.

Tanaya, R. *Cariyos Padhalangan Lampahan Dhalang Kandhabuwana Murwakala.* Kediri: Tan Khoen Swie, 1954.

Tannen, D., ed. *Spoken and Written Language: Exploring Orality and Literacy.* Norwood, N.J.: Ablex, 1982.

———. *Coherence in Spoken and Written Discourse.* Norwood, N.J.: Ablex, 1984.

Tedlock, D. "Toward an Oral Poetics." *New Literary History* 8 (1977): 507–19.

———. *The Spoken Word and the Work of Interpretation.* Philadelphia: University of Pennsylvania Press, 1983.

Timoer, S. *Pakem Padhalangan Ringgit Purwa Warakesthi.* Jakarta: PN Balai Pustaka, 1982.

Tjipto Mangoenkoesoemo. "De Wajang." *De Indische Gids* 36, pt. 1 (1914): 530–39.

Todorov, T. *Genres in Discourse.* 1978. New York: Cambridge University Press, 1990.

Trinh T. Minh-Ha. *When the Moon Waxes Red: Representation, Gender and Cultural Politics.* New York: Routledge, 1991.

Tsuchiya, K. *Democracy and Leadership: The Rise of the Taman Siswa Movement in Indonesia.* Honolulu: University of Hawaii Press, 1987.

———. "Javanology and the Age of Ranggawarsita: An Introduction to Nineteenth Century Javanese Culture." In *Reading Southeast Asia.* Ithaca: Cornell Southeast Asia Program, 1990.

Turner, V. *From Ritual to Theatre.* New York City: Performing Arts Journal Publications, 1982.

Uhlenbeck, E. M. "The Words Morphologically Related with Javanese *Rasa*: A Contribution to Javanese Lexicology." *Oriens Extremus* 6 (1954): 104–15.

———. *A Critical Survey of Studies on the Languages of Java and Madura.* 's Gravenhage: M. Nijhoff, 1964.

Vansina, J. *De la Tradition Orale.* Tervuren, Belgium: Musée Royale de L'Afrique Centrale, 1961. English version, *Oral Tradition.* Chicago: Aldine Publishing Company, 1965.

———. *Oral Tradition as History.* Madison: University of Wisconsin Press, 1985.

Vreede, A. C., ed. *Drie Teksten van tooneelstukken uit de wajang poerwa voor den druk bezorgd door A. C. Vreede.* 2de Deel. *Verhandelingen van het Bataviaasch Genootschap van Kunsten en Wetenschappen* 44. Batavia, 1884.

Selected Bibliography

Wagner, R. *The Invention of Culture.* 1975. Chicago: University of Chicago Press, 1981.

Wahid, Abdurrahman. "Pengantar." In *Perang Tipu Daya antara Bung Karno dan Tokoh Tokoh Komunis*, by H. Ahmad Muhsin. 1989.

Wang Gungwu. "The Study of the Southeast Asian Past." In *Perceptions of the Past in Southeast Asia*, ed. Anthony Reid and David Marr. Singapore: Heinemann Educational Books (Asia) Ltd., 1979.

Weatherbee, D. E. "Raffles' Sources for Traditional Javanese Historiography and the Mackenzie Collections." *Indonesia* 26 (October 1978): 63–93.

White, H. *Tropics of Discourse: Essays in Cultural Criticism.* Baltimore: The Johns Hopkins University Press, 1978.

Wibisono, Singgih. "Konvensi dan Invensi Dalam Sastra Pedalangan." *Gatra* 16 (1987): 7–9.

Wignyawiryanto. *Kusuma Lelana.* Solo: Toko Buku к.s., n.d.

Wijaya, Putu. *BOMB: Indonesian Short Stories*, ed. Ellen Rafferty and Laurie J. Sears. Madison: University of Wisconsin Center for Southeast Asian Studies, 1988.

———. *Perang.* Jakarta: Pustaka Utama Grafiti, 1990.

Wilkens, J. A. "Wajangvoorstelling." *Tijdschrift voor Nederlandsche-Indië* 8, no. 2 (1846): 1–107.

Williams, P., and L. Chrisman, eds. *Colonial Discourse and Post-Colonial Theory: A Reader.* New York: Harvester Wheatsheaf, 1993.

Williams, R. *Marxism and Literature.* Oxford: Oxford University Press, 1977.

———. *Keywords: A Vocabulary of Culture and Society.* 1976. Rev. ed., New York: Oxford University Press, 1983.

Winter, C. F., Sr. *Javaansche Zamenspraken.* 3d ed. Amsterdam: Muller, 1882.

———. *De Brata-Joeda, de Rama en de Ardjoena-Sasra.* Uitgegeven door T. Roorda. Amsterdam: Johannes Muller, 1845.

Winter, J. W. "Beknopte Beschrijving van het Hof Soerakarta in 1824." *Bijdragen tot de Taal-, Land- en Volkenkunde* 54 (1902): 15–176.

Wolters, O. W. *History, Culture and Region in Southeast Asian Perspectives.* Singapore: Institute of Southeast Asian Studies, 1982.

Woodward, K., ed. *The Myths of Information: Technology and Postindustrial Culture.* Milwaukee: University of Wisconsin Center for Twentieth Century Studies, 1980.

Woodward, M. R. *Islam in Java.* Tucson: University of Arizona Press, 1989.

Yampolsky, P. *The University of Wisconsin-Madison Collection of Materials on Modern Indonesian Culture: Handlist of the 1985 Acquisitions.* Wisconsin Bibliographies on Southeast Asia, no. 11. Madison: University of Wisconsin Southeast Asia Program, 1987.

———. *Lokananta: A Discography of the National Recording Company of Indonesia, 1957–1985.* Wisconsin Bibliographies on Southeast Asia, no. 10. Madison: University of Wisconsin Southeast Asia Program, 1987.

Yoewono, Yoen. *Sumbadra Larung* [Cergam]. Jakarta: Yayasan Nawangi & P. T. Inaltu, 1976.

Zarkasi, H. E. *Unsur Islam dalam Pewayangan*. Bandung: P. T. Alma'arif, 1977.

Zoetmulder, P. J. *Kalangwan: A Survey of Old Javanese Literature*. The Hague: M. Nijhoff, 1974.

———. *Pantheism and Monism in Javanese Suluk Literature*. 1935. Ed. and Trans. by M. C. Ricklefs. Leiden: KITLV Press, 1994.

———, with S. O. Robson. *Old Javanese-English Dictionary*. 2 vols. 's Gravenhage: Nijhoff, 1982.

Zurbuchen, M. S. *The Language of Balinese Shadow Theater*. Princeton: Princeton University Press, 1987.

Index

Index

Index

Index

Index

Index

Index

About the Author

Laurie J. Sears is Associate Professor of Southeast Asian History at the University of Washington. She is editor of *Fantasizing the Feminine in Indonesia* (Duke, 1996) and *Autonomous Histories, Particular Truths: Essays in Honor of John R. W. Smail* (1993), and has co-edited a number of other books including *Boundaries of the Text: Epic Performances in South and Southeast Asia* (with Joyce B. Flueckiger).

Library of Congress Cataloging-in-Publication Data

Sears, Laurie J.
Shadows of empire : colonial discourse and Javanese tales / Laurie
J. Sears.
p.   cm.
Includes bibliographical references and index.
ISBN 0-8223-1685-4 (cl : alk. paper). — ISBN 0-8223-1697-8
(pa : alk. paper)
1. Wayang.   2. Wayang plays—History and criticism.   3. Tales—
Indonesia—Java—History and criticism.   4. Java (Indonesia)—
History.   I. Title.
PN1978.153S43   1996
791.5'3—dc20   95-30518   CIP

Photographs on pages 39, 41, 137, 162, 221, 249, 263, and 295 by Nancy Donnelly